AMENDING
AMERICA

AMENDING AMERICA

If We Love the Constitution So Much,
Why Do We Keep Trying
to Change It?

Richard B. Bernstein
with Jerome Agel

UNIVERSITY PRESS OF KANSAS

Published by the University Press of Kansas (Lawrence, Kansas 66049),
which was organized by the Kansas Board of Regents and is operated and
funded by Emporia State University, Fort Hays State University, Kansas
State University, Pittsburg State University, the University of Kansas, and
Wichita State University, by arrangement with Times Books, a division of
Random House, Inc.

Library of Congress Cataloging-in-Publication Data

Bernstein, Richard B.
        Amending America: if we love the Constitution so much, why do we
keep trying to change it?/Richard B. Bernstein with Jerome Agel.
        p.   cm.
        ISBN 0-7006-0715-3 (pbk.)
        1. United States—Constitutional law—Amendments—History.
I. Agel, Jerome.   II. Title
KF4555.B47   1993   342.73'03—dc20   92-50499   [347.3023]

Book Design by Barbara Balch

Printed in the United States of America

10 9 8 7 6 5 4 3 2 1

The paper used in this publication meets the minimum requirements of
the American National Standard for Permanence of Paper for Printed Library
Materials Z39.48-1984.

This book is for
HENRY STEELE COMMAGER
with abiding esteem and affection,
to mark the ninetieth birthday
of a "choice and master spirit of the age."
—R.B.B.

The Congress, whenever two thirds of both Houses shall deem it necessary, shall propose Amendments to this Constitution, or, on the Application of the Legislatures of two thirds of the several States, shall call a Convention for proposing Amendments, which, in either Case, shall be valid to all Intents and Purposes, as Part of this Constitution, when ratified by the Legislatures of three fourths of the several States, or by Conventions in three fourths thereof, as the one or the other Mode of Ratification may be proposed by the Congress; Provided that no Amendment which may be made prior to the Year One thousand eight hundred and eight shall in any Manner affect the first and fourth Clauses in the Ninth Section of the first Article; and that no State, without its Consent, shall be deprived of it's equal Suffrage in the Senate.

ARTICLE V OF THE UNITED STATES CONSTITUTION

TABLE OF CONTENTS

INTRODUCTION

AMERICANS HAVE SHAPED THEIR LIVES through law, and for more than two hundred years the Constitution has been the core of the nation's law. We make many demands on our Constitution: it sets forth the structure of our government, allocates powers and duties among our public institutions and officials, and defines our rights and responsibilities. Just as important, the Constitution declares the nation's central principles—the goals for which we came together to create this nation; the purposes of its grants of power and limits on power; and the kinds of public and private lives that we want to foster under its protection.

The Constitution is thus an expression of the American national character, but, more than that, it is the root of American national identity. In an age of resurgent nationalism, our brand of nationalism is unique. More than any other nation, we have defined ourselves through our political values, our institutions and practices of government, and our balancing of individual rights and responsibilities. Lacking a common ethnic heritage or a single shared religious tradition, we have come together as a people to protect that remarkable diversity through our politics. What we share is a set of political ideals, institutions, and customs, all of them forming an intricate web undergirding our identity as a nation and a people, all of them simultaneously growing out of and reinforcing the Constitution.

What is especially remarkable about the ways that our Constitution defines and holds together our national identity is that it has done so for so long. The Constitution of the United States is the world's oldest written charter of government in continuous effect.

In 1787, when the Constitution was written, the United States was a large, fragile country—rich in natural resources, desperately poor in hard cash and native industries, nearly overwhelmed by a crushing burden of debt. Only eleven years before, the American people had become the first colonists in history to rebel against their mother country—and win. In Philadelphia, then a small town on the fringes of the Atlantic Civilization, a group of farmers, lawyers, merchants, and politicians gathered to frame a new form of government that would

xi

preserve the fruits of their revolution for themselves and their descendants. In the eyes of leading political observers, the hopeful experiment was doomed to failure. Practically every word of the new charter flew in the face of the conventional wisdom of the Western political tradition—even though its designers engaged in a profound and creative dialogue with the best that tradition had to offer.

More than two centuries later, it is a commonplace to observe that the United States is the world's only surviving superpower. We are—or claim to be—the "leader of the world," "the richest and most powerful nation on Earth." Our population is more than eighty times that of 1787, with a social, religious, ethnic, racial, cultural, and linguistic diversity that would have staggered the Revolutionary generation of Americans. Yet we still govern ourselves according to the Constitution drafted by a few dozen former colonists in the Pennsylvania State House in 1787, laboring in the shadow of a hard-fought war for independence from the world's greatest colonial and military power.

The Constitution has changed, to be sure. And the history of those changes is, in many ways, the most remarkable aspect of American history. Changes in the Constitution both kindle and disclose changes in the ways we see ourselves and what we stand for, changes in the process by which we govern ourselves, and changes in the values animating that process.

In all societies, but especially in our own, constitutional change takes place on several distinct though interrelated levels. The highest level is the way we alter the form of the Constitution itself—the amending mechanism set forth in the Constitution's Article V. This book explores the procedure by which the American people amend the Constitution—whether by adding new provisions or by repealing or replacing old ones—and why we have or have not done so. It examines the many ways that we have used the amending process to keep our fundamental charter in pace with changing social, political, and economic realities—to reshape the Constitution to meet our changing needs. It also elucidates why, when we amend the Constitution, we are "amending America."

The twenty-seven amendments adopted between 1791 and 1992 and the six proposed by Congress but not ratified by the states make up about one-third of one percent of the more than ten thousand proposals introduced in Congress since the beginnings of government under the Constitution. Not only do these numbers indicate how difficult the amending process is to use but they also suggest how high the stakes are when we consider using it.

When we amend the Constitution, we alter the matrix of law within which we live our lives and govern ourselves. When an amendment expands the power of government, it shows what we expect and trust our government to do. When an amendment restricts the power of government, it indicates what we want to safeguard from official interference. When an amendment defines rights and brings them within the protection of the Constitution, it suggests how we intend to redefine the nature of liberty.

The consequences of amending the Constitution are neither obvious nor simple. Amendments act retrospectively as well as prospectively—that is, with as much attention to the problems they resolve and thus remove from public life as to the problems and issues to which they give rise. An amendment intended to solve one problem may produce a wide range of unexpected difficulties. The amendment's language also can become a staging area for the development of doctrines of constitutional law that those who framed and adopted the provision may not have expected or intended. The Constitution and American society exist in what the late Buckminster Fuller would have called a synergistic relationship. They shape and reflect each other, and the total effect is greater than the sum of the separate effects. When we amend the Constitution, we and it launch a long, complex process of amending each other.

IF WE LOVE THE CONSTITUTION so much, why do we keep trying to change it?

The amending process is a major theme of our political, social, and cultural history. The work of constitutional creation and change did not end with the framing and adoption of the Constitution in 1787–1788, its implementation in 1789–1791, or the ratification of the first ten amendments (the Bill of Rights) in 1791. Rather, the amending process is a means for enabling us and our government to keep the Constitution ready to meet the challenges of the present and the future.

It is not surprising that we have tried so many times, and in so many ways, to amend the Constitution. Because we venerate it so much, we want the Constitution to fit ever more closely with our hopes and expectations for American life; we thus have a powerful urge to resolve whatever discrepancies we perceive between the "is" of the Constitution and the "ought" of our national aspirations. Moreover, as generations of foreign visitors to America have observed, Americans always have been fond of tinkering. The history of amending the Constitution is a record of recurring trips to the repair shop, putting the Constitution up on blocks with its hood open and Uncle Sam plunging his hands into the engine.

How relevant the history of amending the Constitution can be was dramatized in the spring of 1992, when we discovered that we had amended the Constitution almost in a fit of absentmindedness, and watched as another effort to do so failed:

> • On May 7, 1992, the Michigan legislature added the Twenty-seventh Amendment to the Constitution. Proposed by Representative James Madison on June 8, 1789, and all but neglected for two centuries, the

amendment prevents any law adjusting the salary of Senators and Representatives from taking effect until after an election of Representatives. Its ratification was a triumph for Gregory D. Watson, a thirty-year-old aide in the Texas legislature, who waged a lonely ten-year campaign to add the amendment to the Constitution despite the belief of most politicians, historians, and legal scholars that the proposal was a dead letter.

• On June 11, 1992, the House of Representatives voted, 280 to 153, to adopt an amendment to the Constitution setting forth procedures to require a balanced federal budget, offered by Representative Charles Stenholm (Democrat–Texas). Although the proposal captured a sizable majority, it failed to meet the two-thirds requirement specified in Article V—despite frequent and angry demands from President George Bush and public-opinion polls indicating the approval of more than three fourths of the voters for such an amendment. Even if the House had approved the Stenholm amendment by the necessary margin, the Senate leadership vowed to stall and defeat it. Undaunted, President Bush and his allies pledged to renew the struggle.

These battles are but two of a series of bitter but inconclusive struggles in the 1970s, 1980s, and 1990s to add new amendments to the Constitution.

The changing roles played by Article V in American political life—and the newfound appeal of the amending process to politicians frustrated by the ordinary workings of government—indicate the degree of public confidence in the constitutional system. Key moments of constitutional crisis spur dozens or even hundreds of proposals to amend the Constitution to resolve the crisis. The more strongly we come to believe that the government created by the Constitution is not responding to the nation's needs, the more eagerly we search for ways to change the document. Yet increases in the number and variety of demands for constitutional change reflect a strong public commitment to the Constitution as much as they do growing public discontent with the actual workings of the constitutional system.

THE AMENDING PROCESS HAS SIGNIFICANCE for reasons ranging beyond its place in the American story. While Article V has become a political football at home, its example is bearing fruit abroad. Today, peoples throughout the world strive to redesign their governments and politics, restoring ideals of liberty and principles of self-government long banished from their public lives. Many democratic movements, such as Solidarity in Poland and Civic Forum and Public Against Violence in the Czech and Slovak Federative Republic, look to American examples as they reestablish democratic government and politics. They do not seek to copy American solutions to the perennial problems of government; rather, they draw encouragement from the American experience. Thus, the history of the American people's creative engagement with their Constitution through the amending process contributes to greater understanding, both here and abroad, of the enduring challenge of democratic governance. This book is a contribution to furthering that growth of understanding.

We are a nation because we chose to be. The Constitution of the United States, the fundamental charter of the American polity, shaped the development of an American nation. What kind of government—what kind of nation—have we crafted over the past two hundred years by amending the nation's organic law? Are we truly aware of the consequences of "amending America"?

ACKNOWLEDGMENTS

MANY PEOPLE HAVE HAD A HAND IN THIS BOOK.

My parents, Fred and Marilyn Bernstein, my brother, Steven, and my sister, Linda, bore with me during irascible moments. At various times, and for various reasons, they all have urged me to amend myself; I offer this book as a short-term substitute. I am especially grateful for my father's vigilant and good-humored proofreading.

Friends and colleagues provided intellectual and moral support: Maureen K. Phillips and Joseph Newpol, Dennis G. Combs, Joanne B. Freeman, Allan Blumenthal, Kathleen E. Spencer, Nathan D. Spencer, Ene Sirvet (editor of *The Papers of John Jay* at Columbia University), Professor Thomas C. Mackey of the University of Louisville, Marilee B. Huntoon and Jim Wasklewicz, Phillip G. Haultcoeur, Stephanie A. Thompson, Linda Faulhaber of *Constitution* magazine, Peter S. Kohlmann and Wanda Gaillard of Operation Welcome Home—NYC, Bob Greene and Clarice Joynes of the Mayor's Office of Veteran Affairs—City of New York, Edward D. Young III and Gina Tillman-Young, Bob and Barbara Tramonte, April E. Holder, Patricia Rosten and Jeffrey Pascal, Eva M. Menon, Ron Blumer and Muffie Meyer, Larry Woodbridge, Michael Psareas and Andrew Rubenfeld, Diantha and Walter Schull, Joan Challinor, Kym and Mark Rice, Ellen S. Shapiro, and many others. Special thanks to George Poulos, Louise Child, Jan Perlin, Courtnay Pitt, and Marguerite Shea of the Promenade Coffee Shop's Committee on the Fate of Civilization. Christa, Adam, Noah, Luke, and Mary Maya Tillman-Young, Megan and Daniel Hanford, Kelly Thompson, Claire Rice, and Emma Sarah Blumer all deserve to see their names in print.

The vigorous yet collegial criticisms of Professors William E. Nelson, John Phillip Reid, and Christopher N. Eisgruber of New York University Law School, Professor William P. LaPiana of New York Law School, Professors Martin Flaherty and Robert J. Kaczorowski of Fordham Law School, Professor Peter C. Hoffer of the University of Georgia, Professor Paul Finkelman of Brooklyn Law School, Sarah Barringer Gordon, Elizabeth Wiltshire, and Philippe Uninsky made this a better book. Responding to my presentation of drafts of the introduction and of the present Chapters 2, 4, 5, 11, and 14 at two sessions of the New York University Law School Colloquium on Legal History, they persuaded me both to sharpen the text that now appears and to drop text that the reader should be thankful to have been spared. Special thanks are due to Bill Nelson and John Reid for bearing with the birthing of this book while I should have been completing another one. (It's on the way.)

Professor Stephen L. Schechter of Russell Sage College and Timothy L. Hanford, Esq., assistant minority tax counsel of the House Committee on Ways and Means, provided special aid and valuable research materials in exploring the history and theory of the amending process. Their friendship, interest, and support sustained me at critical moments.

I also am deeply indebted to two great national treasures, the *Documentary History of the Ratification of the Constitution* at the University of Wisconsin–Madison and the *Documentary History of the First Federal Congress* at George Washington University, and to the people who make these monuments of scholarship both scholarly and human: Gaspare J. Saladino, John P. Kaminski, and Richard Leffler in Madison and Kenneth R. Bowling, Charlene Bangs Bickford, and Helen E. Veit at GWU.

I was privileged to interview several people who have played important roles in modern amendment battles. Their names appear in the text and notes. I want to give special thanks, however, to Gregory D. Watson, the stepfather of the Twenty-seventh Amendment, who occupies a unique place in the history of Article V. He bore patiently with countless questions, and I am deeply grateful for his enthusiasm for chronicling the intricate travails of the Twenty-seventh Amendment and discussing the knotty problems of Article V.

Without the generous support of Operation Welcome Home—NYC and New York Law School, this book could not have been completed. Thanks also to Jeffrey Gmelch, Edd Sutton, Dennis Robbins, Tom Elias Weatherly, and their colleagues at the Strand Book Store.

Finally, Paul Golob of Times Books (and his assistant, Andrew Fabens), and Susan Brown, copy editor *extraordinaire,* saw what this book could be; their discerning, imaginative, and tactful labors helped it get there. All writers should be so lucky in their editors.

THIS BOOK IS DEDICATED TO Henry Steele Commager, recently retired as Simpson Lecturer in History at Amherst College. More than twenty years ago, when I was a high-school dilettante in American history, he captured my loyalty and admiration and set me on the winding path to become a historian. In 1974–1975, when I was a student in his upper-level seminar "Rewriting the Constitution," he taught me to appreciate the difficulty and importance of constitution-making and constitutional reform.

Throughout my career, Professor Commager has been my model as a historian—in the clarity and felicity of his prose, in the patience and enthusiasm of his teaching, and in the creativity, rigor, and deep compassion of his scholarship. I hope that *Amending America* is true to the Commagerian tradition.

—R.B.B.

I wish to add undying gratitude to M.H.J., J.G.S., and N.H.O. for their neonatal resuscitation, truly without which . . .

—J.A.

Errors that slipped by these friendly critics are ours alone.

PART I

DEVISING THE AMENDING PROCESS

CHAPTER I

ANTECEDENTS OF ARTICLE V

[W]henever any Form of Government becomes destructive of
these ends, it is the Right of the People to alter or to abolish
it; and to institute new Government, laying its foundation
on such principles and organizing its powers in such form,
as to them shall seem most likely to effect their Safety and
Happiness.

DECLARATION OF INDEPENDENCE
July 4, 1776

THE DOORS OF THE NATIONAL Archives—two bronze slabs, each nearly forty feet tall and weighing six and one half tons—open at ten o'clock each morning. Brooding relics of the distant past or the far future as imagined by Hollywood circa 1935, the doors rumble as hidden machinery rolls them apart.

Visitors walk between metal detectors operated by grim security guards and through the cavernous foyer, looking at the ceiling seventy-five feet above them. The room is solemn and gloomy; the dominant impression is one of polished stone. Two large frescoes, bearing the hallmarks and drawbacks of "official" commemorative art, loom dimly overhead. The eighteenth-century philosopher-statesmen they depict look uncomfortable and awkward—like relatives grouped for a family portrait they would rather not sit for.

More guards, tense and unsmiling, herd the growing queue into the central exhibition hall, toward the left end of the arc-shaped exhibition. The flat glass cases display original documents and facsimiles, tracing the creation of a nation by men whose chosen tools were words and ideas.

At the crest of the arc is an intimidating spectacle of marble, metal, and shatterproof glass. Voices, already hushed in the rotunda, sink to whispers or fade into silence as the sightseers approach the altar-like structure. Guards regularly snap, "Please do not lean on or touch the glass." These cases have a story of their own, detailed in the brochure the visitors study while waiting in line, describing how the cases are lowered each evening into a reinforced vault. If the nation's capital is attacked, that vault will continue to protect its contents—perhaps long after the city above it has ceased to exist. These details reinforce the reverence that the rotunda was designed to elicit.

3

Shielded by tinted glass and inert gases, the founding documents of the American nation seem anticlimactic. The Declaration of Independence is all but illegible, a casualty of patriotic pride. In 1819, when Secretary of State John Quincy Adams ordered that facsimiles of the Declaration be made for general distribution, the process required the removal of some of the ink from the original parchment. Nearly a century of exhibition in direct sunlight in the State Department reading room, with nothing more than a pane of ordinary glass for protection, faded the document still more. Only faint traces of lettering remain.

The other three parchment pages on display are far more legible, because they were not shown until the twentieth century, when technology made protected exhibition possible. For most of its history, the Constitution rested, all but forgotten, in a locked tin box in the files of the State Department. It was first placed on display, in a protective glass case, in 1921; more than thirty years later, in 1952, a solemn procession of military vehicles and armed soldiers escorted the Constitution from the Library of Congress to the National Archives, its home ever since.[1] Only the first and last pages of the Constitution are on regular exhibit, the other two pages emerging from the vault only on September 17, Constitution Day. In the far-right-hand case is the Bill of Rights, the only representative of the Amendments on display.

When we stand before the originals of the Declaration, the Constitution, and the Bill of Rights, we are in the presence of the mainspring of American public life. Our nation's identity is defined by principles, shaped by institutions, and held together by customs and usages founded on the labors of the Revolutionary generation—all of which are codified in or based on these parchment pages.

The reverence inspired by the nation's founding documents carries with it the impression that they are permanent and enduring. We cannot imagine the United States without them. Our nation was given shape and direction by the self-conscious deliberations of men engaged in nation-building and constitution-making. And they deemed it an integral part of their labors to ensure that their handiwork include a mechanism of formal constitutional change. Only when the origins of the Constitution and of its amending process are restored to their historical context does their revolutionary character become apparent.

WHEN WE EXAMINE THE AMENDING process codified in the Constitution, we confront a cluster of ideas arranged like a set of nesting boxes. Changing the text of a written constitution, itself a pathbreaking idea, is but an outgrowth of the concept of a written charter of government outlining the institutional framework and guiding principles of a polity. And, in turn, the idea of a written constitution grew out of the bedrock principle that people can, and ought to, choose how to govern themselves.[2]

These fundamental principles of American government are enshrined in the

Constitution's Preamble, which declares that "We the People of the United States" are the authority promulgating the Constitution.[3] Even more important, both as prior authority for the Preamble and as the foremost testament to the validity of and the need for these principles, is the Declaration of Independence, drafted by Thomas Jefferson and adopted by the Second Continental Congress in 1776.[4]

The Declaration's opening passage is not ceremonial throat-clearing. Rather, it expounds the right of the people to govern themselves (which is the root of constitutional change) and states that changes in forms of government must be explained and justified. Its avowal of the importance of explaining the unprecedented act of rebellion incorporates the idea that the dissolution of allegiance to the former mother country is but an application of fundamental rights:[5]

> We hold these truths to be self-evident, that all men are created equal, that they are endowed by their Creator with certain unalienable Rights, that among these are Life, Liberty, and the pursuit of Happiness.—That to secure these rights, Governments are instituted among Men, deriving their just powers from the consent of the governed,—That whenever any Form of Government becomes destructive of these ends, it is the Right of the People to alter or to abolish it; and to institute new Government, laying its foundation on such principles and organizing its powers in such form, as to them shall seem most likely to effect their Safety and Happiness.

Jefferson further acknowledged the novelty of the action proposed by Congress, and sought to define the appropriate timing of such revolutions:

> [W]hen a long train of abuses and usurpations, pursuing invariably the same Object evinces a design to reduce [the people] under absolute Despotism, it is their right, it is their duty, to throw off such Government, and to provide new Guards for their future security.

Thus, the symbolic founding document of the American nation included as one of its key elements a theory of constitutional change.

The invention of the written constitution is one of the greatest achievements of the Anglo-American political tradition. Previously, the term "constitution" signified the complex of institutions, laws, customs, and principles that made up the way a nation was governed.[6] When, for example, Aristotle described the Athenian constitution and Polybius analyzed the Roman constitution, these classical writers actually were discussing comprehensive structures of government and politics.

The traditional usage of "constitution" prevails to this day in Great Britain.[7] Principles of politics and governance, and common-law doctrines, derived from the unwritten "British constitution" helped to form the Americans' views of politics and constitutional government.[8] However, the key distinction remains true: British constitutionalism began with, and retains its dependence on, an unwritten constitution, whereas the Americans began with, and continue, history's most creative series of experiments with a written constitution.*[9]

THE DECISION OF THE CROWN to pursue dreams of empire in the Western Hemisphere had profound and unexpected consequences for the history of constitutional government, for it was in the English colonies in North America that the idea of a written constitution took root. Under English law, all territories identified and claimed for England fell under the control of the Crown. To encourage the development of the New World in the interests of the mother country, the Crown awarded charters to explorers and promoters, granting them limited sets of rights to those regions they claimed for England and helped to settle.

Charters conferred powers of government (belonging as of right to the monarch) on those to whom the charters were issued, for the regions that they claimed or that had been marked out by previous exploration. They also specified the rights and the duties of English subjects recruited to settle the colonies, thus establishing limits on the monarch's grants of partial sovereign power. Charters were necessary for the expansion of the realm into new and previously inaccessible or unknown territories. These documents both asserted the ultimate claims of the Crown to the colony and its territory and allotted rights and responsibilities to the Crown, to the organizers of the colony, and to the settlers who were to make the colony work.

Charters were of various types, depending on the person or group receiving them. Sometimes the Crown granted a charter to an individual, known as a "proprietor" (the most famous being the Quaker and religious dissident William

---

*The only English experience with a written constitution took place during the English Civil War (1638–1649), which pitted royalists supporting the Stuart monarchy against Parliamentary forces in a constitutional crisis resolved by force of arms. With the deposing and execution of Charles I in 1649, the leaders of the Puritan Revolution struggled to frame a written constitution to replace the unwritten constitution that had the monarchy as its focus. In 1660, the Restoration of Charles II broke off this abortive series of experiments with a written constitution.

Penn, the founder of Pennsylvania), to a company of investors (as in Virginia), or to a group combining investors and settlers (as in Massachusetts). Or the sovereign appointed a governor and dispatched him to North America to organize a colony—as in 1733, when George II sent Governor James Oglethorpe, armed with a royal appointment and a charter confirming it, to found a colony that Oglethorpe loyally named Georgia.

Charters became central to the political life of British North America. By the time of the American Revolution, the thirteen colonies that broke away from Great Britain had amassed more than a century of experience of self-government, most of them under written charters. Much of that experience revolved around disputes between the colonists and the royal government about the rights of individuals, the powers of government, and the limits on powers and rights codified in those charters and in the principles of the unwritten British constitution.[10]

One of the starkest of these conflicts came in 1685–1691, when James II decided to bring all the New England colonies and New York under one imperial government, to be known as the Dominion of New England. In creating the Dominion, the Crown revoked the charters of the colonies that were to constitute it. The colonists rejected the Crown's argument that efficiency of administration justified the creation of the Dominion. Resenting the abrogation of their charters, they did their best to hamper the Dominion's workings. When news arrived of the deposing of James II and the coronation of William and Mary, the colonists dismantled the Dominion and jailed its officials. The colonists' uprisings complemented the Glorious Revolution of 1688.[11]

Throughout the eighteenth century, two distinct types of conflicts dominated colonial politics: disputes between royal governors and colonial legislatures over charters, and controversies about the powers of Parliament over the colonists under the unwritten British constitution. In the 1760s and 1770s, disagreement over the nature, extent, and meaning of the British constitution gave rise to an ominous dispute between the colonists and Great Britain. All attempts to resolve this crisis failed, in large part because none of the proposed means of solving it possessed legitimacy in the eyes of both the British government and the colonists.[12]

The collapse of British authority in 1775 and 1776 did not catch the leaders of colonial resistance unprepared. Almost from the day the Second Continental Congress convened in May 1775, John Adams of Massachusetts insisted that Congress authorize the people to topple their colonial governments and frame new constitutions for themselves; he also urged that Congress fashion a new form of government for the united colonies. Adams's demand reflected a new reality of American public life: American politics was beginning to develop on two levels—within each colony (after independence, state) and in a new, as yet untried, national political theater. In May 1776, a full year after the Second Continental Congress had assembled, it passed a resolution (written by Adams) authorizing and directing the people of the colonies to adopt new constitutions; the delegate from Massachusetts proudly regarded his handiwork as the actual instrument of independence. Less than two months later, Congress formally declared the colonies' independence from Great Britain.

The state constitutions created between 1776 and 1780 are the first examples of the political principles and methods that would inform the creation of the United States Constitution and its amending process.[13] It was at the level of the states that Americans first articulated a theory of constitution-making requiring that a constitution be framed and adopted in a manner more formal, solemn, and difficult than that by which ordinary laws were made. Under this theory, it is the people who possess the power to constitute their form of government—known as the constituent power.[14]

By 1780, when the people of Massachusetts framed their constitution, the theory of Revolutionary constitutionalism required that the body charged with framing the constitution be a special assembly, chosen for that sole purpose, rather than an ordinary legislature. A legislature could not exercise the constituent power; only the people themselves, or a body of delegates they chose for that purpose, could wield it. Moreover, the assembly framing the constitution—known as a constitutional convention—did not and could not possess the authority to promulgate its work. Rather, it had to submit the proposed constitution to the people, who then would decide whether to adopt or reject it.

In 1780, the people of Massachusetts demonstrated that this process worked by conducting the first free debate by a people on how they were to govern themselves.[15] A convention elected by the people framed the constitution and sent it to the town meetings for review by the voters; after the town meetings sent their tabulated votes and comments back to the convention, and after the delegates engaged in some dexterous vote-juggling, the convention announced that the people had approved the new constitution and declared it to be in effect. In 1787, the framers of the United States Constitution drew on the theory of constitutional framing and ratification rooted in the Massachusetts experience.

As to the means adopted to amend and revise state constitutions, the available evidence was slight. Only eight state constitutions in effect in 1787 contained some provision for amendments, and many of these documents had not yet had a chance to prove their worth. Three state constitutions vested this power in the legislature, with requirements exceeding those for the enactment of ordinary legislation,* while the other five delegated it to specially elected conventions.** The Massachusetts constitution provided for the calling of conventions at twenty-year intervals to assess the workings of the document; if the convention determined that amendments were needed, it would frame them for submission to the people. Professor Gordon S. Wood of Brown University has noted, "These were beginnings, rudimentary efforts to make effective the distinction between the fundamental principles of the constitution and positive law."[16]

Perhaps the most unusual form of constitutional revision was that codified in the Pennsylvania constitution of 1776. Every seven years, the legislature would name a Council of Censors to investigate how the government had been administered and in what ways the constitution had been upheld or violated. Based on the report of the Council, the legislature would decide whether to call a convention to revise the constitution. In 1783, the Council of Censors embarked on its first investigation. Its report listed dozens of violations of the letter and spirit of the constitution, most owing to that document's rejection of the principles of separation of powers and checks and balances. But the bitter politicization of constitutional issues in Pennsylvania buried the Censors' catalog and prevented any changes to the constitution. (In 1788, the failure of the 1783 Censors' report furnished powerful ammunition to James Madison in *The Federalist No. 48*, in which he defended the doctrines of separation of powers and checks and balances built into the federal Constitution.) Not until 1790 did growing dissatisfaction with the 1776 charter, and the triumph of the anticonstitution Republican party, result in the adoption of a new state constitution for Pennsylvania.[17]

The Americans had an easier time framing and adopting new constitutions for the states than forging a constitutional framework for an American Union. Although they came together to oppose British colonial policy and violations of the British constitution in America, they were not used to thinking of themselves as a united people. Many considered their state as their "country" and thought of citizens of other states—despite their common cause, common language, and

---

*Maryland (1776) (amendments effective only when passed by two successive separately elected legislatures); Delaware (1776) (certain constitutional provisions, including Declaration of Rights, immune from amendment power; vote of five-sevenths of Assembly and seven members of the legislative Council necessary for effective amendment); and South Carolina (1778) (ninety-days' notice and majority of both houses of legislature required for effective amendment).

**Pennsylvania (1776); Georgia (1776); Vermont (1777 and 1787); Massachusetts (1780); and New Hampshire (1784).

common heritage—as the equivalent of subjects of the Russian Czar or the Emperor of China. States regularly imposed tariffs on goods imported across state borders; some states fought trade wars with their neighbors; all issued their own money.[18]

The outbreak of hostilities between British and colonial forces in 1775 at one stroke severed the colonies' shared allegiance to the mother country (which had held the colonies together) and forced the Americans to explore Union anew as a bulwark of independence. As Congress sent an army into the field to oppose British forces, it wrestled with the problems of forging an American Union. How was it to fill the void left by the disintegration of British governance?

After months of agonized debate, the Second Continental Congress adopted three resolutions in June 1776. The first (and most famous) authorized a declaration of American independence; the second set in motion diplomatic missions to secure European allies for the new nation; the third directed the naming of a committee to frame "articles of confederation and perpetual union."

It took the delegates more than a year to invent a form of government that they felt would preserve the Union and secure American independence—the Articles of Confederation. Yet when Congress finished its task, on November 15, 1777, it could only propose the Articles to the states; the state governments had the responsibility to bring the new government into being by ratifying the Articles. And because all thirteen states had to agree to put the first constitution of the United States into effect, the Articles rested in limbo for four years—until Maryland (the last state to ratify) acted on March 1, 1781. During those four years, the Continental Congress continued in existence as an ad hoc body. Once the Articles were ratified, Congress recast itself as the Confederation Congress.

Historians of the Articles have agreed that their framing was dominated by the struggle to create a government strong enough to coordinate the American war effort against Britain, yet not so strong as to threaten the rights of the people or the sovereignty of the individual states.[19] The Articles created a weak central government having only one institution—the Confederation Congress. Though there was no independent national executive or judiciary, Congress did create executive departments and an admiralty court, despite its members' worries that these bodies lacked legitimacy. Having no power to operate directly on individual citizens, the Confederation was forced to depend on state enforcement of its policies and on the states' willingness to comply with its requisitions for money, men, and supplies. Confederation officials often were forced to dispatch begging letters to reluctant governors and legislatures, or even to place advertisements in newspapers announcing a state's failure to comply with congressional requisitions.

Article 2 stated the Confederation's central problem:

> Each State retains its sovereignty, freedom and independence, and every power, jurisdiction and right, which is not by this confederation expressly delegated to the United States, in Congress assembled.

Although state politicians claimed that the Articles recognized the states as having the sovereignty and independence of separate nations, others recognized the inherent ambiguity of the Articles—designed to duck the issue of whether the states or the Confederation would be paramount. Whatever use this ambiguity might have had in winning adoption of a frame of government for a new nation, it hobbled that government's workings at virtually every stage.[20]

Even before their adoption, the Articles appeared radically defective to many friends of an American nation. Such politicians as Alexander Hamilton (then an officer on General George Washington's staff) urged repeatedly that the United States required a government strong enough to hold the nation together—one far more powerful than that created by the Articles. Hamilton's view, which he first expressed in a series of letters in 1780, became the core of the nationalist political agenda throughout the decade.

Despite frequent demands for revision of the Articles by nationalists within Congress and without, Article 13 posed an insuperable obstacle to constitutional reform:

> [T]he articles of this confederation shall be inviolably observed by every State, and the Union shall be perpetual; nor shall any alteration at any time hereafter be made in any of them; unless such alteration be agreed to in a Congress of the United States, and be afterwards confirmed by the Legislatures of every State.

Thus, one state could frustrate a reform endorsed by the other twelve.

Article 13 was a consequence of the political constraints under which the Articles were framed and adopted. The British had given the Americans fearful object lessons in the dangers of central government; the states therefore were all the more jealous of the "sovereignty, freedom and independence" that Article 2 was supposed to protect. Only a few politicians thought of the Americans as one united people acting in concert for their independence and liberty. It was natural that so far-reaching an act as amending the Articles should require the consent of all members of the Confederation.

Even though at least four attempts were made between 1781 and 1786 to amend the Articles of Confederation in order to give Congress an independent source of revenue through the power to tax imported goods, they all failed because of the unanimity requirement built into Article 13. Two of these proposals (in 1781 and 1783) came within one state of adoption. However, Rhode Island rejected both, and Virginia withdrew its adoption of the 1783 measure after Rhode Island had acted. Indeed, tiny Rhode Island became the foremost adversary of amending the Articles because it feared its neighbors and suspected the motives of those who wished to strengthen the Confederation. The resistance of "Rogue Island" enraged many Americans, who for decades had been offended by the turbulence, factionalism, and extreme democracy of Rhode Island politics.[21]

Because attempts to amend the Articles had failed, advocates of a stronger central government proposed more sweeping measures. They first aired their proposals at the Annapolis Convention of 1786, called by Virginia's legislature to explore the possibilities of joint action to promote interstate commerce and to protect that commerce from discriminatory state laws. The Annapolis Convention issued a Report (prepared by Alexander Hamilton with the assistance of James Madison) urging that a general convention be called in Philadelphia in May 1787 to "render the federal constitution adequate to the exigencies of Government and the preservation of the Union." The Report sidestepped the procedures of Article 13, preserving a discreet silence on the method by which the general convention's proposals would be considered.

Of the twelve states that sent delegations to the Federal Convention in 1787 (Rhode Island boycotted the gathering), eight followed the Annapolis formula. The other four demanded that the Confederation Congress authorize the Convention before they would act. On February 21, 1787, Congress gave that sanction but limited it with care—directing the Convention to operate under the authority and the limitations of Article 13:

> Whereas there is provision in the Articles of Confederation & perpetual Union for making alterations therein by the Assent of a Congress of the United States and of the legislatures of the several States; And whereas experience hath evinced that there are defects in the present Confederation, as a mean to remedy which several of the States and particularly the State of New York by express instructions to their delegates in Congress have suggested a convention for the purposes expressed in the following resolution and such Convention appearing to be the most probable mean of establishing in these states a firm national government
>
> Resolved that in the opinion of Congress it is expedient that on the second Monday in May next a Convention of delegates who shall have been appointed by the several states be held at Philadelphia *for the sole and express purpose of revising the Articles of*

> *Confederation* and reporting to Congress and the several legislatures *such alterations and provisions therein as shall when agreed to in Congress and confirmed by the states* render the federal constitution adequate to the exigencies of Government & the preservation of the Union.[22] [emphasis added]

Following this resolution, the remaining four states named delegations to go to Philadelphia. Only Rhode Island rejected the proposed convention out of hand.[23]

The calling of the Federal Convention was the most damning commentary on the failure of the Articles of Confederation. The defects of the Confederation may have been self-evident, but that was no guarantee that the remedy was equally obvious. As the delegates chosen to attend the Federal Convention traveled to Philadelphia by horse, stage, or ship, they realized that they were about to confront the greatest challenge yet to the future of the American Revolution. On their efforts hinged the success or failure of the American nation.

CHAPTER 2

"AN EASY, REGULAR, AND CONSTITUTIONAL WAY"

The plan now to be formed will certainly be defective, as the Confederation has been found on trial to be. Amendments therefore will be necessary, and it will be better to provide for them, in an easy, regular and Constitutional way than to trust to chance and violence.

GEORGE MASON OF VIRGINIA
Speech at Federal Convention
June 11, 1787

IN THE EVENING OF SEPTEMBER 17, 1787, David Claypoole labored in his Philadelphia print shop, setting in type a special edition of the *Pennsylvania Packet, and Daily Advertiser.* Laying aside the usual advertisements, announcements of ship and coach arrivals and departures, foreign dispatches, reprints of learned essays, and entertaining anecdotes, Claypoole decided to devote the entire four pages of the September 19 issue to what later generations would regard as the most important national news story of its time.[1] The Federal Convention had adjourned that day, and the fruit of its labors, the proposed Constitution, was taking shape under the printer's ink-stained fingers. The Convention had entrusted its printing business to Claypoole all summer, and his reward for prompt and confidential service (other than his fees, which he would have to carry on his books, unpaid, for three years)[2] was an exclusive—the right of first publication of the Constitution.

The sputterings of an oil lamp and the clicking of type being slid into place were the only sounds in the print shop. But the quiet in which Claypoole worked was, for the Constitution, the eye of the hurricane. After four months of vigorous, often bitter debate within the Convention and anxious speculation without, the document that Claypoole was preparing for his readers was about to become the focus of the first "great national discussion." Soon the results of the delegates' labors behind closed doors would be available for the entire citizenry to read—and to pick apart. Each feature of the Constitution would become an epicenter of political dissension: a new national legislature, apportioned according to a novel scheme designed to preserve sectional peace and possessing large yet limited grants of power; a new chief executive for the United States, to be chosen by a system totally unlike anything yet seen in American politics; a host of compromises between large and small states, free and slave states, and national and state authority; and a new means of adopting and amending constitutions.

ARTICLE V OF THE CONSTITUTION, which codifies the amending process, was at once a creative response to the actual problems of the era in which the document was written and a major reformulation of the idea and functions of a written constitution. In devising the amending process, as in creating the other components of the Constitution, the framers combined attention to issues of practical politics with theoretical sophistication in the devising of political technology.[3]

The designers of Article V had two goals in mind. First, recalling that the impossibility of amending the Articles of Confederation had made them ineffective as a form of government, the Constitution's framers hoped to render the new document adaptable to changing circumstances and needs. At the same time, they sought to ensure that the amending process would operate only when the polity had reached a consensus that it was necessary to change the constitutional text. They tried to strike a balance, seeking to create a process more easily used than that of the Articles of Confederation, yet not so easy as to leave the Constitution prey to passing majorities or to reduce it to a catalog of "special provisos."[4] Article V is thus an unappreciated linchpin of the solution propounded by the framers of the Constitution to the difficulties facing the United States in 1787.

THE FEDERAL CONVENTION DEVISES ARTICLE V

ALL THE DELEGATES AT THE Federal Convention recognized that the unanimity required by Article 13 of the Articles of Confederation was unworkable as a means of amending the nation's form of government. Indeed, in a pamphlet collecting his "observations" on the task confronting the Convention, delegate Charles Pinckney of South Carolina attributed the desperate state of the Confederation to its self-defeating amending process:

> [I]t is to this unanimous consent, [that] the depressed situation of the Union is undoubtedly owing. Had the measures recommended by Congress and assented to, some of them by eleven and others by twelve of the States, been carried into execution, how different would have been the complexion of Public Affairs?[5]

As a delegate to the Confederation Congress, Pinckney had chaired the committee that in 1786 had proposed the last attempt to amend the Articles; he therefore spoke with authority on the deficiencies of Article 13.

The delegates spent their first few days drafting rules to guide the Convention's proceedings; one of these, the rule closing sessions to the public and the press, freed them to consider even the most sweeping reforms without worrying about popular approval or disapproval. On May 29, four days after the Convention opened, the delegates concluded, without dissent and almost without debate, that a fresh start was needed to form a federal government adequate to the nation's problems. They therefore bypassed the Articles entirely and based their labors on a set of resolutions drafted by James Madison of Virginia and formally proposed by Governor Edmund Randolph.

The "Virginia Plan" listed a new amending process as one of its goals but did not explain how that process should operate:

> Resd that provision ought to be made for the amendment of the Articles of Union whensoever it shall seem necessary, and that the assent of the National Legislature ought not to be required thereto.[6]

Although Article 13 was one of the most serious defects of the Confederation, and thus attracted extensive and harsh criticism during the Convention, little drama or incident appears in the delegates' discussion of how the new amending process might work. The Convention's debates on this question were vague and desultory, but, in some ways, the Convention's ambiguity and terseness are understandable. The problem the delegates faced was clear. An amending process requiring the consent of all the state legislatures had proved unworkable; therefore, majority consent was the solution—not so small a majority that it could be easily obtained, not so large that it would be impossible to achieve. The principal problem was placating delegates who were wary of any process that might injure the vital interests of individual states.

To the consternation of those who have looked in vain to the surviving records of the Convention for guidance to resolve subsequent constitutional controversies, the Convention was able to address only those problems that its members could anticipate and, within that category, those that they deemed most pressing and most easily settled. Nonetheless, some delegates, notably James Madison, protested to no avail that the Convention should devote more attention to the potential difficulties of the amending process.

Organizing themselves as a Committee of the Whole House (a useful device of parliamentary procedure permitting informal discussion to arrive at a consensus to be the basis of formal debate), the delegates spent the first weeks of the Convention reviewing the Virginia Plan, resolution by resolution. On June 5, they began their examination of the thirteenth resolution, on the amending process, but soon voted to postpone the question, with Virginia, South Carolina, and Georgia disagreeing.[7] Six days later, the amending process resurfaced in the Committee of the Whole House. George Mason of Virginia argued in favor of the resolution:

> The plan now to be formed will certainly be defective, as the Confederation has been found on trial to be. Amendments therefore will be necessary, and it will be better to provide for them, in an easy, regular and Constitutional way than to trust to chance and violence. It would be improper to require the consent of the Natl. Legislature because they may abuse their power, and refuse their consent on that very account. The opportunity for such an abuse, may be the fault of the Constitution calling for amendmt.[8]

The delegates used their power under the Convention's rules to split the proposition into its component clauses, to deal with or postpone each in turn. They accepted the idea of an amending process but deferred their discussion of the role the national legislature would have in it.[9] When the Committee of the Whole House finished its review of the Virginia Plan, the cycle of discussion began again in the full Convention, which, on July 23, agreed unanimously and without debate that the Constitution should include "provision for . . . future amendments . . ."[10]

This was all the guidance the Convention gave to its Committee of Detail, which prepared the first draft of the Constitution between July 26 and August 6. The committee's members were John Rutledge of South Carolina (who acted as chairman), Edmund Randolph of Virginia, Nathaniel Gorham of Massachusetts, Oliver Ellsworth of Connecticut, and James Wilson of Pennsylvania. Although Randolph was assigned principal responsibility for the draft, he worked closely with his colleagues, especially Wilson, a distinguished lawyer and constitutional theorist.[11]

At one point, Wilson scribbled the following draft language—the first recognizable antecedent of Article V:

> This Constitution ought to be amended whenever such Amendment shall become necessary; and on the Application of the Legislatures of two thirds of the States in the Union, the Legislature of the United States shall call a Convention for that Purpose.[12]

The provision authorized only one means for amending the Constitution—a convention, to be called by Congress on application of two-thirds of the states.

(It thus resembled the five state constitutions, particularly that of Massachusetts, that provided for a convention as the principal or sole means of amendment.) In keeping with the Virginia Plan's language, Wilson's draft did not grant Congress any power to propose amendments—or, indeed, any role in the amending process other than calling a convention when required to do so. Wilson's draft was incorporated into the text of the committee draft:

> On the application of the Legislatures of two thirds of the States in the Union, for an amendment of this Constitution, the Legislature of the United States shall call a Convention for that purpose.[13]

Working quickly, the Convention approved this provision on August 30 without comment, except that Gouverneur Morris (a New Yorker who had wangled himself a seat in the Pennsylvania delegation) suggested "that the Legislature should be left at liberty to call a Convention, whenever they please."[14]

Two weeks later, on September 10, Elbridge Gerry of Massachusetts moved to reconsider the provision, touching off the first of two serious discussions of the amending process in the Convention. Gerry, who was gradually defining himself as an opponent of the Constitution, feared the provision's potential to threaten the state constitutions. Madison summarized Gerry's challenge:

> This Constitution . . . is to be paramount to the State Constitutions. It follows, hence, from this article that two thirds of the States may obtain a Convention, a majority of which can bind the Union to innovations that may subvert the State-Constitutions altogether. He asked whether this was a situation proper to be run into—[15]

Agreeing that the provision should be reconsidered, Alexander Hamilton of New York shifted the focus of debate from the danger highlighted by Gerry. Rejecting the possibility that an amending convention might endanger the state constitutions, Hamilton pointed out that the principle of majority rule should work as well for the American people as it did for the people within a given state. The means of proposing amendments was "not adequate," the nationalist Hamilton argued, because only state legislatures had the power to propose amendments:

> The State Legislatures will not apply for alterations but with a view to increase their own powers— The National Legislature will be the first to perceive and will be most sensible to the

necessity of amendments, and ought also to be empowered, whenever two thirds of each branch should concur to call a Convention— There could be no danger in giving this power, as the people would finally decide in the case.[16]

Madison interjected his own reason for reconsidering the proposal, pointing out that it left a host of questions unanswered: "How was a Convention to be formed? by what rule decide? what the force of its acts?"[17] The delegates adopted the motion to reconsider, nine states to one (New Jersey), with New Hampshire divided.*

After a skirmish over a proposal by Roger Sherman of Connecticut to confer power on the national legislature to propose amendments and to require the consent of the states to put amendments into effect, Madison (seconded by Hamilton) offered a substitute for the Committee of Detail proposal:

> The Legislature of the U—— S—— whenever two thirds of both Houses shall deem necessary, or on the application of two thirds of the Legislatures of the several States, shall propose amendments to this Constitution, which shall be valid to all intents and purposes as part thereof, when the same shall have been ratified by three fourths at least of the Legislatures of the several States, or by Conventions in three fourths thereof, as one or the other mode of ratification may be proposed by the Legislature of the U.S.:[18]

Rutledge, the acknowledged leader both of the South Carolina delegation and of the defenders of slavery in the Convention, objected that this draft would permit the federal government to tamper with the constitutional provisions protecting the slave trade for twenty years. He offered an amendment to the proposal to guard against interference with the slave trade before 1808. The delegates agreed without comment, and the amended Madison-Hamilton substitute was adopted, nine states to one (Delaware), with New Hampshire again divided.[19]

Doubtless hopeful that its deliberations were nearing completion, the Convention ended that day's work by referring its amassed resolutions and revisions to the Committee of Style and Arrangement (which the delegates had appointed on September 8 to prepare a final draft of the Constitution). Named to the

---

*By this point, two of the three New York delegates had returned home, leaving eleven voting delegations and only one New Yorker, Hamilton, who could take part in debate but could not cast his state's vote.

committee were Madison, Hamilton, Gouverneur Morris, William Samuel John-son of Connecticut, and Rufus King of Massachusetts. The committee turned over the task to Morris, who prepared a draft of seven articles. Morris's version of the amending process appeared as Article V:

> The Congress, whenever two-thirds of both houses shall deem necessary, or on the application of two-thirds of the legislatures of the several states, shall propose amendments to this constitu-tion, which shall be valid to all intents and purposes, as part thereof, when the same shall have been ratified by three-fourths at least of the legislatures of the several states, or by conventions in three-fourths thereof, as the one or the other mode of ratifica-tion may be proposed by the Congress: Provided, that no amend-ment which may be made prior to the year 1808 shall in any manner affect the [ ] and [ ] sections of article [ ][20]

In the days between the committee's submission of this draft to the Conven-tion and the Convention's last discussion of Article V, George Mason prepared a list of disputed points and suggested revisions. Disturbed by the nationalizing and anti-liberty tendencies he descried in the Constitution, Mason was moving (with Gerry and Randolph) into opposition to the document. His analysis of Article V focused on the proposing of amendments and reflected his truculent commitment to democratic government:

> Article 5th. By this Article Congress only have the Power of proposing Amendments at any future time to this Constitution, & shou'd it prove ever so oppressive, the whole people of Amer-ica can't make, or even propose Alterations to it; a Doctrine utterly subversive of the fundamental principles of the Rights & Liberties of the people[.][21]

On September 15, the longest day of the Convention and the final day of discussion of the Morris draft, the delegates reviewed Article V. Reviving Gerry's specter of threats to the state governments, Sherman asked that the exception already granted to protect the slave trade until 1808 be extended in scope "to provide that no State should be affected in its internal police, or deprived of its equality in the Senate"—thus immunizing both of the major compromises built into the Constitution. Mason also objected to Article V, drawing on his outline just cited. Seeing merit in one of Gerry's points, Gouverneur Morris joined him in proposing that Congress be required to call a convention when requested to do so by two-thirds of the states. Madison agreed that the Morris-Gerry sugges-tion might be a good idea but warned again about the uncertainties of procedure;

such "difficulties . . . as to the form, the quorum, &c. . . . in Constitutional regulations ought to be as much as possible avoided." Despite Madison's qualms, the Convention adopted the proposal unanimously.[22]

Undeterred by the Convention's rejection of his principal criticisms of the amending process, Gerry moved to strike the clause authorizing ratification by state conventions, but only Connecticut supported him.[23] Sherman renewed his call for a limitation on the amending process "that no State shall without its consent be affected in its internal police, or deprived of its equal suffrage in the Senate." Madison protested, "Begin with these special provisos and every State will insist on them, for their boundaries, exports &c." The Convention agreed with Madison; only the small states of New Jersey and Delaware supported Sherman. Sherman thereupon demanded that Article V be struck altogether, but he gained the support only of Connecticut and New Jersey, with Delaware divided.

Perceiving that some olive branch would be in order to settle the worries of Sherman and his allies, Gouverneur Morris suggested a modification of Article V preserving equality of representation in the Senate. Madison recorded in his notes, "This motion being dictated by the circulating murmurs of the small States was agreed to without debate, no one opposing, or on the question, saying no."[24] Madison's comment suggests his attention to the demands of history and his sputtering resentment of the ability of the small states to urge their claims on the Convention.

Thus the Convention approved the final text of Article V:

> The Congress, whenever two thirds of both Houses shall deem it necessary, shall propose Amendments to this Constitution, or, on the Application of the Legislatures of two thirds of the several States, shall call a Convention for proposing Amendments, which, in either Case, shall be valid to all Intents and Purposes, as Part of this Constitution, when ratified by the Legislatures of three fourths of the several States, or by Conventions in three fourths thereof, as the one or the other Mode of Ratification may be proposed by the Congress; Provided that no Amendment which may be made prior to the Year One thousand eight hundred and eight shall in any Manner affect the first and fourth Clauses in the Ninth Section of the first Article; and that no State, without its Consent, shall be deprived of it's equal Suffrage in the Senate.

The September 15 debate was characteristic of the last days of the Convention. Time and again, individual delegates' objections failed because a consensus had emerged within the Convention whose momentum was spurred by the delegates' weariness and impatience. Still, the Convention accommodated the insistent demands of groups of delegates having the power to derail the fragile consensus.

Exhaustion was the principal reason for another decision that would bear significantly on the future of the amending process: the delegates' unexplained rejection of the last-minute bid by Gerry and Mason to add a declaration of rights to the Constitution (although Sherman noted that he did not see its necessity). Later events would brand this decision a ghastly political mistake, which nearly doomed the Constitution in the ratification campaign of 1787–1788. That the document's supporters were able to avert the potentially disastrous consequences of the delegates' omission was thanks largely to the existence of Article V.

ARTICLE V IN THE RATIFICATION CONTROVERSY

ARTICLE V PROVED ITS WORTH by helping to clinch the adoption of the Constitution. Its inclusion in the Constitution enabled the document's supporters to work to change the Constitution and substantiated their pledges to do so, thus mollifying the Constitution's opponents.

On its last day, September 17, the Federal Convention set in motion what we now know as the ratification process. Under the terms of Article VII, as supplemented by resolutions adopted by the Convention, the Constitution would go into effect once it had been ratified by conventions in nine of the thirteen states. Both the framers of the Constitution and their fellow citizens throughout the nation recognized that Article VII was a major departure in two respects from Article 13 of the Articles of Confederation: Article VII required consent by only nine out of thirteen, rather than all thirteen states, and it required that the states choose conventions to grant or withhold that consent rather than leave the decision to the state legislatures.

Opponents of the proposed Constitution claimed in vain that Article VII illegally superseded Article 13, and that this illegality extended by implication to the entire Constitution. But on September 28, after three days of debate, the Confederation Congress voted to transmit to the state legislatures both the proposed Constitution and the Convention's resolutions outlining the ratification procedure. Neither camp's delegates in Congress could claim complete victory; such opponents of the Constitution as Richard Henry Lee of Virginia and Melancton Smith of New York unsuccessfully fought for the chance to reject or rewrite the Constitution, and such pro-Constitution delegates as James Madison could not secure the formal endorsement they had craved. On balance, however, the decision of Congress favored the Constitution, effectively legitimating it and the procedure by which it was to be considered and adopted.

Twelve of the thirteen states elected ratifying conventions in 1787–1788; Rhode Island, as expected, did not.[25] Despite the unanimous early endorsements of the Constitution by the Delaware, New Jersey, and Georgia conventions, the two-to-one majority in the Pennsylvania convention, and the preponderance of pro-Constitution sentiment in the nation's newspapers,[26] eight conventions—a clear majority—exposed deep divisions between supporters of the Constitution (who called themselves Federalists) and the document's adversaries (saddled, against their will, with the name Anti-Federalists).[27]

Few Anti-Federalists made references to Article V. Instead, they stressed the need to amend the Constitution before its adoption. What comments they made on the proposed amending process were disparaging and skeptical. By contrast, Federalists, who argued that the Constitution had to be adopted as it was and that its defects would emerge only from actual experience, often invoked Article V, praising it as more flexible and useful than Article 13 of the Articles of Confederation and promising that it would provide an effective means to repair any defects in the constitutional framework once the need for repair arose.

The early stages of the ratification controversy left Federalists overconfident of the likelihood of success, but several hard-fought battles in early 1788 sobered them considerably, giving heart to Anti-Federalists in key states throughout the Union. Moderate Federalists began to realize that they needed to make more of an effort to woo undecided voters and delegates, as well as moderate Anti-Federalists.

The vehicle they chose for their new ratification strategy was the amending process set out in Article V, the need for which had become apparent at the Massachusetts ratifying convention in February 1788. Days of debate had revealed a bitter impasse in that body: the Anti-Federalists insisted that the Constitution had to be amended before its adoption, and the Federalists retorted that the Constitution had to be accepted as it was, with no previous or conditional amendments. Moderate delegates in both camps—Governor John Hancock and Samuel Adams for the Anti-Federalists and a group of Federalists led by William Cushing (later an associate justice of the United States Supreme Court)—united on a compromise: the convention would recommend amendments to be considered by the first Congress to convene under the Constitution. Should that Congress approve the recommendations, it would propose them to the states, using the mechanisms of Article V.

The agreement on recommended amendments cut through the stalemate; the convention voted, 187 to 168, to adopt the Constitution and a list of six recommended amendments. In the service of this compromise, the Federalists pledged to support amendments in the new Congress, and the Anti-Federalists agreed to put aside their opposition to the new government, should it ever go into effect. Every state ratifying the Constitution after Massachusetts followed this example and adopted a list of recommended amendments. These lists, setting forth more than two hundred proposals, became the raw material from which Representative James Madison would fashion the first draft of the federal Bill of Rights in the spring of 1789.[28]

As the Federalists' vehicle to satisfy the people's fears about the lack of a federal declaration of rights, Article V played a vital part in the people's decision to adopt the Constitution.[29] Just as important, the conciliatory character of the strategy of recommended amendments reconciled many Anti-Federalists to the adoption of the Constitution and stifled threats to resist its implementation.

SURROUNDING THE CONTEST FOR VOTES in the ratification controversy was a war of words and arguments, and Articles V and VII—and, consequently, Article 13 of the Articles of Confederation—became focal points of that war. The old and new methods of constitutional change competed for public favor.

Proponents and opponents of the Constitution blended arguments over four seemingly distinct issues: (i) the legitimacy of the Convention and the proposed Constitution, (ii) the unsatisfactoriness of the Articles of Confederation, (iii) the supposed need to amend the Constitution before it was adopted, and (iv) the actual workings of Article V. These linked constitutional and political arguments helped to determine the fate of the Constitution. Anti-Federalists tended to discuss Articles V and VII interchangeably, for Article VII's provision that nine state ratifications were sufficient to put the Constitution into effect applied the general principles outlined in Article V to the adoption of the Constitution itself.

As we have seen, the illegality of the Constitution was the Anti-Federalists' first line of defense; they insisted that the entire ratification process outlined in Article VII and the Convention's resolutions was invalid.[30] However, the Anti-Federal camp was divided with respect to the merits of the process set forth in Article 13; they either praised the existing process as a safeguard of freedom or sidestepped the embarrassment of conceding its defects.

Attorney General Luther Martin of Maryland defended Article 13 as a bulwark of liberty; the very difficulty of the process, he argued, protected the people against unwise or desperate innovations. He believed that it was better for the amending process to be deadlocked than that the people's liberty and right to govern themselves be subverted.[31] Martin, a Maryland delegate to the Federal Convention, not only was not a signer of the document but was so opposed to it that he left the Convention long before its close to organize opposition to the Constitution in his home state. Other Anti-Federalists regarded the Articles as a solemn act by the people of the states and believed that breaching Article 13, no matter what the reason, would be a violation of public and private virtue, evidencing "a total want of publick faith and destitution of national honour," which, in and of itself, could damage the American people.[32] Still others sidestepped the issue altogether, preferring to grapple with the Constitution on the merits, arguing for a sweeping array of changes to virtually every provision of the proposed charter.

Federalists focused on the defects of the Articles—what Alexander Hamilton termed "the imbecility of our government."[33] One of the key elements of their case against the Articles was that the old document's defects were so many and so great that they could not be repaired by mere amendment. Edmund Randolph made this point in the Virginia ratifying convention:

> I therefore conclude, that the Confederation is too defective to deserve correction. Let us take farewell of it, with reverential respect, as an old benefactor. It is gone, whether this House says so, or not. It is gone, Sir, by its own weakness.[34]

Similarly, Joseph Barrell, a Massachusetts merchant and supporter of the Constitution, pleaded with his brother, an Anti-Federal farmer in the Maine district who was about to take his seat in the Massachusetts ratifying convention:

> . . . if you are really opposed to it, I will suppose it is from Principal, and if so, I think this one consideration alone will induce you to adopt it, vizt. because the present Confederation cannot be alterd, unless *all the 13 States* agree and I was going to say *Heaven and Earth may pass away before that event will take place!* While the Constitution now proposd may be alterd when ever *Nine* States shall require it, *Is it not therefore better to adopt this Constitution* (even if it was not the best) *which may be alterd rather than to retain the present Wretched System wch. never can?*—[35]

Nathaniel Barrell ultimately voted for ratification, accepting the compromise strategy.

James Madison reminded readers of *The Federalist* (the series of newspaper essays he wrote with Alexander Hamilton and John Jay defending the Constitution) of the impossibility of using Article 13 to effect needed changes in the Articles. Explaining why the Convention abandoned the rule of unanimity codified in that provision, he mocked

> the absurdity of subjecting the fate of twelve States to the perverseness or corruption of a thirteenth [meaning Rhode Island]; . . . [and] the example of inflexible opposition given by *a majority* of one sixtieth of the people of America to a measure approved and called for by the voice of twelve states, comprising fifty-nine sixtieths of the people—an example still fresh in the memory and indignation of every citizen who has felt for the wounded honor and prosperity of his country.[36]

In defending the legitimacy of the proposed Constitution, Federalists used a range of arguments, of greater or lesser persuasiveness.[37] First, they emphasized that the Constitution was only a proposal that the people were free to accept or to reject as they pleased, and that no harm could come from considering it.[38] On a higher plane, Madison maintained in *The Federalist No. 40* that the Convention had acted in conformity with a higher law—the principles of the American Revolution articulated in the Declaration of Independence, chief among which was the right of the people to alter or abolish their government and to replace it with one better suited to secure their liberty and happiness. There was no doubt, the Federalists declared, that the Articles could not secure American liberty and happiness.[39]

Perhaps the most effective Federalist argument was that the time to challenge the Constitution's legality had passed. They pointed out that the Confederation Congress had laid the proposed Constitution before the states, the states had called elections for ratifying conventions, the people had taken part in those elections, and the conventions were meeting as regularly constituted bodies—all without challenging the Constitution's legitimacy. It was too late to raise this issue after so many institutions of government and groups of citizens had, either explicitly or implicitly, set it aside.[40] Moreover, the Federalists maintained, all Americans agreed on the need to replace the Articles, and the Constitution was the only alternative before the people. Where they could, Federalists backed up this forensic posture with all the political resources they could muster. For example, the presiding officer of the Virginia ratifying convention, Edmund Pendleton, ruled Patrick Henry out of order when the Anti-Federal orator sought to impeach the legality of the Constitution.[41]

Regardless of where they stood on the legitimacy issue, the Anti-Federalists could not or would not separate their assessments of Article V from their demands that the Constitution be amended before it was adopted. They made three linked points:

- There was no time to consider amendments better than the present, when the Constitution was the focus of the people's attention and not yet the shield of designing, ambitious politicians conspiring against the people's liberties.

- The present was the only practicable time to amend the document, for once it was in effect government officials could not be trusted to propose amendments that would deprive them of powers acquired through its adoption.

- The process outlined in Article V would not work as easily as the Federalists maintained. The newspaper essayist "An Old Whig" wrote:

Let us for a moment consider the propriety of adopting it first, and trusting to its being afterwards amended. These necessary amendments, after the constitution is adopted, can only be made in one of two ways:—either by our future rulers in the continental legislature by their own act—or in the way provided for in the fifth article. . . . This latter mode is so intricate, that an attempt to investigate it is like endeavouring to trace the windings of a labyrinth, and I have therefore observed that people willingly turn aside from the subject, as confused and disgusting. . . .[42]

After spinning out "these strainings, and filtrings, and refinings," An Old Whig asked rhetorically whether any amendments produced by the Article V process would be "of any essential importance." He answered: "For my part I would full as soon sit down and take my chance of winning an important privilege to the people, by the casting of the dice 'till I could throw sixes an hundred times in succession." He concluded that he understood why the framers of the Constitution had made it so difficult to amend the document, yet he insisted that precisely for this reason it was vital to amend the document before it went into effect, and before the people got used to "the chains of slavery."[43]

Similarly, the anonymous "Federal Farmer" insisted that "[w]hile power is in the hands of the people, or democratic part of the community," it is easier to work changes in forms of government than "when power is once transferred from the many to the few."[44] And "Centinel" rejected his fellow Pennsylvanian James Wilson's citations of Article V as a means to reassure the people that amendments could be procured. Centinel inquired: "Does history abound with examples of a voluntary relinquishment of power, however injurious to the community? No; it would require a general and successful rising of the people to effect anything of this nature.—This provision therefore is mere sound."[45]

Moving from general principles to specific cases, New England Anti-Federalists attacked the proslavery exclusions in Article V. Three unrepentant Anti-Federalist delegates to the Massachusetts ratifying convention—Consider Arms, Malichi Maynard, and Samuel Field—explained their opposition to the Constitution in the *Hampshire Gazette* in April 1788. They were particularly offended, they declared, by the many features of the Constitution, including the exceptions clause of Article V, born of compromises with slaveholding states; they rejected both the particular provisions and the Constitution as a whole as a betrayal of the American Revolution.[46]

Recognizing the strength of Article V as an element of the case for the Constitution, Hamilton and Madison defended the provision with skill and energy. Madison used the provision with great effect as the capstone of his argument in *The Federalist No. 39* that the Constitution was neither a national government nor a federal government but combined the virtues of each form while avoiding the defects of both:

> If we try the Constitution by its last relation to the authority by which amendments are to be made, we find it neither wholly *national* nor wholly *federal*. Were it wholly national, the supreme and ultimate authority would reside in the *majority* of the people of the Union; and this authority would be competent at all times, like that of a majority of every national society to alter or abolish its established government. Were it wholly federal, on the other hand, the concurrence of each State in the Union would be essential to every alteration that would be binding on all. The mode provided by the plan of the convention is not founded on either of these principles. In requiring more than a majority, and particularly in computing the proportion by *States*, not by *citizens*, it departs from the national and advances towards the *federal* character; in rendering the concurrence of less than the whole number of States sufficient, it loses again the *federal* and partakes of the *national* character.[47]

In *The Federalist No. 43*, Madison defended Article V:

> It guards equally against that extreme facility, which would render the Constitution too mutable; and that extreme difficulty, which might perpetuate its discovered faults. It, moreover, equally enables the general and the State governments to originate the amendment of errors, as they may be pointed out by the experience on one side, or on the other.[48]

Hamilton concluded *The Federalist*, in No. *85*, by urging the virtues of the amending process codified in Article V.[49] He rejected the Anti-Federalists' fears that it would not be possible to amend the Constitution after ratification. Under Article V of a ratified Constitution, Hamilton wrote, not only would a mere nine states have to consent (rather than the thirteen required by the Articles of Confederation) but the debate over an amendment after ratification could focus far more easily on the merits or defects of the proposal itself. This would ensure the reflection and choice necessary to sound constitutional government. By contrast, should the people pursue the route of previous amendments, the argument over their purposes, content, and effects would be hopelessly entangled with that over the virtues and weaknesses of the Constitution.

Hamilton gave three answers to Anti-Federalists' fears that federal officials would be loath to surrender their powers. First, any defects of the Constitution that he perceived did not pertain to the powers of the federal government but to its structure. Second, practical considerations would impose on officials of the federal government the *"necessity"* to work in "a spirit of accommodation" with the state governments, including the need to accept constitutional amendments limiting federal power. Third, if the states demanded a convention under Article V, the federal government would have no choice but to obey. (This, of course, did not prevent Hamilton, Madison, and their colleagues from working diligently to prevent the calling of such a convention.)

WHAT DID THE FRAMERS AND adopters of the Constitution intend the amending process to be used for? Some have suggested that Article V was intended only to provide a means for tinkering with the structure of government authorized by the Constitution, rather than as a way to build new fundamental principles into it.[50] Others describe it as a mechanism of higher lawmaking designed to return the polity at necessary moments to the level of constitutional politics that engages the attention of the People of the United States (or, in eighteenth-century political language, to make it possible to invoke the constituent power of the citizenry).[51] Still others suggest that there are virtually no restrictions on the amending process, and that even the steps and restrictions it specifies might be ignored in the interest of higher lawmaking.[52]

In resolving such questions, we face two related problems. First, the only guidance given by the text of the Constitution appears in Article V. And, as we have seen, the restrictions built into that provision were designed to immunize from later amendment key sectional compromises vital to the success of the framing of the Constitution. Of the immunized subjects, only the equality of state representation in the Senate survives today. The restrictions shielding slavery were rendered void by their own terms in 1808. Any possibility that provisions related to slavery might still be immunized from Article V's reach was dashed by the Civil War of 1861–1865, and by the three Amendments ratified in its aftermath. This has not prevented constitutional scholars from carrying on a vigorous controversy over whether it might be possible for federal judges to rule unconstitutional an otherwise valid amendment—for example, striking down a "flag desecration" amendment as violating the First Amendment.[53]

Second, neither the proponents nor the opponents of the Constitution deemed it in the interest of their cause to present an impartial analysis of the legitimate uses of the amending process. Determined to secure the Constitution's adoption and to avoid attempts to amend, revise, or rewrite the document before it was adopted, the Federalists feared that any discussion of future amendments might raise specters that would dissuade undecided voters and ratifying-convention delegates from approving it. The Anti-Federalists, equally determined to prevent the adoption of the Constitution and seeking to present it in the most threatening terms they could find, did not want anyone to suggest ways to make it more palatable. Convinced that any appeals to Article V were disingenuous, they emphasized the difficulty of the process and the unlikeliness of any valuable changes emerging from it.

Nor do the more than two hundred amendments proposed by the state ratifying conventions in 1788 cast light on the scope of the amending power conferred by Article V, for those proposals attacked virtually every provision of the Constitution. Finally, nowhere in the surviving evidence of the First Congress's debates on the proposed amendments of 1789 is there comment on whether these amendments exceed the power conferred by Article V. As with so many other parts of the Constitution, the scope of the amending process codified in Article V awaited definition by those who would seek to wield it in the future.

THE USE OF RECOMMENDED AMENDMENTS as a device to win adoption of the Constitution was an implied testament to the crucial role of the amending process in the constitutional framework. But neither the Federalists' exaltation of Article V's flexibility nor their recommended-amendments strategy dispelled Anti-Federal doubts about the Constitution. In most states, the politics of conciliation embodied in that strategy could not conceal the closeness of the Federalists' margin of victory—by ten votes in the Virginia (89 to 79) and New Hampshire (78 to 68) conventions, and by three votes in the New York (30 to 27) convention. And two states, North Carolina and Rhode Island, refused to ratify without previous amendments. Even as Anti-Federalists conceded defeat, they expected their victorious adversaries to live up to their promise to secure amendments to the Constitution. The issue of amendments thus became a determining factor in many congressional elections in the winter of 1788–1789. Moreover, the Anti-Federalists of New York and Virginia continued their quest for a second convention to receive the Constitution and the hundreds of recommended amendments generated by the state ratifying conventions.

As the newly elected members of the First Congress made their way to the temporary federal capital in New York City in the first months of 1789, the second-convention movement and the general controversy over amending the Constitution cast a menacing shadow over the establishment of the new government.[54] Federalist strategists had much to preoccupy them, including the possible roles that Article V would play in the launching of the Constitution.

CHAPTER 3

THE FIRST FRUITS OF ARTICLE V: THE BILL OF RIGHTS

The Bill of Rights was not written into the Constitution in order to protect governments from "trouble," but so that the people might have a legitimate method of causing trouble to governments they no longer trusted.

PROFESSOR HENRY STEELE COMMAGER
Letter to *The New York Times*
June 18, 1971

ON JUNE 8, 1789, A SMALL, frail man in his late thirties stood in the United States House of Representatives chamber in Federal Hall in New York City and sought recognition from the chair. Dressed in sober black, he clutched in his left hand a sheaf of papers scribbled over with notes, to which he referred as he spoke. As wagons clattered down Wall Street outside the building, he reminded his colleagues that he had served notice of his intentions several times since the House had convened three months before, and emphasized his belief that his proposal was necessary both to give quiet to the people and to keep his word to those who had elected him. The scholarly, weak-voiced Virginian presented a singular spectacle—a politician seeking to keep a campaign promise. Although some of his colleagues muttered with impatience, others paid him close attention, as did the visitors and journalists looking down at the chamber from the galleries. Representative James Madison had launched his last—and boldest—campaign to secure victory in the controversy over the Constitution: the proposing of constitutional amendments under Article V, specifically a federal declaration or bill of rights.

It is fitting that the Bill of Rights was the first product of Article V.[1] American constitutionalism is based on two linked principles: that the people govern themselves, and that the government they design for that purpose should be strong enough to identify and secure national interests, yet limited enough to protect liberty. The Preamble of the Constitution is the anchor for these principles; the Bill of Rights makes a reality the Preamble's promise to "secure the Blessings of Liberty to ourselves and our Posterity."

RIGHTS IN THE RATIFICATION CONTROVERSY

IN 1787–1788, BOTH THE ANTI-FEDERALISTS and those who sought to remain neutral in the ratification controversy worried that the Constitution authorized a government so powerful that it would destroy the states and the rights of the people. Such Federalists as James Wilson and Alexander Hamilton derided these fears as groundless, explaining that the general government could exercise only those powers conferred on it by the Constitution. Moreover, they contended, the people were the ultimate sovereigns; how could the people violate their own rights? They also cited such provisions as Article I, section 9, cataloging a series of limitations on federal power, to refute the Anti-Federal charge that the Constitution conferred unlimited powers on the general government. Finally, they maintained, the state governments were far from bastions of liberty themselves; throughout the 1770s and 1780s they had been responsible for the most frequent and blatant violations of individual rights.

Unconvinced, Anti-Federalists insisted that the Constitution provided few explicit limitations on governmental power, making even more glaring the document's lack of a bill of rights. They brushed aside the Federalists' attacks on state governments, pointing out that the powers of a new, untried federal government were the issue under debate. And they refused even to consider the argument (so popular with Federalist polemicists) that the people could not violate their own rights. Clinging to the traditional view that the government and the people were and could only be adversaries, Anti-Federalists could not embrace the new Federalist theories of popular sovereignty. And, they knew, many Americans who were otherwise friendly to the Constitution shared their views on the need to limit the federal government's power over rights.

As this debate moved from one state ratifying convention to the next, the Constitution's lack of a bill of rights limiting the powers of the general government over the individual became the Anti-Federalists' most compelling argument. Moreover, Anti-Federalists were able to point to state constitutions that either began with declarations of rights, as in Virginia and Massachusetts, or incorporated rights-protecting provisions, as in New York.[2] That the Constitution created a government possessing the power to operate on individual citizens, they insisted, meant that (like the state constitutions that it resembled) it ought to include provisions defining and protecting rights.

But the defects that Anti-Federalists perceived in the Constitution did not end with the omission of a declaration of rights. The document's opponents also demanded amendments limiting the federal government's powers to levy taxes and to regulate interstate and foreign commerce—changes that would have reduced the Constitution to little more than a redrafted Articles of Confederation. And, as noted in Chapter 2, during the ratification controversy, Anti-Federalists insisted that the proposed charter of government be revised or fully rewritten before its adoption; many favored submitting it to a second constitutional convention.[3] Still, the demand for a bill of rights became the ideological centerpiece (if not the intellectual core) of the case against the Constitution as written.

The amendments proposed by the state ratifying conventions illustrate the neat division between those that would protect individual rights or enshrine fundamental principles of government and those that would cut back the government created by the Constitution. Indeed, the Virginia and New York conventions took pains in their instruments of ratification to separate rights-declaring amendments (or draft declarations of rights) from amendments altering the structure of government.

The proposed rights-declaring amendments covered virtually everything now found in the first ten amendments to the Constitution, but if the structural amendments had been adopted, even in part, the result would have been a dismemberment of the government limned in the Constitution. These proposals would have curtailed the number of terms for the President, Senators, and Representatives; abolished the Vice Presidency; limited the scope of jurisdiction of the federal courts; forbidden Congress to create any court but a Supreme Court and federal admiralty courts; restricted congressional powers of taxation and regulation of interstate and foreign commerce; barred any exercise of federal power to raise revenue unless and until the states refused to comply with congressional requisitions; and required a two-thirds vote of both houses of Congress for any statute regulating commerce, any tax law, and any treaty. Given the unhappy fate of the Articles of Confederation, it is doubtful whether such an eviscerated form of government would have lasted long.

In response to the structural amendments, some Federalists tried to stonewall, linking the call for any amendments to these proposals. They feared that any attempt to answer the public demand for a bill of rights would open the door wide to these other "alterations," especially in light of the New York and Virginia legislatures' threats to demand a second convention to secure the alterations they had specified.

RIGHTS IN THE FIRST CONGRESS

WHEN THE FIRST CONGRESS CONVENED on March 4, 1789 (and assembled its quorum to do business by April 6), it had before it recommendations for amendments from the ratifying conventions of five states—Massachusetts,

South Carolina, New Hampshire, Virginia, and New York.[4] In addition to these, Anti-Federal newspapers and pamphleteers circulated the lists of demands promulgated by the Anti-Federal minority of the Pennsylvania ratifying convention and the amendments demanded by the North Carolina convention, whose Anti-Federal majority had refused even to vote on the Constitution unless it were amended first. (Rhode Island had not yet acted, but its opposition to the Constitution and its support for a declaration of rights were well-known.)

The question of amendments was one of the trickiest and riskiest facing the new government. Those Federalists who were willing to consider rights-declaring amendments in order to promote conciliation and harmony (as well as repair a defect that began to look both obvious and ominous) found themselves divided from those who regarded any attempt to amend a Constitution only just adopted as a conspiracy to commit sabotage. It was essential, they perceived, to stake out a temperate position—one that could secure the support of moderates in both the Federalist and the Anti-Federalist camps, while not goading extremists on either side to action that would cripple the government. Many Federalists agreed that the best course would be to launch the promised campaign to add a bill of rights to the Constitution.

Leadership to obtain a bill of rights from the First Congress came from someone who, only a year earlier, would have been a most unlikely candidate for the role. James Madison had reversed his stand from the opening stages of the struggle for ratification, having made a public commitment at the Virginia ratifying convention to work to amend the Constitution. This about-face was the most noteworthy development in the ratification controversy with respect to future amendments. Madison brought many strengths to the movement for a declaration of rights: his national political stature, his ability to secure President Washington's backing of the call for amendments securing individual rights, and his extraordinary intellectual talents and capacity for hard work.

At first Madison had been cool to the idea of adding a bill of rights to the Constitution. His experience of Virginia politics in the 1780s, and his scrutiny of politics on both state and national levels, had led him to conclude that a bill of rights would be a mere "parchment barrier," insufficient to restrain a government or a popular majority bent on violating rights. Madison explained his thinking in a letter to Thomas Jefferson in 1788:

> [E]xperience proves the inefficacy of a bill of rights on those occasions when its controul is most needed. Repeated violations of these *parchment barriers* have been committed by overbearing majorities in every State.[5]

Such arguments carried great force, especially among veterans of the tumultuous state politics of the 1780s, who had seen firsthand the ineffectiveness of state constitutional provisions guaranteeing rights against determined legislative and popular majorities.

Eighteenth-century opinions on the nature of a declaration of rights and its function in the life of a polity differed profoundly from today's understandings of the same questions. Declarations of rights originally were not legally enforceable limitations on government power. Rather, they were political documents, enshrining the people's values and providing the citizenry a standard for evaluating the performance of elected officials.[6] They were generally phrased as admonitions, stating that the government "ought" to do this or "should not" do that. Government officials could, and did, ignore such political guidelines, however, with virtual impunity from popular reaction and even with popular approval.

In his arguments for the federal Constitution, Madison had used the state governments' inability to abide by their own constitutions with telling effect. In *The Federalist No. 48,* for example, he itemized the many violations of specific provisions of the Pennsylvania constitution of 1776 cataloged by the 1783 report of the state's Council of Censors—abuses that had been, and continued to be, tolerated by the people of the state:

> The conclusion which I am warranted in drawing from these observations is that a mere demarcation on parchment of the constitutional limits of the several departments is not a sufficient guard against those encroachments which lead to a tyrannical concentration of all the powers of government in the same hands.[7]

It is not surprising that Madison found the "parchment barriers" argument congenial. He believed that the plan for representation in the national legislature of an extended republic (which he defended in *The Federalist No. 10*) and the Constitution's devices of checks and balances (which he vindicated in *The Federalist No. 51*) provided a solution to the problem of government abuse of power that was both theoretically satisfying and workable in practice, and on both counts more secure than formal declarations of rights could ever be. Thus, Madison at first resisted adding a declaration of rights to the Constitution at least in part because he believed that the new Federalist "science of politics" he had helped devise could perform the tasks most Americans assigned to a declaration of rights without the problems that such a declaration might cause.[8]

A veteran drafter of constitutions and legislation, Madison understood the limitations of legal and political language—especially vague admonitory language—as a means to achieve political ends.[9] He believed that it would be difficult, if not impossible, to draft a bill of rights that would give sufficient protection to the rights it mentioned, or that might not give protection so broad as to paralyze the needed powers of government. He also feared that it would be all too easy to leave some rights out by mistake, with the result that those rights would not be protected.

Despite his intellectual struggles against the demand for a declaration of rights, in the summer of 1788 Madison determined to lead the effort to amend the Constitution. Four linked reasons explain his about-face, which he announced at the Virginia ratifying convention in Richmond:

• The first was the series of admonishing and persuasive letters Madison received between late 1787 and the summer of 1789 from his friend Thomas Jefferson, then American Minister to France and a keen observer of the ratification controversy.[10] Taking pains to refute each argument that Madison raised against a declaration of rights, Jefferson reminded him that a "bill of rights is what the people are entitled to against every government on earth, general or particular, and which no government should refuse, or rest on inference."[11] He also rebutted his younger correspondent's fears that "a positive declaration of some essential rights could not be obtained in the requisite latitude": "[H]alf a loaf is better than no bread. if we cannot secure all our rights, let us secure what we can."[12] The Jefferson-Madison correspondence served not simply as a source of intellectual and personal leverage on Madison, but also as an indication to him that moderate Federalists throughout the nation might well think as Jefferson did. The correspondence also provided Madison with a valuable catalog of arguments that he would later use to persuade reluctant Federalist colleagues in the House and the Senate to support his amendments.[13]

• Second, Madison's close observation of the American political scene and the communications he received from friends and political allies around the nation in 1788–1789 helped to convince him that Americans of all persuasions would rest easier if a bill of rights were added to the Constitution. Moreover, as the leader of the campaign for amendments within Congress, Madison knew that he would have the most advantageous position from which to deflect any proposed amendments that might go beyond a bill of rights.

• Third, Madison feared the likelihood that diehard Anti-Federalists in New York and Virginia would make good their oft-repeated threat to seek a second general convention. If he could assume leadership of the quest for amendments within Congress, he reasoned, he might be able to deflect the momentum of the second-convention movement, or even stop it altogether. Even though only these two states' legislatures had adopted resolutions making clear their intention to demand a new convention, Virginia and New York were among the most powerful states in the Union.

As the largest and most populous state (and the home state of the likely first President), Virginia wielded extraordinary political and economic power in American affairs. New York, the home of the new nation's fastest-growing port (and of its capital since 1784), was not far behind. Had Anti-Federalists in both states succeeded in making common cause against the Constitution in 1788, they might well have derailed the momentum that the Federalists had managed to build for the new charter of government. Should these two states indeed issue calls for a convention, Madison worried that other states might follow their lead—unless he placed an alternative on the agenda of Congress.

• Fourth, and of most direct personal concern, Madison recalled the role that the demand for amendments had played during the federal elections of 1788–1789, when he ran for a seat in the first United States House of Representatives against his friend (and fellow protégé of Jefferson) James Monroe. Anti-Federalists launched a whispering campaign charging that Madison still opposed a bill of rights, despite his public pledge, which they suspected was only a ruse to lure wavering delegates to support ratification. They hoped that this charge would alienate the Baptist community, who were not only among Madison's staunchest supporters but also among the strongest advocates of a bill of rights. Madison gained election to the House largely because he refuted the charge, in person and in writing, publicly reaffirming his promises to work for the adoption of a federal bill of rights.

Thus, when the First Congress convened the following spring, Madison was already hard at work, studying with great care a pamphlet published by Augustine Davis, a Virginia printer, setting forth the more than two hundred amendments to the Constitution recommended by the ratifying conventions.[14] Madison realized that the existence of this pamphlet and its circulation far beyond its original place of publication confirmed that the question of amendments was still alive. He therefore scoured its pages, noting redundancies and sorting out those amendments designed to identify and protect rights from those that would otherwise alter the structure of government provided by the Constitution.

Madison used other political demands on his time and energies to advance the cause of amendments. At the same time that he immersed himself in the Davis pamphlet, he was deep in consultation with President-elect George Washington, who had arrived in the capital city on April 23. On April 30, in his first inaugural address (either drafted by Madison or approved by him beforehand), Washington made only one substantive recommendation to the First Congress, expressed with the overbalanced, ponderous eloquence characteristic of his formal statements. Acknowledging "the nature of objections which have been urged against the system, or . . . the degree of inquietude which has given birth to them," Washington disclaimed any ability or desire to use his authority to guide the amending process—and then proceeded to do just that:

> Instead of undertaking particular recommendations on this sub-ject, in which I could be guided by no lights derived from official opportunities, I shall again give way to my entire confidence in your discernment and pursuit of the public good. For I assure myself that whilst you carefully avoid every alteration which might endanger the benefits of an united and effective govern-ment, or which ought to await the future lessons of experience; a reverence for the characteristic rights of freemen, and a regard for the public harmony, will sufficiently influence your delibera-tions on the question, how far the former can be more impregna-bly fortified, or the latter be safely and advantageously pro-moted.[15]

With the President firmly in the moderate camp of amendment advocates, Madison judged it a good time to move forward. On May 4, 1789, Madison first gave notice to his colleagues that he would act on the question of amendments, moving that the subject be raised on May 25. He thus stole the thunder of Anti-Federal Representatives who had hoped to focus the attention of the House on the Virginia and New York demands for a second convention.

Still determined to do his part for a second convention, despite Madison's actions, Representative Theodorick Bland of Virginia introduced his state's application for a second convention on May 5, and Bland's New York colleague John Laurance submitted that state's application on May 6. The Virginia applica-tion sparked a brief and occasionally testy debate: should the House appoint a select committee to consider the application or just lay it on the table until enough states' applications were received to compel Congress to call a second convention? Madison proposed that all applications be laid upon the table as they arrived and that Congress wait until constitutional critical mass was achieved. Despite Bland's protests, the House adopted Madison's views, and the Virginia and New York applications were tabled, never to be heard from again, as no other state sent Congress an application for a second convention.

Madison had thus achieved the first of his two goals—the derailing of the second-convention movement. Yet, when the appointed day for discussion of amendments arrived three weeks later, he was forced to postpone the question until June 8 to accommodate his colleagues' desire to complete work on legisla-tion setting up federal systems of customs regulation and revenue legislation. Once again, they did not share his sense of urgency.

When June 8 came, Madison claimed recognition from the floor to fulfill his promise to his colleagues and to the nation to introduce the subject of amendments. He was confident of success, having worked hard to prepare a set of proposals that would satisfy the goals he and the President had set in Washington's inaugural address. With the people's expectations about to be gratified, and the support of the President, how could he fail?

Madison's list of proposed amendments[16] included none that would limit the necessary powers of the general government. The Virginian aimed instead to state basic principles of republican government and to protect individual rights. Virtually every one of the twelve amendments ultimately proposed by Congress in 1789 has roots in Madison's list. He also included four provisions, derived from the Virginia Declaration of Rights and the American Declaration of Independence, affirming that government is derived from the people and is instituted to protect their liberty, safety, and happiness, and that "the people have an indubitable, unalienable, and indefeasible right to reform or change their Government, whenever it be found adverse or inadequate to the purposes of its institution."[17] Finally, he included one other amendment not derived from any proposal, formal or informal, made during the ratification controversy: "No state shall violate the equal rights of conscience, or the freedom of the press, or the trial by jury in criminal cases."

With respect to form, Madison proposed that Congress rewrite the Constitution to incorporate the amendments in their appropriate places in the 1787 text. Thus, for example, the "bill of rights" amendments would have been added to Article I, sections 9 and 10, which limit the powers of Congress and the states.

Madison's success in devising amendments that would meet the objectives defined in Washington's inaugural address is suggested by two letters that he received at the time. In the first, Washington himself praised the draft amendments, knowing that Madison would find the letter useful in persuading his colleagues to stand with him:

> As far as a momentary consideration has enable[d] me to judge, I see nothing exceptionable in the proposed amendments. Some of them, in my opinion, are importantly necessary, others, though of themselves (in my conception) not very essential, are necessary to quiet the fears of some respectable characters and well-meaning men. Upon the whole, therefore, not foreseeing any evil consequences that can result from their adoption, they have my wishes for a favorable reception in both houses.[18]

Three weeks later, the moderate Virginia Anti-Federalist Joseph Jones congratulated Madison:

> [T]he amendments proposed to the constitution . . . are calculated
> to secure the personal rights of the people so far as declarations
> on paper can effect the purpose, leaving unimpaired the great
> Powers of the government.[19]

Madison's colleagues in the House, however, were not so agreeable or well-disposed. Madison ran into the legislative equivalent of a full-body block, as Representatives protested that the business before them—the ever-present revenue and customs bills—was too important to set aside, especially for conjectures as to what reforms the Constitution might require.[20]

After several postponements and a complex series of parliamentary maneuvers,[21] the Representatives spent most of their time on June 8 squabbling over whether amendments were necessary, rather than focusing on the terms of Madison's proposal. James Jackson of Georgia argued that amendments were not needed at all, while Connecticut's Roger Sherman stressed the newness of the government authorized by the Constitution and protested that there had been nowhere near enough time to determine what, if any, defects in the system required amendment.

Madison stuck to his position, protesting, "I am sorry to be accessory to the loss of a single moment of time by the house." In defense of his motion, he made one of the greatest speeches of his career:

> If I thought I could fulfill the duty which I owe to myself and my
> constituents, to let the subject pass over in silence, I most cer-
> tainly should not trespass upon the indulgence of this house. But
> I cannot do this. . . . And I do most sincerely believe that if
> congress will devote but one day to this subject, so far as to satisfy
> the public that we do not disregard their wishes, it will have a
> salutary influence on the public councils, and prepare the way for
> a favorable reception of our future measures. It appears to me
> that this house is bound by every motive of prudence, not to let
> the first session pass over without proposing to the state legisla-
> tures some things to be incorporated into the constitution, as will
> render it as acceptable to the whole people of the United States,
> as it has been found acceptable to a majority of them.[22]

Madison emphasized four objectives: satisfying the people of the trustworthiness of the new government, bringing the dissenting states of North Carolina and Rhode Island back into the Union, redeeming a campaign promise made by Federalists throughout the nation, and remedying a real defect in the Constitution. He then presented the amendments he thought necessary and explained and defended each in turn. It was in this speech that Madison conferred on these amendments the name, so powerful in political controversy at the time and so generally revered afterward: "The first of these amendments, related to what may be called a bill of rights."[23]

The House ended its first debate on amendments by agreeing to set down Madison's proposals for discussion at a later date by the Committee of the Whole House on the State of the Union. So matters rested for six weeks, until July 21, when Madison sought to move that the House go into Committee of the Whole House to take up his amendments. Yet another wrangle ensued over the proper procedure for dealing with the amendments.

The House finally voted, 34 to 15, to appoint a select committee, with one member from each state, to report a set of draft amendments.*[24] The committee worked quickly, producing a report listing seventeen amendments, which on July 28 was ordered printed for the full House.[25] Six days later, on August 3, Madison successfully moved to have the Committee of the Whole House take up the committee report on August 12.

Without explanation, the House delayed this action by a day, but on August 13, the Committee of the Whole House began its detailed debate on the proposed amendments, clause by clause, concluding on August 18. The next day, the House began formal debate, reviewing the accomplishments of the previous week. Throughout this period, Anti-Federal Representatives pleaded without avail for amendments restricting the powers of the federal judiciary and preserving state authority over congressional elections. But the House rejected these requests, as the Representatives were aware both of the need to walk a narrow line between protecting rights and damaging the powers of the government and of the challenge of drafting a declaration of rights that would be neither too constricted nor too expansive.

One key influence on the framing of the amendments was the question whether the Constitution could permit federal intrusions into the spheres of authority of the state governments. For this reason, for example, New England Representatives persuaded Madison to recast his forthright prohibition of religious establishments to limit only the power of the federal government, thereby preventing the establishment of one or more national churches while preserving state religious establishments in New England.

---

*The members were Madison, Jacob Vining of Delaware, Abraham Baldwin of Georgia, Roger Sherman of Connecticut, Nicholas Gilman of New Hampshire, George Clymer of Pennsylvania, Egbert Benson of New York, Benjamin Goodhue of Massachusetts, Elias Boudinot of New Jersey, George Gale of Maryland, and Aedanus Burke of South Carolina.

Once it became clear that the House would propose amendments of some sort, the discussion shifted to the choice of words and phrases, as the Representatives groped for the right constitutional language. The major characteristic of their draftsmanship was haste. For example, what is today one of the most controversial clauses in the Bill of Rights—the Fourth Amendment's prohibition against unreasonable searches and seizures—got through with only a few minutes' debate.[26]

It was at this point that the House, at the urging of Roger Sherman, abandoned Madison's idea of incorporating the amendments in the constitutional text. Sherman had two reasons for his demand. His first indicated his respect for the canons of legal draftsmanship:

> We ought not to interweave our propositions into the work itself, because it will be destructive of the whole fabric. We might as well endeavor to mix brass, iron, and clay, as to incorporate such heterogeneous articles; the one contradictory to the other. Its absurdity will be discovered by comparing it with a law: would any legislature endeavor to introduce into a former act, a subsequent amendment, and let them stand so connected. When an alteration is made in an act, it is done by way of supplement; the latter act always repealing the former in every specified case of difference.[27]

His second reason, one of principle, was grounded in his understanding of the Constitution as an exercise of the constituent power by the People of the United States through their delegates in the Federal Convention:

> The constitution is the act of the people, and ought to remain entire. But the amendments will be the act of the state governments; again all the authority we possess, is derived from that instrument [the Constitution]; if we mean to destroy the whole and establish a new constitution, we remove the basis on which we mean to build.[28]

Despite the resistance of Madison and some of his colleagues,* the House adopted Sherman's point of view. This vote set a precedent for all future

---

*For example, William Loughton Smith of South Carolina insisted that the form of the South Carolina convention's amendments required Congress to incorporate the amendments into the constitutional text.

exercises of the amending power. The House's decision, setting amendments aside from the rest of the Constitution, would lead to the placement of the Bill of Rights at the head of the post-1787 text of the document, thus ensuring its primacy in popular imagination.

On August 24, the House endorsed the seventeen draft amendments, but once the amendments made their way up the stairs of Federal Hall to the Senate the next morning, our detailed knowledge of the debates evaporates. Unlike the House, which had a visitors' gallery and several self-employed reporters recording the proceedings, the Senate met behind closed doors. The only record of its actions appears in its bare-bones Legislative and Executive Journals, which record motions and votes but not debates or individual speeches.[29]

What we do know is that the Senate, containing only two Anti-Federalists out of twenty-two members, was much less responsive to the desirability of amendments than the House, which, despite its Federalist majority, had a significantly high proportion of Anti-Federal members from key states such as Virginia, New York, Massachusetts, and South Carolina. The amendments produced by the Senate on September 9 dramatized the Senators' coolness. The Senate reduced the House's proposals from seventeen to twelve and significantly weakened them. For example, the House version of the religious-liberty provision clearly deprived Congress of any power over religion:

> Congress shall make no law establishing religion or prohibiting
> the free exercise thereof, nor shall the rights of Conscience be
> infringed.[30]

By contrast, the Senate's version only barred Congress from creating an established church like the Church of England:

> Congress shall make no law establishing articles of faith, or a
> mode of worship, or prohibiting the free exercise of religion.[31]

Although Roger Sherman declared that, in his view, the amendments had been "altered for the Better," Madison was angered by the Senate's handiwork, or so Senator Paine Wingate of New Hampshire reported to his colleague John Langdon: "As to amendments to the Constitution Madison says he had rather have none than those agreed to by the Senate." Representative Fisher Ames of Massachusetts noted that the Senate version lacked the "sedative Virtue" of the original House proposals and fretted that a "contest on this subject between the two houses would be very disagreeable."[32]

A "conference committee" of three Representatives and three Senators*
—the usual method of resolving an impasse between the chambers of a bicameral legislature—restored many of the twelve proposed amendments to the form
favored by the House; the House approved the final list of twelve on September
24, 1789, and the Senate concurred in two votes on September 25 and 26. Clerks
prepared fourteen engrossed copies (that is, copies written in clear, formal
calligraphy); one was sent to each of the thirteen states, and the fourteenth was
retained in the files of the federal government.[33]

IN THE HANDS OF THE PEOPLE: 1789–1791

ANTI-FEDERALISTS DIVIDED OVER THE Amendments proposed by Congress.
Some, who had objected to the Constitution because it lacked a declaration of
rights, welcomed the Amendments and abandoned their distrust of the new
government. Others, who wanted to restrict the general government's powers
over taxation and regulation of interstate and foreign commerce, charged that
the Amendments produced by Congress only distracted the people from the
serious flaws still present in the Constitution. Federalists rejected these arguments with scorn, pointing out that those who had painted themselves as friends
of liberty now showed their true colors by opposing the Bill of Rights.

The ratification process started quickly; several states adopted the Amendments almost as soon as the engrossed copies arrived.[34] Among these was North
Carolina, one of the two holdout states. Its legislature ratified the Amendments
on December 22, 1789, one month after its second ratifying convention had
adopted the Constitution (194 to 77). Rhode Island was more stubborn. It took
veiled threats of trade reprisals from Congress, the refusal of President Washington to visit the state during his fall 1789 tour of New England, and secession talk
from the Federalists of Providence and Newport before the state at last called
a ratifying convention to assemble in April 1790. The convention took nearly a
month to adopt the Constitution by a two-vote margin (34 to 32), with dozens
of recommended amendments; less than two weeks later, on June 11, the Rhode
Island legislature adopted the Bill of Rights.

Anti-Federalists in the Virginia legislature were bitterly disappointed by the
Amendments, because they included none reining in the powers of the general

---

*Madison, Sherman, and Vining were the House members of the conference committee;
Oliver Ellsworth of Connecticut, Charles Carroll of Maryland, and William Paterson of
New Jersey were the Senate members.

government over taxation and commerce. Following the lead of their commander, Patrick Henry, they blocked action in the legislature's upper house for
months.

By March 4, 1791, nine states had ratified ten of the twelve proposed Amendments, leaving them one state short of the required three-fourths. On that date,
Vermont joined the Union. The problem was that, with Vermont's addition to
the Union (and even after its ratification of the Amendments on November 3),
the number of necessary state ratifications automatically rose from ten (out of
thirteen) to eleven (out of fourteen). With no word from Connecticut, Massachusetts, or Georgia, the focus shifted back to Virginia.[35] Supporters of the
Amendments in the Virginia legislature revived them, mocking the diehard
Anti-Federalists as obstacles to the amendments they had demanded years
before; caught in an uncomfortable political predicament, the Anti-Federalists at
last gave in to overwhelming pressure. On December 15, 1791, Virginia ratified
all but the first of the twelve proposed amendments and added the third through
the twelfth to the Constitution as the Bill of Rights.[36]

THE LONG SHADOW OF THE BILL OF RIGHTS

MADISON HAD ORIGINALLY DRAFTED WHAT we now know as the Bill of Rights
as a set of Amendments to various provisions of the Constitution. Even in the
final form as proposed to the states, these Amendments appear in the order of
the provisions they were intended to modify.

Of the twelve Amendments proposed by Congress, the first two had nothing
to do with rights. They pertained to the structure of Congress (outlined in the
first sections of Article I), responding to Anti-Federal critiques of that institution. The remaining ten Amendments were intended to revise sections 9 and 10
of Article I, which established limitations on the substantive powers of federal
and state governments, respectively.

The first proposed Amendment, ratified by only ten states,* would have
established a rigid formula tying the size of the House of Representatives to
increases in population. It was designed to protect the principles of representation deemed necessary to guard the people against any danger to their liberties
from the actions of their elected representatives. This proposal provided that
there should be one Representative for every 30,000 people until the House had

---

*New Jersey, Maryland, North Carolina, South Carolina, New Hampshire, New York,
Rhode Island, Vermont, Pennsylvania, and Virginia. Delaware rejected it.

100 members, after which there would be one Representative for every 40,000 people until the House grew to 200 members. Congress then would establish a new ratio, making sure that there was no more than one Representative for every 50,000 people. Two centuries later, when the nation's population exceeds 250,000,000, the proposed Amendment would mandate a House of more than 5,000 members—rather than the present 435. The proposal now seems a quaint anachronism that failed to anticipate the growth of the nation.

The second proposed Amendment, adopted by six states and rejected by five states between 1789 and 1791,* stipulated that no law changing the compensation of members of the House and the Senate could go into effect until after an election to the House had taken place. The purpose of this proposed Amendment was to compel Representatives to go before the voters (and Senators before the state legislatures, which had selected them) to justify their approval of a pay raise. If the voters agreed, they would reelect their Representatives (and the state legislatures would reelect their Senators), who then would receive their pay raise. Its broader purpose was to guard against creating a national government whose officials would prefer their own gain over their duties to the people. After 1791, the amendment languished neglected for more than eighty years, until the outraged legislators of Ohio ratified it to protest Congress's "salary grab act" of 1873. Wyoming followed suit in 1978. In the early 1980s, a movement to ratify the amendment found a new champion—Gregory D. Watson, then a college student at the University of Texas, Austin. On May 7, 1992, the unlikeliest story in the history of the amending process culminated with Michigan's ratification of the 1789 proposal as the Twenty-seventh Amendment.**

Taken together, the ten amendments we know as the Bill of Rights reinforced the basic premise of a written constitution: government must be limited if the rights of the people are to be protected. Even today, when we think of the principles of the American republic, we think first of the cadences of the Bill of Rights: freedom of religion, freedom of speech, freedom of the press, freedom of assembly, the right to keep and bear arms, the ban on unreasonable searches and seizures, due process of law, the prohibition of cruel and unusual punishment, and so forth.

Yet the Bill of Rights differs from the original body of the Constitution in a fundamental way. Instead of spelling out the powers of the national government, it specifies procedures the government must follow when it exercises its author-

---

*Maryland, North Carolina, South Carolina, Delaware, Vermont, and Virginia ratified it; New Jersey, New Hampshire, Pennsylvania, New York, and Rhode Island rejected it.

**See Chapter 13 for the history of the Congressional Compensation Amendment of 1789 and its implications for the law and politics of the modern amending process.

ity over individual citizens and actions it may not take when using that authority. For this reason, the Bill of Rights is framed in a different manner from declarations of rights in the state constitutions of the 1770s and 1780s.[37] Those declarations spelled out the principles of a free polity, expressed as admonitions (using "ought" or "should" language) rather than enforceable commands (using "shall" or "shall not" language). Because the Constitution did not begin with a declaration of rights but with a series of grants of power, the federal Bill of Rights was written in the language of command, establishing limitations on previous grants of government power.

Ironically, however, by March 1, 1792, when Secretary of State Thomas Jefferson certified that the Bill of Rights had become part of the Constitution, the first ten amendments had been transformed from the focus of national politics to a set of shared though unexamined assumptions about American public life. Within a few months after their submission to the states, they were eclipsed by other issues, less elevated but more dramatic: the contest over the location of the temporary and permanent capitals of the United States, the proposals of Secretary of the Treasury Alexander Hamilton to assume the debts of the states and consolidate them with the Confederation and federal debts, the controversy over the bill to create a Bank of the United States, and the foreign policy issues sparked by the French Revolution.[38] Not until the twentieth century would the first ten amendments to the Constitution, and the proposition that rights are at the core of the American constitutional experiment, exert a powerful influence on constitutional law and the public mind.

THE BILL OF RIGHTS has been the single largest grafting of new principles and doctrines in the history of the Constitution and its amending process. At the same time, these first ten amendments codified understandings having deep roots in Anglo-American history and law—the American people's understandings of individual rights and limits on government power.[39]

It would be misleading to think of the Bill of Rights as "amending America," for ideas of rights always have been vital to American national identity and to the American experiment.[40] Demands for a national bill of rights predated, accompanied, and even (because of the existence of Article V) made possible the adoption of the Constitution. Thus, the first ten amendments confirmed, rather than revised, the conception of the American nation held by the American people between 1789 and 1791. But the existence of these amendments as symbols of liberty, and their evolving function as judicially enforceable safeguards, helped to move ideas of rights to the core of American public life. We may well regard the pursuit, definition, and enforcement of rights as a central theme of the history of the United States. And, as we continue our disputes over the appropriate or necessary scope of rights, the Bill of Rights continues to amend America, over two centuries after its ratification.

CHAPTER 4

SETTING THE PATTERN:
THE ELEVENTH AND TWELFTH
AMENDMENTS

*[The] framers [of the Constitution] . . . knew that time
might develop many defects in its arrangements, and many
deficiencies in its powers. . . . They believed that the power
of amendment was . . . the safety valve to let off all
temporary effervescences and excitements; and the real effective instrument to control and adjust the movement of the
machinery, when out of order, or in danger of self-destruc-
tion.*

JUSTICE JOSEPH STORY
*Commentaries on the Constitution,
Abridgment* (1833), § 957

AFTER THE PEAKS OF CONSTITUTIONAL creation of 1787–1791, it comes as
something of a shock to examine the next products of the Article V process, the
first true changes in the government authorized by the Constitution. Far from
ringing statements of constitutional principle or majestic allotments of powers,
duties, and responsibilities, the Eleventh and Twelfth Amendments seem hyper-
technical, crabbed, and trivial.

Narrow procedural questions often mask larger substantive problems. The
Eleventh Amendment is the constitutional legacy of complex legal and political
quandaries that preoccupied the politicians of the early republic; the Twelfth
Amendment is the by-product of the only serious threat to the first peaceful
transfer of authority and power from one national political party to another in
American political history. The history that gave rise to the amendments contains more than its share of gaps and constitutional and historical might-have-
beens. Finally, both these amendments set the pattern for the subsequent history
of the amending process.[1]

48

DEBTS, LAWSUITS, AND FEDERALISM:
THE ELEVENTH AMENDMENT

THE ELEVENTH AMENDMENT, WHICH OVERTURNED a decision of the United States Supreme Court that many at the time saw as a dangerous omen of potential tyranny by the new national government, is the only one altering the Constitution's provisions for the federal judiciary. It emerged from the economic, political, and legal confusion of post-Revolutionary America.

After the War of Independence, one of the most compelling and intractable problems facing the new nation was the mountain of debts owed by American citizens to British creditors and to Loyalists. The Revolution not only had interrupted an extensive network of commercial transactions between colonists and residents of the mother country[2] but also had posed difficult personal questions for creditors and debtors, who discovered that their economic relations now had political consequences. The creation of a new nation, and of thirteen new state governments, raised painful problems for those Americans who wished to remain loyal to King and country—or only to keep out of the way.[3]

At first, the Revolutionaries applied the term "Loyalists" only to those colonists who actively opposed the Revolution. As the war progressed, however, the Continental Congress and the state governments required loyalty oaths and imposed penalties even on those Americans who simply did not want to take a stand. The penalties for refusal to swear allegiance were exile (breach of which would be punished by execution or imprisonment) and forfeiture of real property to the state.[4]

Throughout the war, Loyalists and fence-sitters fled to British strongholds such as New York City. By war's end, tens of thousands had been forced to leave the United States, taking refuge in Canada, the West Indies, or Great Britain. Observing preparations in New York City for the Loyalists' departure, Elbridge Gerry of Massachusetts wrote to his brother Samuel:

> The Refugees are mostly embarked from this Place, & some
> say their Number will not be less (including Women & Children)
> than twenty thousand, which far exceeds my former Ideas of the
> Matter.[5]

Virtually all the Loyalist exiles lost their property as a result of state forfeiture statutes.

The ouster of Loyalists had far-reaching economic consequences for the United States. The state governments sold the confiscated lands, both to reap a fiscal windfall and to replace the pre-Revolutionary system of landholding (which in most states pitted a small number of wealthy landlords against a majority of landless tenants) with widespread freehold ownership. The redistribution of Loyalist estates had two lasting effects: it strengthened the political and economic power of those leading families who had supported the Revolution (and who had seized the opportunity to speculate in land), and it provided thousands of American farmers with the opportunity to acquire their own land for the first time.[6]

In addition to the land expropriated and redistributed by the states, Loyalists lost other significant property interests. Many of the exiles (and their British compatriots) were forced to write off debts owed to them by former friends, neighbors, and business associates who had thrown in their lot with the Revolution. Americans who owed large sums to the exiles and to British creditors, often for debts predating Independence, hoped that the mass emigration caused by the Revolution would make it unnecessary, or impossible, to repay these obligations.[7]

The proper disposition of the debts became a major stumbling block in the negotiation of the Treaty of Paris of 1783 and its ratification by the Confederation Congress. During the peace talks, British negotiators demanded that the Americans pay compensation for property seized through the confiscation statutes; Benjamin Franklin quashed this demand by threatening in turn to submit American claims for property destroyed during the war by British and Loyalist forces. The diplomats agreed to treat the two sets of claims—distinct from legitimate debts owed by American citizens to British subjects—as canceling each other out, and the British government compensated the Loyalists for their losses.[8]

Under the treaty eventually agreed to, the United States acknowledged prewar debts owed to British subjects by individual American citizens as valid obligations and promised, both for the Confederation and for the individual states, not to impose obstacles to British and Loyalist creditors' attempts to recover those sums.[9] This provision alarmed state politicians. Many of them were truly concerned for the debtors among their constituents (and within their own ranks), but, closer to home, a good number of these politicians had supported the confiscation of Loyalist properties and their distribution among the local citizenry, creating thriving land markets and fueling the engine of land speculation. Would these programs of land redistribution be subject to challenge—and would profitable land-speculation ventures be wiped out—as the result of Loyalists' lawsuits to recover property under the Treaty of Paris?

One warning that the treaty might pose problems for state confiscation measures was *Rutgers v. Waddington,* a case decided by the Mayor's Court of New York City in 1784. In 1776, when the British arrived in New York City, Elizabeth

Rutgers fled, abandoning the brewery she owned. The British occupying forces gave Josiah Waddington (who had come to the city with them) a license to operate the brewery under the "laws of war." When, in November 1783, the British left New York, Waddington stayed behind. On her return to the city, Mrs. Rutgers took advantage of the Trespass Act of 1783, a New York state law permitting her to sue Waddington for damages for back rent for the period he occupied and used her brewery. Alexander Hamilton, who represented Waddington, argued that the law was invalid under the treaty; the state's attorney general, Morgan Lewis, appeared for Mrs. Rutgers to defend the statute. The Mayor's Court ducked the issue, interpreting the statute so that it would be consistent with the treaty and the "laws of war." *Rutgers v. Waddington* hinted— but only hinted—that if a state statute could not be "saved" by interpretation, it could be struck down under the treaty; Hamilton had made this precise argument against the New York statute.[10]

In the wake of *Rutgers v. Waddington,* British and Loyalist creditors who did file suit to recover debts owed to them by American debtors found that the treaty gave them almost no protection. State courts—especially juries—were unsympathetic to the claims of "foreign" plaintiffs. Even in those rare cases where a jury could be persuaded to render a verdict for a creditor, some states' legal requirement that all debts be paid only in worthless paper money issued by those states made such judgments laughable.[11]

Another problematic category of debts burdening the new governments was that of debts for supplies sold, and loans made, during the Revolution by citizens and foreign subjects to Congress and the states. The Confederation and many of the state governments had run up huge debts to support the war effort. But in the late 1780s, some states were still clamoring for aid in repaying their loans, while those that had managed to pay off their debts resented the "deadbeat" status of their neighbors. A vast and thorny network of loans among the states, and between the states and the Continental and Confederation Congresses, only complicated matters; both federal and state authorities found it easier to argue over how to set off loans against one another than to determine what was owed to whom and how it would be repaid.[12]

For years, suppliers of arms, ammunition, clothing, food, and property tried to recover compensation for the supplies they had made available in the service of independence. Frustrated by the indifference of the debtor governments, they sought recourse through the courts. Their suits also failed, because the common-law doctrine of sovereign immunity barred a creditor of a state from suing that state in its own courts without the state's consent.[13]

British, Loyalist, and American creditors all yearned, therefore, for an independent system of federal courts, one that would hear cases without being prejudiced in favor of state government or local defendants, or without being barred by sovereign immunity. They had allies in such notable nationalists as Alexander Hamilton, who in 1783 had presented a series of resolutions to the Confederation Congress demanding revision of the Articles of Confederation. In his third resolution, Hamilton focused on the consequences of the state courts' refusal to entertain lawsuits by out-of-state or foreign plaintiffs against state governments:

> In want of a Federal Judicature, having cognizance of all matters of general concern in the last resort, especially those in which foreign nations and their subjects are interested; from which defect, by the interference of the local regulations of particular States militating directly or indirectly against the powers vested in the Union, the national treaties will be liable to be infringed, the national faith to be violated, and public tranquility to be disturbed.[14]

Hamilton's proposals sank into limbo, however, being too centralizing for all but the most militant nationalists.

In 1787–1788, advocates of a national court system that would provide an alternative to hostile state courts took heart. The proposed Constitution authorized (in Article III) a federal supreme court and a system of lower federal courts whose design and jurisdiction were left to the discretion of Congress.

Most Americans, however, and especially Anti-Federalists, dreaded such an independent court system. They grounded their opposition on principle. Comparing the threat posed by Article III with the British courts of the colonial period, which were responsible only to the Crown and its representatives, the royal governors of the colonies, they feared that the new federal courts would swallow up the state courts. On occasion, the Anti-Federalists acknowledged their concerns that the new federal courts would disrupt what they deemed a highly satisfactory state of affairs with respect to outstanding debts.

In January 1788, for example, Melancton Smith, a New York delegate to the Confederation Congress and a staunch Anti-Federalist, outlined the fearsome prospect of a rapacious, all-powerful federal court system:

> It appears to me this part of the system [the judiciary] is so framed as to *clinch* all the other powers, and to extend them in a silent and imperceptible manner to any thing and everything, while the Court who are vested with these powers are totally independent, uncontroulable and not amenable to any other power in any decisions they may make.
>
> What are the cases in *equity* arising under the Constitution? Will

not the supreme court under this clause have a right to enlarge the
extent of the powers of the general government—and to curtail
that of the States at pleasure?[15]

Smith then posed the question of the Loyalist confiscations, with reference to
the Treaty of Paris:

> What are the cases of equity under Treaties? Will they [federal
> courts] not under this power be authorized to reverse all acts of
> attainder heretofore passed by the States, and to set aside all
> Judgments of Confiscation?[16]

For reasons such as these, Anti-Federalists demanded assurances from supporters of the Constitution that the federal courts would not have the power to
hear lawsuits against a state government by citizens of another state or of a
foreign country. Such leading Federalists as Hamilton, James Madison, and John
Marshall willingly gave such assurances.[17]

When Congress framed the Judiciary Act of 1789, the statute that gave shape
to the federal courts, it used Article III as a template, modifying or cutting back
the scope of the original constitutional grant of power to respond to Anti-
Federal objections. However, it left vague the issue of the suability of states,
providing no guidance as to what it had in mind.[18]

Within a year after the first federal judges were nominated and confirmed, the
federal circuit courts (the principal federal trial courts) made clear that the Treaty
of Paris and Article I, section 10, of the Constitution—which bars state interference with the obligations of contracts—prevailed over state laws designed to
protect debtors and to obstruct Loyalist or British creditors.[19] These cases
caused little controversy, and indeed were well-received.*

With but one exception, the federal courts did not confront the question
whether they had jurisdiction to hear a lawsuit against a state. That exception was
the first case filed in the United States Supreme Court, *Van Staphorst v. Maryland.*[20] In 1782, two Dutch bankers named Van Staphorst had negotiated a loan
to the state of Maryland; the state legislature, dissatisfied with the terms, decided
to cancel the loan and repay the money but never got around to acting on these
decisions. In the spring of 1791, the bankers tired of waiting for Maryland to

---

*In 1790–1791, however, a brief and nasty controversy erupted over defining the limits
of federal and state judicial power, leading Representative Egbert Benson of New York
to propose a set of fifteen amendments that would have reshaped the federal court
system. The Benson proposals are discussed in Chapter 10.

repay the loan and brought suit, invoking the original jurisdiction of the Supreme Court (that is, those cases that can begin in the Supreme Court itself) and retaining Attorney General Edmund Randolph to represent them in his private capacity. (In the years before 1870, the Attorney General had no Justice Department to supervise. Because his job was at best part-time, he often retained his private practice.) Maryland responded with circumspection, acknowledging the suit but not making a formal appearance in court. The suit dragged on until early 1792, when both parties agreed to settle. There the matter would have rested but (as is so often the case in American constitutional history) for a lawsuit.

The circumstances of *Chisholm v. Georgia* were depressingly familiar to any creditor of the state governments, and indeed to anyone who had followed *Van Staphorst v. Maryland.* In 1777, at the height of the Revolution, Robert Farquhar, a South Carolina merchant, sold provisions to the government of Georgia but never received payment for them. Until his death in 1784 in a shipping accident, Farquhar repeatedly demanded payment for more than $169,000 worth of merchandise, and the executor of his estate, Alexander Chisholm (also a South Carolinian) continued this quest.[21]

After failing to secure payment from the state of Georgia for his friend's estate, in 1790 Chisholm filed suit against the state in the United States Circuit Court for the District of Georgia. In 1791, the court rejected his suit on jurisdictional grounds. Undeterred, in 1792 Chisholm filed a new lawsuit, this time invoking the original jurisdiction of the Supreme Court and hiring Attorney General Randolph to argue his case.

The filing and argument of *Chisholm v. Georgia,* and the commencement of a series of similar lawsuits against other states, touched off a brushfire of alarm in the press and the state governments; panicked legislators and anonymous essayists expressed fears that the suits would result in the total subordination of the states to the federal government.[22]

On February 5, 1793, in the Mayor's Court Room of Philadelphia's Old City Hall, five robed Justices began a session of the United States Supreme Court. The tall, elegant, and polished Chief Justice, John Jay of New York, nodded to Randolph, who opened his argument in *Chisholm, Exr. of Farquhar, v. State of Georgia.* The vain, handsome Randolph was a gifted public speaker; reprising his role in *Van Staphorst* as counsel for an out-of-state plaintiff in a lawsuit against a state, he was thoroughly familiar with the issues.

The five Justices listened attentively to Randolph's argument. Chief Justice Jay, the linchpin of the team that had negotiated the Treaty of Paris of 1783, was known to view the authority of the federal courts as a bulwark of national supremacy over the states. James Wilson of Pennsylvania, the most scholarly Justice and a fervent advocate of national unity both in his legal and political careers and on the bench, was also a likely vote for Chisholm, as was the tactful and respected William Cushing of Massachusetts. The quiet John Blair of Virginia was a question mark, but he probably would side with Jay, Wilson, and Cushing. Thus, only Justice James Iredell of North Carolina seemed likely to support Georgia; indeed, Iredell had already indicated his stand by rejecting Chisholm's first lawsuit in the circuit court two years earlier.*

The state of Georgia, however, was not present. It had filed no papers, and no attorney stepped forward to present Georgia's case—though it was well-known that the state government had rejected with indignation the very idea that it might be sued in the Supreme Court. At the close of Randolph's argument, Chief Justice Jay asked if anyone present had anything else to say to guide the Court in its consideration of the case. No one answered, and the Justices retired to reach a decision.

The Court waited nearly two weeks to give Georgia a chance to respond, but the state continued to ignore Chisholm's lawsuit. On February 19, 1793, the Supreme Court rendered a decision in Chisholm's favor.[23] As was customary in the Court in its first decade, the case was decided by *seriatim* opinions; that is, each Justice delivered his own opinion, each stressing different points as persuasive or unconvincing. The decision was 4 to 1 to reverse the lower court, with Iredell the sole dissenter. Blair and Cushing delivered brief opinions endorsing the conclusion of the Court. Wilson presented a learned, passionate, but impolitic lecture on the nature of the Union and the supremacy of the Constitution. Jay's opinion, as befitted a veteran diplomat, was at once authoritative and conciliatory; it has generally been taken as the "opinion of the Court" and is the most important opinion Jay delivered during his tenure as Chief Justice.

The Justices ruled that the Judiciary Act of 1789 and Article III of the Constitution indeed authorized the federal courts to hear suits against a state by citizens of another state or a foreign country. Thus, even though Georgia had refused to acknowledge Chisholm's lawsuit, Chisholm could maintain his suit in the Supreme Court and recover a judgment against the state.

The Justices ignored the assurances given by Federalists five years earlier that the judicial power of the United States would not permit federal courts to hear such lawsuits,[24] and contemporaries were convinced that the Court had erred. Georgians were so outraged by the decision that the state legislature debated (but did not adopt) a resolution warning that any federal marshal seeking to enforce *Chisholm* would be hanged as a felon.[25]

Chisholm had consequences, and provoked alarm, outside Georgia as well.

---

*Under the Judiciary Act of 1789, as amended through the date of *Chisholm,* Justices of the Supreme Court "rode circuit," sitting with the U.S. district judge in each state to hold trial courts. Study of the records of the Supreme Court in its first decade indicates that, contrary to modern practice, Justices of the Supreme Court rarely recused themselves from reconsidering decisions of circuit courts in which they had participated.

Throughout the early 1790s, Southern states had become increasingly suspicious of the powers of the federal government; they saw the decision in *Chisholm* not only as a breach of faith but also as an ominous portent of potential tyranny by the federal government over the states.[26] Just as important, state governments feared that British and Loyalist creditors would seize on *Chisholm* as a means to bring suit against the states to recover either the lands seized and distributed during the Revolution or money judgments for the value of those lands. Not only would such lawsuits disrupt the growing market in land speculation that drove so many state economies in the 1790s but they would subject many states to potentially ruinous judgments. Indeed, seizing on the opportunity presented by *Chisholm,* creditors quickly filed lawsuits against five states—Maryland, New York, Massachusetts, South Carolina, and Virginia—and brought more lawsuits against Georgia.[27]

In the public mind, the problem facing the nation was clear: Georgia and the other state governments had to be placated, though whether this need arose from the specific fury over *Chisholm* or from the Supreme Court's overstepping its bounds remained uncertain. The answer was equally clear: it was necessary to amend the Constitution to overturn the result in *Chisholm.* On the day after the Supreme Court announced its decision, the first resolution proposing an amendment to overturn *Chisholm* was introduced in the Senate. Within a month, the legislatures of Massachusetts, Connecticut, and Virginia submitted resolutions to Congress demanding such an amendment. Although these proposals died when the Second Congress adjourned on March 3, 1793, the Third Congress returned to the task in early 1794; by March 4 of that year a proposed amendment (of uncertain parentage) was on its way to the states for ratification:

> The Judicial power of the United States shall not be construed
> to extend to any suit in law or equity, commenced or prosecuted
> against one of the United States by Citizens of another State, or
> by Citizens or Subjects of any Foreign State.

By using the phrase "shall not be construed to extend" rather than "shall not extend," Congress framed the amendment as a rule of constitutional interpretation rather than as an outright limitation on judicial power. The amendment's framers thus intended it to be read as a correction of judicial misreading of an unaltered Constitution rather than a change of the Constitution to remove a disagreeable provision correctly interpreted by the Court. Its framers thus placed the blame for an ostensibly incorrect interpretation of the Constitution squarely on the Justices. In what would prove a firm precedent, politics had guided the task of constitutional drafting.

By February 7, 1795, the Eleventh Amendment had won the support of enough states to be added to the Constitution, though it was not promulgated as such for nearly three years. Why the delay? The principal reason is state and federal inaction. At the time the Amendment was proposed, there were fifteen states in the Union, twelve of which would be needed to ratify the Amendment. Apparently, the ratifying states were astonishingly slow in informing the federal government of their actions. In early 1796, when Congress requested information on the Amendment's status, President Washington was able to send notices of ratification from only eight states. In 1797, when Tennessee became the sixteenth state, Congress asked President John Adams to determine the status of the proposed Amendment. (Tennessee's admission to the Union did not change the number of state ratifications needed.) Only on January 23, 1798 (sometimes the date is given as January 8), was Secretary of State Timothy Pickering able—or willing—to certify that the Eleventh Amendment was part of the Constitution.[28]

The most recent historical scholarship suggests yet another reason for the delay—the Adams Administration's determination to ensure a role for the executive branch in the amending process. The Constitution is silent on who certifies the valid adoption of an amendment, and Adams and Pickering wanted to be sure that the responsibility—and the attendant power—remained in the hands of the executive branch.[29]

Ironically, questions of the executive branch's role in the Article V process cropped up again immediately after the Amendment was declared in effect. Its validity came under fire in the Supreme Court—where all the fuss and bother had started five years before.

At issue in *Hollingsworth v. Virginia*[30] was the validity of a state legislature's vote to cancel a land-speculation company's title to a huge tract of land that, the legislature maintained, was Virginia territory. The lawsuit, which had been filed in the Supreme Court before *Chisholm* (and whose origins predated the Revolution), reached the Justices on February 10, 1798; litigation was a leisurely business in the early years of the republic. Although Virginia cited the Eleventh Amendment as a complete defense to the suit, the plaintiffs' lawyers rejected the Amendment as a defense. They challenged the procedure by which the Amendment had been adopted, arguing that its lack of a Presidential signature made it invalid under Article I, section 7, clause 3 of the Constitution, which requires the submission of every congressional "Order, Resolution, or Vote" to the President for his signature or rejection.

Hollingsworth's assertion had consequences beyond the Eleventh Amendment. The Bill of Rights also lacked a Presidential signature; if his argument were accepted by the Justices, it would cast doubt on the status of the Bill of Rights as well. The Court solved the problem by declaring it solved. Without stating a rationale, the Justices concluded that all eleven Amendments were "constitutionally adopted."[31] Having saved the Amendment—and thereby set a precedent that was set aside only twice in the subsequent history of Article V*—the Justices cited the Eleventh Amendment as grounds to dismiss *Hollingsworth* and all similar cases. Among the cases dismissed by the Court in the aftermath of *Hollingsworth* was *Chisholm v. Georgia*—but the Justices were disposing of a case that already had ended.

Notwithstanding the furor over the Eleventh Amendment, Chisholm's case had dragged on in the Supreme Court. Because Georgia had never made a formal appearance in the case, the Justices had entered a default judgment against the state. The next stage was to begin proceedings to determine the damages that Chisholm could recover. The writ issued by the Court to Georgia was never acted upon, however, and the case was continued from term to term until 1798.[32]

The reason for inaction had become apparent in December of 1794, when Georgia agreed with Peter Trezevant, the husband of Farquhar's daughter, to settle the Farquhar claim for a sum far below that covered by the original contract; the state issued Trezevant eight certificates to satisfy the debt, and Trezevant accepted them, determining that it was the best deal he could make. But for some reason that does not appear in the historical record, he waited until 1838 to redeem five of the certificates. Trezevant's delayed quest touched off another procedural wrangle in the Georgia legislature which lasted until 1845, when the legislature finally enacted a bill for his relief.

Whether because of the Court's inattention or the lawyers' failure to inform the Court's clerk of the settlement, the Supreme Court never removed *Chisholm* from its docket. The case was still awaiting proceedings on the enforcement of the default judgment when, in 1798, the Justices decided *Hollingsworth* and cleared the Court's docket of all similar cases—including *Chisholm*.

All this maneuvering was a matter of profound indifference to Alexander Chisholm himself. Disappearing from the case's records after the Supreme Court's 1793 decision but before Trezevant's 1794 settlement with the Georgia legislature, he died in 1810, thirty-five years before the final resolution of the Farquhar case.

A by-product of *Chisholm*—one that had nothing to do with the merits of the case but everything to do with its fate at the hands of Congress and the states—was the resignation, in 1795, of the nation's first Chief Justice. Already tired and exasperated by the burdensome tasks of circuit-riding, John Jay took the nation's abrupt and hostile reaction to *Chisholm* as a sign of the impotence of the Supreme Court. From early 1794 to the middle of 1795, he served as

---

*See Chapter 5, on the Corwin Amendment, and Chapter 6, on the Thirteenth Amendment.

President Washington's Special Minister Plenipotentiary to Great Britain, where he negotiated a treaty that, he hoped, would resolve the issues left unresolved by the Treaty of Paris. Thus, the highest federal court operated for more than a year without its presiding member, with little effect on its as yet meager business.

On his return to the United States in 1795, Jay learned to his surprise and pleasure that he had been elected governor of New York, without even having campaigned for the office. (He had sought the post in 1792, but vote-stealing by the supporters of Governor George Clinton had cost Jay the election.)[33] The Chief Justice also noted that his absence had not interfered with the Court. Delighted that the office he had for so long hoped to hold was now his, the forty-nine-year-old Jay resigned from the Court to accept what, by all appearances, was a more important post than that of Chief Justice.

In 1801, after Jay had retired from public life following two successful terms as governor, President Adams named him Chief Justice once again, to replace the retiring Oliver Ellsworth. Even though the Senate overwhelmingly approved him, Jay declined the appointment, stressing the grave defects in the federal judiciary.[34] Though he did not mention it, *Chisholm* was also much on his mind. John Jay was thus an unintended victim of *Chisholm* and its nemesis, the Eleventh Amendment.

"THE INTRINSIC DEMERITS OF THE EXISTING PLAN": THE TWELFTH AMENDMENT

THE NEXT SUCCESSFUL AMENDMENT, THE Twelfth, continued the pattern begun with the framing and adoption of the Eleventh Amendment. It was a response to another unexpected constitutional crisis—this one rooted in the Presidential elections of 1796 and 1800.

No problem of design gave the framers of the Constitution more trouble than that of choosing the President.[35] James Wilson of Pennsylvania proposed that the chief executive be elected directly by the people—only to be greeted with derision. The delegates seesawed between two procedures—election by state legislatures and election by Congress. Their tug-of-war was tied to the issue of how long the President should hold office. Those who favored election by Congress wanted a single long term (ranging from seven to twenty years) to immunize the President from pressure by those to whom he owed his election. Those who favored election by the states wanted a short term to ensure the President's dependence on the electorate. They also believed that he should be eligible for reelection as a reward for responsible service—and that he should face the risk of rejection by the voters as a penalty for failing to serve the nation's interests.

In the end, the Convention tossed the matter to its Committee on Postponed Matters, chaired by David Brearley of New Jersey; it was the Convention's workhorse, resolving issues of institutional creation and draftsmanship whose settlement had evaded the delegates. Steering a middle course, the committee turned to another of Wilson's previously unsuccessful proposals: the Electoral College. Acting more out of exhaustion and frustration than as an expression of confidence in the wisdom of the solution, the Convention adopted the Electoral College, which historian Arthur M. Schlesinger, Jr., has dubbed "the vermiform appendix in the American body politic."[36]

Article II, section 2 of the Constitution codifies the mechanism of the Electoral College. Each state was allotted a number of electoral votes equal to the total number of its Representatives and Senators. Each state would choose a group of electors (none of whom could hold any federal office) to cast these votes; most states vested the power to choose electors in the state legislatures. The electors would meet in their respective states (to avoid collusion, bribery, or influence that might result if they all met in the same place) and vote for two men, at least one of whom could not be from the electors' own state.* Congress would count the electoral votes; the candidate receiving the most votes (so long as it was a majority) would become President and the runner-up would become Vice President. In the event of a tie, or the failure of any candidate to secure a majority, the House of Representatives would decide the question. Each state's delegation would have one vote; the candidate to receive a majority of the states would become President, with the runner-up becoming Vice President.

The architects of the Electoral College had sought a nonpartisan system that would elevate the ablest candidates to the nation's two highest offices. They did not anticipate the growth of political parties or the rise of partisan competition for national office—two developments that would combine to expose what Alexander Hamilton despairingly called "the intrinsic demerits of the existing plan."[37]

In 1789 and 1792, George Washington was elected President, each time unanimously; John Adams became Vice President by a bare plurality of votes in

---

*The delegates feared that, without this limitation, the electors would vote for candidates from their own states, resulting in repeated deadlocks. This provision has been interpreted to mean that no two persons from the same state could run for President and Vice President on the same ticket. In fact, it would be possible for two candidates from the same state to run together, and even to win, if their home-state electors cast their votes for some other candidate for Vice President.

1789 and by a majority in 1792. Even in the first Presidential election, the aftershocks of conflict between the Federalists and the Anti-Federalists ensured that partisan rivalries tainted the contest for Vice President.[38] By 1796 the American political landscape was dominated by the first national political parties, the Federalists and the Republicans, rendering obsolete the nonpartisan conception of the Electoral College.

The Federalists, who coalesced around Washington, Adams, and Alexander Hamilton, supported a strong general government dominated by a powerful executive and promoting domestic policies favorable to the growth of commerce, manufacturing, and foreign trade. Federalist foreign policy favored either neutrality in world affairs or opposition to the revolutionary government of France, which Federalists considered an enemy to civilization, order, and liberty. The Republicans gathered around two Virginians—Thomas Jefferson and James Madison—and two New Yorkers—Senator Aaron Burr and Governor George Clinton. They espoused a foreign policy favoring France, which they saw as the world's principal force for human liberty against the tyrannies of the old European order. They argued for retaining the American economy's emphasis on agriculture, distrusting commerce and manufacturing as dangerous to liberty; they also supported what Jefferson called a "wise and frugal" general government, with most domestic problems left to the states, the principal actors in the federal system.*

In the fall of 1796, after Washington had announced his retirement, the Federalists chose Adams for President and Thomas Pinckney of South Carolina for Vice President. The Republicans countered with Jefferson and Burr. Seeking to adapt the election process to the new realities dictated by the evolution of parties, both parties had invented the national ticket—even though it lacked formal sanction in the Constitution or in federal law.

Informal adaptation, however, was not enough. The first contested Presidential election short-circuited the Electoral College. The Federalist Adams was chosen President with 71 electoral votes—a bare majority of the total of 138. The Republican Jefferson, as first runner-up with 68 electoral votes, became Vice President. Pinckney finished a respectable third, Burr a distant fourth.

---

*The Republican party continued until 1824, when it broke apart into four factions. One of these reorganized itself as the Democratic party, which has continued to the present, albeit with major shifts in party doctrines. By 1832, the Whig party was the new opposition party, disintegrating in the mid-1850s. In 1856, a new Republican party formed, drawing together Free-Soil Democrats, Whigs, and others who could not abide the proslavery cast of the Democratic party. The Republicans have continued to the present, although, like the Democrats, they have changed their principles considerably.

The 1796 election alarmed politicians of both parties, for the nation now had a divided executive branch—which, history taught, was a recipe for trouble— and a presiding officer of the Senate at odds with the Federalist majority in that body. A generation of Americans who still did not fully accept the legitimacy of political parties found this prospect difficult to swallow. In January 1797, there- fore, Representative William Loughton Smith (Federalist–South Carolina) pro- posed an amendment requiring electors to vote separately for President and Vice President; in the next two years, Senator Humphrey Marshall (Federalist– Kentucky) and Representative Abiel Foster (Federalist–New Hampshire) revived the idea, but Congress tabled, and killed, all three proposals—despite supportive resolutions from the legislatures of Massachusetts and Vermont.[39]

In 1800, both parties were determined to avoid the embarrassment of 1796. Building discipline and organization, the Republicans renominated Jefferson and Burr. Their campaign capitalized on the bitter split between Adams Federalists and "High" Federalists (whose chief was Hamilton and whose preferred candi- date was Charles C. Pinckney). The Republicans also benefited from the Admin- istration's unpopular undeclared war with France and the government's attempts to suppress dissent through the Alien and Sedition Acts of 1798.[40]

Desperate to prevent a likely Federalist rout, Hamilton did two extraordinarily imprudent things, both of which focused on trying to manipulate the cumber- some machinery of the Electoral College. On May 7, 1800, he sent Governor John Jay of New York a letter pleading that Jay call a special legislative session to enact a new statute dividing the state into electoral districts, each of which would cast its own electoral vote. Hamilton's aim was to ensure at least a handful of Federalist electoral votes from party strongholds in the state—"a *legal* and *constitutional* step, to prevent an *atheist* in Religion and a *fanatic* in politics from getting possession of the helm of the State." Jay chose not to act on Hamilton's letter, noting that it "[p]ropos[ed] a measure for party purposes, which I think it would not become me to adopt."[41] Five months later, having failed to persuade his Federalist colleagues of the need to rework the Electoral College machinery at the state level or to achieve the party's repudiation of Adams, Hamilton published *Letter from Alexander Hamilton, Concerning the Public Conduct and Character of John Adams, Esq., President of the United States*—an outlandish pamphlet attacking the President, apparently seeking both to vent private spleen and to sway Federalist electors to cast their ballots for Pinckney, the ostensible Federalist nominee for Vice President.[42] Hamilton's plan backfired; he alienated those Federalists who had not already chosen Adams's side over his, and presented the nation with the spectacle of a party leader committing political suicide and dragging his party down with him.

The Federalists were routed in the Presidential and congressional elections, but the Republicans were horrified when they learned the results of the vote in the Electoral College. Because no one had taken precautions to avoid a deadlock, the two Republican nominees, Jefferson and Burr, were tied for the Presidency, with 73 electoral votes apiece. (Adams garnered 65, Pinckney 64, and John Jay 1; a Federalist elector in Rhode Island cast his vote for Jay to avoid the quandary that the Republicans now confronted.)

Republicans hoped that Burr would urge the election of Jefferson, but the New Yorker remained silent, creating a mystery that persists to this day. Some historians insist that Burr was scheming to become President; others defend him but offer no explanation for his conduct; still others believe that Burr simply wanted to see what fortune would bring.[43]

Under the Constitution, the responsibility for resolving the electoral deadlock belonged to the House—still dominated by lame-duck Federalists, for the new Seventh Congress had not begun its term of office. After thirty-five ballots in February 1801, neither Jefferson nor Burr had secured a majority. Smarting over their defeat, Federalists saw a chance to humiliate Jefferson—and some of them hoped that Burr might be more sympathetic to their views. Aghast at the prospect of a Burr Presidency, Hamilton begged his colleagues not to support Burr, whom he distrusted on both political and personal grounds, and argued that Jefferson was an honorable man who would better serve the nation than would Burr.

Only two weeks before the close of Adams's term, the House chose Jefferson on the thirty-sixth ballot. Ten states voted for Jefferson, four backed Burr, and two cast blank ballots. (Apparently, the blank ballots reflected Federalist uncertainty about Burr's trustworthiness rather than the persuasiveness of Hamilton's passionate appeals.) Throughout the period between the casting of the electoral votes and the House's final vote, Jefferson maintained public calm. In private letters to Madison and Monroe, however, he speculated on whether the Federalists might seize the opportunity to try to throw the election to Pinckney; he even floated, in strictest confidence, the possibility of calling a constitutional convention in the event of a Federalist attempt at usurpation.[44]

The 1801 nightmare convinced the Republicans and some Federalists to begin an overhaul of the Electoral College machinery. Congress wrestled with several alternatives. Brooding in New York over the electoral disaster, Hamilton tried to revive his idea of dividing the states into electoral districts, each to cast one electoral vote; he also proposed "[t]hat in all future elections of President and Vice President the persons voted for shall be particularly designated by declaring which is voted for as President and which as Vice President."[45] DeWitt Clinton, then a member of the New York state senate, persuaded the state legislature to propose the amendment to Congress.[46]

Agreeing that the Constitution needed to be revised, Congress decided to take the second part of Hamilton's proposal—that requiring a distinction between

Presidential and Vice Presidential candidates—and make it the core of an adjusted Electoral College mechanism. Politicians of the time quickly dubbed the proposal the "discrimination" amendment, from the idea that electors would discriminate between candidates for President and those for Vice President. But the first attempt to adopt such an amendment, in the fall 1802 session of the Seventh Congress, failed; despite the nearly unanimous support the House gave to the proposal, the Senate majority was one vote short of the two-thirds required by Article V. Senator Gouverneur Morris (Federalist–New York) cast the vote that doomed the amendment. He had two reasons for opposing the discrimination proposal. First, it would devalue the Vice Presidency, by creating the impression that candidates for that office were and should be somehow inferior to candidates for the Presidency. Second, it would promote sectional rivalries and behind-the-scenes bidding with the Vice Presidency as the prize.[47]

Undaunted, friends of the amendment tried again in the Eighth Congress. This time, Republicans were determined to get the amendment through Congress to fend off a potential attempt in 1804 by Vice President Burr to reenact the crisis of 1800–1801; the goad to their efforts was Burr's series of increasingly public flirtations with the Federalists of New York. Proposed by Congress to the states on December 9, the amendment was ratified by thirteen of the seventeen states only six months later, on June 15, 1804, and, on September 25, Secretary of State James Madison declared it to be in effect.[48] Surviving "circular letters" from the period, written by Representatives to inform their constituents of the doings of the federal government, praise the Twelfth Amendment, focusing on its elimination of what Representative Joseph Winston (Republican–North Carolina) called "such pernicious intrigues as were exhibited on a late occasion."[49]

Under the Twelfth Amendment, each state's electors cast separate ballots for President and Vice President. If no clear winner emerges, the House chooses the President from among the top three contenders, and the Senate picks the Vice President from the top two vote-getters. If the House remains deadlocked by Inauguration Day, the Vice President assumes the Presidency until the House resolves its deadlock.* To this day, the people of the United States do not vote directly for President and Vice President.

Ironically, one of the amendment's unacknowledged architects, Alexander Hamilton, died on July 12, 1804, without ever seeing his handiwork written into the Constitution. Hamilton was fatally wounded in a duel by Vice President Burr, the man whose devious ambitions had spurred Republicans and Federalists to secure the amendment. The duel killed Burr's political career as effectively as Burr killed Hamilton.[50]

---

*The amendment does not indicate what Congress should do if the deadlock persists and appears unresolvable. Section 5 of the Twentieth Amendment resolved that problem.

Federalists fought a doomed holding action against the amendment, objecting to its recognition of the force of party in Presidential elections. Representative Benjamin Hillhouse of Connecticut asserted that having a President and Vice President of different parties would be a valuable check on executive authority; he thus turned a deliberate blind eye to the unhappy Adams-Jefferson "partnership" of 1797–1801. The Federalists also appealed to the idea of state equality, arguing that separating the elections for President and Vice President would yield control of the national electoral process to the largest states. Indeed, they maintained, the Electoral College had been a critical component of the Great Compromise between the large and small states in the drafting of the Constitution; to modify it in this way was to gut the work of the Convention of 1787. And some Federalists proposed the abolition of the Vice Presidency altogether.[51] Despite their efforts, the Twelfth Amendment was adopted in more than enough time to govern the 1804 Presidential election.[52]

In addition to preventing a replay of the deadlock of 1800–1801, the Twelfth Amendment became an insuperable obstacle to Federalist hopes in subsequent Presidential elections. Reduced by larger political forces to a sectional party (rooted in New England) and thus deprived of any possibility of contesting Presidential elections on a national basis, the Federalists could only seek to throw elections into the House, where they might have a chance of dictating the outcome. The Twelfth Amendment was thus a major factor in the disintegration of the Federalists as a political force.[53]

LESSONS AND PORTENTS

As noted at the beginning of this chapter, narrow procedural issues often conceal larger substantive problems. The histories of the Eleventh and Twelfth Amendments demonstrate that the same is true of seemingly narrow procedural reforms.

The Eleventh Amendment brought with it the resolution of two unsettled procedural issues of the amending process. Its framing and adoption helped to establish both the role of the executive branch as certifier of the adoption of amendments and the validity of dispensing with a Presidential signature on amendments proposed by Congress to the states.

The Eleventh and Twelfth Amendments' larger significance is that they crystallized the pattern of successful uses of Article V. That pattern, however, raises as many questions as it solves. Though the process was designed to raise formal constitutional change beyond the level of ordinary politics, it did not and could not insulate the workings of Article V from ordinary political pressures, as the states' and Congress's panicked response to *Chisholm* made clear, and as the equally distraught responses to the Jefferson-Burr electoral deadlock confirmed.

Reviewing the origins of these Amendments, we find features that are familiar from the origins of the Bill of Rights and that reappear in later instances of formal constitutional change:

- The *stimulus* that sets Article V in motion is a specific crisis that usually raises a significant, long-term constitutional problem to fever pitch. In the case of the Bill of Rights, the crisis was the combination of the ratification of the Constitution with the promise to add a bill of rights and the Anti-Federalists' threats to seek a second constitutional convention to rewrite the document. Likewise, the Eleventh Amendment grew out of the confluence of *Chisholm v. Georgia,* of the threat of a wave of similar lawsuits, of the virtual certainty of Georgia's refusal to comply with a Court decision against the state, and of the risk that other states would follow Georgia's lead in cases brought against them. Similarly, the Twelfth Amendment was rooted in the tie vote in the Electoral College, followed by the nearly disastrous contest within the House of Representatives to determine who would become the nation's third President.

- The *response* is an almost spasmic burst of activity in Congress, which develops into a frenetic struggle for control of the congressional agenda and the amending process. The three invocations of Article V between 1789 and 1804 mark out the poles between which later uses of the provision have oscillated. The Bill of Rights represents one pole—the open-ended effort to define and protect constitutional principle, which gives rise to a wide range of proposals that in turn become the focus of the battle to direct the amending process. The Eleventh and Twelfth Amendments stand for the other pole—the repair of a real or perceived defect in the constitutional system. If, as with *Chisholm v. Georgia* and the Jefferson-Burr deadlock, the defect is easily defined, the response is focused and an amendment proposed with comparable ease.

- The *result,* paradoxically, is an amendment that goes before the states with an abrupt falling-off of public and political interest. The proposing of the amendment by Congress gives the appearance that the problem has been solved; and the states' responses are mercurial and fragmented— though, in the first decades of the Constitution, their inconsistent behavior was the result mostly of the primitive state of communications, transportation, and the administration of government. With the passage of time, technological progress, and the improvement of governmental record-keeping, the states' erratic responses to later uses of Article V have more to do with state legislatures' abrupt flip-flops echoing equally abrupt shifts in public opinion.

• The Eleventh Amendment added one more stage to the pattern followed by the Article V process. The *aftermath* of ratification is a matter for the courts; judges consider and reconsider the amendment in concrete cases, articulating and refining doctrines rooted in the amendment's provisions, sometimes discerning principles not apparent to the framers or adopters of the provision but clearly permitted by the new constitutional text. In those cases questioning the validity of the amendment by attacking the process that produced it, the courts either avoid the issues or resolve them by fiat rather than judicial reasoning. By contrast, the Twelfth Amendment resolved the *specific* problem it was intended to solve; we have never had a deadlock comparable to the crisis of 1800. To be sure, the Amendment did not iron out all the defects of the Electoral College mechanism, but, again, it was not framed for that purpose.

The Eleventh and Twelfth Amendments staved off two federalism-based crises threatening the Union and the Constitution. Despite the relative speed of their reversal through the use of Article V, the depth and emotional intensity of these crises suggested the risk of other sectional dangers. Threats of disunion overshadowed American politics for several decades, culminating in the "secession winter" of 1860–1861, which was dominated by repeated—though vain—attempts to use the amending process to avert the disintegration of the United States.

PART II

THE AMENDING PROCESS AND THE DEVELOPMENT OF THE CONSTITUTION

CHAPTER 5

"TAKE CARE OF THE UNION"

*My principle, and the doctrine I teach, is—take care of the
Union; compromise it; do anything for it; it is the palladium—so General Washington called it—of your rights;
take care of it; and it will take care of you. Yes, sir; let us
take care of the Union, and it will certainly take care of us.
That is the proposition which I teach.*

SEN. JOHN J. CRITTENDEN (WHIG–KENTUCKY)
March 2, 1861[1]

IN FEBRUARY 1861, WILLARD'S HOTEL glistened in the pale winter sunlight of
Washington City. A few years before, the famed hotel, the center of the capital's
informal political life as well as its social life, had absorbed an adjoining structure,
a former Presbyterian church built on the plan of a Greek temple, for use as a
dancing hall and convention center; the building immediately acquired the name
Willard's Hall.

Now serious-looking men bundled in overcoats tramped up the steps of
Willard's Hall. Their destination: the Washington Peace Conference, proposed
the previous December by the Virginia legislature, just as that assembly had
called for the Annapolis Convention in 1786, almost seventy-five years before.
Their goal: to set the political and constitutional agenda of the Union, just as the
Annapolis Convention had done. Their method: to seize the means that the
Annapolis Convention had helped to make possible—the amending process
defined in Article V of the Constitution.[2] Their reason: for at least the fifth time
since the adoption of the Constitution, the Union was in jeopardy, and this time
the threat seemed mortal.[3]

On December 20, 1860, South Carolina had declared its secession from the
Union. Over the next two months, six other Southern states had followed suit.[4]
On February 4, 1861, the same day that the Washington Peace Conference
opened at Willard's Hall, representatives of these seven states convened in the
state capitol in Montgomery, Alabama, to form a new general government to
secure their independence.[5]

Bent on saving the Union from impending calamity, the Peace Conference
delegates picked their way through the mud and frost, striving to avoid the

treacherous patches of ice that were slick against the cobblestoned streets. Keeping one's balance was a physical as well as a political necessity in this secession winter, and focusing on this task made it easier for the delegates to ignore the shouted questions of journalists and the taunts of loiterers.

Inside Willard's Hall, lit by four chandeliers and the weak sunlight filtering through the tall, many-paned windows, 132 delegates from twenty-one of the thirty-four states argued over commas and phrases, struggling to produce a formula to hold the nation together. The subject of their anxious editorial and political surgery was a set of constitutional amendments designed to define and preserve an imprecise equipoise between free and slave states. The very imprecision of that balance, they hoped, would help it survive; too much insistence on definitions of rights and powers had brought the nation to its latest and severest sectional crisis.

Two blocks away from Willard's Hall, the Executive Mansion also echoed to the murmurings of men wrestling with the problem of preserving the Union. Counting the days until his retirement from the Presidency, James Buchanan fretted over the secession crisis with his patchwork Cabinet. Every now and then, he distracted himself from the emergency by brooding over choosing replacements for the Southern members, who one by one had resigned to return home and cast their lot with the Confederacy. Buchanan and his supporters also nursed their bitterness toward President-elect Abraham Lincoln, who seemed unwilling to lift a finger to aid the President in seeking to stave off the crisis. Lincoln and his allies saw the matter differently: they did not want to tie their hands and thus avoided even the appearance of joining a repudiated Administration's last-minute search for a way out.[6]

Lincoln had better reason to understand the nation's ugly mood than his critics realized.[7] He knew that pro-Southern, pro-secession men and women wanted nothing more than to see him prevented from assuming the Presidency. On the railroad journey from Illinois to Washington, he had yielded to the request of his security guards and assumed a disguise for the changing of trains at Baltimore, a hotbed of secessionist sentiment. But the President-elect was infuriated and embarrassed by that midnight incident, which had touched off a spate of jokes about his disguising himself as an old woman.[8]

In Suite 6 at Willard's Hotel, where he stayed until his inauguration on the morning of March 4, Lincoln conducted private discussions with officials of the departing Administration, candidates for his Cabinet, other ambitious office-seekers, and delegations from the Peace Conference—all of them importunate. In every meeting, he sought to charm his visitors with humor and self-deprecating references to his family and his new beard, but on substantive matters he kept his own counsel.

At the other end of Pennsylvania Avenue, brooding under the Capitol's unfinished dome, Representatives and Senators huddled in committee rooms and smoking-rooms, in corridors and alcoves, often giving way to impotent anger and despair. At regular intervals, they would return to the House and the Senate chambers to hear their Southern colleagues announce their departures.

Observers such as the young Henry Adams, a political journalist for the Boston *Advertiser,* shook their heads in dismay at the spectacle of the Union tearing itself to pieces. In scribbled private letters and telegraphic dispatches to their editors, they fumed that none of the politicians of the day seemed capable of avoiding the debacle.

Previously, the American genius of compromise had asserted itself in the persons of such statesmen as Henry Clay of Kentucky. These men had spent their careers in national politics working to deflect the catastrophe of disunion.[9] Now they were dead, and in February 1861 appeals for and proposals of compromise did not receive the public welcome or the respect accorded the efforts of Clay and his contemporaries. Compromise now struck the nation not as heroism but as a cowardly evasion of issues and a betrayal of principle.[10]

In this atmosphere of threat and counterthreat, the search continued for a way to avert disunion. In the President's Mansion, the Capitol, and Willard's Hall, politicians struggled with the intractable materials out of which they hoped to fashion yet another compromise. Time was short, however, and the would-be saviors of the Union grew more and more convinced that they had no chance of success.

Most agreed on the need to preserve the Union, yet there was little if any agreement about the character of the Union they wanted to preserve. It was this uncertainty that kept lamps burning far into the night and made politicians old before their time. For it was precisely this question—the nature of the Union and of the people, societies, economies, and states composing it—that was threatening to tip the nation into chaos and bloodshed.[11]

THE UNION AS A CONTESTED CONSTITUTIONAL CONCEPT

FROM 1776 THROUGH 1865, THE American people struggled to preserve the Union and to define its character; they deemed the Union an element of American national identity and a vital guarantor of American liberty.[12] (The word's customary initial capital symbolized its moral and political force.) Indeed, the colonists had recognized the need for and desirability of preserving their union even before they began to contemplate independence from Great Britain. Three times between 1643 and 1754—twice on their own initiative and once under duress imposed by the Crown—they had experimented with Union.[13] The efforts to resist British colonial policy in the 1760s and 1770s led almost naturally to colonial efforts to coordinate their responses—in such bodies as the Stamp Act Congress of 1765, the First Continental Congress of 1774, and the Second Continental Congress of 1775.[14]

If anything, the Americans' attachment to the ideal of Union grew and flourished with the American Revolution. The first objective defined in the Articles of Confederation was the achievement of "perpetual union," and the strongest argument for revising or replacing the Articles was that the Confederation was failing in the task. The Constitution's Preamble built on this tradition, citing as the document's first goal the formation of "a more perfect Union," and Union was a popular and persuasive card that the Constitution's supporters played with great skill.

Leading politicians often invoked Union as a political talisman. Throughout his career, George Washington praised the Union as the palladium of American liberty, and in the eyes of his countrymen he became the apotheosis of Union. Chief Justice John Marshall used the preservation of the Union as justification for federal judicial review of state laws and government actions. Similarly, in his "Advice to My Country," penned in 1835, the venerable James Madison stressed the overriding importance of the Union and the need to preserve it against enemies open and secret. Daniel Webster made his nationalist vision of the Union the hallmark of his political philosophy; in 1830 he ended his greatest speech with the call for "Liberty *and* Union, now and forever, one and inseparable!"[15] Yet, among and despite all these paeans, the Union had come repeatedly to the brink of dissolution.

Why should an ideal so generally shared be at the same time so fragile and endangered? It is easy to forget that the period between the framing of the Constitution and the outbreak of the Civil War was brief enough to be encompassed in a single lifetime,* and that threats to the Union were both numerous and serious until the 1865 meeting between Grant and Lee at Appomattox Court House.[16]

The principal threats to the Union emerged from a confluence of demographic and economic factors with constitutional and political issues. The size of the Union daunted those who would weld it into the world's largest republic; the Union of 1787 was larger than any European nation except Russia, and even a modest-sized state such as New York could easily contain the whole of

---

*Senator John J. Crittenden of Kentucky, for example, was born in 1787, the year the Federal Convention framed the Constitution. He died in 1863, an opponent of President Abraham Lincoln's Emancipation Proclamation.

England. James Madison, the nation's most creative political thinker, developed his theory of factions and the compound republic—his most original and profound contribution to politics—in response to the size of the Union and the diversity of people and interests composing it.[17] During the controversy over adoption of the Constitution, the authors of *The Federalist* devoted their first fourteen essays to celebrating the glories of Union and asserting that the only way to preserve the Union was to ratify the Constitution. Although no evidence exists to support the Federalists' charge that opponents of the Constitution wanted to break up the Union into three or four distinct confederacies, the accusation carried powerful weight in the struggle for ratification.[18]

The size and diversity of the Union was a reliable measure of either the Framers' achievement or their hubris, depending on one's point of view. In creating a vast, heterogeneous federal republic, containing so many different interests, religions, sections, and peoples, the Framers made it imperative that the American people answer not only the question "Are we to be a nation?" but its corollary, "What kind of nation are we to be?"[19]

The problem of holding together a vast, diverse union had existed long before independence. Throughout the colonial era, American colonists and visitors from abroad strained to discern something they called an "American identity" but were more convinced that the American colonies made up a loose network of polities and societies founded at different times, by different groups, for different reasons, with just as much dividing them as uniting them.[20]

Intercolonial (and, after 1776, interstate) conferences, which began as responses to discrete problems, became learning experiences for the delegates who attended them and for the politicians who appointed the delegates and received their reports. In many cases, these were the first times that these men had met residents of different regions and sections, let alone worked together to define and advance a common cause.[21] Patrick Henry might declaim in the Virginia House of Burgesses, "I am not a Virginian—I am an American!" But Henry and his contemporaries from New Hampshire to Georgia always were aware of the cultural, religious, and political differences separating the colonies. Residents even of neighboring colonies—and certainly those of different sections—viewed one another with mutual incomprehension and even hostility, as though they were residents of different countries. The same Henry who in 1775 could call himself an American also declared time and again that Virginia was his "country."[22] This consciousness of diversity and the wide range of competing interests and loyalties preoccupied the architects of the new nation.

Sectional divisions persisted during and after the Revolution—flowing from differing economic interests, differing constellations of beliefs and cultural practices, and differing political cultures.[23] Contests between states and between the Confederation and the states flared repeatedly through the 1780s. Often those seeking to derail interstate or federal ventures invoked and exploited such schisms.

Sectionalism and the competing claims of Union and state sovereignty cropped up repeatedly in the Federal Convention. During the struggle to design the Presidency, some delegates proposed a three-member chief executive, one each from the three great sections of the Union—Eastern (that is, New England and New York), Middle (New Jersey through Maryland), and Southern (Virginia through Georgia). These men feared that a one-man executive would become both a "foetus of monarchy" and a likely source of bitter sectional rivalry. Recalling the destruction of the Roman Republic by competition among the members of the First and Second Triumvirates, the Convention rejected this plan for a three-member executive as unworkable.[24]

As national politics evolved under the Constitution and the federal government's power over interstate and foreign commerce grew, sectional rivalries continued to sputter and burn. At times, they threatened to consume the nation, despite the efforts of prophets of compromise to put out the fires of discord.

But there was one sectional division that possessed moral, legal, and constitutional implications transcending mere geographic rivalry. In 1787, about 650,000 men, women, and children of African descent were held as slaves in the United States. Although slavery was principally a Southern domestic and agricultural institution, and although the institution was virtually dead in the states north of Maryland, slaves were held in every state from New Hampshire to Georgia but one: only Massachusetts, whose Supreme Judicial Court in 1783 had declared slavery void, was free from the institution.[25]

Under the law of most states, Northern as well as Southern, slaves were viewed as personal property and thus were denied the most basic of human freedoms.[26] Even those such as Thomas Jefferson, who believed that slavery as an institution might well die out, could not accept the continuing presence of blacks in the United States after the institution's demise. In the first decades of the nineteenth century, the racism prevalent among white Americans, their alarm lest free blacks serve as an example to the slaves, and their fear of resentment and reprisal at the hands of freed slaves led to the perennial suggestion that both slaves and free blacks be colonized outside the United States.[27]

Slavery injected itself not only into the culture and the politics of the United States but into its fundamental law as well. Issues having to do with slavery surfaced several times during the Federal Convention and led to compromises that the delegates built into the core of the constitutional framework.[28] Southern delegates pressed to have slaves counted along with free Americans in the ratio for determining representation in the House of Representatives, arguing that the slaves embodied an important Southern interest deserving representation in the national legislature. Delegates from Northern states resisted counting slaves for representation, insisting that if slaves were to be included in the population count for purposes of representation, they should also be included, as valuable income-producing property, in the formulas determining the states' shares of federal taxation.

After weeks of bitter debate, the delegates agreed on a compromise method of accounting: for purposes of both representation and taxation, Article I, section 2, clause 3 provided that three-fifths of the total number of slaves in each state would be added to the total number of free inhabitants (including free blacks). The Convention also authorized the federal government to enact laws providing for the return of fugitive slaves to their owners and prevented the federal government from banning American involvement in the international slave trade for twenty years (until 1808).[29] As noted in Chapter 2, this last compromise was also immunized from the Article V amending process.

The lines dividing the factions hardened with each clash between free and slave states.[30] Northern states repealed their slavery laws; some enacted "personal liberty laws," which state courts invoked to free any slave who set foot within their borders.[31] The sectional rift widened further with the rise of abolitionism in the 1830s. Demanding the outright ending of slavery, abolitionists gained prominence in American politics and at the same time became objects of fear and loathing from both moderate and proslavery politicians.[32] Many abolitionists dismissed the Constitution as a "covenant with death" because of its provisions protecting slavery, and leading abolitionists such as William Lloyd Garrison and Wendell Phillips burned copies of the Constitution at abolition rallies.[33] Frederick Douglass, himself a runaway slave, argued that the greatest American statement on human freedom, the Declaration of Independence, meant nothing to blacks because of the nation's toleration of slavery, which the Constitution made explicit.[34] Other antislavery advocates of both races made powerful arguments based on the Declaration and the Constitution. Reading these documents as charters of human liberty, they demanded that the nation live up to its principles of freedom, justice, and equality by ending slavery.[35]

Three of the major contests between the sections in the nation's first half century—those over the Alien and Sedition Acts in 1798,[36] the War of 1812,[37] and the "Tariff of Abominations" in 1832–1833[38]—had nothing to do with slavery. Even so, politicians recognized the threat implicit in these confrontations, all of which carried a latent time bomb in the ways they framed the incendiary questions of federal versus state sovereignty. A federal government powerful enough to limit the freedom of expression of citizens (including citizens of a state dominated by the opposition party), to begin a war that would injure citizens of one section for the perceived benefit of the others, or to impose a tariff discriminating against the interests of an individual state could be powerful enough to abolish slavery nationwide or to encourage its spread nationwide—despite the wishes of residents of individual states.

Any sectional crisis sparked fears of disunion, but none was more terrifying than those implicating the issue of slavery. Prudent politicians rarely called for the abolition of slavery—or for augmenting its constitutional protection. Two seemingly peripheral issues, however, had the potential to fix slavery at the heart of the nation's politics. Both had to do with the development of the nation and of the ways that its parts were knitted together—in particular, the growth of methods of transportation that made travel throughout the Union cheaper, quicker, and easier.

First: What happened when slaveowners traveled through free states with their slaves? Did the free states' laws operate to liberate slaves in transit? Or did the principles of "interstate comity" and federalism protect what slaveowners considered to be their property rights?

Second: What was slavery's status in the unorganized territories? It was this issue that nearly tore the Union apart in the years before 1861.

The United States first grappled with the territory issue in 1783, after acquiring British territory between the Allegheny Mountains and the Mississippi River under the terms of the Treaty of Paris. The Confederation Congress had to decide whether to permit or restrict the expansion of slavery into the territories and the new states that would take shape there. The Northwest Ordinance, adopted in 1787 and confirmed by the First Congress in 1789, seemed to exclude slavery from all territory northwest of the Ohio River—though a recent careful study of the Ordinance's provisions, and of the territories' history under it, suggests that slavery was suffered to continue because of careless draftsmanship and a prevailing indifference to the plight of slaves in the region.[39]

By 1820, slavery's position in the territories had become critical to the character of the evolving Union. The Louisiana Purchase in 1803 had added vast lands to the young republic, including territory seemingly ripe for the transplantation of slavery as the economic basis for new states. The petition of Missouri to be admitted as a slave state resulted in the first great constitutional crisis over slavery since the Convention of 1787. Congress resolved it through the first of two landmark compromises.

One of the two elements of the Missouri Compromise was the concurrent admission of Maine, formerly a district of Massachusetts, to the Union. The free state of Maine and the slave state of Missouri balanced each other, and in turn preserved the balance between free and slave states in the Senate. The other element was the drawing of the famous 36°30' North Latitude line (the southern border of Missouri), north of which slavery would be excluded and south of which it would be authorized.

The acquisition of the Louisiana Territory did not sate the territorial hunger of American politicians, nor did the Missouri Compromise still the contest over the expansion of slavery. Slavery lay fallow for a generation as a national issue, until the Mexican War of 1846–1848 resulted in the acquisition of vast territories in the Southwest, reopening the quarrels over the extent to which slavery would be allowed to spread into the territories.[40]

Most efforts to resolve or defuse the issue of slavery in the territories took place at the level of ordinary politics rather than at the level of constitutional change.[41] The principal battleground was the maintenance in the Senate of a balance between free and slave states, achieved through the paired admissions of free and slave states along the lines of the Maine-Missouri precedent from 1820. This practice was followed until the Compromise of 1850, when additional securities for slavery (such as a strengthened fugitive slave law) were part of the price the South exacted as compensation for the loss of free-slave parity in the Senate.

However, in 1854, Democratic Senator Stephen A. Douglas of Illinois proposed that Congress abandon the geographic method of determining whether new states would permit or exclude slavery in favor of the doctrine of "popular sovereignty" (first popularized in 1848 by Democratic Senator Lewis Cass of Michigan). Under his plan, the people of each territory would decide whether to sanction or to prohibit slavery in organizing their state. Douglas's proposal, codified in the Kansas-Nebraska Act of 1854, masqueraded as a principled solution but actually was an attempt to remove the federal government from the mare's nest of slavery in the territories. Opponents of popular sovereignty mocked Douglas for calling it an application of democratic principle; they condemned it instead as an abdication of principle.[42]

The first application of popular sovereignty produced a gory fiasco in the Kansas Territory. Proslavery and antislavery settlers streamed into Kansas, beginning a terrible conflict over which group would elect the territorial legislature and organize a government. Throughout the 1850s, the territory was known as "Bleeding Kansas." Douglas, outraged that proslavery "border ruffians" and their supporters had manipulated popular sovereignty to stage a proslavery coup in Kansas, opposed recognition of the proslavery constitution they sought to impose on the Territory.[43] (Only in 1861, when Congress was dominated by Republicans eager to halt the spread of slavery, did Kansas join the Union as a free state. By contrast, Nebraska developed quietly as a free Territory and, eventually, a free state.)

Because geographic and "democratic" solutions had failed, the Supreme Court sought to resolve the conflict over slavery through an authoritative decision on the meaning of the Constitution.[44] The vehicle the Justices proposed to use was *Dred Scott v. Sandford.*[45] In 1837, Scott, a slave, had been taken from Missouri to Fort Snelling in the free Territory of Wisconsin by his master, Dr. John Emerson, a U.S. Army surgeon. Emerson and his family and slaves— including Dred Scott and his wife—bounced back and forth between free Territories and slave and free states until Emerson's death in 1843. At his death, his wife's brother, John F. A. Sanford, became his executor and the nominal owner of Dred Scott. Scott first sued Mrs. Emerson, and then Sanford, for his freedom on the basis of his brief sojourn in the Wisconsin Territory. The case climbed the federal judicial ladder, its ascent quiet and almost unnoticed, until in early 1857 it reached the Supreme Court.[46]

Chief Justice Roger B. Taney sought to present an unanswerable restatement and affirmation of the protections the Constitution afforded slavery as a property right of slaveowners, and to strike down once and for all federal attempts to limit the spread of slavery into the Territories or anywhere else, thus invalidating the Missouri Compromise. To achieve this goal, he wrested control of the Court's majority opinion from his moderate colleague, Associate Justice Samuel Nelson of New York. The elderly Chief Justice penned a stark proslavery opinion, cloaking itself in the supposed intent of the framers of the Constitution and of the Declaration of Independence to exclude blacks from citizenship and constitutional protection.[47]

The Court's attempt to solve the slavery controversy backfired. Taney only goaded antislavery forces into fury, persuading abolitionists and their allies to look for ways to evade, challenge, or ignore the decision. In the process, he damaged for over a generation the Court's authority as an interpreter of the Constitution.

The bitterness of the contest over slavery led some leading spokesmen on both sides of the contest—abolitionist Northerners and fire-eating Southerners—to welcome disunion. Such extremists as Robert Barnwell Rhett of South Carolina and Horace Greeley of New York agreed that the slavery issue so weakened the Union that the abolitionist and slaveowning interests should be allowed to go their own ways. Rhett savored the prospect of a weak Southern confederation whose member states would be free to govern themselves without interference from the general government; Greeley was willing to settle for a reconstituted Union free to purge itself of the taint of slavery.

Still other politicians believed that contests between federal authority and vital local interests could be headed off by amending the Constitution rather than sundering the Union; they maintained that constitutional revision might be the only thing that *could* preserve the Union. Article V's mechanisms were ready to hand, and politicians anxious to save the Union through constitutional reform were eager to make use of them.

Some would have altered the executive branch to ensure that all interests were equally represented in it, whether by resurrecting the idea of a plural executive or by requiring the rotation of the Presidency among the sections. At the height of the crisis of 1850, Senator John C. Calhoun of South Carolina implied that only constitutional revision of the executive branch could save the Union and the vital interests of his beloved South. Calhoun's recipe—a two-headed executive, one appointed by the North, one by the South, with each possessing the power to check the other—was treated with the respect due its author, but not even he believed that his proposal would succeed.

Other proposals to refashion the executive to preserve sectional peace would have left the Presidency in the hands of one man but would have required a "concurrent majority" for his election—that is, a majority including all the major interests in the polity, rather than a simple numerical majority.[48] In 1822, for example, a Kentucky Representative proposed to divide the Union into four "Presidential sections"—the North (New England and New York), the Middle States (New Jersey to Virginia), the South (North Carolina to Louisiana), and the West (then Kentucky, Ohio, Indiana, Illinois, and Missouri). Each section would elect the President in a regular rotation. (Though its author insisted that he was serious, his proposal was received with derision and quickly forgotten.) During the "secession winter" of 1860–1861, Senator Andrew Johnson of Tennessee suggested that the choice of President and Vice President alternate between the slave states and the free states, beginning in 1864 with the slave states.[49]

Other proposed amendments would have exacerbated rather than eased sectional tension, by tilting the constitutional machinery firmly in a proslavery or antislavery direction. At the height of the "secession winter," for example, Representative Clement L. Vallandigham (Democrat–Ohio) urged that the sectional method be used to ensure that whoever was chosen President would be acceptable to all four sections of the nation. This amendment would have given the Southern states the power to block the election to the Presidency of anyone hostile to slavery. It also would have ensured that the slave states could block any proposed laws that threatened slavery, both implicitly (through a reliance on a Presidential veto) and explicitly, because it would have given Senators of any one section the power to demand sectional voting on legislation, with the concurrence of all sections needed to enact a bill into law.[50] (During the Civil War, Vallandigham became a notable antiwar Democrat suspected of pro-Confederate activity.)

Similarly, several times before 1861, New Englanders had suggested the repeal of the three-fifths ratio. The closest this idea ever came to fruition—and the time that it emerged most clearly as an antislavery rather than a sectional effort—was in 1843, when Representative (and former President) John Quincy Adams introduced it at the request of the Massachusetts legislature; it was the latest of a series of antislavery amendments he had introduced in the House beginning in 1833. The outrage of the Southern states, including the South Carolina legislature's formal denunciation of the proposal, led to its burial by the House the following year.[51] By contrast, in 1860, to conciliate the Southern states and to prevent their departure from the Union, moderate Northern Senators and Representatives proposed amendments designed to make the three-fifths ratio unamendable—with as little success as Adams's proposals had had.

Some amendment advocates sought declarations making what they saw as the states' powers to resist federal encroachment so explicit that they could not be denied any longer. In response to the nullification crisis over the Tariff of Abominations, which, in 1832–1833 pitted South Carolina against President Andrew Jackson, Georgia demanded a constitutional convention to consider thirteen proposals for amendments. The first and second were

> That the powers delegated to the General Government, and the right reserved to the States or to the people may be more distinctly defined.
> That the power of coercion by the General Government over the States, and the right of a State to resist an unconstitutional act of Congress may be determined.[52]

Georgia thus wanted to write into the Constitution the doctrines of nullification and interposition, which held that a state has the power to block any federal measure that strikes directly at its vital interests. These doctrines flowered in the 1820s and 1830s, and hovered over the nation like vultures until 1861.[53]

As the 1850s wound to a close, the stakes and the level of rancor in the slavery controversy increased geometrically. Seeking ways to stave off disaster, politicians cast about for solutions commensurate with the challenge to the survival of the Union and the Constitution.

THE "SESSION OF AMENDMENTS"

THE ELECTION OF 1860 RESURRECTED the specter of disunion. The Republicans, a new political party contesting only its second Presidential election, had captured the Presidency and both houses of Congress.[54] Derided by many Democrats, especially in the South, as the party of "Black Republicans" and rabid abolitionists, the Republicans prevailed because of the three-way split of the Democratic party that year. Unionist Democrats in the North and the West backed Senator Stephen A. Douglas of Illinois; Southern Democrats rallied behind Vice President John C. Breckinridge of Kentucky; and those who remembered the compromising successes of Henry Clay adhered to yet another Kentuckian, Senator John Bell, a former Whig running as a "Constitutional Unionist." In this four-way race, Republican candidate Abraham Lincoln was able to garner a majority of electoral votes, despite tallying less than 40 percent of the popular votes cast. Indeed, he was not even on the ballot in some Southern states.

The 1860 Presidential election was the first in American history in which the losers did not accept with grace the verdict of the electorate. South Carolina was the first to act; reacting in fury to the news of Lincoln's election, the state legislature adopted resolutions of secession on December 20, 1860, and called on other slave states to follow suit. In fifteen tumultuous days in January 1861, six more states emulated South Carolina and declared their intention to organize a new confederation.

President James Buchanan watched, weary and sad, as the nation drifted toward the abyss. To one visitor, the sixty-nine-year-old President complained, "I think it is very hard [that] they can not let me finish my term of office in peace, at my time of life."[55] It was a shattering conclusion to a political career that, four years earlier, had been generally hailed as among the most distinguished in the nation's history. Having held a dazzling array of government posts, including Secretary of State in the Polk Administration and American Minister to Great Britain in the Pierce Administration at the time of his election to the Presidency in 1856, Buchanan had portrayed himself as the most experienced man ever to become Chief Executive. But he crippled himself almost immediately by giving in his inaugural address an implied endorsement of the Supreme Court's impending decision of *Dred Scott v. Sandford,* which—he predicted—would be the definitive solution to the crisis over slavery. By approving the decision two days before it was handed down, he laid himself open to charges of conspiring with Chief Justice Taney to sell out the Constitution to the forces of slavery. Moreover, his prediction of the decision's success rebounded to his discredit when Taney's opinion proved a dismal failure.

The national firestorm over *Dred Scott* and slavery wrested the direction of events from the President's grasp. He chose not to run for a second term—in large part because he knew that the otherwise disunited Democrats would reject his candidacy. In 1860, he put his fading prestige behind the candidacy of Vice President Breckinridge; the Kentuckian's defeat was a repudiation of Buchanan as well, especially because Breckinridge Democrats emerged after the election as leaders of the campaign for secession.

As Buchanan's Cabinet disintegrated in the wake of the seven secession resolutions, the pro-Southern old guard competed with new Unionist members in a tug-of-war for the President's loyalty. If the President and his Cabinet agreed on anything, it was the federal government's constitutional and practical inability to resist secession. Southern Cabinet members resigned and went home to join the Confederate cause. The new Secretary of War, Joseph Holt, wrote to a friend on January 14, 1861:

> The thought of employing force to oblige a state to remain in
> the Union has never been entertained by the President or any
> member of his cabinet—He has held, as I do, that it is his duty

to protect the public property in his charge as well as he can—But this principle is virtually an abstraction since with two or three exceptions the arm[orie]s and forts of the Un[ited] States have been seized throughout the South. . . . No effort to regain them will be made. . . . The Union is passing away like a band of fog before the wind—But the fate of the South will be that of Sampson—She will pull down the temple, but she will perish amid the ruins.[56]

In his last annual message to Congress, Buchanan declared that the Union could not be broken by secession but that the federal government lacked the power to prevent such unconstitutional acts. Republican Senator William Seward of New York delivered a mocking summary of Buchanan's position: "[It] is the duty of the President to execute the laws—unless somebody opposes him—and no state has the right to go out of the Union—unless it wants to."[57]

Taking refuge in proposals that he hoped would bear fruit after he stepped down from the Presidency, Buchanan recommended that Congress call a constitutional convention to increase the protections given slaveholders in their efforts to recover fugitive slaves and to augment protection of slavery in the territories. He regarded his suggestion as statesmanlike, but the nation did not agree.

The most determined opponent of secession among the President's new advisers, Attorney General Edwin M. Stanton of Ohio, was outraged by the threats to the Union and the indecisiveness of Buchanan. Stanton denounced secessionists as traitors to the Union and the emerging Confederacy as a treasonous conspiracy against the Constitution. In a private letter, he predicted that "there will not be a semblance of a Union left by March 4," the date Lincoln was to take office. Exasperated by the President's irresoluteness, Stanton met behind the scenes with representatives of the President-elect and the Republican party, assuring them of his firm commitment to the Union, keeping them up to date on the waverings of Buchanan's Cabinet, and urging them to take positive steps to preserve the Union.[58]

Those who looked to Lincoln for leadership against secession were confused and disappointed by his reticence. Lincoln was all too aware that he had been elected by less than a majority of the popular vote. The President-elect therefore was reluctant to act before he possessed the constitutional power to do so. Nor did he want to dissipate his authority by joining forces with the discredited Buchanan, or by endorsing a faltering policy bound to be overtaken by events. Finally, like most members of his party, Lincoln suspected that talk of secession was the latest in a long series of empty Southern threats. He believed that South Carolina was "crying wolf" in 1860–1861, much as it had done in 1832–1833. In February 1861, as Lincoln traveled to the nation's capital from his home in

Springfield, Illinois, he contented himself with repeating his endorsement of two key Republican positions: opposing the expansion of slavery and assuring slaveholders that the institution would not be disturbed where it already was legally established.[59]

In the face of the President's weakness and the President-elect's taciturnity, other politicians decided to explore the possibilities of constitutional compromise to resolve or suspend the crisis. In the second session of the Thirty-sixth Congress (December 1860 to March 1861), which the historian Herman V. Ames dubbed the "session of amendments," over two hundred proposals were laid before Congress—some moderate, others farfetched, all of them desperate.[60]

To manage the flood of proposals, each chamber of Congress created its own select committee. On December 4, 1860, the House of Representatives established its Committee of Thirty-three; two days later, the Senate formed its Committee of Thirteen. Meanwhile, Senator Seward, the de facto leader of Congressional Republicans, worked with moderate Unionist Democrats to persuade states considering secession to hold back from that step "until every opportunity for compromise had been exhausted."[61]

The Senatorial leader of the quest for compromise was the chairman of the Committee of Thirteen, John J. Crittenden of Kentucky. The white-haired, seventy-three-year-old Crittenden was four years older than Buchanan but far more active and hopeful. He behaved as if he had inherited the mantle of compromiser from his revered predecessor Henry Clay, and his assumption of Clay's role augmented his stature in the Senate.

Crittenden's counterpart in the House of Representatives was the chairman of the Committee of Thirty-three, Thomas Corwin of Ohio. A former Whig Senator, Corwin seemed an unlikely voice of reason and compromise. In 1846, during the debates over declaring the Mexican War, he had opposed the war as an amoral grab for Mexican territory; he had even expressed his hope that Mexican soldiers would welcome invading United States forces "with bloody hands, to hospitable graves."[62] However, once Corwin joined the Republicans following the disintegration of the Whig party in the mid-1850s, he became more comfortable with moderate politicians and impatient with extremists of all stripes; he hated Democrats and abolitionists equally. In a letter to President-elect Lincoln, Corwin vented his exasperation with the process of compromise he was desperately trying to advance:

> I cannot comprehend the madness of the times. Southern men
> are theoretically crazy. Extreme Northerners are practical fools.
> The latter are really quite as mad as the former. Treason is in the
> air around us *every* where. It goes by the name of patriotism.[63]

On the last day of 1860, culling the hundreds of suggestions put forth throughout the month, the Senate's Committee of Thirteen produced a report outlining four sets of proposals. Each had at its core proposed amendments and drafts of laws complementing the amendments.[64] Three of these clusters got nowhere.

The first two sets, the handiwork of Jefferson Davis of Mississippi and Robert Toombs of Georgia, were acceptable only to stiff-necked Southerners. They provided that the right to own slaves, like any other property right, would be protected throughout the Union; that fugitive slaves would not have such rights as habeas corpus and jury trial (thereby writing into the Constitution the holdings of the Court's principal fugitive-slave-law decision, *Prigg v. Pennsylvania*);[65] that a majority of Senators and Representatives from slave states would have to consent to any federal statute affecting slavery; that every slave state had to ratify constitutional amendments affecting the institution; and that Northern states' "sojourner" laws (freeing any slave who was brought into a free state by his or her master, no matter how briefly) were invalid.

The third set of amendments, offered by Stephen Douglas, catered to racism among white Americans. They would have disenfranchised blacks, disqualified them from any political office, required freed blacks to be colonized outside the United States, preserved slavery in the District of Columbia, and commanded the federal government to provide compensation to owners of fugitive slaves evading capture. Hoping to defuse Northern fears that Southerners would agitate to find new territory where they could plant slavery, he also proposed to freeze the territorial growth of the nation and to require that no existing territory be considered for admission to the Union until its population should reach 50,000.

The fourth set in the committee's report, devised by Crittenden himself, had an authority that the others lacked, thanks to the political seniority of their sponsor. Crittenden proposed that all new states be admitted without condition, leaving it to them to decide for or against slavery—thus offering to write into the Constitution the principle of popular sovereignty. His other proposals would have immunized slavery from abolition, adjusted fugitive slave statutes to protect slaveowners' rights, protected the interstate slave trade, and provided federal compensation for slaveowners who could not recover their runaway slaves.

But what attracted the most attention among Crittenden's recommendations was his proposal that the 1820 Missouri Compromise line be revived, excluding slavery from all future states north of 36°30′ North and permitting it south of that line. Viewing the Missouri Compromise as the most successful attempt to produce a nation permanently half slave and half free, Crittenden proposed, in effect, to overturn that portion of *Dred Scott v. Sandford* that had invalidated the Missouri Compromise.

Finally, Crittenden aimed to bypass existing federal and state institutions by submitting his proposals to a national popular referendum rather than to the state legislatures or conventions as required by Article V. It may seem odd that this defender of constitutional Union would try to evade these constitutional requirements, but Crittenden believed that the traditional amending process would break down, because the established institutions were too blinded by ideology to see the necessary solution. "My confidence in the intelligence and public virtue of the people," he explained in March, during the last stages of congressional debate, "is greater than it is in any body of their representatives."[66]

The House's Committee of Thirty-three submitted two proposals of its own that week.[67] The first, offered by Representative Henry Winter Davis of Maryland, the "gilded aristocrat and political boss of Baltimore,"[68] was an ordinary bill that would have authorized the admission of New Mexico to the Union as a slave state. However, rupture between "border-state" Representatives and their Southern colleagues over the bill's silence on the larger issues of slavery derailed the measure.

The other House proposal was the handiwork of the committee's chairman, Representative Corwin, who offered an "unamendable" amendment to the Constitution protecting slavery in the existing states:

> No amendment shall be made to the Constitution which will authorize or give to Congress the power to abolish or interfere, within any State, with the domestic institutions thereof, including that of persons held to labor or service by the laws of said State.

Briefly tabled (so that it could be held in reserve if nothing better emerged), the Corwin amendment then became a focus of debate in the House, but on February 27 it apparently failed; the Representatives could not muster a two-thirds vote to approve it.

The plethora of amendment proposals in the House and the Senate, none of which marked out a basis for compromise between the sections and all of which were tabled after fruitless debate, exhausted Congress and frustrated the American people. Because the committees had failed to identify grounds on which to base a sectional compromise, public attention focused on the Washington Peace Conference, which convened on February 4, 1861. Despite its serious agenda, the Conference was mocked by some as the "Old Gentlemen's Convention" because of its members' age and political eminence (and, perhaps, their senescence).

Virginia's senior delegate, the elderly former President John Tyler, presided. Other delegates who typified the tone of the Conference included Justice Thomas Ruffin of the North Carolina Supreme Court, author of *State v. Mann,*[69] an 1829 decision upholding the right of persons entrusted with slaves to inflict battery on those slaves but decrying the brutality of slavery; James B. Clay of Kentucky, a son of Henry Clay; and William C. Rives of Virginia, a protégé of James Madison.[70] Most of the delegates were (and thought of themselves as) moderates, though some Northern Republican delegates such as David Wilmot of Pennsylvania and Salmon P. Chase of Ohio saw it as their duty to block any compromise proposals that conceded too much to the Southern states. In an ominous development for the Conference, the seven states that had voted to secede did not send delegations. (Because of logistical difficulties, Oregon and California—the two West Coast states—did not send delegations, and political disagreements blocked the naming of delegations in four other states.)

President Buchanan assured Tyler that he would support any proposals offered by the Conference; as a result, Tyler held repeated meetings with Buchanan, which accomplished nothing more than giving the two elderly, querulous gentlemen opportunities to play on each other's nerves. Attorney General Stanton was dubious that the Conference would produce anything of value. In a private meeting ten days before it opened, he assured Massachusetts Senator Charles Sumner that it would come to nothing, and "that Virginia would most certainly secede—that the conspiracy there was the most wide-spread & perfect." Virginia's purpose, Stanton averred, was "to constitute a Provisional Govt. which was to take possession of the Capital & declare itself a nation. . . . [W]e are in the midst of a revolution."[71]

After nearly four weeks behind closed doors, during which delegates met with President-elect Lincoln and other key figures, the Conference issued a report at the end of February presenting and explaining a "Proposed Amendment XIII to the Constitution of the United States" to be submitted to Congress. Despite the announcement of their labors, the delegates somehow omitted to take a formal vote to adopt this "amendment" or the report presenting it, a blunder that reflected the disarray with which the Conference concluded its efforts.

The Peace Conference's report began with an address cloaking the confusion that marked its proceedings:

> The Convention assembled upon the invitation of the State of Virginia to adjust the unhappy differences which now disturb the peace of the Union and threaten its continuance, make known to the Congress of the United States that . . . they have approved what is herewith submitted, and respectfully request that your honorable body will submit it to conventions in the States as an article of amendment to the Constitution of the United States.[72]

The seven sections of the proposed amendment read like a sectional treaty of peace, and that is precisely what the delegates hoped it would become:

(i) It would revive the Missouri Compromise line, except that the status of slavery in the territories would depend on the decisions of federal courts, "according to the course of the common law." Just what this phraseology meant was unexplained; in this period, federal courts could enunciate their understandings of the common law in cases not governed by federal or state statutory law.[73]

(ii) It would require the support of a majority of Senators from the slaveholding states for the acquisition of territory and for the ratification of any treaty by which territory would be acquired.

(iii) It would deny the federal government any power to affect slavery within states or territories where it was already established. Moreover, slavery could not be abolished in the District of Columbia without the consent of Maryland and the resident slaveowners, and without providing just compensation to nonconsenting slaveowners.

(iv) It would permit state governments to use their powers to assist slaveowners seeking to recover fugitive slaves under the federal fugitive slave laws, thus overturning Justice Joseph Story's antislavery dictum in the Supreme Court's generally proslavery decision in *Prigg v. Pennsylvania.*

(v) It would continue and strengthen the ban on the foreign slave trade.

(vi) It would render its first, third, fifth, and sixth provisions unamendable except by consent of all the states.

(vii) It would require the federal government to compensate slaveowners for unrecovered runaway slaves.

Bickering and parliamentary obfuscation swirled around the report of the Washington Peace Conference when it arrived on the desk of the Speaker of the House on March 1. Under the rules of the House, a two-thirds vote was required to take up the report, and radicals and secessionists united to oppose any motion to bring it to the floor. Northern members refused even to recognize the legitimacy of the Peace Conference; Representative Owen Lovejoy of Illinois, brother of the murdered abolitionist Rev. Elijah Lovejoy, proclaimed, "It is not a peace congress at all. There is no such body known to this House." The vote of 93 to 67 failed to satisfy the two-thirds requirement, and the House went on record as refusing even to receive the proposed amendment.[74]

In the Senate, Crittenden had the report referred to a select committee of five (which he chaired), despite the mocking recommendation of Senator Jacob Collamer of Vermont "not only that it be made the order of the day for twelve o'clock to-morrow, but that it be adopted by three-fourths of the States the next day." Collamer's colleagues shared (but did not acknowledge) his sense of the ridiculousness of using the slow-moving amending process to head off a fast-worsening sectional crisis.[75]

The committee voted, 3 to 2, to endorse the Conference's proposed amendment. The dissenters, William Seward of New York and Lyman Trumbull of Illinois, recommended the calling of a constitutional convention under Article V, leading one Virginia newspaper to attack the New Yorker:

> Seward has somewhat betrayed his Richmond Confederates. He led them to suppose that he would do something in the way of conciliating the South. Perhaps he designed to do so; but finding that he could not get his party to follow him, he forfeited his promise and took ground against Crittenden and against the Peace Conference, and fell back on a recommendation to the States to *take into consideration* the *propriety* of holding a National Convention—which is *"nothing* whittled down to a point."[76]

At this point in the Senate's deliberations, Crittenden realized that his own proposals, which he had sought to revive only a few days earlier, were doomed to failure. He therefore carried out a heroic act of self-denial, asking on March 3 that the Peace Conference report be substituted for his own proposal. A few minutes after 4:00 A.M. on March 4, the last day of the Thirty-sixth Congress and the day on which Lincoln was to be inaugurated, the substitute was defeated in the Senate, 28 to 7, by a prickly alliance of radical Northerners and fire-eating Southerners.

In the end, the only accomplishments of the Peace Conference were to provide a basis to dissuade border states such as Kentucky and Missouri from voting to secede, and to delay the ultimate clash between the Union and the Confederacy long enough to permit Lincoln's peaceful inauguration. While significant, these achievements were far short of what the Conference's organizers had hoped for. The Southern delegates returned home to lend their support to secession (with Tyler becoming a Virginia member of the Confederate Senate that November); the Northerners returned home either to face scorn and obloquy from their fellow politicians or to join forces with the Lincoln Administration to resist secession.[77]

The Thirty-sixth Congress ended in chaos and discord. Those sitting in the galleries during the tumultuous first days of March would have seen knots of legislators, arguing bitterly, sawing the air with windy and futile gestures as it grew gray and heavy with tobacco smoke.

One last card, however, remained to be played in the effort to stave off disunion. The Corwin Amendment, forgotten since February 27, was innocuous enough that all factions in Congress might be able to agree on it—and Senator

Seward, the prime mover to revive the Amendment, realized this. On Saturday, March 2, the House reversed its decision of a week earlier and endorsed the Amendment by a vote of 133 to 65. The House probably approved the Amendment because its members realized that nothing else available to them had any chance of success. A bare two-thirds majority of the Senate (24 to 12) followed the House's lead minutes later.

Once the Corwin Amendment had cleared the congressional hurdles, Congress agreed to reconsider Senator Crittenden's proposals, out of respect for the Kentuckian and those of his colleagues who had worked so hard for sectional compromise with so little result. The proposal failed in both chambers, however, despite Crittenden's emotional last-minute appeal.[78]

While Congress spent its dissipating energies on the Crittenden proposal, a messenger carried the Corwin Amendment to the President. Even though the Supreme Court had ruled in 1798 that a proposed amendment does not need a Presidential signature, Buchanan signed it, seeking to place what was left of his authority behind it. The exhausted Pennsylvanian was convinced, however, that it would not work, confiding to friends his belief that he would be the last President of the United States.

On Monday, March 4, the doddering Buchanan accompanied his successor to the Capitol, where Lincoln took the oath of office from Chief Justice Taney. Lincoln began his inaugural address, knowing that it would be scrutinized by all sides in the secession controversy. He spoke to the apprehensive crowd in a firm voice, though some were surprised by his high pitch and Kentucky accent. Lincoln commented publicly for the first time on the frantic search for a constitutional amendment that had dominated the secession winter:

> This country, with its institutions, belongs to the people who inhabit it. Whenever they shall grow weary of the existing government, they can exercise their *constitutional* right of amending it, or their *revolutionary* right to dismember, or overthrow it. I can not be ignorant of the fact that many worthy, and patriotic citizens are desirous of having the national constitution amended. While I make no recommendation of amendments, I fully recognize the rightful authority of the people over the whole subject, to be exercised in either of the modes prescribed in the instrument itself; and I should, under existing circumstances, favor, rather than oppose, a fair opportunity being afforded the people to act upon it.[79]

Lincoln then focused on the Corwin Amendment, which he believed was consistent with the 1860 Republican platform and was not a concession to the slaveowning interests:

I understand a proposed amendment to the Constitution—which amendment, however, I have not seen, has passed Congress, to the effect that the federal government, shall never interfere with the domestic institutions of the States, including that of persons held to service. To avoid misconstruction of what I have said, I depart from my purpose not to speak of particular amendments, so far as to say that, holding such a provision to now be implied constitutional law, I have no objection to its being made express, and irrevocable.[80]

Only the Ohio and Maryland legislatures ratified the Corwin Amendment; a third ratification came by the vote of a constitutional convention in Illinois, which arguably violated the terms set by Congress for its adoption (which required the vote of the state legislature). No one else even bothered to consider it, and the Corwin Amendment was forgotten within months after Buchanan had affixed his trembling signature to it.[81]

THUS THE ONE TIME WHEN every faction agreed on the need to amend the Constitution resulted in the most catastrophic failure of amendment politics in American history. The search for amendments compromising issues of slavery and sectionalism was as unlikely to succeed as was the medieval alchemists' quest for the Philosopher's Stone.

While the Corwin Amendment misfired, other events intervened. Lincoln's inauguration did nothing to dispel the secessionist fever sweeping the upper South, and four more states joined the Confederacy. The emboldened Confederacy wrote its own constitution (discussed in Chapter 12), began to organize its military resources, and elected its own president—the gaunt, frail former Senator Jefferson Davis of Mississippi, who thirty years earlier had been Lincoln's commander in the Black Hawk War.[82] Davis issued an ultimatum to Lincoln, demanding the withdrawal of Union forces from all forts and military posts in Confederate territory. In some instances, Lincoln agreed, but in other cases, he held firm.[83]

In the early hours of April 12, 1861, Fort Sumter crouched, quiet and somber, in the harbor of Charleston, South Carolina. Above it still waved the United States flag, despite the angry demands of Confederate officials for the fort's surrender. Along the shoreline, behind fortifications shielding primed and loaded cannon, onlookers watched the preparations of militiamen under the command of Pierre G. T. Beauregard.

At Beauregard's gesture, Edmund Ruffin of Virginia, the patriarch of Southern secessionism and an honorary member of the Palmetto Guards of South Carolina, stepped forward to a waiting cannon.[84] Stooped and lank-haired, the sixty-seven-year-old Ruffin was a distant cousin of Judge Thomas Ruffin, who had returned home from the Washington Peace Conference despairing of any further attempts to preserve the Union. Edmund Ruffin had expressed grim satisfaction at the Conference's failure, having long believed and argued that the Union was a fatal threat to the interests of the slaveholding South. Having made a name for himself as a leading expert on agriculture, a respected writer and journalist, and a passionate advocate of state sovereignty and the doctrines of John C. Calhoun, Ruffin now proudly pulled the cannon's lanyard, venting his hatred for a government that, he believed, was hell-bent on destroying his beloved South. As he fired the Confederacy's first shot at Fort Sumter, Ruffin consigned to a historical footnote the quest for a constitutional formula to prevent civil war.

CHAPTER 6

REDEFINING THE UNION: THE CIVIL WAR AMENDMENTS

[T]his mighty convulsion, mightier by far than the old Revolution . . . is a new birth of the nation. The Constitution will hereafter be read by the light of the rebellion; by the light of the emancipation; by the light of that tremendous uprising of the intellect . . . going on everywhere around us. . . . This struggle has been as organic in its great meaning as the Constitution itself.

REP. IGNATIUS DONNELLY
(Republican–Minnesota)
February 1, 1866[1]

AFTER SO TRAUMATIC A STRUGGLE as the Civil War, it is no wonder that the victors sought to write the results of the cataclysm into the Constitution. The antebellum Constitution was as dead as the more than six hundred thousand Union and Confederate men who had lost their lives.

The war made the character of the Union a question just as important as its preservation. President Abraham Lincoln had recognized the defining nature of the war, and his many eloquent speeches and letters succeeded so well precisely because he used them to help guide his countrymen to understand what the war was doing to them, what they were doing to one another, and where they were tending.[2] What we now know as the Civil War Amendments (the Thirteenth, Fourteenth, and Fifteenth)—of which Lincoln helped to guide only the Thirteenth into existence before his assassination—were a political and constitutional necessity as much as a symbolic victory for the friends of emancipation and Union.

Yet these Amendments were neither the natural nor the ideal consequences of the war. They were neither conceived nor adopted as a unit. Each emerged from a complex and inconsistent array of proposals, the scope and dimensions of which were dictated as much by transient political circumstances as by questions of national purpose and constitutional principle.

The proponents of each Amendment were themselves bitterly divided. Some worked only to eradicate the stain of slavery; others hoped to raise the freed slaves (and the free blacks) to full legal and social equality with whites; still others labored to transform the political life of the nation. Each Amendment's supporters thought that it alone would be sufficient to achieve their goals. This turned out not to be the case, however, requiring another trip to the well of amendments. And, when the nation lost interest in bringing the "unfinished revolution" of Reconstruction to a successful close, the Civil War Amendments—once so contested and so acclaimed—languished for decades.

The debates over the framing and the adoption of the Civil War Amendments, and over what shape the United States should take following Appomattox, were as bitter and difficult as any in the nation's history. Few were satisfied with the final result; fewer still were happy with the Amendments' interpretation by the Supreme Court. Only in the twentieth century, as the surviving grizzled, bent veterans of the war were breathing their last, did a consensus develop around the Thirteenth, Fourteenth, and Fifteenth Amendments and the nation they helped to shape.

The Civil War Amendments remade the Constitution of 1787, so that it could serve as the charter of a unified nation in "the world the War made."[3] The Amendments codified the formal lineaments of that world, giving them the protection of the Constitution, stripping away the remnants and relics of the antebellum world from the text of the Constitution.

The substantive components of the Amendments, however, remained dormant for generations after their ratification. Blacks faced massive obstacles to the achievement of social or economic independence, despite the Thirteenth Amendment. They could not claim or enjoy the equal protection of the laws, despite the Fourteenth Amendment. And they could not vote, despite the Fourteenth and Fifteenth Amendments. Even so, these Amendments, though at first neglected or ignored, would prove to be versatile and effective tools in the hands of later generations seeking to redeem their promise.

ERASING THE STAIN OF SLAVERY: THE THIRTEENTH AMENDMENT

THE PROCESS OF OUTLAWING SLAVERY, which culminated in the ratification of the Thirteenth Amendment, followed a tortuous path during the Civil War, despite Republican control of the executive branch and both houses of Congress. As they struggled to direct the war to suppress the rebellion in the South, Republican politicians gingerly began to grope for a means to reconfigure the Constitution for a post-slavery era. Not everyone shared this objective; stubborn border-state Representatives and Senators persisted in their efforts to preserve the antebellum Constitution. In July of 1861, for example, as President Lincoln challenged Congress to save the Union by raising money and men to put down the rebellion, Senator Willard Saulsbury (Democrat–Delaware) quixotically proposed the revival of the Crittenden Compromise, believing that the threat of actual war would so terrify the opposing parties that the nation might unite on what Congress had previously rejected.[4]

Lincoln, too, concentrated his efforts at first on preserving the Union, but he understood that the character of the Union and of the American people would be changed forever by the Confederate attempt at secession. He also realized that striking a blow against slavery would simultaneously rally the forces of the Union, persuade foreign nations to reject Confederate overtures for recognition and aid, and damage the rebel war effort. He therefore spent most of 1862 deliberating how to use emancipation against the South.

Believing that the people were ready for emancipation, Lincoln backed away from his 1860 campaign position that slavery should not be molested where it already existed. His first step on this route was private; in November 1861, he experimented with drafting a law for Delaware to establish compensated emancipation for that state, but his draft never saw the light of day.[5] Four months later, he sent a message to Congress proposing compensated emancipation, and he continued to air schemes to that end throughout the spring and summer of 1862, while giving clear signals that he was ready to use the full power of the Union against slavery.[6]

Lincoln sought to chart a moderate course—one whose radicalism angered Democrats, yet whose caution disappointed abolitionist Republicans. Abhorring the prospect of what he called "a violent and remorseless revolutionary struggle," Lincoln nonetheless came to accept the need for extreme measures to cripple the rebellion against the Union—measures that might also result in the destruction of an institution that he had hated all his life.

The President made good his warnings on September 22, 1862, when he issued his Preliminary Emancipation Proclamation.[7] In consultation with his Cabinet, he timed the announcement to capitalize on the ambiguous results of the Battle of Antietam, in which Union armies had prevented rebel advances into Maryland but had not crushed Robert E. Lee's forces. Using the Union "victory" as the occasion, Lincoln thought and the Cabinet concurred, would give the Proclamation added force; otherwise, it would look like the last desperate measure of a floundering Administration.[8] Abolitionists, freed slaves, and advocates of equal rights on both sides of the Atlantic welcomed the Proclamation, and news of it spread throughout the South, where it galvanized the slaves' hopes and their masters' fears. It blocked the efforts of those in Britain who sought to persuade their government to recognize the Confederacy as an independent nation; the great mass of Britons welcomed Lincoln's action as a landmark in the history of freedom. They recognized, as he did, that the Proclamation put slavery in the course of ultimate extinction.[9]

Not everyone in the Union, however, approved the Proclamation. Moderate Republicans and Democrats, who sought only to preserve the Union and regarded abolitionists as visionary fools, thought it an act of supreme folly by a President they despised. This group included such men as General George B. McClellan, who had been fired by Lincoln as commander of the Army of the Potomac. Antiwar "doughface" and "Copperhead" Democrats (many of them borderline Confederate sympathizers) were outraged by the Preliminary Emancipation Proclamation and by what they saw as its twin—Lincoln's proclamation two days later suspending the writ of habeas corpus.*[10] The combination of this massive expropriation of property (that is, slaves) without compensation and the suspension of one of the central rights of Anglo-American law substantiated their fears that Lincoln was bent on becoming a dictator.[11]

Like many of his predecessors in the Presidency, Lincoln recognized the need to maintain the appearance of legality and constitutionality, even if he might believe that he already had the authority he needed.[12] He expostulated with his critics about the specific problem of slavery and emancipation and the general legalities of the war: "To state the question more directly: are all the laws, *but one*, to go unexecuted, and the government itself go to pieces, but that one be violated?"[13] At the same time, Lincoln explored ways to legitimate some of his bolder measures. Removing doubts about his suspension of habeas corpus was easy; Congress passed a law retroactively endorsing it and extending it into the future.

Abolishing slavery was a different matter. Realizing that the Proclamation's principal justification—as a war measure—might expire once the rebellion was put down, Lincoln was convinced that a constitutional amendment was the only sufficient means to abolish slavery. He worried that declaring the slaves free by executive order or legislation would leave the federal government open to claims by former slaveowners that they had been deprived of their "property" without just compensation or due process. He also hoped that an amendment authoriz-

---

*The writ of habeas corpus is a judicial order requiring a government official holding a person in custody to produce the person before the court to justify the detention. If the court is not satisfied with the justification offered, it may order that the detained person go free. While Article I, section 9, clause 2 of the Constitution prohibits the suspension of the writ except "when the public safety may require it," it is silent on who has the power to suspend the writ.

ing gradual, compensated emancipation might win over some of the states in rebellion, disrupt the Confederacy (if not dissolve it), and thus bring the war to an early close.

To this end, therefore, in his 1862 annual message to Congress, Lincoln proposed three amendments to the Constitution. The first offered a system of federal compensation for slaveowners resident in states that agreed to abolish slavery before January 1, 1900; the second declared that slaves "who shall have enjoyed actual freedom by the chances of war . . . shall be forever free," providing compensation to loyal owners of slaves who had thereby gained freedom; and the last authorized the colonizing of blacks, both those born free and the freed slaves, outside the United States.[14] Lincoln explained that he intended this trio of amendments to form constitutional common ground on which friends of the Union could unite, whatever their views on slavery:

> By mutual concession we should harmonize, and act together. This would be compromise; but it would be compromise among the friends, and not with the enemies of the Union. These articles are intended to embody a plan of such mutual concessions. If the plan shall be adopted, it is assumed that emancipation will follow, at least, in several of the States.[15]

The Southern states refused the bait, however, and Lincoln therefore felt justified in proceeding with the final Proclamation. On January 1, 1863, after spending most of the day shaking the hands of well-wishers during the New Year's reception at the Executive Mansion, Lincoln withdrew to his office and, making certain that his weary hand would not tremble, signed the Final Emancipation Proclamation. With a stroke of his pen, he freed all the slaves in those states under rebellion (but not in the loyal border states)—that is, three out of every four slaves in the United States.*[16]

The Final Emancipation Proclamation was greeted with joy by abolitionists, by free blacks, and by freed and runaway slaves throughout the Union. Even those who were disappointed that slavery was left untouched where Union authority was unchallenged or reestablished realized that slavery could not last there if it were abolished everywhere else. Moreover, the Proclamation recognized a state of affairs already given its impetus by the war. As Union forces

---

*In 1863, there were over 3,000,000 slaves in the Confederate states; 450,000 in Delaware, Kentucky, Maryland, and Missouri; 275,000 in the reconquered state of Tennessee; and several hundred thousand in the conquered sections of Virginia and Louisiana.

moved through Southern territory, slaves flocked to join their ranks (though, at first, they were rebuffed). Slaves often played a prominent role in their own emancipation, in some instances taking over plantation houses and expropriating their masters' property.[17]

But the Proclamation remained a war measure. Although Lincoln declared that he would not withdraw it, advocates of abolition shared his view that a more permanent, impregnable basis to do away with slavery was required. Determined to extirpate slavery once and for all, they sought to devise an abolition amendment diametrically opposed to the moribund Corwin Amendment of 1861.

Supporters of such a measure maintained that only an amendment could put an end to slavery because the institution and the racial prejudices it engendered were integral to the framework established by the Constitution of 1787. No mere Presidential proclamation could supersede the "three-fifths" clause or the fugitive slave clause, or the risk of former slaveowners' demands for compensation for their seized "property." Refusing to let that issue rest, intransigent border-state Senators and Representatives persisted in their attempts to attach schemes for compensation to all proposed abolition amendments.[18]

Undaunted, foes of slavery proposed several abolition amendments in Congress in the winter of 1863 and the spring of 1864, seizing the opportunity presented by the absence of their traditional adversaries, the Southern Democrats, to use the powers of Congress to reshape the nation.[19] On December 14, 1863, Representative James Ashley (Republican–Ohio) proposed the first abolition amendment, which would "prohibit slavery or involuntary servitude in all of the States and Territories now owned or which may be hereafter acquired by the United States," echoing the language of the Northwest Ordinance of 1787. Another proposal, offered on the same day by Representative James Wilson (Republican–Iowa), read:

> Slavery being incompatible with free government, is forever prohibited in the United States; and involuntary servitude shall be permitted only as a punishment for crime.

Wilson's proposal also would have conferred power on Congress to enforce the amendment by "appropriate legislation."[20]

Senator Charles Sumner (Republican–Massachusetts), the tough-minded abolitionist, weighed in with a proposal modeled on the French Declaration of the Rights of Man and the Citizen. He began his amendment with a ringing proclamation of the equality of all men, justifying the abolition of slavery on the ground that no one man had the right to own another. This wording was ultimately rejected by legislators eager to strip the amendment down to its bare legal purpose of abolishing slavery; they deemed language recognizing racial equality too explosive to win adoption. (Two years later, however, the principle of equality found its way into the Fourteenth Amendment.)

By 1864, as Union victories multiplied, only Senators and Representatives from the border states still resisted abolition. The most bitter and the most desperately ingenious opponent was Senator Garret Davis (Democrat–Kentucky), who threw a welter of proposals into the path of the abolition amendment. His eight "singular and factious amendments" included proposals to exclude blacks from citizenship and public office; to withhold freedom from the slaves until after they had been removed from the United States (and sent either to the Caribbean or to Latin America); and to scatter the freed slaves throughout the United States, giving each state and territory its proportionate share (by population). His oddest proposal would have redrawn the map of New England, rejoining Maine and Massachusetts as the state of East New England and merging Connecticut, Rhode Island, New Hampshire, and Vermont as the state of West New England. Davis's stated objectives were to remedy what he saw as the disproportionate influence of New England on American life and to punish Massachusetts because "the most effective single cause of the pending war has been the intermeddling of Massachusetts with the institution of slavery." In a similar spirit, Senator Saulsbury introduced an intricate twenty-section amendment designed to derail the abolition amendment by reviving the obsolete Crittenden Compromise.[21]

None of these uses of amendment politics to fend off constitutional abolition succeeded. It was plain to everyone, even to Davis and Saulsbury, that the rebellion was destined to fail and that slavery would have no place in the postwar American republic. This realization sapped the strength of the opposition to the abolition amendment. The Senate approved the measure in the summer of 1864, but it failed to receive a sufficient majority in the House.

After the Union victories of 1864 in Georgia and South Carolina, the reelection of Lincoln, and the election of a solid Republican Congress, the abolition amendment's supporters revived it in the House in the lame-duck session which convened in December 1864. On February 1, 1865, the House endorsed the Thirteenth Amendment by a lopsided majority. The gallery, newly opened to blacks who wished to see their government in action, erupted in wild cheers; on the floor, the joyful Representatives staged a demonstration of their own, embracing one another and weeping openly.[22]

President Lincoln signed the Amendment the same day. Although there is no definitive explanation why he signed, two reasons suggest themselves. He may have wanted to put himself on record as endorsing the constitutional provision that would do away with slavery. He also may have wanted to wipe out the memory of the Corwin Amendment, the only other proposed amendment to receive a Presidential signature.

In what during the war had become a popular custom to celebrate Union victories, a large and jubilant crowd gathered before the Executive Mansion that evening to serenade the President; a reporter took down Lincoln's off-the-cuff response:

> He thought this measure was a very fitting if not an indispensable adjunct to the winding up of the great difficulty. He wished the reunion of all the States perfected and so effected as to remove all causes of disturbance in the future; and to attain this end it was necessary that the original disturbing cause should, if possible, be rooted out. . . . [T]his amendment is a King's cure for all the evils. [Applause.] It winds the whole thing up. He would repeat that it was the fitting if not the indispensable adjunct to the consummation of the great game we are playing. He could not but congratulate all present, himself, the country . . . and the whole world upon this great moral victory.[23]

Lincoln's remarks typified the joy of most Americans and their unexpressed belief that the job was done with the proposing of the Thirteenth Amendment. That February, few gave any thought to the problem of ratification.

Engravings commemorating the Amendment's passage through Congress proliferated to meet a growing and soon insatiable public demand. Even the text of the Amendment became the centerpiece of prized souvenirs. As a way to raise funds for medical aid for Union soldiers and relief for the families of those who had died in the war, politicians swiftly prepared elaborate printed versions of the Amendment, which each Representative and Senator voting for it signed, along with President Lincoln.[24]

The Thirteenth Amendment is expressed in muted language that downplays its sweeping effects:

> Section 1. Neither slavery nor involuntary servitude, except as a punishment for crime whereof the party shall have been duly convicted, shall exist within the United States, or any place subject to their jurisdiction.
>
> Section 2. Congress shall have power to enforce this article by appropriate legislation.

By putting an end to slavery, the Amendment helped to cause a social revolution in the former slave states by abolishing, root and branch, one of the South's key social, legal, and political institutions. It also expanded the scope of federal constitutional authority, both by outlawing a purely domestic institution and by conferring enforcement authority on the federal government. Finally, it erased the contradiction (a favorite abolitionist debating point) between the principles of the Declaration of Independence and the provisions of the original Constitution safeguarding slavery and slaveowners' interests.[25]

The Thirteenth Amendment was the first to move beyond defining individual rights or correcting technical defects in the structure of the federal government.[26] Its provisions not only expanded the federal government's powers but also broadened the scope of Article V. Thereafter, the amending process could be employed to achieve major national objectives, even to the extent of reworking the states' internal affairs.

The Amendment's ramifications were not lost on either its supporters or its opponents during its framing and adoption. As the debate moved from Congress to the states, controversy focused as much on the proposed Amendment's legality as on the merits of abolition. Rallying behind the slogan "The Union as it was and the Constitution as it is," those opposed to the measure claimed that the power lodged in Article V was applicable to the federal government only; thus, they contended, it did not extend to what they deemed tampering with the states' governments, legal systems, or "domestic institutions."[27] These arguments were to no avail, however, for public opinion had moved beyond the assumptions of antebellum politics and constitutional law; slavery no longer commanded its former legitimacy anywhere outside the conquered South, and within the South those who clung to slavery were powerless to enforce their views.

Leaving aside the problem of defining its scope and impact, the Thirteenth Amendment posed an immediate practical problem: the number of state ratifications needed to put it into effect. Because the Union won the Civil War, its position—that the Confederate States of America was an illegal conspiracy seeking to accomplish an unconstitutional purpose—meant that twenty-seven of the thirty-six states had to ratify the Amendment for it to take effect. But eleven states were under military occupation by Union forces, their civil governments having toppled in the face of Union advances or having been ousted as agencies of the rebel conspiracy. True republican government had yet to be restored, so it was an open question whether these states could—or would—ratify. The problem was complicated further when Delaware rejected the Amendment on February 8, followed by Kentucky on February 24.

The proposal's backers realized that, even if every one of the other twenty-three Union states ratified the Amendment, the support of at least four former Confederate states would still be needed. They therefore brought pressure to bear on the occupied states, demanding ratification before Congress would consider receiving their Senate and House delegations. On this basis, Virginia,

Louisiana, Tennessee, Arkansas, South Carolina, Alabama, North Carolina, and Georgia adopted the Thirteenth Amendment; Georgia's ratification, on December 6, 1865, put it into effect.[28] Florida and Texas ratified after Secretary of State William H. Seward had declared the Amendment in effect (Florida in 1865, Texas in 1870), leaving Mississippi as the only former Confederate state that did not ratify. The wrangles over the validity of the ratifications provided by eight of the occupied states petered out without resolution; whether strictly legal or not, the ratification of the Amendment was an accomplished fact by the end of 1865, and slavery was dead.

RIGHTS, CITIZENSHIP, AND EQUALITY: THE FOURTEENTH AMENDMENT

MONCURE DANIEL CONWAY, A NOTED author who later wrote distinguished biographies of Thomas Paine and Edmund Randolph, was a former slaveowner who welcomed the Thirteenth Amendment. In 1866, he pleaded with his compatriots to turn away from the constitutional dogmas of the past:

> Lift up your hearts. . . . There is not a thinking man in America
> but must see that any permanent "reconstruction" must imply a
> reconstruction of the whole organic law of the country.[29]

Conway hoped that Congress would seize the opportunity—whether through statutes or through Amendments—to restore the principles of the Declaration of Independence as the central components of American public life.

At least some of the Thirteenth Amendment's framers had hoped that the abolition of slavery would, all by itself, raise the freed slaves to full and equal citizenship with free citizens and recognize their entitlement to the suffrage. Within a few months of the Amendment's ratification, however, they realized that abolition was not enough; the Thirteenth Amendment needed constitutional reinforcement.

The Fourteenth Amendment was framed by the Thirty-ninth Congress (1865–1867), elected in November 1864, as Union forces under Grant and Sherman slowly ground the rebel armies into powder. This Congress was far different from the querulous and palsied Thirty-sixth Congress (1859–1861), which proposed the stillborn Corwin amendment; the quarrelsome Thirty-seventh Congress (1861–1863), which heard the news of the Emancipation Proclamation; or the jubilant, tearstained Thirty-eighth Congress (1863–1865), which proposed the abolitionist Thirteenth Amendment. The Thirty-ninth Congress was a grim, fractious body that had lost its patience with the South and with the version of Reconstruction offered by Lincoln's successor, President Andrew Johnson. It was ready to take the bit between its teeth—but was uncertain in which direction it should go. The product of its eagerness to act, and of its uncertainty, was the constitutional text we know as the Fourteenth Amendment.

Lincoln's assassination on April 14, 1865, had changed the world the Civil War made. No one could describe with accuracy the slain President's plans for rebuilding the Union. Although Lincoln was the first national politician to use the term "Reconstruction," he had not had a chance to think through the dimensions of the problems that Reconstruction posed, or the lineaments of the policies that would be needed to answer the call of his Second Inaugural Address "to finish the work we are in." Vague comments and off-the-cuff remarks were all the advice that fate permitted Lincoln to leave the American people.

Whatever Lincoln may have intended was made irrelevant by the thoughts and deeds of the man who succeeded him as President, Andrew Johnson of Tennessee.[30] Johnson was a ferocious War Democrat, an advocate of crushing the rebellion and those who had fomented it. In 1864, while serving as military governor of his reconquered home state, he attained national prominence when the Republicans chose him as Lincoln's running-mate in an effort to attract Unionist Democrats and War Democrats to the "National Union" ticket. At the inauguration, the fever-ridden Johnson was falsely rumored to have disgraced himself by showing up drunk. Five weeks later, John Wilkes Booth's derringer made the Tennessean President.[31]

Johnson's first actions as President—his orders for the harshest punishment for Lincoln's assassins and for the captured leaders of the Confederacy—reassured vindictive Republicans in Congress who wanted to punish the South. But by the end of 1865, the President seemed to be showing his true colors as a Southerner. On the heels of the ratification of the Thirteenth Amendment, Johnson sought to end the Union occupation of the rebel states, and he advanced plans to restore them to full status as members of the Union with minimal changes in their governments and politics.

Republicans in Congress grew alarmed. They worried that their former adversaries would return to the House and the Senate in full strength. Indeed, the Thirteenth Amendment implicitly mandated the end of the three-fifths clause and required that former slaves be counted as full persons for purposes of representation and taxation. The Republicans knew, however, that those who governed the South would not permit freed slaves to take part in choosing the new congressional delegations. General Alfred H. Terry, the Union commander in Virginia, declared that most Southern whites wished to reduce blacks "to a condition which will give the former masters all the benefits of slavery, and throw upon them none of its responsibilities."[32] Thus, to readmit the Southern states might actually require the *expansion* of their delegations in the House, giving those who had plotted to destroy the Union at least as much power in Congress as the party that had preserved the Union. As Senator Lyman Trumbull (Republican–Illinois) protested in 1866, it was out of the question to restore authority and control to "the very men who causelessly inaugurated a civil war and brought upon the land, North and South, unnumbered evils—the very men who, although overcome by force of arms, are still as hostile as ever in their hearts to the Union."[33] If Johnson's readmission ploy went unchallenged, Republicans fretted, the victories at Gettysburg, Vicksburg, and Appomattox might go for nought.

Dominated by a quarrelsome and divided group that later historians have labeled "Radical Republicans," Congress determined to put into effect its own views of what Reconstruction should accomplish, and by what means.[34] Concerned, nonetheless, that the Supreme Court might not accept mere legislation to this end without constitutional sanction, and seeking to place their goals beyond the reach of Presidential vetoes or later Congressional repeals, Congress augmented its quest to include the framing of a new constitutional amendment.

The intent of the framers of the Fourteenth Amendment and the extent to which that intent (once identified) should be given effect make up the single bloodiest battleground of American constitutional history. What the Amendment's "due process" and "equal protection" clauses were supposed to do and how far they were supposed to reach are questions of constitutional law as much as of constitutional history. Rivers of ink have been spilled over these questions, for their answers remain unclear.[35] Professor William E. Nelson of New York University Law School, the Amendment's leading historian, has pointed out the central problem plaguing all attempts to find the key to the Fourteenth Amendment's meaning in the "intent" of its framers:

> [H]istory can only begin the task of finding meaning with the framing and ratification of the amendment because the framers and ratifiers themselves only began the creative task of transforming constitutional rhetoric into constitutional law. The debates on the Fourteenth Amendment were, in essence, debates about high politics and fundamental principles—about the future course and meaning of the American nation. The debates by themselves did not reduce the vague, open-ended, and sometimes clashing principles used by the debaters to precise, carefully bounded legal doctrine. That would be the task of the courts once the Fourteenth Amendment, having been enacted into law, was given over to them to reconcile its ambiguities and its conflicting meanings.[36]

What were the "fundamental principles" that the Congressional debaters of 1866 invoked in framing the Amendment? Some emphasized the fundamental rights either codified in the Bill of Rights or subsumed in the words "liberty" or "natural rights";[37] others gave pride of place to the concept of equality and its legal twin, equal protection of the laws;[38] still others defined the Amendment's reach by sole reference to the Civil Rights Act of 1866, which was making its way through Congress at the same time.[39]

Most of the modern debates over "intent" are conducted with a weather eye cocked toward judicial interpretation of the Amendment. If, for example, it can be shown that the framers and adopters of the Amendment intended to outlaw racial segregation, then the verdict of history supports modern uses of the Amendment to strike down laws segregating school systems and public accommodations. If, however, it can be shown that the framers and adopters of the Amendment did not intend to outlaw segregation, then the verdict of history defends it from legal challenges based on the Fourteenth Amendment.[40]

Both in the Thirty-ninth Congress and throughout the nation, the debates on the Amendment yielded much heat but little light—thanks, in part, to the goals and purposes of those who took part. The debates of the framers of the Fourteenth Amendment were no more principled or sacred than are modern political debates. Politics was at work even in the midst of the efforts to formulate a constitutional text that would expound and protect vital principles of free government.

Those who sought to block the Amendment's passage or to limit its reach attacked both the process by which the Amendment would be proposed and the substance of the proposal. For example, as part of their process challenge, they charged that the absence of the defeated Confederate states meant that no amendment could be proposed by Congress because nearly one-third of the states were not present.[41]

The Amendment's opponents voiced two categories of substantive objections: first, that blacks were not and could not be treated as equal to whites, and, second, that the Amendment would so expand the powers of the federal government that the states would be destroyed and liberty consumed by despotism. During the war itself, Senator James A. McDougall (Democrat–California) deftly mixed racism and eugenics to suggest that requiring equality between the races would result in miscegenation and the "race suicide" of the American people (by which he meant white Americans), themes repeatedly sounded by opponents of the Amendment in Congress, in the newspapers, and in state legislatures.[42] Those deploying racist arguments against the Amendment sounded a consistent note: because blacks were (allegedly) inferior to whites by nature, it was both futile and wrong to set aside nature's judgment by law.[43] Even defenders of the Amendment who rejected these arguments about blacks were willing to apply them to other groups. Senator John Conness (Republican–California) accepted the terms of the Amendment while holding white supremacist views regarding the Chinese in California and the other Pacific Coast states:

We are fully aware of the nature of that class of people, and their influence among us, and feel entirely able to take care of them and to provide against any evils that may flow from their presence among us. We are entirely ready to accept the provision proposed in this constitutional amendment, that the children born here of Mongolian parents shall be declared by the Constitution of the United States to be entitled to civil rights and to equal protection before the law with others.[44]

Opponents also proffered overly broad interpretations of the Amendment designed to terrify its moderate supporters. In his message to the Alabama legislature recommending against ratification, Governor R. M. Patton painted a horrid picture of an engulfing federal government, a recurring theme of Southern political discourse since the Revolution (and a theme of the amending process since the proposing of the Bill of Rights in 1789 and of the Eleventh Amendment in 1794):

[Section one] would enlarge the judicial powers of the General Government to such gigantic dimensions as would not only overshadow and weaken the authority and influence of the State courts, but might possibly reduce them to a complete nullity. It would give to the United States courts complete and unlimited jurisdiction over every conceivable case, however important or however trivial, which could arise under State laws. Every individual dissatisfied with the decision of a State court, might apply to a Federal tribunal for redress. . . . The granting of such an immense power as this over the State tribunals would, at the very best, subordinate them to a condition of comparative unimportance and insignificance.[45]

By contrast, those who supported the Amendment backed and filled, paying little attention to overall coherence or clarity, focusing instead on meeting each challenge as it presented itself. It is customary among historians of the origins of the Amendment, for example, to mock the vagueness and supposed incoherence of Representative John Bingham of Ohio, the Amendment's floor manager in the House. Such derision, however, does not acknowledge the difficulty of Bingham's principal task: to preserve a two-thirds majority in support of the Amendment in each house of Congress.

Bingham and his colleagues had to walk an intellectual and political tightrope, for they faced three recurring challenges: (i) to keep conservative and moderate supporters from bolting, (ii) to avoid alienating progressive and radical supporters, and (iii) to refute the most extreme and dangerous charges of the Amendment's adversaries. That Congress eventually approved the Amendment is a testimony to their success as political managers, regardless of their failures as clear-speaking constitutional theorists—a task that the debates rendered difficult, if not impossible.

President Johnson made no secret of his opposition to the Fourteenth Amendment and the civil rights bill that was so closely linked to it. He vetoed the bill on March 27, 1866, while Congress was still wrestling with the language of the amendment. His veto message enraged Congress, which on April 6 overrode the veto by the necessary two-thirds vote in both houses and turned with renewed vigor to the task of constitutional drafting.

After repeated attempts to build a constitutional text on which a sufficient majority could agree, the Senate Republican majority named a five-member committee that, by the end of May, established the text of the Amendment. On June 3, the Senate approved it and sent it to the House, which concurred on June 13. Representative Thaddeus Stevens of Pennsylvania, a veteran abolitionist and Radical Republican, voted for the Amendment, but he mourned the lack of provisions guaranteeing the vote for freed slaves and other blacks:

> I find that we shall be obliged to be content with patching up the worst portions of the ancient edifice, and leaving it, in many of its parts, to be swept through by . . . the storms of despotism.
>
> Do you inquire why, holding these views and possessing some will of my own, I accept so imperfect a proposition? I answer, because I live among men and not among angels.[46]

President Johnson would have been astonished by Stevens's description of the Amendment, for what was too moderate for the Pennsylvania Republican was far too radical for the Tennessee Unionist. Johnson spurned the Amendment, declaring in a special message to Congress on June 22 that he believed it invalid; because Congress had done nothing to bring the occupied Southern states back into the Union, Johnson charged, it therefore had sought to propose an Amendment without the requisite two-thirds vote.

In the winter of 1866–1867, Johnson met with informal representatives of the Alabama government. "Leo," the pseudonymous Washington correspondent of the Charleston (S.C.) *Courier,* reported that the President "expressed the hope that the Southern States would remain firm in their position as regards the [Fourteenth] amendment, and steadfastly reject it."[47] These reports spread throughout the nation. Infuriated and embarrassed by the leaks, Johnson neither endorsed nor repudiated them. At the same time, the President's allies in the Northern Democratic party complicated matters by seeking to play a double game. While publicly supporting the most radical proposals offered by the

Republican party, they secretly exhorted Southern states' legislatures to stand fast against the Amendment. Their plan was to split the Republican majority along ideological lines, but the scheme backfired, resulting in the election in November 1866 of a Congress dominated by advocates of the harshest and most sweeping Reconstruction measures—a Congress so infuriated by Southern rejection of the Fourteenth Amendment that it was determined to compel ratification.[48]

In the end, ratification was achieved through a public campaign on the high ground of principle concurrent with the naked exercise of political power. Despite President Johnson's 1865 proclamation welcoming the former Confederate states back to full membership in the Union, Republicans in Congress had successfully delayed the question of that status. But by June 1868, Congress was exasperated beyond measure by the failure of the Amendment to garner the support of the necessary three-fourths of the states. It therefore abandoned all pretense of civility and spelled out the conditions for the Southern states: ratify the Amendment or face continued exclusion from Congress. Congress thus achieved the adoption of the Fourteenth Amendment at constitutional gunpoint.*[49]

In the same spirit, Congress determined to take vengeance for Johnson's refusal to enforce the Reconstruction laws it had passed over his vetoes. In February 1868, the House voted articles of impeachment—the first time it had used that constitutional process against a President. Johnson probably deserved impeachment—though not necessarily on the charges that actually were brought against him. Although the Senate voted to convict, several Radical Republican Senators, concerned to preserve the Presidency from congressional dominance, backed Johnson, leaving the advocates of impeachment one vote short of the two-thirds needed to remove the President from office.[50]

The failure of the campaign to oust Johnson coincided with the last stages of the ratification of the Fourteenth Amendment. Hypnotized by the Senate's impeachment trial, the nation did not pay much attention to the adoption of an amendment that has become the most important feature of the post–Civil War Constitution.

AT THE TIME OF ITS ratification, the Fourteenth Amendment was seen primarily as continuing the work of the Thirteenth in rooting out vestiges of slavery in the

---

*Three states had complicated matters; in January 1868, Ohio withdrew its ratification, followed in April by New Jersey and in October by Oregon. The official stance of the federal government, then and afterward, is that a state may refuse to adopt an amendment and then change its collective mind but that a state may not rescind a ratification. This question is discussed in detail in Chapter 13.

original Constitution and confirming the Union victory in the Civil War by writing the illegitimacy of the Confederacy into the Constitution. Sections 2, 3, and 4 of the Amendment also indicate how the Thirty-ninth Congress stitched together dozens of proposals pertaining to Congressional Reconstruction, emancipation, and the fate of the former Confederate governments and those who had held office under them.

Removing all doubt about the status of the freed slaves for purposes of representation in the House and taxation, section 2 explicitly repealed the "three-fifths" clause of Article I of the Constitution. At the same time, the section established a remedy that could be applied to punish any state that discriminated against those who sought to exercise the right to vote—punitive reapportionment (that is, reducing the population represented in the House by the number of voters denied access to the polls):

> Representatives shall be apportioned among the several States according to their respective numbers, counting the whole number of persons in each State, excluding Indians not taxed. But when the right to vote at any election for the choice of electors for President and Vice President of the United States, Representatives in Congress, the Executive and Judicial officers of a State, or the members of the Legislature thereof, is denied to any of the male inhabitants of such State, being twenty-one years of age, and citizens of the United States, or in any way abridged, except for participation in rebellion, or other crime, the basis of representation therein shall be reduced in the proportion which the number of such male citizens shall bear to the whole number of male citizens twenty-one years of age in such State.

Section 3 barred from any federal or state government position those who had held federal office before the Civil War and repudiated their oaths of office to join the Confederate cause, unless both houses of Congress, by a two-thirds vote, removed the disability:

> No person shall be a Senator or Representative in Congress, or elector of President and Vice President, or hold any office, civil or military, under the United States, or under any State, who, having previously taken an oath, as a member of Congress, or as an officer of the United States, or as a member of any State legislature, or as an executive or judicial officer of any State, to support the Constitution of the United States, shall have engaged in insurrection or rebellion against the same, or given aid or

comfort to the enemies thereof. But Congress may by a vote of two-thirds of each House, remove such disability.

This process, which was trimmed repeatedly by Congressional action in the 1870s and rendered moot by 1898,[51] was aimed at such former Confederate leaders as Jefferson Davis and Robert E. Lee. Lee applied for removal of the disability. (Because of a clerical error, his application was not discovered until more than a century after his death. Davis similarly languished in limbo until the 1970s.)[52]

The framers of the Fourteenth Amendment hoped that sections 2 and 3 would operate in tandem to increase Republican voting strength (black voters) and reduce Democratic voting strength (former Confederates) to prevent the resurgence of the prewar Democratic majority. However, neither provision worked as intended. Section 3 never applied to more than a few hundred men, and the passage of time made it increasingly irrelevant to the nation's public life. Likewise, the federal government has never used its power of punitive reapportionment codified in section 2.

Section 4 rejected federal or state responsibility for Confederate war debts and is thus a counterpoint to Article VI, section 1 of the original Constitution, in which the new federal government agreed to assume as its own the debts amassed by the United States under the Articles of Confederation. The distinction is that the Confederation was a legitimate government, whereas the Confederate States of America was not. Section 4 also closed the door on any possibility that former slaveowners might demand reimbursement for the property interests they claimed in slaves freed by the Thirteenth Amendment:

> The validity of the public debt of the United States, authorized by law, including debts incurred for payment of pensions and bounties for services in suppressing insurrection or rebellion, shall not be questioned. But neither the United States nor any State shall assume or pay any debt or obligation incurred in aid of insurrection or rebellion against the United States, or any claim for the loss or emancipation of any slave; but all such debts, obligations and claims shall be held illegal and void.

Though the middle sections of the Amendment were the most bitterly contested during its framing and adoption, the intervening decades have seen the first and fifth sections of the Fourteenth Amendment become the most controversial parts of the Constitution. (Their consequences are discussed at length in Chapter 11.) The first section contains a network of clauses, each of which has given rise to a complex and contentious body of constitutional doctrine:

> All persons born or naturalized in the United States and sub-
> ject to the jurisdiction thereof, are citizens of the United States
> and of the State wherein they reside. No State shall make or
> enforce any law which shall abridge the privileges or immunities
> of citizens of the United States; nor shall any State deprive any
> person of life, liberty, or property, without due process of law;
> nor deny to any person within its jurisdiction the equal protection
> of the laws.

The fifth section, usually known as the "enforcement" section, may look clear
and simple, but it too has become a focus of controversy, in large part because
the enforcement authority of Congress is inextricably linked to what Congress
is, or is not, authorized to enforce:

> The Congress shall have power to enforce, by appropriate
> legislation, the provisions of this article.

The immediate results of the Fourteenth Amendment, however, were virtually nil; what counted far more in securing black rights in the South was the
presence of Union armies of occupation. Should those armies ever be with-
drawn, the freed slaves worried, they would have no protection against trium-
phant and vengeful Southern whites. With the end of Reconstruction nine years
after the ratification of the Amendment, this came to pass.

CONSTITUTIONALIZING THE SUFFRAGE:
THE FIFTEENTH AMENDMENT

THE FIFTEENTH AMENDMENT, RATIFIED IN 1870, followed the pattern of the
Thirteenth and Fourteenth Amendments in reworking the constitutional structure of American federalism.[53] Until the adoption of the Fifteenth Amendment,
the federal government never claimed power to regulate the franchise. The right
to vote was a matter of state sovereignty; Article I, section 3 of the Constitution,
for example, set the qualifications for voting in House elections to match those
standards imposed on voters for the most numerous branch of their state's
legislature.[54]

In the midst of the national debate over Reconstruction, few issues proved
more potentially explosive—or politically risky—than "Negro suffrage." Most
Northern states excluded blacks from the franchise; only the New England states
(except Connecticut) recognized their right to vote. New York's 1777 constitu-

tion had not contained a race-based exclusion from the franchise, but the state's 1821 constitutional convention imposed such a limit, which lasted through the Civil War.

During the framing of the Fourteenth Amendment, the Thirty-ninth Congress had wrestled with various suggestions to include in it a provision forbidding race-based restrictions on the franchise. What is now section 2 of that Amendment, giving the federal government the power of punitive reapportionment (as described in the previous section), was the most that advocates of enfranchising blacks could secure from a stubborn and apprehensive Congress. The nation was not ready, they judged, to write full political equality into the Constitution, or to invade what was generally seen as a prerogative of the states.

Throughout 1867, a series of referenda in Northern states indicated that most white Americans remained averse to extending the vote to blacks. These results suggested that it was in the interest of incumbents not to recognize blacks' right to vote. By contrast, nervous Republican congressional leaders deduced from the returns of the regular elections in 1866 and special elections in 1867 that the Democrats could drive them from power unless the Republican party could secure the support of black voters.

The Congressional genesis of the Fifteenth Amendment is yet another story of confusion, again pitting political advantages and liabilities against principle. Members of the House of Representatives, which took the lead in drafting the Amendment, were concerned mostly with its effects on their districts. An unlikely alliance of political moderates, both Republicans and Democrats, carried the Amendment through the House and the Senate over the protests of Radical Republicans, who wanted a broader amendment, and diehard Southerners, who opposed any suffrage amendment.

The supporters of the Amendment sought two objectives, which united expedience and principle: to enfranchise the black electorate in the Northern states and to protect the freed slaves' right to vote. They stripped the Amendment to its essentials, fending off other proposals (for example, provisions protecting the right of blacks to hold elective office and outlawing state tests of literacy, property, and "nativity"—that is, whether one was a native-born citizen) that might jeopardize it when it was sent to the states.

Another matter that the Amendment's supporters dumped over the side was women's suffrage.[55] The managers had to choose between the feasible goal of protecting blacks' right to vote and the establishment of universal suffrage, which they judged had no chance of success. Their decision infuriated leaders of the women's suffrage movement. Already angered by the Congressional failure to include in the Fourteenth Amendment language prohibiting discrimination on account of sex and by the Amendment's explicit wording recognizing only males as participants in the political process, the women's movement broke with their longtime allies, the male abolitionists. The noted suffragist Susan B. Anthony promised "to cut off this right arm of mine before I will demand the ballot for the Negro and not the woman."[56] Her colleague Lucy Stone wrote an anguished letter to Abby Kelley, a veteran antislavery organizer and woman suffragist who had decided to accept the Fifteenth Amendment:

> O, Abby, it is a terrible mistake you are making. You, and [Wendell] Phillips & [William Lloyd] Garrison and the brave workers, who for thirty years have said "let justice be done if the heavens fall" now believe that the nation's peril can be averted if it can be induced to accept the poor half loaf of justice for the Negro, poisoned by its lack of justice for every woman of the land. Tears are in my eyes, and a wail goes through my heart akin to that which I should feel, if I saw my little daughter drowning with no power to help.[57]

Fighting her failing health, Kelley replied:

> [T]he only question has been which shall take precedence in time. The slave is more deeply wronged than woman and while a nation can keep him a chattel it cannot be induced to allow political rights to woman. I should look on myself as a monster of selfishness if, while I see my neighbor's daughter treated as a beast—as thousands still are all over the rural districts of the South—I should turn from them to secure my daughter political equality.[58]

The dream of women's suffrage would have to wait half a century to be realized, and the long-hoped-for Equal Rights Amendment still awaits its moment.

Taking the principles of the Fourteenth Amendment one step further, the Fifteenth Amendment established the first constitutional limitation on the states' power to regulate access to the franchise.

> Section 1. The right of citizens of the United States to vote shall not be denied or abridged by the United States or by any State on account of race, color, or previous condition of servitude.
>
> Section 2. The Congress shall have power to enforce this article by appropriate legislation.

The drafters of section 1 hoped that its terms would ensure that once blacks had the vote, no state could repeal it; in this way, they hoped, they could shore up

Republican federal hegemony. Section 2 empowered favorably disposed federal administrations to enact enforcement legislation. Its authors hoped that political circumstances (including those assisted by the Amendment itself) would ensure the election, at the national level, of Republican executives and legislators who then would avail themselves of section 2.

Within a year after it was proposed, the Fifteenth Amendment was ratified by the states,* although its supporters again had to resort to compulsion, persuading Congress to require those Southern states that had not yet been readmitted to Congress (Georgia, Texas, Virginia, and Mississippi) to ratify as a condition of readmission.[59]

The Fifteenth Amendment seemed to consummate the constitutional settlement of the Civil War and the interment of the antebellum Constitution. It was the final step in overruling the part of *Dred Scott v. Sandford* that declared that blacks were never intended to be part of the American polity or to have any rights that white Americans were bound to respect. Moreover, it greatly expanded the "political population"[60] of the United States, declaring that that population could not be restricted or limited based on the race of prospective male voters. But not until the twentieth century did the Fifteenth Amendment fulfill the promise that its authors saw for it.

Finally, the Fifteenth Amendment set a precedent for future uses of the amending process to expand the protection given by the Constitution to the right to vote. Building on the Fifteenth, a series of Amendments has defined as a matter of federal constitutional law those limitations on the franchise that the American nation will no longer tolerate: the Nineteenth (votes for women), the Twenty-third (enfranchising residents of the District of Columbia voting in Presidential elections), the Twenty-fourth (abolishing the poll tax), and the Twenty-sixth (lowering the voting age in all elections to eighteen). Chapters 7 and 8 take up this story.

IN 1864, SENATOR CHARLES SUMNER of Massachusetts declared, "Let the people change, and the Constitution will change also; for the Constitution is but the shadow, while the people are the substance."[61] He was only partly correct. The

---

*New York ratified the Amendment in April of 1869 but rescinded its ratification in January of 1870 and rejected it a month later. Thus, although the official ratification date of the Amendment is generally agreed to be February 3, 1870 (the day after Georgia ratified), that date is valid only if New York's ratification is counted. Nebraska and Texas ratified two weeks later. New Jersey ratified a year later; Delaware acted in 1901; Oregon ratified in 1959 (after having rejected it in October of 1870); and California ratified in 1962, also having previously rejected it.

history of the Constitution teaches that language planted in the document also contains the potential to change the nation, and changes in the Constitution can in turn shape a changing polity and society.

When finally activated in the twentieth century, the Civil War Amendments reshaped the United States—establishing principles of individual rights and equal justice as the nucleus of American national identity. The framers of these Amendments did more than secure the Union and write that victory into the Constitution. The terms of these Amendments set in motion ideas, arguments, and events that ultimately reconceived the Union and the American republic.

CHAPTER 7

DEMOCRATIZING THE CONSTITUTION: THE PROGRESSIVE AMENDMENTS

Here, Sir, the people govern.

ATTRIBUTED TO ALEXANDER HAMILTON,
showing a visitor the House of Representatives
1791

THE ADOPTION OF THE CIVIL War Amendments dramatically enlarged the scope of the amending process, extending its reach into areas of American life that had not before been subject to the power of government or that had been within the exclusive authority of state and local governments. After the ratification of the Fifteenth Amendment in 1870, however, the next successful use of Article V did not occur for over forty years.

Some scholars assign political factors as the principal reason for this "quiet period," the second longest in the history of the amending process. (The longest gap between amendments was sixty-one years, between the Twelfth Amendment's ratification in 1804 and the Thirteenth Amendment's adoption in 1865.) The Democrats controlled the Southern states whereas the Republicans controlled the North and West, making it all but impossible to assemble the broad consensus in both Congress and the nation required to steer an amendment through the stages of the Article V process.[1] Undaunted by these political realities, advocates of various types of changes in the Constitution did propose hundreds of amendments during this period, but none amassed sufficient support to be sent by Congress to the states; indeed, only four secured the endorsement of even one house of Congress.[2]

By contrast to the fallow period between 1870 and 1913, the people amended the Constitution four times between 1913 and 1920. Each Amendment had been a key goal of the Progressive movement, the multifarious reform effort that dominated American politics and society from the late 1890s through the First World War. Three of the Amendments reinforced the growing democratization of American politics in complementary ways:

- The Sixteenth Amendment (proposed in 1909 and ratified in 1913) subjected the government to the people's control by authorizing

Congress to levy and collect taxes on income. This Amendment shifted the burden of financing the federal government from the states to the people, and thus gave the people a direct stake in the government's spending of public funds.

• The Seventeenth Amendment (proposed in 1912 and ratified in 1913) broadened the people's control over government by subjecting a key institution of the federal government to their authority: it provided that Senators be elected directly by the people rather than chosen by state legislatures.

• The Nineteenth Amendment (proposed in 1919 and ratified in 1920) enlarged the people's power by expanding the "political population." On the model of the Fifteenth Amendment's protection of the right of blacks to vote, the Nineteenth Amendment recognized women's right to vote.

Even the Eighteenth Amendment, granting constitutional authorization for Prohibition, was a Progressive victory. Ratified in 1919, it outlawed the sale and use of alcoholic beverages, thereby (or so its adherents believed and hoped) encouraging sobriety, hard work, and virtue among all classes of society but especially among the working people of America. And the Twenty-first Amendment (1933), which repealed the Eighteenth and thereby ended Prohibition, exemplified the capacity of the people to acknowledge and correct even mistakes they had previously written into the nation's fundamental law—another basic assumption of the Progressive movement. (We discuss these Amendments in Chapter 10.)

But it was the Sixteenth, Seventeenth, and Nineteenth Amendments that set the themes followed by most later Amendments to the Constitution.

DEMOCRATIZING PROCESSES OF GOVERNANCE: THE SIXTEENTH AMENDMENT

THE SIXTEENTH AMENDMENT DID NOT arise with much fanfare, but it is the Amendment that most directly affects the greatest number of Americans every day. For the Sixteenth Amendment places the responsibility for financing the government on the shoulders of the individual citizen—the taxpayer.

The Framers of the Constitution wanted to avoid the prospect of revenue measures that discriminated in favor of some states and against others. For this reason, they crafted the Constitution to require apportionment of taxes among the states based on population (modified by the now-infamous three-fifths ratio for slaves). During the ratification controversy, Anti-Federalists claimed that Article I, sections 2 and 9 gave too much power to the general government; they unsuccessfully demanded a supermajority requirement on Congress's power to levy tariffs (taxes on imports). Once the Constitution went into effect, its revenue provisions made it possible in the 1790s for Treasury Secretary Alexander Hamilton to bring order and stability to the nation's finances for the first time since independence.[3]

For most of the history of the United States, the federal government's chief source of revenue was customs duties (revenue collected under tariff legislation), supplemented by excise taxes (taxes on specific items, such as liquor). During the years 1797 to 1802, 1862 to 1870, and 1898 to 1902, the federal government also levied death taxes.[4]

The idea of an income tax was introduced in Great Britain in 1799, to finance that nation's wars against the French; the tax was imposed, then repealed, at irregular intervals until the 1880s, when it became a permanent part of the British revenue system. The United States followed the British example of using a tax on incomes as a wartime measure. In 1862, in response to the financial emergency caused by the Civil War, Congress adopted a tax collected on wages, salaries, interest, and dividends, with a flat $600 exemption (not including any allowances for children). In 1865 and 1866, Congress enacted new legislation graduating the tax, with a 5 percent tax on incomes over $600 but under $5,000 and a maximum level of 10 percent on incomes over $5,000. To counteract fraud, the income-tax laws required all returns to be made public—a measure repealed in 1870. In 1866, the tax's most successful year, it accounted for nearly one-fourth of internal revenue collections, and during its history it produced $376 million in revenue. Even so, more than three-fourths of the 1866 income-tax revenues came from taxpayers in only seven states.

In 1870, Congress revised the tax law; the new measure, scheduled to expire in 1872, levied a tax of 2.5 percent on incomes over $2,000. Not content with the built-in time limit, several Representatives and Senators sought without success to repeal the unpopular tax before its expiration date. In 1872, Congress decided to let the statute die—although Democrats throughout the 1870s and 1880s would urge the desirability of the measure as a way to keep tariff rates down and combat the unequal distribution of wealth.

In 1892, the Populist party, formed to defend the interests of farmers and workers in the Midwestern and Western states, adopted this last justification in its campaign for a new income tax.[5] Two years later, dissatisfaction with the tariff system and anger over the increasing inequity of the distribution of wealth in the United States led to a rebellion in Congress, one of whose leaders was a young Representative, William Jennings Bryan (Democrat–Nebraska).[6]

Bryan fought an epic forensic duel in behalf of the income tax. Representative Bourke Cockran (Democrat–New York) denounced the measure as "Socialistic . . . , directly hostile to the whole spirit of our institutions, . . . [and] objection[able] in a commercial community, because it is necessarily inquisitorial in character." A wealthy corporation lawyer and celebrated orator, Cockran charged that enactment of the tax would lead to class warfare, pitting the government and the poor against "the true patriots of this country, . . . the men by whose industry land is made valuable, by whose intelligence capital is made fruitful."[7] Despite Cockran's appeals, Bryan carried the debate, emphasizing the inequity of expecting the nation's poor to carry the burden of financing the government by paying excise and customs taxes. The tax's opponents, Bryan thundered, "weep more because fifteen millions are to be collected from the incomes of the rich than they do at the collection of three hundred millions upon the goods which the poor consume."[8]

The 1894 income tax, which Bryan tacked on to that year's tariff legislation, established a tax of 2 percent on personal income above a $4,000 exemption and a tax of 2 percent on corporate income. Within a year, the United States Supreme Court heard a challenge to the income tax. In *Pollock v. Farmers' Loan and Trust Company* (1895),[9] the Justices struck down the tax (by a vote of 5 to 4) as a violation of the Constitution's requirement that such taxes be apportioned among the states on the basis of population. The Court's decision provoked vigorous dissents from the minority Justices and heated criticism from the nation as a whole.

Infuriated by the decision, Congress began to consider amending the Constitution to authorize an income tax. Public opinion maintained that the Court had erred; nothing in the Constitution explicitly barred an income tax, and taxes on income had been enacted and collected before without judicial challenge. Nonetheless, supporters of the income tax agreed, an amendment would remove all doubt. The first such proposal was introduced in December 1895, and by 1909 thirty-three amendments had been offered to overrule *Pollock*—all of them thwarted by vigorous lobbying by corporate and other special interests.[10]

On June 28, 1909, Senator Joseph Bailey (Democrat–Texas) proposed an addition to a controversial tariff bill; his rider would impose a 3 percent tax on all incomes over $5,000. In response to Bailey's explosive challenge to *Pollock,* the Senate Committee on Finance proposed an amendment to the Constitution:

> The Congress shall have the power to lay and collect taxes on incomes, from whatever source derived, without apportionment among the several States, and without regard to any census or enumeration.

The chairman of the committee, Senator Nelson W. Aldrich (Republican–Rhode Island), presented the amendment as a measure designed to overrule *Pollock;* however, what the wealthy Aldrich really sought was to derail the Bailey proposal. Convinced that an amendment never would be ratified by the states, Aldrich hoped that the controversy would distract opponents of what eventually became the Payne-Aldrich tariff. After a struggle over whether it would not be better to amend the Constitution to delete its clauses requiring apportionment of direct taxes (the foundation of *Pollock*), the Senate voted unanimously to approve the Aldrich amendment. On July 1 2, the House added its endorsement (3 1 8 to 1 4).[11]

Aldrich was in for a rude surprise. The growing agitation for an income tax, which had received endorsements from Presidents Theodore Roosevelt (in 1906 and 1907) and William Howard Taft (in 1909), propelled the Sixteenth Amendment through most of the thirty-six states needed for ratification. The strongest argument for the measure was that it was a fairer and more effective way of raising revenue than the regressive customs duties and excise taxes. The Amendment had easiest going in the South and the West, facing lingering opposition only in the Northeast.[12]

On February 4, 1913, *The New York Times* reported the ratification of the Sixteenth Amendment. Ratification the previous day by Delaware, Wyoming, and New Mexico, the *Times* declared in its headline, meant that "Congress [is] Now Free to Act." Delaware's legislature had disposed of the Amendment (by a unanimous vote in both houses) in twenty-five minutes, apparently aiming to win the honor of being the state to ensure the Amendment's adoption.

On February 2 5, 1913, the Secretary of State declared the Sixteenth Amendment in effect, but even before ratification, the House Committee on Ways and Means had been preparing to write the first income-tax legislation in twenty years. One Representative noted that the committee's chief task was to devise an income tax that would fit with the nation's other sources of revenue, in particular making up expected revenue losses resulting from tariff reductions. Representatives also declared that they "favored making the new tax an integral part of the financial system of the United States to remain in full force without regard to the character of tariff bills that Congress may enact from time to time."[13]

Following the precedents of the 1862 and 1894 income-tax legislation, the first federal income-tax law authorized by the Sixteenth Amendment was added to a tariff bill—as Section II of the Tariff Law of 191 3. The measure established exemptions of $3,000 for an individual and $4,000 for a married couple (but none for children); the rates of taxation began at one percent for income over the exemption but under $20,000, with an additional percent levied for income over $20,000 but under $50,000, and so forth, up to a 6 percent levy on income over $500,000.[14] This first income-tax law inaugurated a new era in American domestic politics, one whose reverberations continue to affect Presidential and Congressional elections eighty years later.

DEMOCRATIZING INSTITUTIONS: THE SEVENTEENTH AMENDMENT

THE SEVENTEENTH AMENDMENT, WHICH TRANSFERRED the election of Senators from the state legislatures to the voters, is the most drastic alteration in the system of federalism since the Civil War Amendments. The power to choose Senators long was a cherished prerogative of the state governments, and it shaped the character of the Senate and of national politics for generations.

The Federal Convention's greatest political challenge had been the design of the national legislature. Delegates from small states fought to preserve the rule of equality of representation that had governed all previous intercolonial and interstate assemblies; Delaware's legislature had instructed its delegates to oppose any deviation from the principle of state equality.[15] Delegates from large states insisted that representation had to reflect the diversity of population and wealth in the several states, and they therefore denounced the rule of state equality as unjust.

Throughout June and July 1787, the Convention hammered out a compromise between large-state delegates' demands for proportional representation and small-state delegates' efforts to preserve state equality. One historian of the Convention pointed out: "The problem . . . was not for constitution-makers to find the solution but for politicians to learn to live with it, and that process of learning . . . was a hard one."[16]

The bicameral Congress authorized in Article I of the Constitution was designed to satisfy both the large-state and small-state camps. The people of the states were to be represented in the House of Representatives, and the states themselves would be represented in the Senate. James Wilson of Pennsylvania urged that Senators be elected by the people of each state, but the Convention rejected his proposal. State legislatures would choose two Senators apiece— though, in a departure from the "unit rule" of previous Congresses and the Convention, each Senator, and not each state, would have one vote.[17] The Great Compromise ensured that Senators would take up an important function formerly performed by delegates to the Continental and Confederation Congresses—representing the interests of their states to the general government. Although it drew fire during the ratification controversy of 1787–1788, the Great

Compromise was so successful that the rivalry between large states and small states never broke out again.

In addition to using their power of election to control Senators' conduct, some state legislatures sought to bind Senators through instructions.[18] Two future Presidents—John Quincy Adams of Massachusetts (in 1807) and John Tyler of Virginia (in 1836)—resigned from the Senate when the instructions of their state legislatures conflicted with their personal views; Adams supported President Thomas Jefferson's embargo on trade with the warring powers of Europe despite the prevailing view among the Senator's constituents that the embargo would destroy their economy, and Tyler refused to back a Senate resolution expunging from the Senate's records a vote of censure against President Andrew Jackson.[19] However, the practice of instructing Senators had died out by midcentury.

The profound revolution wrought by the Civil War in virtually every aspect of American society reached into the Senate as well.[20] The knitting together of a national economy and transportation system impelled by the war brought with it the rise of peacetime industries and economic organizations operating on a national scale.[21] In turn, these enterprises exerted powerful influences on the nation's political life, seeking to block or divert government actions harmful to their interests.

Few methods of influencing government were as effective as the manipulation of state legislatures' choice of Senators. State legislatures had long used this power to reward prominent politicians who could be trusted as zealous advocates of their state's interests or to punish those who "betrayed" their constituents. By the 1880s and 1890s, advocates of constitutional reform charged, special interests had conspired to hold the Senate hostage; the documentation they presented to the public painted a horrifying picture of a widespread network of corrupt bargains, in which wealth and power were exchanged for influence and votes.[22] By the end of the nineteenth century, reformers of all parties united in demanding change in the method of electing Senators.

Senate elections had become three-ring circuses. Some mired state business in days, weeks, or even months of elaborate parliamentary wrangling; others gave rise to what a leading historian of the Senate called "riotous demonstrations more appropriate to a prize-fight than to a senatorial election."[23] A noteworthy example of the latter is the Missouri legislature's 1905 struggle over choosing a Senator:

> Lest the hour of adjournment should come before an election was
> secured, an attempt was made to stop the clock upon the wall of the
> assembly chamber. Democrats tried to prevent its being tampered

with; and when certain Republicans brought forward a ladder, it was seized and thrown out of the window. A fist-fight followed, in which many were involved. Desks were torn from the floor and a fusillade of books began. The glass of the clock-front was broken, but the pendulum still persisted in swinging until, in the midst of a yelling mob, one member began throwing ink bottles at the clock, and finally succeeded in breaking the pendulum. On a motion to adjourn, arose the wildest disorder. The presiding officers of both houses mounted the speaker's desk, and, by shouting and waving their arms, tried to quiet the mob. Finally, they succeeded in securing some semblance of order.[24]

The Missouri case was also an example of a growing tendency in state legislatures' choice of Senators: "It is ridiculous to suggest that amid scenes like these the choice of a senator retains anything of the character of an exercise of cool judgment."[25]

Such quarrels also led to institutional paralysis that prevented the selection of a Senator, often leaving a state either partly or totally unrepresented in the Senate. In the Fifty-seventh Congress (1901–1903), Delaware was not represented at all because of its legislature's failure to elect Senators.[26]

In other states, money and other forms of political corruption subverted rational choice. Consider New York's 1897 choice of a Senator:

On January 14, the Republican members of the Legislature of New York met in caucus and selected their candidate to succeed Mr. D. B. Hill. The most eminently qualified man in the State of New York (the Hon. Joseph H. Choate) was duly presented to the caucus. No other names were presented or mentioned. There are 151 Republican members of the present state legislature. A vote was taken, and seven members were found to be in favor of Mr. Choate. All the rest, with a notable exhibition of spontaneity, declared themselves in favor of Thomas C. Platt. A few days later Mr. Platt was formally elected. His control of the legislature is more complete than his control of any office boy in his private employ; for the office boy, after all, is not owned by Mr. Platt, and could quit work if he did not find that the place suited him, but the legislature seems to be his, both soul and body.[27]

One legislator described to a reporter the dilemma he faced:

I am uncertain what to do. I have various important measures which I desire to introduce in the assembly, and if I do not vote for Platt, none of them will be allowed to go through. You have no idea of the pressure which has been brought to bear upon me to vote for Platt, and I am not sure that it is the part of wisdom for me to refuse to support him.[28]

What kind of institution resulted from these distorted processes of Senatorial election? A 1906 analysis of the Senate in the Fifty-eighth Congress (1903–1905), using confidential evaluations obtained from numerous observers of the national political scene, concluded that four out of every nine Senators possessed either "high powers of leadership" or "qualities of courage, intelligence and integrity"—qualities traditionally identified as central values of the Senate. But the analyst also presented disturbing judgments of the Senate:

> [O]ne senator out of every three owes his election to his personal wealth, to his being the candidate satisfactory to what is coming to be called the "System," or to his expertness in political manipulation—qualifications which make their usefulness as members of the dominant branch of Congress decidedly open to question.[29]

Reformers maintained that a constitutional amendment authorizing direct election of Senators was the best means to end the corruption of the Senate—a suggestion first made in 1826, and championed in the 1850s and 1860s by Senator (and later President) Andrew Johnson (Democrat–Tennessee).[30] But the obstacles to an amendment seemed insuperable. The Senate itself had to approve any amendment originating in Congress by a two-thirds vote. Moreover, even if the required number of states adopted applications for a constitutional convention, the Senate could still block action to call a convention or could interfere with its results. Nevertheless, as one historian wrote in 1897, "[s]carcely a session of Congress passes in which one or more resolutions are not offered to secure this amendment."[31]

Assuming that the amending process was foreclosed by the selfishness of the Senate, advocates of reform pursued other avenues to the same goal. The first such innovation was the introduction of political parties into the Senate electoral process; state conventions of the party faithful designated their party's nominee, and the party's candidates for the state legislature would be pledged to support that nominee for the Senate. (This injection of party politics into Senatorial contests produced, among other things, the Lincoln-Douglas debates of 1858.)[32]

In time, the limitations of the party-caucus method led to a more democratic development: the invention of primary elections. Under this system, the voters would choose their state's Senators, and the state legislature would officially "elect" the winner of the primary to the Senate to preserve the fiction of compliance with the Constitution.[33] This "Oregon system," developed in that state between 1901 and 1904, was adopted in many other states; by 1910, fourteen of the thirty Senators to be chosen by state legislatures already had been designated by popular vote.[34]

Despite these inventive attempts to introduce the voice of the electorate into the choosing of Senators, the demand to amend the Constitution to achieve this goal persisted; "the number of resolutions proposing this change," one observer exclaimed in 1897, "is unprecedented."[35] The House of Representatives welcomed the proposal, adopting it five times between 1893 and 1902, each time by the requisite two-thirds margin.[36] Each time, however, the Senate blocked the measure, as few Senators were willing to abolish the electoral system to which they owed their seats.

Anticipating this result, in 1893 state legislatures began the process of seeking a convention to amend the Constitution to provide for the election of Senators by direct popular vote.[37] By 1905, thirty-one of the forty-five states (more than two-thirds) had taken some form of action endorsing a direct-election amendment. Some legislatures' resolutions requested that Congress propose an amendment to the states; others asked for referenda on the issue; still others demanded a convention to propose an amendment; and some resolutions proposed that the states confer on the best means of securing an amendment. Only the New England and Middle Atlantic states did not join the general demand for the reform, but even within those states vigorous movements arose supporting the proposal.*[38]

Supporters of a direct-election amendment urged that the existing system was an obsolete relic of the antebellum Constitution and that its abolition would actually strengthen the principle of state equality. They maintained that direct election would elevate the Senate's tone and membership, improve its functioning, and increase its responsibility to the people. It also would enhance the functioning of state government by separating it from national politics and ensure the full representation of the states in the Senate.[39]

Opponents of a direct-election amendment denounced it as unnecessary in and of itself, an invasion of states' rights, and a distraction from the truly grave issues affecting the nation. The existing system, they maintained, was the product of wise planning and thorough deliberation. It had worked far better than its

---

*Two other proposals, one from 1882 and one from 1892, would have added an element of proportional representation to the Senate, undermining the Great Compromise. One sought to confer an additional Senator for each "million of inhabitants of any State in excess of two million," and the other would have given each state one Senator with another Senator for each additional million inhabitants.

adversaries represented; the spirit of the party introduced by popular elections would damage the Senate, and the virtues of conservatism built into the Senate in 1787 would be lost if a system of popular election were adopted. One skeptical commentator observed, "[I]t may be said in support of the present method that it has secured to the United States the only effective second chamber in the world."[40]

In addition, the amendment's opponents declared, the direct-election measure would be "the first change in the organic structure of the government under the Constitution"; for this reason alone, it should be resisted. They sought to play on the growing public suspicion that the products of the amending process almost never fulfilled the hopes of amendment advocates. The Constitution was better modified, they contended, through custom and interpretation. In response, the amendment's supporters claimed that reform of the process of choosing Senators would augment the legitimacy of the Senate in the eyes of the people and thus would increase the favor with which the Constitution was generally regarded.

In late 1910, the House swiftly passed yet another direct-election amendment, which ran into a firestorm in the Senate. Although the leadership assigned the amendment to the Judiciary Committee rather than the Committee on Privileges and Elections, which had killed all previous attempts, the Judiciary Committee reported a modified version of the amendment on January 1, 1911. The modification, quickly dubbed the "race rider," became the focus of debate for the rest of the session.

The race rider would have vested control of Senate elections entirely in the hands of state governments, thereby limiting the reach of Article I, section 4 of the Constitution, which authorized Congress to make or alter regulations of Congressional elections. Democrats from Southern states favored the race rider, claiming that it would compensate the state legislatures for the loss of their power to choose Senators. Others were ready to accept the race rider as the price of a direct-election amendment. The rider's opponents denounced it as a veiled means to remove federal power to bar racial discrimination in access to the polls, thus overturning the Fifteenth Amendment.

The fight over the race rider regularly overshadowed what was supposed to be the major issue—direct election of Senators. Both the House and the Senate shifted their positions on the rider with bewildering frequency. Some observers have speculated that the Senate was playing the race rider card to slow down or even stop the drive for a direct-election amendment. For two solid months, battle raged over the rider, which Northern Senators managed to delete by a vote of 50 to 37 on February 28. However, the Senate's vote for the amendment, taken that same day, failed (by 54 to 33) to reach the needed two-thirds majority.

Undeterred, in April 1911 Representative Walter Rucker (Democrat–Missouri) reintroduced the proposed amendment (this time with the race rider) in the House. The measure sailed through the House (296 to 14), but ran into extraordinary opposition in the Senate—even though that body was more sympathetic to the direct-election movement than any of its predecessors had been. On a 45 to 44 roll-call vote decided by Vice President James S. Sherman, the Senate adopted the motion of Senator Joseph Bristow (Republican–Kansas) rejecting the amendment with the race rider. It then adopted the 1910 House version without the race rider; the vote of 64 to 24 overcame the two-thirds requirement. This time the House balked, apparently viewing the deletion of the race rider from its original version as an insult to its prerogatives; it was not until the next session of Congress that Representative Rucker moved that the House recede from its support of the provision in order to achieve the desired goal.

On April 8, 1913, the Seventeenth Amendment was added to the Constitution; ironically, in light of Congress's repeated battles over the race rider, the rider's absence proved no bar to the swift adoption of the Amendment. Moreover, the state legislatures accepted their loss of control over Senatorial elections without a murmur of complaint. They deemed it a small price to pay for the increased order, coherence, and democracy of choosing Senators under the amendment. By 1919, every member of the Senate owed his election to that body to the people, rather than the legislature, of his state. However, the growing popularity of primary elections even before the Amendment rendered it an open question whether the Seventeenth merely codified in law a development—the democratization of the Senate—that already was settled fact.[41]

WOMEN'S SUFFRAGE:
THE NINETEENTH AMENDMENT

THE FIFTEENTH AMENDMENT HAD OPENED a new sphere of previously sacrosanct legal and political issues to the reach of the amending process. Not even the most ambitious and nationalist-minded of the framers of the Constitution had been prepared to assert federal jurisdiction over the suffrage—regulation of which was a treasured prerogative of the state governments. The Fifteenth Amendment showed that Congress could use Article V to establish constitutional limits on the range of state restrictions of the suffrage. The Nineteenth Amendment was the first to follow in the path blazed by the Fifteenth, and the debates over its adoption revolved around one central question: What further restrictions on the states' control of access to voting—if any—should be added to the Constitution? The Nineteenth Amendment raised the issue of how far Congress and the state legislatures were willing to go to expand the "political population"[42] of the United States, and what sorts of restrictions should not be tolerated in a modern democratic republic.

ON AUGUST 26, 1920, Secretary of State Bainbridge Colby conducted a small, private meeting at his residence in Washington, D.C. The aristocratic Colby signed with a flourish of an ordinary steel pen the certification that the Nineteenth Amendment had been adopted by enough states to add it to the Constitution and declared, "I say to the women of America, you may fire when ready." It is not clear whom Colby was addressing, for only men were present at the ceremony. Colby, who did not seem especially pleased by his duties that day, explained the absence of leaders of the women's suffrage movement: "It was decided not to accompany this simple ministerial action on my part with any ceremony or setting . . . I have contented myself with the performance in the simplest manner [prescribed] by law." He then set aside his pen to be sent to the Smithsonian Institution. Thus ended over a century of struggle by the women of America for a voice in the governance of their nation.[43]

What role women should play in public life is a question far older than the American republic. When in 1776 Abigail Adams pleaded with her husband, John, then a delegate to the Second Continental Congress, to "Remember the Ladies" in the design of the new independent states, he responded with indulgent mockery. One of the most brilliant and tough-minded Americans of her generation, Abigail Adams found herself disabled by her sex from being taken seriously when she raised the issue of the disenfranchisement of half the human race.[44]

The one state that had not denied women the vote had acted more by accident than by design. In 1776, New Jersey's constitution established qualifications for voting but left out the qualifying words "male" and "men." Single women throughout the state took advantage of the omission and voted in elections for thirty years, until the 1806 constitution established that only men could vote.[45] But even in New Jersey, the common-law doctrine of coverture effectively (though not explicitly) forbade voting by married women. Coverture provided that when a man and a woman married, they formed one household with one voice to address outside concerns, whether political, economic, or legal—and that voice was the husband's. A wife's property became her husband's upon marriage; even if a wife conducted a business independent from that of her husband, she could not sign contracts and could not sue or be sued—unless her husband signed, sued, or was sued with her.[46]

Despite these restrictions, women throughout the nation played vigorous and open parts in the public life of the new nation. Mary Katherine Goddard was the first printer to produce the Declaration of Independence in Maryland and successfully won several contracts to do printing business for the Confederation Congress. The learned, eloquent, and fiercely democratic Mercy Otis Warren of Massachusetts wrote a notable pamphlet opposing the Constitution (anonymous, as was the custom) that generations of later scholars mistakenly attributed to Elbridge Gerry. She also published plays, poems, and a massive history of the United States.[47] Women throughout the Republic showed themselves to be at least equal to men in assuming the burdens of active participation in political life.[48]

Women's rights, scanty as they were during the Revolutionary and early national periods, diminished further during the nineteenth century.[49] Even so, in the decades before the Civil War women were increasingly active in such social and political reform movements as temperance and abolition, both of which they explicitly connected to the issue of women's rights.[50] A long and difficult campaign in New York State resulted in the enactment in 1848 of the first of several Married Women's Property Acts designed to roll back at least part of the doctrine of coverture; these statutes became models for other states, so that by 1900 every state had enacted at least one statute providing for separate treatment of married women's property.[51]

Three months after the 1848 Married Women's Property Act made its way through the New York legislature, a group of women and like-minded men gathered in Seneca Falls, New York, to begin the first Women's Rights Convention. The leaders of the gathering included the noted suffragists and abolitionists Lucretia Mott, Elizabeth Cady Stanton, and Frederick Douglass. The Declaration of Sentiments that the convention adopted, "the first female legal text in U.S. history," was modeled explicitly on the Declaration of Independence.[52] The Declaration and its accompanying resolutions pointed an accusing finger at American men, just as the 1776 document had targeted George III:

> When, in the course of human events, it becomes necessary for one portion of the family of man to assume among the people of the earth a position different from that which they have hitherto occupied, but one to which the laws of nature and of nature's God entitle them, a decent respect to the opinions of mankind requires that they should declare the causes that impel them to such a course. . . .
>
> The history of mankind is a history of repeated injuries and usurpations on the part of man toward woman, having in direct object the establishment of an absolute tyranny over her.[53]

The movement had its charter and manifesto, but charters and manifestos are not equivalent to legal and political victories. Despite the remarkable efforts of women in the North and West in support of the Union during the Civil War, and despite the devotion of American women to the cause of abolition, they could not persuade the men of America—and, in particular, the politicians of America—to recognize their right to equal treatment and their right to vote.

In 1866–1867, women and their allies pleaded to no avail to remove the words "men" and "male" from the proposed Fourteenth Amendment. This controversy obscured the demands for women's suffrage in Congress. All but unnoticed, on January 23, 1866, the subject of women's suffrage was first mentioned in that body when Representative James Brooks (Republican–New York) made a vain attempt to include in what became the Fourteenth Amendment language recognizing women's right to vote.[54]

With their defeat over the Fourteenth Amendment fresh in their minds, advocates of women's rights regrouped in 1869. During the legislative battles over the Fifteenth Amendment, they tried to rework the amendment's language to include sex as one of the categories protected against discrimination. Republican legislators bluntly told women that the choice was between enfranchising the freed slaves and enfranchising women; both goals could not be achieved, and a war had been fought in behalf of the slaves. Women would have to wait.

These battles were only preliminaries to a larger and more anguished contest, as women concluded that the new additions to the Constitution effectively excluded them from American citizenship. They chose to emphasize women's suffrage as their main goal and charted a new array of political and legal tactics. In Rochester, New York, Susan B. Anthony attempted to vote in the Presidential election of 1872; she knew that she was violating the terms of the Civil Rights Act of 1870, but she hoped to turn her trial into a public forum from which she could argue that women should have the right to vote. To her dismay, however, federal Judge Ward Hunt (later a Justice of the United States Supreme Court) denied her the right to testify on her own behalf, delivered an opinion (which he had prepared before the trial began) ruling against her on the law, and directed the jury to find her guilty. When her attorney questioned the constitutionality of his action, Judge Hunt discharged the jury, denied motions for retrial, and fined Anthony one hundred dollars and the costs of the prosecution—which she refused to pay, hoping that she would be sentenced to jail. Judge Hunt did not oblige.[55]

Virginia Minor also attempted to vote in the 1872 election—in St. Louis, Missouri. She and her husband sued the local registrar of voters, Reese Happersett, and this case reached the United States Supreme Court in 1874. In *Minor v. Happersett* (1875),[56] the Justices unanimously rejected Mrs. Minor's claim that the disenfranchisement of women was a denial of their rights as citizens of the United States under the privileges and immunities clause of the Fourteenth Amendment. The sweeping language of *Minor v. Happersett* wrought as much damage to the rights of women as *Dred Scott v. Sandford* had done to the rights of black Americans nearly twenty years before.[57]

In 1876, in Philadelphia, another convention of women's rights advocates noted the injustice of restrictions on women's inability to take part in politics. Choosing to "strike the one discordant note, on this one-hundredth anniversary of our country's birth," the delegates proclaimed:

> *Universal manhood suffrage,* by establishing an aristocracy of sex, imposed upon the women of this nation a more absolute and cruel despotism than monarchy; in that, woman finds a political master in her father, husband, brother, son. The aristocracies of the old world are based upon birth, wealth, refinement, education, nobility, brave deeds of chivalry; in this nation, on sex alone; exalting brute force above moral power, vice above virtue, ignorance above education, and the son above the mother who bore him.[58]

Just as it took a constitutional amendment to overturn *Dred Scott,* it would take an amendment to overturn *Minor v. Happersett.* Efforts to secure constitutional protection for women's right to vote resumed in 1878. Over the following thirty-three years, at least one amendment—sometimes as many as four—was proposed in each Congress to recognize women's right to vote. At the same time, two suffragists' organizations, the National Woman Suffrage Association (NWSA) and the American Woman Suffrage Association (AWSA), adopted contrasting strategies—AWSA urging low-key, state-level lobbying and NWSA pursuing a highly visible, even confrontational strategy through political and legal action. They ended their rivalry by merging, in 1890, to form the National American Woman Suffrage Association.

Meanwhile, the women's suffrage movement gained unexpected allies at the state level. Pressures in the Western territories for statehood (a territory's readiness for statehood was measured by the number of voting inhabitants it could claim) combined with a growing conviction of the equality of women and men to produce territorial statutes and state constitutional provisions extending the suffrage to women. Wyoming Territory was the first to do so, in 1869; Utah and Washington Territories followed, only to have their statutes nullified (Utah's by Congress, Washington's by a federal judge). In 1893, Colorado held a binding referendum that conferred the vote on the state's women. Several states extended limited franchise—in school board elections and on other issues connected with schools—in the 1890s.[59] By 1897, twenty-seven states and two Territories had authorized women's suffrage in various forms.[60] In the first decade of the twentieth century, more and more states began to recognize women's unrestricted right to vote. By June 4, 1919, when Congress proposed the Nineteenth Amendment to the states, seventeen states recognized women's right to vote in all elections; thirteen permitted women to vote in Presidential elections; and eighteen did not recognize women's right to vote at all.[61]

As women narrowed the focus of their campaign and thereby excluded references to the range of "causes and consequences of women's inequality," they won more and broader political support for their movement.[62] Still other factors helped swell the ranks of those supporting the suffrage amendment—dubbed the "Anthony amendment" to honor Susan B. Anthony, who had died in 1906. These included the participation of women in political and social reform movements, the important roles played by American women in domestic activities supporting American involvement in the First World War, and the dawning recognition by American men of the validity of at least some elements of women's case for political equality.

Nonetheless, the growing pressure for women's suffrage continued to raise various kinds of objections in the national political arena. Some politicians, such as President Woodrow Wilson and the authors of the 1916 Democratic and Republican platforms, declared their belief that the reform should be achieved through state action and not through a federal constitutional amendment that would sap the powers of the state governments. Other politicians opposed women's suffrage because it would inspire members of minority races—specifically Asians and blacks—to seek enforcement of their rights. Representative Frank Clark (Democrat–Florida) declared:

> Make this amendment a part of the Federal Constitution and the negro women of the Southern States, under the tutelage of the fast-growing socialistic element of our common country, will become fanatical on the subject of voting and will reawaken in the negro men an intense and not easily quenched desire to again become a political factor.[63]

Proponents of women's suffrage, led by the redoubtable Carrie Chapman Catt and Alice Paul, addressed these objections directly. First, they retorted, the goal of expanding the franchise could be more easily secured through constitutional amendment than through seeking the cooperation of the individual states. Second, women's suffrage was "a war measure of the most definite sort," strengthening the cause of democracy for which the war ostensibly was being fought.[64] Third, it would increase the number of intelligent voters in the nation—because illiterate men far outnumbered illiterate women.[65]

On January 30, 1918, after two months of debate, the House passed the suffrage Amendment by a vote of 274 to 136, precisely the two-thirds majority needed. Both President Wilson and former President Theodore Roosevelt pledged their support for the measure. Several Representatives had themselves carried to the floor of the House from their sickbeds to vote on the measure, and one left his wife (an ardent suffragist) on her deathbed to cast his vote for the proposal in her honor.[66] But the Senate's vote for the Amendment (53 to 31) fell just short of the needed two-thirds majority.

With the armistice in November 1918, ending hostilities in Europe, the public renewed its interest in the question of women's suffrage, and the suffrage movement renewed its pressure on the nation's politicians. On May 19, 1919, the Sixty-sixth Congress convened in an extraordinary session, and Representative James Robert Mann (Republican–Illinois) introduced the proposal that would become the Nineteenth Amendment. President Wilson again endorsed the proposal, declaring to Congress his belief that "every consideration of justice and of public advantage calls for the immediate adoption of that amendment and its submission forthwith to the legislatures of the several states."[67]

The resolution cleared the House of Representatives (304 to 89), but once again ran into opposition in the Senate. Southern Senators (the South was the only region of the nation where states did not recognize women's right to vote) demanded that the first clause of the Amendment read "The right of white citizens to vote," but the Senate rejected this change. Other Senators clamored to have the amendment submitted not to the state legislatures but to popularly elected ratifying conventions, believing that opponents of the Amendment would have a better chance to defeat it under that procedure. Despite these last-minute stratagems, the Amendment was approved by a vote of 56 to 25, with 15 not voting. Once the Amendment emerged from Congress, it was swiftly adopted by the states, with Tennessee, the thirty-sixth, voting to ratify on August 18, 1920. In the end, twenty-four-year-old Harry Burn, a Tennessee state representative, held the Amendment's fate in his hands; bowing to the pleas of his mother to "help Mrs. Catt," he voted for ratification, helping his chamber to pass the Amendment by a vote of 49 to 47.[68]

WHEN BAINBRIDGE COLBY CERTIFIED THE Nineteenth Amendment, he put the finishing touches on a transformed Constitution that both shaped and reflected a nation far different from the one that had ratified the Civil War Amendments. The American nation was much more willing to make use of national government power to achieve its goals, to acknowledge democracy as a central principle of its public life and government, and to revise its fundamental law to respond to changing conditions.

The Progressive Amendments adopted between 1913 and 1920 thus lay the groundwork for the further democratization of the Constitution—and the nation. Just as important, the framing and adoption of three amendments (four, counting the Prohibition Amendment discussed in Chapter 10) suggested the newfound versatility and utility of the Constitution's amending process, and helped to spur increased interest in later decades in using the process to respond to a wide variety of national concerns.

Chapter 8

TESTING THE LIMITS
OF DEMOCRATIZATION

*The framers of the Constitution meant to give intense,
sizable minorities a near veto on constitutional amendments,
and they succeeded. This raises a democratic paradox. We
sometimes think of the rights-oriented amendments to the
Constitution as having the function of protecting politically
disadvantaged groups from the power of the majority. Yet
the Constitution requires much more than a majority to pass
these amendments. How, politically, can one persuade not
only a majority but a supermajority to thwart its own will,
or the will of future majorities?*

JANE J. MANSBRIDGE
Why We Lost the ERA (1986)[1]

FIFTY YEARS AFTER THE FLURRY of Progressive Era amendments, politicians and citizens joined forces to revive the principles of bolstering the democracy of the constitutional system and making that system more responsible to the electorate. In the 1960s and 1970s the cause of democratization won renewed prominence, as the Twenty-third (1961), the Twenty-fourth (1964), and the Twenty-sixth (1971) Amendments continued the project of augmenting federal constitutional protection of the franchise. However, despite the high hopes of would-be amendment framers during those years, the Twenty-sixth Amendment has turned out to be the last successful Amendment proposed in modern times.*

In the 1980s, for the first time in American history, democratizing amendments failed to clear the hurdle of ratification—the Equal Rights Amendment in 1982 and the D.C. Statehood Amendment in 1985. It seemed that, for the moment at least, the American people had reached the limits of their willingness to democratize the constitutional system.

---

*The Twenty-seventh Amendment, ratified in 1992, was proposed in 1789. See Chapter 13.

SUFFRAGE AND SOCIAL CHANGE

BETWEEN 1960 AND 1971, TWO major social and political movements convulsed the nation and left their marks on virtually every feature of American society, including the Constitution. The Twenty-third and Twenty-fourth Amendments ranked among the principal achievements of the civil-rights movement; the Twenty-sixth Amendment, which protected the right of American youth to take part in politics, was a response to the movement against the Vietnam Conflict.

The Twenty-third and Twenty-fourth Amendments

The amending process sometimes produces results different from the expectations of those who set it in motion. In the early 1960s, the Twenty-third and Twenty-fourth Amendments grew out of a proposed amendment seeking something entirely different, which in turn led to a combination of proposals designed to effect a series of reforms in the suffrage. Partisan politics within Congress dismantled the package, and two distinct Amendments went to the states, two years apart.

Both Amendments were concerned with expansion of the "political population" of the United States. The Twenty-third was designed to grant at least some measure of self-governance to the three-quarters of a million residents of the nation's capital (according to the 1960 census), enabling them to vote in Presidential elections. It was supposed in this way to remedy, in part, the failure in foresight of the Revolutionary generation, who, as The New York Times observed in 1961, had "provided only for national electoral machinery within the state framework."[2] They also had not expected the nation's seat of government to acquire a large permanent population.[3]

The Twenty-fourth Amendment was designed to eradicate the last vestige of a once-powerful Anglo-American political principle: a prospective voter had to demonstrate financial independence, which was a guarantee of the political independence he needed to be able to vote. Throughout the colonial and Revolutionary periods, the colonies (and later the states) used a rudimentary means test—the poll tax. But, by the mid–twentieth century, the tax had degenerated into a weapon in the hands of conservative local officials to bar blacks and poor whites from the polls.

A tangled, elaborate set of circumstances sent the amending process lurching into motion.[4] The cold-war hysteria of the 1950s led some members of Congress to ruminate on what would happen to their institution should the capital come under nuclear attack—specifically, how would members of the House of Representatives be replaced? (The Constitution provided that Senators would be replaced by special appointments made by state governors.)

In 1960, Senator Estes Kefauver (Democrat–Tennessee) proposed an amendment to authorize state governors to appoint temporary Representatives until a new election could be arranged. His suggestion spurred Senator Spessard Holland (Democrat–Florida) to bring forward his proposal to abolish the poll tax; it also prompted Senator Kenneth Keating (Republican–New York) to seek an amendment enfranchising federal officials residing in the District of Columbia. The ensuing legislative maelstrom combined Kefauver's, Holland's, and Keating's suggestions in an omnibus proposal that also would have given residents of the District representation in the House of Representatives—though not in the Senate.[5]

Despite thinly disguised racist opposition to enfranchising the largely black population of the capital and to removing a barrier keeping blacks from the polls in the South, the omnibus package passed easily in the Senate. The House followed a different path; its amendment, proposed by Representative Emanuel Celler (Democrat–New York), provided only for residents of the District to be able to vote in Presidential elections. The clash between the two proposed amendments touched off a brisk though polite political storm between the chambers, exacerbated by the resistance of Southern conservatives in both chambers to the Holland amendment. In the resulting compromise, Holland withdrew his proposal and endorsed Celler's version, and Celler in turn pledged his aid to get a separate version of the Holland anti-poll-tax amendment through the House. (Somewhere along the line, the Kefauver proposal had dropped through the cracks, never to be seen again.)[6]

Celler's proposal emerged from Congress on June 17, 1960, winning ratification as the Twenty-third Amendment when Kansas approved it on March 29, 1961. President John F. Kennedy hailed the ratification of the Amendment, declaring that it "demonstrates the interest of the nation at large in providing to all American citizens the most valuable of human rights," and he urged the enactment of home-rule legislation for the District.[7]

Meanwhile, Senator Holland prepared to reintroduce his proposal to abolish the poll tax, which he brought forward in March 1962. After a series of parliamentary maneuvers that briefly entangled the proposal with a resolution to make Alexander Hamilton's house in New York City a National Monument, the Holland resolution came before the Senate. Opposition came from both ends of the political spectrum. Liberals argued that to propose an amendment served only to make the task more difficult; the same objective could be achieved more easily by a federal statute abolishing the poll tax in federal elections. Holland rejoined that a mere statute could be struck down as unconstitutional; even if the statute survived the tests of constitutionality in the federal courts, its progress through the judicial system would be at least as slow as, if not slower than, the adoption of a constitutional amendment. Southern conservatives charged that the Holland measure was yet another attempt to destroy states' rights, a charge that Holland rejected as a mask for race prejudice, his opponents' true motivation. The Senate finally voted to approve the Holland amendment by a comfortable margin (77 to 16, with 7 not voting).

In the House, the leadership had difficulty coordinating its efforts on the poll-tax amendment with those of the Senate (again because of skilled manipulation of House rules by the amendment's critics), but on August 27, 1962, the House suspended its rules and brought forward the joint resolution proposing the amendment. The leadership also limited debate to forty minutes and barred any attempts to amend the measure. The amendment's sponsors defended its halfway character as being better than no action at all. Conservatives (who opposed any amendment) continued their resistance to interference with states' rights, some liberals (who were bent on an amendment that would outlaw poll taxes at all levels of government) declared their willingness to abandon the amendment as inadequate, and all denounced the restrictions imposed on the debate. Other adversaries of the measure noted that states would have to set up two sets of electoral records—one for national elections and the other for state elections (which would be unaffected by the amendment). Even so, the House managed to adopt the amendment, 294 to 86, with 1 voting "present" and 56 not voting.

The Twenty-fourth Amendment was ratified on January 23, 1964, in time for the Presidential election that fall. By that date, only five of the fifty states retained poll-tax requirements for state elections, and the Voting Rights Act of 1965 soon threatened the validity of even these measures.[8] In 1966, two years after the adoption of the Amendment, the Supreme Court struck down Virginia's state poll-tax statute as a violation of the Fourteenth Amendment's equal protection clause.[9]

The Twenty-sixth Amendment

The Twenty-sixth Amendment represents the intersection of two seemingly unrelated topics: the suffrage and service in the armed forces.[10] In 1942, during the Second World War, Representative Jennings Randolph (Democrat–West Virginia) proposed an amendment to lower the voting age to eighteen; he reintroduced it in every succeeding Congress. In his 1954 State of the Union message, President Dwight D. Eisenhower also proposed that the Constitution be amended to mandate eighteen as the minimum age for voting. Fresh from supervising the negotiation of the truce that ended the Korean Conflict, and recalling the brave young men who had served under his command during the Second World War, Eisenhower urged Congress to recognize that those old enough to fight and die for the United States should have the right to take part in governing it. Eisenhower's call was later endorsed by two of his successors, Lyndon B. Johnson and Richard M. Nixon.

In the 1960s, one of the key arguments against the Vietnam Conflict was that most of the men and women who were fighting and dying in Southeast Asian jungles were too young to vote in national elections and thus had no voice in choosing the Presidents or members of Congress who had sent them into battle. The case for the amendment was captured in the slogan "Old Enough to Fight, Old Enough to Vote." The states were no more progressive on this issue than the federal government. At decade's end, only four states had extended the vote to those under twenty-one—Hawaii (twenty), Alaska (nineteen), and Kentucky and Georgia (eighteen).

In 1970, responding to the political pressure of the anti-war movement and the demographic pressure of the maturing "baby boom" generation, Congress enacted a Voting Rights Act lowering the voting age to eighteen for federal, state, and local elections. Oregon challenged the constitutionality of the statute's coverage of state and local elections, and in *Oregon v. Mitchell,*[11] a divided Supreme Court agreed. In one of the first of many split decisions on serious constitutional issues handed down under Chief Justice Warren E. Burger, four Justices held that Congress could adopt statutes establishing minimum voting ages for federal and state elections, four Justices denied that Congress had any such power for any elections, and Justice Hugo L. Black maintained that congressional power extended to regulating qualifications (including age) for federal but not state elections—absent a constitutional amendment.

Oregon v. Mitchell posed a difficult problem for those states maintaining the traditional twenty-one-year-old limit for state and local elections. To be consistent with federal law, such states would have to keep two sets of voting records and registration—one for those who were old enough to vote in state and local elections, and one for those who were old enough to vote only in federal elections. Paradoxically, the issue of the eighteen-year-old vote was easier to solve via the amending process than by ordinary legislation in forty-eight of the fifty states.

Now a Senator, Jennings Randolph reintroduced his amendment. After brief discussion, the Senate accepted the Randolph amendment, tabling a proposal by Senator Edward M. Kennedy (Democrat–Massachusetts) to attach a provision authorizing representation for the District of Columbia in the House of Representatives. The House swiftly concurred with the Senate, and on March 23, 1971, three months after the Court's decision in *Oregon v. Mitchell,* Congress sent the proposed Twenty-sixth Amendment to the states. The needed three-fourths of the states ratified the amendment on June 30, 1971—the same day that the United States Supreme Court decided *New York Times v. United States,* the "Pentagon Papers" case (another constitutional landmark emerging from the Vietnam Conflict).[12] The adoption of the Amendment only three months after its proposal by Congress was the swiftest in the history of the amending process.[13]

THE LIMITS OF DEMOCRATIZATION

IN CONTRAST TO THE PROGRESSIVE Era and the 1960s, when the American political system was expanded to include previously excluded groups, the decade following the adoption of the Twenty-sixth Amendment marked the first time in American history that democratizing amendments were proposed by Congress yet failed to win ratification by the states. The history of the Equal Rights Amendment (ERA), proposed in 1972, and the D.C. Statehood Amendment, proposed in 1978, reveals the current limits of democratization.

The Equal Rights Amendment

Although most leaders of the women's movement rejoiced at the adoption of the Nineteenth Amendment, others recognized that the crusade's focus on the suffrage had had the unintended consequence of dissipating feminists' focus on other issues of importance to women. The women's movement split between those, such as Alice Paul, a founder of the National Woman's Party, who believed that the law should recognize full equality between men and women and do away with "special benefits" for either sex, and those, such as the socialist reformer Florence Kelley, who, having fought for decades for laws protecting women in the workplace and the home, maintained that full equality between the sexes would not be achieved by establishing "identity of treatment under the law"—although she did not indicate what, in her view, *would* suffice or, indeed, whether that goal was worth achieving.[14] Undeterred, in 1923 Paul drafted the first Equal Rights Amendment (ERA):

> Men and women shall have equal rights throughout the United States and in every place subject to its jurisdiction. Congress shall have power to enforce this article by appropriate legislation.[15]

Although the Paul Amendment (as it was known) was submitted to every Congress for the next twenty years, opposition by such groups as the National Consumers' League and labor unions combined with the resistance of conservative interests to ensure its defeat. During the next three decades, opposition to the Paul Amendment among women's groups abated, and both major political parties endorsed the proposal in their Presidential platforms starting in 1940. The parties thus recognized what Paul and her allies had always maintained—that the principle of equality between men and women deserved explicit constitutional recognition.

Conservative politicians still insisted that the Paul Amendment was dangerous because it would provide a basis to invalidate laws conferring special benefits and protections on women, such as maximum-hour statutes and immunization from the draft. They repeatedly demanded the addition of language declaring that the amendment "shall not be construed to impair any rights, benefits, or exemptions now or hereinafter conferred by law upon persons of the female sex." This "Hayden rider," named for Senator Carl Hayden (Democrat–Arizona), eviscerated the amendment and was a major obstacle to Congressional endorsement of ERA until the adoption of the Civil Rights Act of 1964.

Title VII of the Civil Rights Act, which prohibited sex discrimination in the workplace, marked a turning point in the fortunes of ERA. The courts' use of the provision to invalidate protective legislation and to mandate equal treatment for men and women removed this major obstacle to the amendment, for it was clear that protective laws were dead even without ERA. In 1970, therefore, the unions reversed themselves, and activists from feminist organizations such as the National Organization for Women (NOW) pressured Senator Birch Bayh (Democrat–Indiana) to revive ERA before the Senate Judiciary Committee.

That same year, the House seized the initiative by pulling the revised ERA out of the House Judiciary Committee and adopting it by a near-unanimous vote of 350 to 15. The Senate, meanwhile, was mired in a debate over exemptions and riders, focusing its attention on a provision that would exempt women from the draft. Noting an impending battle between feminist supporters of an unamended ERA and Senate backers of the draft exemption, Senator Bayh tried to cut off the dispute by proposing his own version:

> Neither the United States nor any State shall, on account of
> sex, deny to any person within its jurisdiction the equal protection
> of the laws.

Bayh maintained that the new wording would meet the objections of ERA's critics, and he hoped that his evocation of the equal protection clause of the Fourteenth Amendment would increase ERA's apparent familiarity—and acceptability—in the eyes of his Senate colleagues. Women's organizations rejected the substitute, however, distrusting Bayh's flexibility.

Noting the problems that enmeshed the Senate, in 1971 the House revived ERA, proposing a version that included exemption language crafted by Representative Charles Wiggins (Republican–California):

> [This Amendment shall] not impair the validity of any law of the
> United States which exempts a person from compulsory military
> service or any other law of the United States or any state which
> reasonably promotes the health and safety of the people.

Again, feminist leaders resisted the restriction on the ground that it offered no greater protection than women had already received from the United States

Supreme Court. The House ultimately rejected the Wiggins rider and once more adopted ERA, this time by a vote of 354 to 23.

When the revived ERA reached the Senate, Senator Samuel J. Ervin, Jr. (Democrat–North Carolina), chair of the Judiciary Committee's Subcommittee on Constitutional Amendments, tried to attach riders and qualifications that would have gutted the amendment, but Senator Bayh, chairman of the full committee, led his colleagues in rejecting the Ervin proposals. On March 22, 1972, the Senate finally approved ERA by a vote of 84 to 8:

> Section 1. Equality of rights under the law shall not be denied or abridged by the United States or by any State on account of sex.
>
> Section 2. The Congress shall have the power to enforce, by appropriate legislation, the provisions of this article.
>
> Section 3. This amendment shall take effect two years after the date of ratification.

As was customary with virtually every proposed amendment in the twentieth century, the Congressional resolution setting forth the text of ERA included a seven-year time limit for ratification. At first, this provision appeared overly cautious, as states seemed eager to adopt the amendment. Hawaii's legislature acted within twenty minutes of the Senate's vote; Delaware, Nebraska, and New Hampshire followed the next day; and Idaho and Iowa ratified two days after that. By mid-1973, thirty of the necessary thirty-eight states had ratified the amendment, often after brief and desultory debate and without the usual referrals to committees.

Despite this remarkable progress, several factors in the mid-1970s dissipated ERA's momentum and ultimately led to its defeat. First, the Supreme Court's *Roe v. Wade* decision (1973)[16] caused many voters to link the explosive issue of abortion rights with ERA, as both were key goals of the women's movement. *Roe v. Wade* rekindled conservative activists' strong distrust of expanding constitutional rights in an age of judicial activism. What might the Supreme Court do, they wondered, with a full-blown Equal Rights Amendment?[17] Moreover, as other Supreme Court decisions struck down laws and practices discriminatory against women, articulating an "intermediate scrutiny" standard under the Fourteenth Amendment, ERA began to seem less necessary to undecided voters and politicians.

Organized by conservative activists such as Phyllis Schlafly, a veteran of right-wing causes since the 1964 Goldwater campaign, the "Stop ERA" campaign combined skilled use of political and constituent pressure with insistent repetition of alleged horrors that ERA, interpreted by an "ultra-liberal" Court, might foster: drafting women into combat forces, unisex bathrooms, homosexual marriages, and the like. Although some supporters of ERA did maintain that women should not be excluded from combat service, and others worked for gay rights and an end to discrimination against gay men and women, the parade of horribles (a forensic tactic familiar to any law student) tainted ERA beyond repair.

The increasing polarization of the ERA debate along ideological and party lines doomed the forging of the broad consensus that any successful constitutional amendment needs. Republican state legislators retreated from their party's 1940 endorsement of ERA, stressing instead the dangers that the amendment would pose to "traditional family values" and to traditional relationships between men and women. The party's growing conservatism, and the prominent place of "Stop ERA" activists in its right wing, helped to crystallize Republicans' opposition to the amendment.

Finally, conservative opponents of ERA, well-organized at the state level, brilliantly exploited the difficulty of the amending process. Anti-ERA activists managed to persuade state legislatures in five states (Idaho, Nebraska, Tennessee, Massachusetts, and South Dakota) to rescind their ratifications—a step of dubious constitutionality which nonetheless sent a clear message to states that had not yet ratified.[18] When in 1978 Congress voted to extend the ERA deadline from 1979 to 1982,[19] opponents charged that Congress was trying to change the rules in the middle of the game, because (they insisted) ERA clearly could not win on the merits. Proponents of ERA argued in vain that Congress had the power to revise its resolution, which was distinct from the text of the amendment itself.[20]

No state ratified ERA after Indiana—the thirty-fifth—approved it in 1977 (though the Utah legislature rejected it in 1979). The original and revised deadlines elapsed without incident, and (as of this writing) Congress has not seen fit to revive ERA.

The D.C. Statehood Amendment

The ratification of the Twenty-third Amendment animated another amendment campaign—this time, for an amendment to achieve full self-government and representation in Congress for the people of the District of Columbia. An amendment was needed to set aside Article I, section 8, clause 17 of the Constitution, which placed the District under the exclusive jurisdiction of Congress. This clause gave Congress power

> To exercise exclusive Legislation in all Cases whatsoever, over
> such District (not exceeding ten Miles square) as may, by Cession

of particular States, and the Acceptance of Congress, become the
Seat of the Government of the United States, and to exercise like
Authority over all Places purchased by the Consent of the Legisla-
ture of the State in which the Same shall be, for the Erection of
Forts, Magazines, Arsenals, dock-Yards and other needful Build-
ings . . .

The federal district clause was intended to remedy the nation's lack of a fixed
capital during and after the American Revolution. Not only had the Continental
Congress moved from city to city during the war to avoid capture by the British,
but in 1783 Congress was almost taken hostage in Philadelphia by mutinying
Pennsylvania militia, whose purpose was to capture the state's lawmakers to
force them to make good on months of back pay the men had never received.
Congress left Philadelphia and by the end of 1784 had established itself in New
York City.

During the ratification controversy, Anti-Federalists alleged that the federal
district would become an impregnable fortress where the people's oppressors
would shelter themselves from the people's wrath. The Constitution's opponents also maintained that the new government's officials would lose touch with
the people they were to govern and fail to heed the effects that their policies
would have on the citizenry—charges that the Federalists indignantly rejected.

Once the Constitution was ratified, the newly elected Senators and Representatives engaged in a grim struggle to pick the site of the permanent federal district.
The capital issue had extraordinary significance for the Revolutionary generation. On the level of "pork-barrel" politics, it was a coveted prize. Cities from
Albany, New York, to Alexandria, Virginia, competed for the honor. President
George Washington, who in all other things preserved evenhanded impartiality,
promoted a site on the Potomac River (close to his home, Mount Vernon, and
to adjoining lands he owned), and he made his preference known to members
of Congress and the executive branch. Even such diehard opponents of urban
life as Thomas Jefferson sought the capital for their home states, reasoning that
the benefits of a great city might as well redound to the folks back home.[21] On
the level of principle, the site of the capital could determine the kind of nation
that the United States would become. If the capital were established in a large
city, manufacturing, commercial, and speculating interests would influence the
government; if it were sited in farming territory, agricultural interests would exert
influence.

The capital issue soon became entangled with other controversies within the
new government. In 1790, Treasury Secretary Alexander Hamilton proposed
that the federal and state debts left over from the Revolution be assumed by the
federal government, consolidated, and used as the basis of new federal securities;

traffic in debt certificates would stimulate economic growth and unite the inter-ests of the wealthy with those of the federal government. Hamilton's former ally, Representative James Madison of Virginia, led vigorous congressional opposi-tion to Hamilton's program. In the spirit of compromise, Secretary of State Jefferson and Senator Robert Morris of Pennsylvania (a backer of Philadelphia as the site of a permanent capital) arranged congressional acceptance of Hamil-ton's program in exchange for moving the capital to Philadelphia for ten years, and then establishing its permanent home on the banks of the Potomac River. The Compromise of 1790, the first great sectional compromise, resolved the capital question.[22]

The federal district disappointed those who had predicted that it would become a great center of culture, politics, and commerce. Washington City (named for President Washington after his death in 1799) remained a sleepy, hot, provincial village whose inhabitants deserted it during its muggy summers. Foreign visitors mocked the city's pretensions to greatness and the contrast between the huge marble buildings and the muddy, rutted streets. The burning of Washington in 1814 by British forces during the War of 1812 (in revenge for the Americans' destruction of York, Canada, the predecessor of Toronto) fur-ther damaged the hopes of those captivated by "Potomac fever."

Nobody expected Washington to acquire a large, permanent population inde-pendent of government officials and staffers. The two contributing factors to this explosion of growth were the New Deal and the Second World War, which brought a proliferation of government agencies charged with coordinating a massive program of economic recovery and the largest war effort in American history. Others have suggested a third factor—the invention of air-conditioning, which made it possible to have a year-round federal government on the site of what was once festering swampland.[23]

In 1788, writing in *The Federalist No. 43,* James Madison had predicted that "a municipal legislature for local purposes, derived from their own suffrages, will of course be allowed" residents of the federal district.[24] But Madison's optimism was not to be borne out by subsequent history. It was not until 1802 that Congress granted the city a charter establishing the office of mayor (to be filled by Presidential appointment) and an elected council. In 1820 Congress approved election of the mayor by direct popular vote, but democracy only held sway in the capital until 1874, when Congress responded to a procurement scandal within the District by placing its government under the direct control of House and Senate committees, who appointed a three-member board of commission-ers.[25]

By 1960, the population of Washington, D.C., numbered more than 750,000, none of whom could play any part in their own governance. The nation's capital city was a fief under the control of congressional committees, which often were chaired by conservative Southerners unsympathetic to the needs of the District's black majority. In 1966, President Lyndon B. Johnson issued an Executive Order reorganizing the District's government and giving himself the power to appoint a mayor and a council. Johnson then named Walter Washington the District's first mayor in nearly a century. In 1971, Congress also permitted the District to name a nonvoting delegate to the House of Representatives. After a decade of further struggle and lobbying by District residents, Congress enacted limited home rule, permitting the popular election of the mayor and the council and allowing the government to enact some laws but not others. Most notably, Congress prohibited the District from adopting laws to tax commuters from Virginia and Maryland, to establish procedures to select judges and prosecutors, to define the structure of the courts, and to set the maximum heights of buildings. Those laws it could pass had to lay before Congress for thirty working days, during which time Congress could overrule the legislation by resolution. And Congress still retained the discretion to revoke even this partial grant of home rule.

Because District residents regarded the limited home rule recognized by Congress as little better than the governance of the American colonies by Great Britain, they began to work for statehood for what they called "America's last colony."[26] Walter Fauntroy, the District's nonvoting delegate to Congress, lobbied his colleagues to amend the Constitution to permit the District to apply for statehood. His efforts bore fruit on March 2, 1978, when the House approved the D.C. Statehood Amendment by a vote of 289 to 127, with the Senate following suit (67 to 32) on August 22, 1978. Its terms ran as follows:

> Section 1. For purposes of representation in the Congress, election of the President and Vice President, and article V of this Constitution, the District constituting the seat of government of the United States shall be treated as though it were a State.
>
> Section 2. The exercise of the rights and powers conferred under this article shall be by the people of the District constituting the seat of government, and as shall be provided by the Congress.
>
> Section 3. The twenty-third article of amendment to the Constitution of the United States is hereby repealed.*

---

*Section 3 would repeal the Amendment making special provision for the District's participation in Presidential elections, because section 1 presumably would have given the District a number of electoral votes equivalent to its representation in the House and the Senate, thus making the Twenty-third Amendment unnecessary and potentially inconsistent.

Section 4. This article shall be inoperative, unless it shall have been ratified as an amendment to the Constitution by the legislatures of three-fourths of the several States within seven years from the date of its submission.

The residents of the District responded enthusiastically to the prospect of their enfranchisement. In 1980, a referendum approved a D.C. Statehood Initiative by a 60 percent majority. In 1981, the movement organized and elected a D.C. Statehood Constitutional Convention, which in early 1982 drafted a constitution for what its members called the State of New Columbia.[27]

But the Amendment ran into serious trouble when it reached the states. By 1981, only ten states had ratified it, ten had rejected it (four of these adopting further resolutions disapproving it), and more than a dozen other state legislatures had buried it in committee.[28]

Some opponents of the D.C. Statehood Amendment maintained that it was unconstitutional, because it directly violated the proviso of Article V that "no State, without its consent shall be deprived of its equal Suffrage in the Senate." Their argument was based on the contention that the D.C. Statehood Amendment would have conferred only "nominal" statehood on the District. Under the terms of section 2, Congress would retain control over the District's governance, thus barring the District from being considered a true state within the meaning of the Constitution. Maintaining that the Constitution created the Senate as an institution in which the states alone shall be represented, these opponents insisted that Article V requires the consent of all fifty states to permit the representation in the Senate of an entity that would be accorded only nominal statehood. Their conclusion: the Amendment would require the unanimous endorsement of the states, not the three-fourths specified by Article V.

The opponents of the Amendment suggested that there are two better solutions to the problems posed by the District. The first would be to do away with the District as a federal entity and enact a statute admitting the territory as a state, but such action might conflict with the claims of Maryland, which had ceded the territory solely for the purpose of establishing a federal district. The second would be "retrocession," a procedure by which the District would be reabsorbed by the state of Maryland. Its residents thus would become citizens of Maryland and could vote for Maryland state officials, for their own voting Representatives and Senators in the Maryland congressional delegation, and in Presidential elections conducted by Maryland. Either of these solutions might require a constitutional amendment, but it would be more narrowly drawn and thus more precise (and perhaps more acceptable) than the 1978 proposal.[29]

Like the Equal Rights Amendment, the D.C. Statehood Amendment labored under a seven-year time limit. After a flurry of state ratifications in the fall of

1978, the pace slowed considerably. By the expiration of the time limit in 1985, only sixteen states had approved the amendment; four had rejected it, and legislatures in the other thirty states showed no inclination to act on the proposal. Congress made no attempt to extend the time limit because it was built into the amendment's text, and thus beyond the power of Congress to adjust.[30]

Although theoretical arguments against the amendment were unexpectedly strong, politics and issues of race also doomed the D.C. Statehood Amendment. Not only would the District's admission as a state entitle it to one or two Representatives but it also would have two Senators—all but certainly black, in a body that had had no black members between Reconstruction and 1966, and none from the defeat of Senator Edward Brooke (Republican–Massachusetts) in 1978 until the election of Carol Moseley Braun (Democrat–Illinois) in 1992. Moreover, the domination of District politics by the Democratic party did not recommend the statehood measure to the nation's Republicans, who feared that should the District achieve the goal of statehood, its new Representatives and Senators would swell the Democratic majority in both houses. Undeterred, supporters of statehood for the District vowed to revive the amendment in later Congresses, but as of this writing they have not yet done so. The expiration in 1985 of the D.C. Statehood Amendment brought the second great wave of constitutional democratization to an ignominious, untidy end.

As would-be amendment architects struggled to democratize the Constitution, they also faced the challenges posed by the nation's highest-ranking elective office—the Presidency of the United States. Often praised as the peak expression of American democratic principles,[31] the Presidency has posed many problems for the constitutional system—and has sparked many attempts to solve those problems through the amending process. Chapter 9 examines the recurring struggle to adjust the Constitution's outline of the Presidency—to reinforce its democracy, efficiency, and responsibility.

CHAPTER 9

THE FIRST CITIZEN: ADJUSTING THE PRESIDENCY

Tho we cannot, affirmatively, tell you what we are doing;
we can, negatively, tell you what we are not doing—we never
once thought of a King.

FEDERAL CONVENTION,
"leak" to newspapers
August 1787[1]

OF ALL THE COMPONENTS OF the Constitution of 1787, the single most innovative was the Presidency. Judging by the history of the amending process, the Presidency is also the Constitution's most troublesome feature. Four of the seventeen Amendments after the Bill of Rights adjusted the Presidency. The Twelfth Amendment (whose origins are discussed in Chapter 4) and the Twenty-second Amendment were designed to rectify real or apparent defects in the process of choosing the President; the Twentieth Amendment authorized a comparatively minor change in the beginnings of Presidential and congressional terms of office; and the Twenty-fifth Amendment was intended to clarify the processes for dealing with Presidential illness and disability. As it has turned out, the Twelfth, Twenty-second, and Twenty-fifth Amendments all have sparked further controversy.

None of the four adopted Amendments—indeed, none of the thirty-three proposed by Congress to the states—would limit Presidential powers. In fact, many of the Amendments have indirectly expanded Presidential powers. Enforcement clauses in the Thirteenth, Fourteenth, Fifteenth, Sixteenth, Eighteenth, Twenty-third, Twenty-fourth, and Twenty-sixth Amendments confer power not only on Congress but also on the executive branch, which is charged with enforcing laws enacted by Congress. Demands for amendments to define and limit Presidential powers have persisted, but to little practical effect.

By focusing on the means of electing, retaining, and ousting Presidents rather than on the powers of the Presidency, the delegates to the Federal Convention established the terms and boundaries of later attempts to revise the office.[2] Wary of executive power, yet desirous of the benefits of a vigorous executive, the framers steered a cautious path in the shadow of two Georges: King George III of Great Britain and George Washington of Virginia.[3] The framers hoped to create a constitutional chief executive office that would encourage the greatness of spirit and devotion to the public good that were characteristic of George Washington—and that would guard against the corruption and arbitrariness that they associated with George III.

Both at the Convention and during the ratification debates of 1787–1788, objections to the Presidency fell into two categories. Some emphasized the dangers that executive power posed to a republican form of government, charging that a unitary executive presented a threat to liberty. Others, focusing on the office limned in the Constitution, stressed issues having to do with the selection of the President: method of election, duration in office, and reeligibility.

Thomas Jefferson, then serving as American Minister to France, thought that the problem of Presidential selection was the most troubling issue raised by the Constitution—after the lack of a declaration of rights. Prophesying to Madison that a President could be reelected, term after term, for life, Jefferson worried that the great European nations would intrude themselves into American elections, backing pro-French against pro-British candidates and corrupting the electoral process with bribery and threats of force.[4]

Still other fears emerged from the ratification controversy. The Virginia, New York, and North Carolina conventions proposed amendments prohibiting the President from serving more than two terms; New York also sought to strip the President of the quasi-kingly authority to lead the nation's armed forces in the field.[5] In August 1789, as the First Congress debated amendments, Anti-Federalist Representative Thomas Tudor Tucker of South Carolina sought to revive these amendments to Article II, but the House rejected his motion.[6] Washington's two terms as the first President (and his refusal to seek a third) reconciled the people to the institution.

Although later Presidents (including Andrew Jackson, Abraham Lincoln, Franklin D. Roosevelt, and Richard M. Nixon) have had to suffer being denounced as dictators by political opponents, these attacks almost never went beyond the President to arraign the institution of the Presidency. Rather, by a combination of custom, usage, interpretation, and concession by the other two branches of government, the Presidency has grown in power and authority to become the focus of American public life.[7]

FILLING AND REFILLING THE PRESIDENCY

As NOTED IN THE PREVIOUS section, most attempts to adjust the Presidency through Article V focus on the processes of electing the President, installing him in office, and determining when, whether, and how he must depart.*[8] By far the most discussion has focused on the Electoral College,[9] as revised by the Twelfth Amendment.

Although the framers of the Twelfth Amendment had hoped that it would resolve the outstanding defects of the Electoral College, it solved only the specific problems posed by the electoral short-circuits of 1796 and 1800–1801. In 1824, when the four fragments of the disintegrating Republican party each fielded a candidate for the Presidency, the Twelfth Amendment knocked out of contention the fourth-place candidate, Speaker of the House Henry Clay. Because no candidate amassed an electoral majority, the House had to choose among the three leading candidates—General Andrew Jackson, Secretary of State John Quincy Adams, and Secretary of the Treasury William Crawford (who was disqualified as a practical matter by a series of crippling strokes). Expressing his confidence in Adams and his loathing for Jackson, Clay threw his support to Adams. Once elected, Adams named Clay Secretary of State, touching off Jacksonian charges of a "corrupt bargain" that proved critical in Jackson's defeat of Adams four years later.[10] The three-candidate rule in the Twelfth Amendment gives any third-place or fourth-place candidate the power to decide a Presidential election, but such a problem has not arisen since 1824.

The Electoral College system has been revised only once since 1804—by the Twenty-third Amendment (discussed in Chapter 8), which added the District of Columbia to the pool of electoral votes. But Senators and Representatives have introduced hundreds (some estimate thousands) of proposed amendments to rework or abolish the Electoral College system.

Although there is a broad (and largely quiescent) consensus that the Electoral College should be replaced, no proposed amendment has succeeded in amassing the political and popular support needed to emerge from the Article V process. Rather, critics of the Electoral College regularly present their arguments against the institution, hoping to spark the broad-based constitutional and political discussion necessary to jump-start Article V. They regularly invoke several arguments against the Electoral College:

- The "wrong winner" argument is a favorite of those who would adopt a system of direct popular vote. In 1888, Republican Benjamin Harrison

---

*There have been a few suggestions to modify the system of choosing a President to take account of sectional and regional interests—for example, a recurring suggestion to prohibit two Presidents in succession coming from the same state, or proposals (discussed in Chapter 5) to rotate the Presidency among the sections. None of these has emerged from Congress.

won a majority of the electoral vote even though his opponent, incumbent President Grover Cleveland, received more popular votes (5,537,857 to 5,447,129). Though Cleveland received 90,728 more popular votes (49 percent to 48 percent) than Harrison, they were grouped in eighteen states (most of them in the South) with only 168 electoral votes; Harrison's close victories in twenty states throughout the nation gave him an electoral majority of 233. The election of 1888 is unique in American political history; it is more common to find, in elections such as 1860 (Lincoln), 1912 (Wilson), 1960 (Kennedy), 1968 (Nixon), and 1992 (Clinton), that the victor won a lopsided electoral majority with only a plurality of the popular vote. The risk that a future President might receive an electoral majority but a popular minority—a prospect that sparked speculation in 1960, 1968, 1976, 1980, 1988, and 1992—could damage the people's faith in constitutional government.[11] Defenders of the present system dismiss the prospect as remote.[12]

• The "faithless elector" argument is a relic of the early years of the Constitution, when electors were chosen to exercise their best judgment as to who should be President and Vice President.[13] In each of the elections of 1796, 1820, 1948, 1956, 1960, 1968, 1972, and 1976, one elector refused to vote for the candidate to whom he or she was pledged—a total of 8 electors out of the more than 16,000 men and women who have served as electors since 1789. Of the fifty-one jurisdictions that choose electors, only five (New Mexico, North Carolina, Oklahoma, South Carolina, and Washington) bind them to vote according to the results of the popular election and impose a penalty if the electors violate their pledge; nineteen states and the District of Columbia bind their electors but impose no penalty for violations of the pledge; and twenty-six states do not bind their electors at all. The penalties generally are fines ranging from $500 to $1,000, and at least one state provides that a "faithless elector" shall be deemed to have resigned his or her office, and that another elector will be named to cast that vote.[14]

The risk that faithless electors might thwart the will of the people has prompted two proposals. One would abolish the Electoral College, replacing it with a system of direct popular vote. The other would keep electoral votes but do away with electors; electoral votes would be cast automatically in line with the results of the popular vote in each state. Defenders of the present system contend that the faithless elector problem, never more than a minor distraction, does not warrant the abandonment of a system that basically has worked well.

• Still other opponents of the Electoral College denounce its unfairness. When a candidate carries a state, even if by one ballot, he or she wins all its electoral votes. This winner-take-all, or unit, rule does not appear in the Constitution; it is a matter of state electoral law. Critics charge that the unit rule exaggerates the majority of the successful candidate and disenfranchises the voters in that state whose votes for the defeated candidate might as well not have been cast at all. Defenders of the unit rule argue that majority rule (and minority acquiescence) is a basic American political principle, making it unnecessary and undesirable to reconfigure the Electoral College simply to soothe the minority's feelings.

Under one proposal to replace the unit rule, each candidate would receive electoral votes equal to the number of House districts he or she carried in the state; the two electoral votes representing the state's Senate seats would be awarded as a bonus to the winner of the greater number of House districts within the state. Another proposal, first and most enthusiastically advocated by Alexander Hamilton,[15] would strike a balance between the Electoral College and direct popular vote, dividing each state into electoral districts, each with one vote; a district's electoral vote would be awarded to the candidate carrying the district.

Critics of the unit rule also contend that lopsided Electoral College majorities give a President who wins a close election the misleading impression that his electoral landslide indicates a popular mandate. They point out that a President's belief in such a mandate (founded or unfounded) tempts him into rash policies that can hamstring or even destroy his Administration—for example, Franklin D. Roosevelt's 1937 proposal to "pack" the Supreme Court, or Richard M. Nixon's conduct during the Watergate affair.[16]

A principal argument for retaining the Electoral College is that its abolition would do violence to federalism in unexpected ways.[17] Were a system of direct popular vote to replace the Electoral College, modern means of communication and transportation would induce candidates to focus their efforts on the nation's most populous areas to secure the most efficient return of votes for campaign resources. Concentration on largely urban regions, such as the Northeast, Florida, Texas, and California, would ignore large parts of the country, skewing elections by failing to take account of the interests of the entire nation.[18] It is also possible, as Arthur M. Schlesinger, Jr., has suggested, that abolition of the Electoral College "would hasten the disintegration of the party system" by encouraging the growth of single-issue movements that, in turn, could capitalize on the pervasiveness of the electronic media.[19]

Every four years, the American people scratch their heads in puzzlement as they try to unravel the intricacies of the Electoral College, and every four years, Representatives and Senators introduce amendments to reform or abolish it. To date, no proposal has emerged from committee. Most observers believe that only a serious electoral dislocation, on the order of the Harrison-Cleveland election of 1888, could spur an effective campaign to do away with the Electoral College.

TURNING FROM ELECTING TO INAUGURATING the President, we come to the Twentieth Amendment, proposed in March 1932 and ratified the following January. For nearly a century and a half under the Constitution, the beginnings and endings of federal terms of office were matters of custom, not constitutional law. The traditional inauguration date of March 4 was in fact a relic of the transition from the Articles of Confederation to the Constitution. Upon receiving the news in June 1788 that nine states had ratified the Constitution (thus satisfying the condition specified in Article VII), the Confederation Congress adopted an election ordinance directing that the new government convene on the first Wednesday of the following March, which turned out to be March 4, 1789.[20] From that time forward, Presidential and Congressional terms were deemed to begin on that date.

Yet this seemingly innocuous arrangement turned out to have several unsatisfactory side effects. Because elections were held in early November and electoral votes were not counted until the middle of December, Presidents-elect had to wait more than three full months before assuming office, fostering stagnation and drift as the nation waited for the new administration to take office. At that time, government was a part-time affair at all levels. Legislative sessions lasted only a few months, and federal and state legislators grumbled about the duration of their service and the time they wasted traveling between their districts and the state and national capitals. Federal and state courts met only at stated times, and for brief sessions. A President could spend weeks or even months away from the nation's capital and the nation's business. That months elapsed between the election and the inauguration of a President may have been acceptable in the slower days of the eighteenth and nineteenth centuries, but in the twentieth century events moved at a quicker pace, and the government needed to be adaptable enough to keep up with them.

The March 4 date also created a particularly odd situation with respect to how Congress did business. Article I, section 4 of the Constitution mandated that the annual sessions of Congress begin on the first Monday in December. Thus, the Seventy-second Congress, elected in November 1930, officially began its term on March 4, 1931, but did not convene for its regular session until December 7, thirteen months after its election. Stranger still, its second session began in December 1932, after the Seventy-third Congress already had been elected. Such "lame-duck" sessions, in which politicians about to leave office (many of whom had been defeated for reelection) could pass legislation, were seen by many reform-minded Americans as an affront to democracy.

The Twentieth Amendment's abolition of lame-duck government was one of the final achievements of the Progressive movement; its architect, Senator George W. Norris (Republican–Nebraska), urged its adoption to promote efficiency and accountability in government—values that were at the core of Progressivism. The Amendment provided for the President to be inaugurated on January 20 and for Congress to begin its term and its annual sessions on January 3. Simple as these changes seem, they could not have been brought about by ordinary statute because their practical effect was to trim by two months the terms of the President, Senators, and Representatives who would be in office at the time of its adoption. Because the Constitution specifies terms of federal office as whole numbers of years, an amendment was required.

While traditionalists argued that it did not matter much that a few months elapsed between the election and the inauguration of a President, supporters of the Twentieth Amendment could cite examples from the earliest days of the republic as well as from contemporary headlines to justify its adoption. The four-month transition period in 1800–1801 between the Adams and Jefferson Administrations was rife with mischief on the part of the defeated Federalist party. During that time, Adams and the lame-duck Federalist Congress enacted the Judiciary Act of 1801, creating new federal courts and other judicial posts to which they appointed loyal members of their party. By this tactic, the Federalists sought to secure control of the national judiciary, despite their loss of the executive and legislative branches. Adams spent his last day and night as President signing commissions for these "midnight judges."[21]

More recently, the 1932–1933 transition between Herbert Hoover and Franklin D. Roosevelt (which was taking place even as the Amendment was being ratified by the state legislatures) dramatized vividly the need for the Twentieth Amendment. The repudiated Hoover, believing that he could not stave off the worsening Depression unaided, appealed to his victorious rival to join forces with him before the transition of power—much as James Buchanan had sought Abraham Lincoln's support during the "secession winter" of 1860–1861. President-elect Roosevelt, stung by what he considered the departing President's attempts to tie his hands (as Lincoln had been seventy-two years earlier), fumed that Hoover was seeking to win through manipulation what he had not been able to win at the polls—a continuation of Republican policies and a renunciation of any deviation from them.

Although the Twentieth Amendment has been nicknamed the lame-duck Amendment, half its sections were designed to resolve questions about Presidential succession, having to do with deaths of victorious Presidential and Vice Presidential candidates during the period between the election and the inauguration. Three weeks after the Amendment was adopted, a stunned nation missed by a hair's breadth the need to invoke sections 3 and 4. On February 15, 1933, President-elect Roosevelt was addressing a crowd in Miami from a parked car;

Chicago's Mayor Anton Cermak was at his side. Giuseppe Zangara, an unemployed bricklayer, fired several shots at Roosevelt to dramatize his hatred of people in authority. Roosevelt escaped unhurt, but Cermak was mortally wounded. In a testament to the unwitting foresight of its framers, the succession mechanism embodied in sections 3 and 4 of the Amendment was available to resolve the imbroglio that would have resulted had Zangara been a better shot. Had Zangara slain Roosevelt before the ratification of the Twentieth Amendment, it was unclear who would have become President on March 4; once the Amendment was in effect, Vice President–elect John Nance Garner would have become President on Inauguration Day. Fortunately for the nation, sections 3 and 4 have never been tested.

Section 3 of the Amendment also resolves what would happen if the House and Senate were to deadlock on choosing a President and Vice President should the Electoral College mechanism break down. This section empowers Congress to establish by statute the officer who shall act as President pending the resolution of a deadlock, and "the manner in which one who is to act shall be selected."

THE TWENTY-SECOND AMENDMENT, proposed in 1947 and ratified in 1951, began as what its opponents termed a backhanded posthumous attack on the memory of the only President ever to be elected to more than two terms of office, Franklin D. Roosevelt. Nonetheless, it enshrined in the Constitution the principle of rotation in office, a doctrine having its roots in the era of the American Revolution.

Rotation in office rejected a tendency that many Americans and Englishmen perceived in eighteenth-century Great Britain: a belief that offices were the personal property of those who held them, rather than trusts vested in them as long as they performed their duties with attention to the public good. Most state constitutions and the Articles of Confederation set limits on the number of times a person could be elected to a given office. For example, Article 5 of the Articles barred any delegate from serving in Congress longer than two out of any three years.

Supporters of rotation in office declared the principle necessary to liberty and free government. It would ensure that officials were obliged to experience as citizens the effects of the laws they had made and the policies they had put into effect. Moreover, the principle would prevent these officials from believing that they held their posts as of right, and would forestall the development of incumbents' interests opposed to the interests of those to whom they were in fact responsible. No one opposed the idea of rotation in office, but many Americans, including the Framers of the Constitution, believed that mandating it might force officials to return to private life just as they were beginning to master the duties and responsibilities of their posts.

The Framers concluded that repeated eligibility for a short term of office would balance the two goals they sought in designing the Presidency—a President powerful enough to administer the government and secure national objectives, yet limited enough that he would not become a tyrant or a monarch.

One of the principal focuses of the ratification debates of 1787–1788 was the supposed risk that a President could win reelection, term after term, for life, thereby fastening an elective monarchy on the American republic. However, the likelihood that George Washington would become the first President of the United States eased most citizens' minds about the potential threat that a strong President might pose to the nation's liberty.[22]

Washington was aware of the risks posed by the Presidency. At first he was determined only to serve one term, but in 1792 his two principal advisers, Hamilton and Jefferson, put aside their growing partisan animosity to persuade him to stand for a second term. Only his nonpartisan presence at the head of the government, they argued, could forestall a ruinous contest between the emerging Federalists and Republicans. Four years later, embittered, exhausted, and obdurate, Washington decided to retire to Mount Vernon and to wash his hands of politics.

Washington's rejection of a third term set a precedent that stood for nearly one hundred fifty years. Presidents Jefferson, Madison, Monroe, and Jackson endorsed Washington's precedent and adhered to it. (This, however, did not prevent anti-Jacksonian Representatives and Senators from seeking to limit future Presidents to one four-year term.)[23]

Not until 1880 did a President consider challenging the two-term tradition. Republican powerbrokers dissatisfied with President Rutherford B. Hayes sought to persuade former President Ulysses S. Grant (who had served from 1869 to 1877) to put his name forward at the Republican convention that year. Although Grant professed his interest in another term, he made only a half-hearted effort and deferred to Representative James A. Garfield of Ohio, the eventual Republican nominee. Grant probably agreed to put his name forward more because he was at a loss for anything else to do with his life than because he truly wanted to return to the Presidency.[24]

In 1912, the split in the Republican party between supporters of President William Howard Taft and adherents of former President Theodore Roosevelt resulted in the first serious test of the two-term tradition. Roosevelt had served nearly two full terms as President, having succeeded the assassinated William McKinley only six months after the Ohioan's second inauguration in 1901 and winning election on his own three years later. However, Roosevelt regarded his 1904 campaign as only his first run for the Presidency and therefore believed that his candidacy in 1912 would not violate Washington's precedent.

Charging that Taft had betrayed his legacy on reform, economic regulation, and conservation, Roosevelt challenged the incumbent for the Republican nomination. The party regulars, however, gave Taft the nomination, and a major factor in their decision was their concern about Roosevelt's temerity in contesting the two-term tradition. The indignant Roosevelt stormed out of the convention, launching the most successful third-party Presidential campaign in American history. Running on the Progressive or "Bull Moose" ticket, he denounced the Republicans for betraying the party's heritage of reform. Although he outpolled Taft in both the popular and the electoral vote, he was unable to overcome the two-term precedent, as the Democratic nominee, Governor Woodrow Wilson of New Jersey, took advantage of the Republican-Progressive split to win the Presidency.

Twenty-eight years after the Bull Moose campaign, another Roosevelt succeeded in shattering the two-term tradition. For over a year before the 1940 election, Franklin D. Roosevelt kept the nation, and the members of his party, guessing about whom he would support as his successor, giving no hint that he might consider a third term for himself. But, as the months wore on, Roosevelt decided that no sufficiently strong or popular candidate for the Democratic nomination had emerged, and the nation's place in world politics proved so threatening that he felt obliged to put himself forward.[25]

Roosevelt's candidacy stunned the nation and outraged his opponents. Republicans and anti-third-term Democrats adopted the slogan "Washington Wouldn't, Grant Couldn't, Roosevelt Shouldn't." They drew ominous parallels between Roosevelt's place in American politics and the ambitions of European dictators who had replaced democracy with personal tyranny. The Republican nominee in 1940, Wendell Willkie of Indiana, charged that Roosevelt's candidacy was an insult to the memory of George Washington and the later Presidents who had followed Washington's example. Although Roosevelt won a convincing victory, his popular vote was several million votes below the levels set by his victories in 1932 and 1936. Having exploded the two-term tradition in 1940, Roosevelt ran for a fourth term in 1944 without the same level of controversy; the campaign owed its muted tone to its timing—the closing year of the Second World War.

Two major political developments gave resentful Republicans the chance to strike a blow at their great nemesis: Roosevelt's sudden death, on April 12, 1945, and the 1946 Congressional elections, which gave the Republicans control of both the House and the Senate. In January 1947, in the first week of the first session of the Eightieth Congress, seven House Joint Resolutions were introduced calling for an amendment limiting Presidential terms. Debate was brief, sharp, bitter, and partisan; within two months, the Twenty-second Amendment, restricting all future Presidents to two four-year terms, was on its way to the states for ratification. The succeeding four years of debate was desultory, with opponents of the Amendment stressing its partisan roots and supporters insisting that it was necessary to prevent executive dictatorship.[26]

Critics of the Twenty-second Amendment focus on its partisan roots, calling it a mean-spirited Republican slap at a great Democratic President whom the party could not defeat in life. In the years since its ratification in 1951, however, the Amendment has won grudging respect from many of its former adversaries. (One reason is purely partisan: Democrats note that the only Presidents who have been blocked from repeating Roosevelt's feat have been Republicans—Eisenhower, Nixon [before the outbreak of the Watergate scandal that drove him from office], and Ronald Reagan.) The revisionist view of the Amendment has two bases.

> • The Presidency exacts a fearful strain on those who hold the office. Indeed, it may not be possible for a President to survive more than two terms. As one observer has declared, "I have talked with doctors in Washington, and they say that if the American public knew what the strain does to even the toughest, they would be horrified."[27]

> • Further, Presidents' second terms (no matter what the era or the party) have been less successful than their first terms, both before and after the adoption of the Amendment. This phenomenon makes it less likely that a President would be strong enough politically to win a third term, even if he could seek one.

Even so, there is a small but vocal movement within Congress and the academic and journalistic communities favoring the repeal of the Twenty-second Amendment.[28] Ironically, Republican advocates of repeal find themselves citing arguments by liberal Democrats who had opposed the Amendment's adoption more than four decades before.[29] Then–Representative Guy Vander Jagt (Republican–Michigan), who spearheaded this movement, introduced a succinct repeal amendment each year from 1972 to 1991.[30] But in February 1992, Representative Vander Jagt's chief of staff, James M. Sparling, Jr., observed:

> The outlook never has been all that good. Literally nothing happened to the amendment. Republicans in the House tried to promote it; President Reagan endorsed it, though he said he would not take advantage of it. As of today, it still has made no progress and it still has had no hearings. We recognize it's not exactly a burning issue. It's something a Congress might consider when there are no unemployment problems, no war and peace problems, no economic problems.

Sparling noted the strong relationship between Presidential and Congressional term limitations (an issue discussed in Chapter 10):

> The purpose of the amendment is not merely political; it's unfair to restrict the President but not members of the House and the Senate. President Reagan just made it clear that the change was desirable. In today's mood of term limitations, an awful lot of people are saying that the demand for congressional term limits suggests that the Twenty-second Amendment should not be disturbed.[31]

At the same time that Representative Vander Jagt and his allies are pursuing their dream of repeal, former Presidents Gerald R. Ford and Jimmy Carter have endorsed a proposal to amend the Constitution to limit future Presidents to a single six-year term. This amendment has been introduced 160 times in Congress since 1826 and secured the backing of fifteen Presidents.[32] Advocates of the six-year term maintain that it would free the President from the burden of tailoring policies to the needs of reelection, that it would provide greater opportunity to master the demands of the Presidency, and that it would enhance the President's credibility on policy choices, because voters would know that the President is not speaking for mere political advantage. Opponents stress the need to retain an electoral check on the President; the inducement of good performance provided by the reward of a second term; and the potential decline of presidential legitimacy that might result if the President is perceived as a "lame duck" from Inauguration Day onward. As with the attempt to repeal the Twenty-second Amendment, none of the proposals to create a single, six-year Presidential term has yet emerged from Congress.

THE TWENTY-FIFTH AMENDMENT, adopted in 1967, also responded to particular crises of the era in which it was written (the illnesses of Presidents Dwight D. Eisenhower and Lyndon B. Johnson and the assassination of President John F. Kennedy), while resolving constitutional ambiguities dating back to the origins of the document. In practice, however, the Amendment has raised more questions than it answers.[33]

The Framers of the Constitution devoted little attention to the question of what happens when a President dies or otherwise cannot carry out the duties of his office. The Convention created the office of Vice President only in its last days—and only because it could not devise a means of choosing a member of the Senate to preside over that body without costing one state half its Senate delegation. There were precedents in state constitutions for offices resembling the Vice Presidency—in particular, the office of lieutenant governor in the

Massachusetts constitution of 1780—but, unlike the Vice Presidency, these offices were vested with significant additional powers.

Vice President John Adams is famous for his many comments about the insignificance of his office; in April 1789 he plaintively asked, "*In esse* I am nothing; *in posse,* I may be everything. I pray, Gentlemen—what shall I be?" While in office, President Washington suffered two serious illnesses that terrified the nation—and Vice President Adams—but Washington recovered from both ailments.

No President died in office during the Constitution's first half century, but two Vice Presidents did—George Clinton of New York in 1812 and Elbridge Gerry of Massachusetts in 1814. Ironically, both men were regarded at the time as healthier than their President, the frail and hypochondriacal James Madison, and far more likely to outlive him than he was to outlive them. In addition, John C. Calhoun resigned in 1832, the last year of his second term as Vice President, to protest President Jackson's opposition to South Carolina's resistance to the 1828 "tariff of abominations" and to accept election as a Senator from South Carolina so that he could speak for the interests of his state. None of these matters caused more than passing concern about the vacancies in the nation's second-highest elective office.[34]

In 1841, however, the Vice Presidency moved to center stage. The previous fall, sixty-seven-year-old William Henry Harrison of Ohio became the first successful Presidential candidate of the Whig party and the oldest man elected to the Presidency up to that time. On April 4, a month after his damp and drizzly inauguration, President Harrison died—in part because of his insistence on delivering a long and ponderous inaugural address, leading his inaugural parade up Pennsylvania Avenue to the Executive Mansion, and doing his own shopping. The President's sudden death shifted public attention to Vice President John Tyler. A former Democrat from Virginia who had opposed Andrew Jackson's policies, Tyler had been named to the Whig ticket to balance Harrison.

Arguing that, upon the President's death, the office of President itself—not merely its powers and duties—passed to the Vice President, Tyler had himself sworn in as President. He then set to work with a will, using his veto to wreak havoc on the Whigs' legislative program. Although his conduct in office prompted several attempts to amend the Constitution to curtail or abolish the veto power, Tyler served out the balance of Harrison's term.[35]

The Harrison-Tyler precedent foretold what happened when seven later Presidents died in office—in 1850, 1865, 1881, 1901, 1923, 1945, and 1963. In each case, the Vice President had been selected to balance the ticket with the Presidential nominee. In all cases but two (Theodore Roosevelt and Lyndon B. Johnson), he was an obscure politician who had made little impression on the electorate: Millard Fillmore, Andrew Johnson, Chester A. Arthur, Calvin Coolidge, and Harry S Truman. On assuming the Presidency, each of these new Presidents posed surprises for supporters of his predecessor, many of them unwelcome. Virtually all of them found themselves unprepared for the burdens of the Presidency; having contributed to the election of the ticket, they had languished, neglected by the President, until fate catapulted them into prominence.[36] But only in the case of Andrew Johnson was the new President's performance so unsatisfactory that his political opponents sought not only to impeach him (see Chapter 6) but also to propose amendments to abolish the office of Vice President.[37]

In all but one instance, the President had died suddenly or after a few days, limiting the uncertainties of succession. But the shooting of President James A. Garfield in July 1881 posed precisely the questions that the Constitution did not answer. Shot while walking through a railroad station in Washington, D.C., Garfield lingered in agony for two months, dying in September. During his illness, the nation was in political limbo. It was not clear until the end that Garfield was dying; Vice President Chester A. Arthur had no idea what to do and therefore determined to do nothing unless and until the President died.

Other incidents, some of them kept secret when they occurred, posed grave questions about the Presidency and the mechanisms of Presidential succession.[38] President Grover Cleveland, informed during his second term that he had cancer of the jaw, decided that he would undergo an operation, which was performed aboard the Presidential yacht during an ostensible vacation. Nobody outside the immediate family circle, not even Vice President Adlai E. Stevenson of Illinois, was informed of Cleveland's ailment or the treatment; news of the operation was not made public until 1917, nine years after Cleveland's death.[39]

A more serious crisis unfolded in the fall of 1919, when President Woodrow Wilson suffered a series of crippling strokes. Although he recovered his mental alertness, he was paralyzed and weak. His wife and physicians screened him from the outside world—even from his Vice President, Thomas R. Marshall of Indiana, who was unaware just how ill Wilson really was. Political opponents, such as Senator Albert B. Fall (Republican–New Mexico), sought to prove that Wilson could not continue as President, though they had no clear suggestions on how to remove him short of impeachment. Charges abounded that Mrs. Wilson was the actual Chief Executive, damaging the legitimacy of executive actions during the last eighteen months of Wilson's term.[40]

In 1944, Franklin D. Roosevelt's physicians realized that the President's health was failing but decided to keep the news from him and his family. That year, Roosevelt shouldered the exhausting ordeal of a fourth Presidential campaign—not knowing that he would not serve out his term.[41] He had little contact with his running-mate, Senator Harry S Truman of Missouri, and the pattern continued during Truman's three months in the Vice Presidency. Nervous aides realized that something was wrong with "the Boss"—but kept their opinions to themselves—when, on January 20, 1945, the President had his inauguration ceremony held on the White House balcony rather than at the Capitol, the traditional site. A month later, when he returned from the Yalta conference, Roosevelt made his first public reference to his leg braces, apologizing for not standing when addressing Congress. Nonetheless, when Roosevelt died on April 12, Truman was totally unprepared for the burdens of the Presidency, and he admitted as much to the nation.[42]

Dwight D. Eisenhower learned from Truman's baptism by fire. The sixty-two-year-old former general recognized that the invention and deployment of nuclear weapons dramatically increased the importance of establishing a swift, certain, and reliable plan for dealing with issues of Presidential disability and succession. Although he and his Vice President, Richard M. Nixon of California, disliked each other,[43] they determined to avoid the problems that had beset Truman in 1945. Aided by Eisenhower's trusted adviser and first Attorney General, Herbert Brownell, Eisenhower and Nixon exchanged letters that established procedures to be followed should the President fall ill. Eisenhower also took pains to keep Nixon informed of major policy decisions and other burdens that the Vice President might have to shoulder. As a result, during Eisenhower's several major illnesses, Nixon was far better prepared than any of his predecessors to cope with the crisis.[44]

The problems posed by Eisenhower's illnesses worried many observers of the Presidency, who were not reassured by the smooth transition after John F. Kennedy's assassination in 1963, especially in light of public concern about the health of Lyndon B. Johnson, who had a history of chain-smoking and heart trouble.[45]

In this period, too, questions about the health of candidates for the Presidency began to manifest themselves at the margins of the campaigns for the White House. In 1952, for example, Eisenhower's age kindled repeated speculation about his health and his life expectancy—speculation which would have flamed into controversy had the full details of the General's health been disclosed. For example, during Eisenhower's tenure as president of Columbia University, he once pulled Professor Richard B. Morris back from crossing a street, saving him from being run over by a truck. The infuriated Eisenhower bellowed at the astonished Morris, "You idiot! Don't you realize that I have a heart condition? You almost gave me a heart attack!" Morris believed that he could not reveal this story in 1952, even given its relevance to Eisenhower's fitness for the Presidency, because he felt that he owed his life to Eisenhower.[46] Similarly, throughout the 1950s and 1960s, John F. Kennedy and his family engaged in a shrewd and successful campaign to maintain Kennedy's public persona of youthful vigor—despite his history of frail health and his long battle against the potentially fatal Addison's disease. Not only did Kennedy's campaign issue misleading press releases denying that the Senator suffered from Addison's disease but Kennedy himself misled his close aide and "official historian," Arthur M. Schlesinger, Jr.[47]

Beginning with the drawn-out illness and death of James Garfield in 1881, scholars and legislators have experimented with drafting an amendment to solve problems of succession and disability, spurred on by each subsequent episode of known Presidential disability.[48] In 1956, Attorney General Brownell appeared before a subcommittee of the House Judiciary Committee to propose a constitutional amendment that was a recognizable antecedent of what became the Twenty-fifth, but it got nowhere.[49] Only the assassination of President Kennedy was enough to galvanize Congress into action. Lawmakers realized that, should President Johnson die in office, the 1947 Presidential Succession Act provided that the next two men in line were the Speaker of the House of Representatives, seventy-two-year-old John W. McCormack (Democrat–Massachusetts) and the president *pro tempore* of the Senate, eighty-six-year-old Carl Hayden (Democrat–Arizona).

Senator Birch Bayh (Democrat–Indiana), the new chairman of the Senate Judiciary Committee's Subcommittee on Constitutional Amendments, took the lead in the effort to resolve the problems of succession and disability. In 1964, his subcommittee began extensive exploratory hearings on the possibility of an amendment.[50] Bayh declared:

> Here we have a constitutional gap—a blind spot, if you will. We must fill this gap if we are to protect our Nation from the possibility of floundering in the sea of public confusion and uncertainty which ofttimes exists at times of national peril and tragedy.[51]

Former President Truman, who more than most Americans had reason to understand what was at stake, concurred, telling the committee: "I don't think, in the enormous emergency that we would be faced with under the circumstances if the President did become disabled, that we can wait much longer in meeting the problem. We must face it and solve it."[52]

The Twenty-fifth Amendment did several things. First, it resolved the issue first posed by John Tyler's succession to the Presidency in 1841. Section 1 states that, if the President dies, resigns, or is removed from office, the Vice President becomes President. Section 2 establishes a procedure for filling vacancies in the Vice Presidency, empowering the President to nominate a new Vice President subject to confirmation by a majority vote of both houses of Congress.

Sections 3 and 4, the Amendment's most elaborate—and controversial—provisions, choreograph the steps of a complex institutional dance to be performed by the President, the Vice President, the Cabinet, and Congress in the event that the President "is unable to discharge the powers and duties of his office." Either the President, or the Vice President together with a majority of the Cabinet, informs Congress's presiding officers of the disability, in which case the Vice President takes over as Acting President. But if the President then sends word that he is not disabled (or that the disability has ended), the President may resume his office, unless the Vice President and the Cabinet (by majority vote) stick to their position that the President is still disabled. If such a conflict arises, Congress has the responsibility to determine the question—but the amendment requires a two-thirds vote of both houses of Congress to remove the President from office. (Many politicians, however, notably Representative Henry Gonzales [Democrat–Texas], have observed that sections 3 and 4 are more likely to create crises in Presidential disability and succession rather than resolve them.)

Yet the first use of the Twenty-fifth Amendment was not to resolve a problem of Presidential illness and disability, and its operations during the Watergate crisis of 1973–1974 surprised its inventors. In the fall of 1973, while President Richard M. Nixon was under legal and political siege, Vice President Spiro T. Agnew was accused of bribery and violations of federal tax laws committed while he was Governor of Maryland and during his first term as Vice President. On October 10, after lengthy negotiations with federal prosecutors, Agnew resigned his office and pleaded "no contest" to the charges.[53] Nixon then activated section 2 of the Amendment, nominating to the Vice Presidency an old friend and staunch supporter, House Minority Leader Gerald R. Ford of Michigan. After detailed confirmation hearings, Ford was confirmed by both houses of Congress and sworn in on December 6, 1973. Eight months later, on August 9, 1974, Ford took a second oath of office—the Presidential oath—following Nixon's resignation. He then nominated former Governor Nelson A. Rockefeller of New York to succeed him as Vice President; Rockefeller was confirmed and sworn in on December 19, 1974. Thus, through the end of Ford's term on January 20, 1977, the two highest elective offices in the nation were held by men who had not been elected to them.

The Twenty-fifth Amendment has been the focus of considerable controversy at least twice in the two decades since its first applications. In March 1981, after John W. Hinckley, Jr., shot President Ronald Reagan, it appeared that Vice President George Bush might have to assume the duties of Acting President under sections 3 and 4. Reagan's aides rallied around the stricken President, however, convincing the nation that he was able to function as President from his hospital bed (even though later accounts have suggested that he was far more seriously wounded than his advisers were willing to reveal).*[54] In 1986–1987, during the Iran-contra controversy, some of the President's aides considered invoking the Twenty-fifth Amendment to supplant Reagan, because of fears that he was too old and detached from the cares and responsibilities of his office. Again, Reagan and his closest advisers managed to dispel such worries.[55]

George Bush, who became President in 1989, experienced two episodes of illness. During an operation in early 1991, he followed the pattern with Vice President Dan Quayle that Reagan had followed with him, disclaiming formal use of the Amendment but using informal procedures paralleling the Eisenhower-Nixon precedents; Bush's second illness, during his trip to Japan in January 1992, was brief enough that the issue of disability never arose.

In sum, the Twenty-fifth Amendment poses at least as many questions as it answers. The experience of the Reagan Administration suggests that a President's aides may determine, for reasons of their own, to mislead the nation about the President's condition. Supposedly, indications that a President is ill might diminish his or her political effectiveness and perhaps make it more difficult for a President to resume the duties of the office once the disability has passed.

WHAT PRESIDENTS CAN AND CANNOT DO

AS THE PRESIDENCY HAS INCREASED in importance in American political life, politicians have sought to reshape the office via the amending process. But such attempts to expand, restrict, or restructure Presidential powers have been unavailing.

Demands to restructure the Presidency are closely related to uses, abuses, or failures of power by specific Presidents. When a President has moved to expand the office's powers and responsibilities, critics of Presidential power resort to constitutional remedies, charging that the President is so distorting the political process—and the constitutional framework—that ordinary politics cannot be relied on to save the constitutional system. Similarly, when it appears that the Constitution stands in the way of the President's ability to implement policies, the President's supporters maintain that a constitutional amendment is needed

---

*During the crisis set in motion by the Hinckley shooting, the Reagan Administration was unprepared to deal with issues of Presidential disability—and unwilling, for short-term political reasons, to invoke section 3. White House aide Richard Darman even seized documents prepared (pursuant to the Twenty-fifth Amendment) to give effect to a transfer of power to Bush and locked them in a White House safe.

to remedy the defect and arm the President with the powers necessary to "get things done."[56] The same political currents and pressures that give rise to such calls for amendments make it unlikely that the proposals will pass through Congress, let alone be ratified by the states, however, for a politicized amending process defeats the attempt to put together the broad consensus that is necessary for a successful amendment.

The sole serious attempt to strip the President of power via a constitutional amendment arose during the mid-1950s.[57] Senator John W. Bricker (Republican–Ohio), a silver-haired, mellifluous party stalwart who in 1944 had been Thomas E. Dewey's running-mate, repeatedly proposed amendments to limit or do away with the President's power to make treaties or executive agreements—informal accords with foreign nations that do not require the consent of the Senate to go into effect. At first, Bricker sought to write into the Constitution a vague requirement that any treaty or agreement be consistent with the Constitution before it could go into effect. His goal was to ensure that no treaty or executive agreement could have force within the United States without supporting legislation enacted by Congress. Later, he and his allies presented varying forms of his original proposal that would have given the House as well as the Senate power to exercise a congressional veto over treaties and executive agreements. At one point, Bricker rallied fifty-seven of the ninety-six Senators to his side, but skillful lobbying by the Eisenhower Administration, in consultation with the bipartisan leadership of Congress, scuttled the proposals.

Just as proposals to limit Presidential powers via the amending process have not succeeded, so, too, proposals to amend the Constitution to expand the powers of the office have not. The most celebrated of these are the repeated demands by Presidents Reagan and Bush for an amendment permitting the President to exercise a line-item veto—that is, to approve or reject portions or clauses of a bill, such as an appropriations measure, rather than the all-or-nothing veto power the President now has.

Championed by Republican members of Congress, who note that many state governors already possess this power, the line-item veto dates back to the Confederate Constitution of 1861, and to the postwar pleas of Presidents Ulysses S. Grant, Rutherford B. Hayes, and Chester A. Arthur for power to pick and choose items in omnibus appropriations bills.[58] These Presidents, and many of their successors, resented the power of the majority in Congress to "piggyback" controversial or parochial measures onto vital or popular appropriations bills. Lacking the line-item veto, Presidents face the unpalatable choice of signing bills they desire and accepting provisions they oppose, or vetoing necessary legislation to force Congress to reenact it without the unwanted baggage. Opponents of the proposal argue that it would seriously unbalance the roles of President and Congress in the legislative process.

In 1992, all three of the major candidates for the Presidency—Republican incumbent George Bush, Democrat Bill Clinton, and independent H. Ross Perot—favored the line-item veto, a rare instance of unanimity. It is not clear, at this writing, whether President Clinton will press the issue with Congress, or whether Congressional leaders will cooperate.

HOWEVER WE MAY FEEL ABOUT the conflation in the public mind of the Presidency with the whole of American government, the Presidency has become the preeminent national political institution, a unifying national symbol as compelling as Uncle Sam and the bald eagle—and its modern occupants have regarded it that way, despite ideological commitments or party affiliation.[59] Questions about the nature, structure, and functions of the Presidency go to the heart of the kind of government the American nation has, and the nature of American politics.

Implicit in controversies over how the President is chosen is a deeper question: where does ultimate authority in American politics lie? Disputes over Presidential power are at root skirmishes in the enduring conflict between the desire for an effective, vigorous executive and the fear of executive power as a danger to liberty—a conflict dating back to 1787 and beyond. The problems of Presidential disability, succession, and removal pose the risks of destabilizing the legitimacy and predictability that are vital components of American constitutional government and the rule of law. Attempts to use the amending process to alter or revise the Presidency thus raise issues of the proper definition, or redefinition, of the American character.

CHAPTER 10

ROADS NOT TAKEN:
PROPOSED AMENDMENTS
TO THE CONSTITUTION

*A customer asked a bookseller: "Have you a copy of the
[French] Constitution?" "No," the bookseller replied, "we
do not deal in periodical literature."*

NINETEENTH-CENTURY FRENCH JOKE[1]

ADMIRERS OF THE UNITED STATES Constitution cite this old French jest to illustrate what they deem a major virtue of the American constitutional system—that it has persisted, with comparatively few adjustments and additions, for over two hundred years. That the amending process has been used infrequently and only in serious cases, they maintain, is vital to the stability of the Constitution.

The Framers of the Constitution designed Article V to occupy the middle ground between too-easy change—that is, treating the Constitution as an ordinary law subject to the whims and fancies of later lawmakers—and the insuperable difficulties of the unanimity mandated by the Articles of Confederation. In over two hundred years, the Constitution has been amended only twenty-seven times; if we lump together the provisions of the Bill of Rights as one "mega-amendment," the number drops to eighteen. When compared with the more than ten thousand proposed amendments introduced in or formally recommended to Congress since 1789,[2] the chances for an amendment to be added to the Constitution are little better than one in one thousand.[3] Six other amendments have vaulted the hurdle of Congressional approval, only to fail the test of ratification by the states. Thus, the odds of an amendment surviving the Congressional gantlet are a little better than one in five hundred.[4]

Each proposed amendment represents a potential course of development of the Constitution. When Congress rejects a proposal, therefore, or when the states spurn an amendment that Congress has agreed to propose, that proposal becomes a "road not taken" by the constitutional system. These roads not taken teach valuable lessons about the evolution of American public life. Each embodies an attempt to reshape the Constitution to the nation's changing needs. As in so many other areas of constitutional law, the real challenge for would-be directors of the amending process is to persuade a sufficient number of legislators and citizens that the perceived need is substantive, immediate, and serious enough to require the use of the amending process.

Writers have played for laughs the thousands of proposed amendments. Sometimes they have proposals of their own in mind; the cartoonist Matt Groening offered a set of five proposals in 1987, two of which called "for the judicious use of canned laughter during televised congressional hearings" and "for the immediate lawful thrashing of anyone whose hourly beeper alarm watch goes off in the middle of a movie theater."[5] Also in 1987, the humorist Charlie Haas published a "Bill of Improvements" containing ten proposed amendments, including:

> AMENDMENT XXVII: Freedom of Speech shall not be granted to the Dashboards of Automobiles.
>
> AMENDMENT XXX: In their Prosecution of Grave and Sordid Crimes by Citizens, States shall have Power to reduce the Penalties for any Offenses that are not made into mini-series starring Richard Chamberlain, Elizabeth Montgomery or Both.[6]

Those who would use the amending process have often provoked humor and derision in response, as with the 1893 proposal to change the name of the nation to "the United States of the Earth."[7] Nonetheless, the proponents of these measures were not lunatics but well-meaning Americans who sought to enshrine their values in the nation's fundamental law. The prominence and recurrence of certain issues—balancing the budget, protecting (or rescinding) the right to an abortion, regulating what it means to be an American—reveal important truths about what kind of nation we wish to become. But before examining the current crusades to change the Constitution, we must first turn our attention to the most famous crusade of all: Prohibition.

"THE NOBLE EXPERIMENT": THE EIGHTEENTH AND TWENTY-FIRST AMENDMENTS

THE EIGHTEENTH AMENDMENT, KNOWN AS the Prohibition Amendment, is the most spectacular failure in the history of Article V, for it was the only constitutional amendment that provoked another, the Twenty-first, repealing it entirely.

Most Americans associate the word "prohibition" with the 1920s—with gangsters, G-men, flappers, speakeasies, bathtub gin, and the tall, gaunt, black-clad sourpuss "Old Man Prohibition" popularized by political cartoonists such as Rollin Kirby. But campaigns against intoxicating beverages date back to the earliest days of the American republic.[8] In 1788, for example, the *American Museum* magazine described Philadelphia's July 4 celebration of the adoption of the Constitution, stressing a message of temperance and virtue:

> IN HONOUR of AMERICAN
> BEER and CYDER,
>
> It is hereby recorded, for the information of strangers and poster-ity, that 17,000 people assembled on this green, on the 4th of July, 1788, to celebrate the establishment of the constitution of the United States, and that they separated at an early hour, without intoxication, or a single quarrel.—They drank nothing but Beer and Cyder. Learn, reader, to prize those invaluable FEDERAL LIQUORS, and to consider them as the companions of those virtues that can alone render our country free and respectable.
>
> Learn likewise to despise
> SPIRITOUS LIQUORS, as
>
> *Anti-federal,* and to consider them as the companions of all those vices, that are calculated to dishonour and enslave our country.[9]

Similarly, in a document dating from the early 1830s, former Presidents James Madison and John Quincy Adams joined President Andrew Jackson in declaring:

> Being satisfied from observation and experience, as well as from Medical testimony that ardent spirit, as a drink, is not only needless, but hurtful; and that the entire disuse of it would tend to promote the health, the virtue, and the happiness of the com-munity, We hereby express our conviction that should the citizens of the United States, and especially all *young men,* discontinue entirely the use of it, they would not only promote their own personal benefit but the good of our country and the world.

Temperance advocates persuaded every President through Abraham Lincoln to endorse this pledge;[10] Lincoln's decision to sign it capped more than twenty years of his commitment to encouraging temperance.[11]

The repeated linkage between the national good and the renunciation of spiritous liquors was a common theme of the temperance movement, and of its offspring, the campaign for prohibition. The career of Neal Dow illustrates how prohibition evolved from temperance. A Maine politician, Dow began as an advocate of temperance. In the mid-1840s, as he later recalled, Dow sought to rehabilitate a relative who had fallen prey to drink. Finding him a job, he went to a nearby saloon to ask the innkeeper not to serve his relative if the former inebriate fell once more to temptation. The innkeeper refused, declaring that he had a license to sell liquor to anyone he pleased and would continue to do so to support his family. Dow vowed, "With God's help, I will change all this," and in 1851 he succeeded in pushing through the Maine legislature "An Act for the Suppression of Drinking Houses and Tippling Shops," the most stringent prohibition law yet enacted. The Maine law became a rallying cry for prohibitionists on both sides of the Atlantic, and twelve states enacted similar laws (all but five of which were struck down under various clauses of those states' constitutions by 1865); Maine's statute continued on the books until 1933, when it was swept away by the forces behind the Twenty-first Amendment.[12]

While Dow became a hero to many Americans, not everyone viewed his crusade with enthusiasm. Some Americans (even the most sober and respectable) resented the idea of prohibition as an assault on American liberty. At the same time that Madison, Adams, and Jackson were able to come to rare agreement on their call for temperance, the conservative New York jurist James Kent is said to have spurned a request to sign a petition calling for the outlawing of spiritous liquors, saying, "Gentlemen, I do not get drunk, I have never gotten drunk, and I will not get drunk. But I have a constitutional right to get drunk, and that right I will not sign away!" Thus were the constitutional boundaries of the argument over prohibition defined—the desirability of encouraging sobriety versus the dangers of infringing personal liberty.

In 1872 the Prohibition party (founded in 1869 by Dow and his allies) nominated its first Presidential candidate (James Black of Pennsylvania) and included in its platform the first demand for a constitutional amendment to establish prohibition as a national policy. The Prohibition party thus sought to make prohibition a key component of the constitutional system. (The party has continued its activities ever since but has never garnered more than 2 percent of the vote.)

Other like-minded organizations, such as the Women's Christian Temperance Union (WCTU), chose to work with the established political parties, promising or withholding support for candidates based on the party's willingness to endorse their agenda. Members of the WCTU also appreciated the power of dramatic public incidents. They invaded saloons and bars, singing and praying and blocking access to liquor. The WCTU's tactics, and those of allied groups such as the Anti-Saloon League, foreshadowed the public civil disobedience practiced by the civil rights movement, opponents of the Vietnam Conflict, and prochoice and prolife activists.[13]

An argument for prohibition that grew stronger in the late nineteenth century was the supposed connection among urban saloons, political bosses, and easily manipulable immigrant voters. Prohibitionists maintained that corrupt politicians held sway in the bars and saloons of the nation's cities, exchanging favors for votes, with impressionable and befuddled immigrants as their raw material and liquor as an effective lubricant of the process. While the prohibition movement thrived in urban areas, federal and local authorities adopted and policed measures barring the sale of intoxicating beverages to Indians on the reservations; thus, prohibition became a rallying point "wherever there was a conspicuous, identifiable underclass in or near the established society."[14]

In the early years of the twentieth century, prohibition became a key element of the Progressive agenda. Two further political developments signified that a prohibition amendment might succeed: first, the admission of twelve Western states to the Union, nearly all of which were "dry" and Progressive, and, second, the congressional reapportionment of 1910, which increased the power of rural (and "dry") districts in national politics.[15] American participation in the First World War helped spur the spirit of national sacrifice. The demands of the war effort for such staples as grain and sugar made it imperative to rechannel raw materials from the manufacture of liquor to the nourishment of the people at home and the soldiers abroad.

In 1919, therefore, the United States was ripe for a prohibition amendment—a measure first proposed in the Senate in 1876 and revived, unsuccessfully, eighteen more times before 1913. In the Sixty-third Congress (1913–1915), fourteen resolutions called for an amendment abolishing the liquor traffic; twelve prohibition proposals were introduced in the Sixty-fourth Congress (1915–1917), and thirteen were submitted in the Sixty-fifth Congress (1917–1919)—thirty-nine attempts in only six years.[16]

Under the firm and dexterous prodding of the godfather of constitutional Prohibition, Wayne Wheeler of the Anti-Saloon League, the Sixty-fifth Congress mustered the political muscle and organization to act on a national prohibition amendment. In its debates over the amendment, introduced (for the fifth time in his career) by Senator Morris Sheppard (Democrat–Texas), supporters of national morality confronted defenders of individual liberty.

Prohibition pitted two key Progressive goals against each other—democracy versus virtue. Opponents charged that the proposal was undemocratic, pointing out that an amendment could be ratified by thirty-six states having an aggregate population nine million fewer than that of the other twelve states. Advocates retorted that they were only using the procedures devised by the Founding Fathers and insisted that the amendment had strong support throughout the population.

Senator Warren G. Harding (Republican–Ohio) tried to slow the process with a motion to add a clause to the proposed amendment requiring that it be ratified by January 1, 1923—a deadline that was relaxed, at Sheppard's suggestion, to seven years from the date the amendment was proposed to the states. Noting that all previous amendments had been adopted within that time, advocates of the measure agreed to the inclusion of a time limit—even though the noted Progressive Senator William E. Borah (Republican–Idaho) insisted that any time limit would be unconstitutional because Article V did not require one. Thus, on December 18, 1917, Congress proposed the Amendment; within thirteen months, on January 29, 1919, the Secretary of State declared it ratified by the necessary thirty-six states; eventually, over 80 percent of the legislators of forty-six states would vote to adopt the Eighteenth Amendment. And, on January 16, 1920, pursuant to the year delay mandated by the opening clause of its first section, the Eighteenth Amendment went into effect. Harding's attempt to set an impossible time limit had failed.[17]

Following the ratification of the Eighteenth Amendment and the enactment in 1919 of the Volstead Act to enforce it, an unlikely alliance of liquor and beer manufacturers, "personal liberty leagues," and constitutional scholars joined forces to resist the Prohibition Amendment in the courts. Even after ratification, the coalition argued that federal courts could declare a proposed amendment unconstitutional.

The seven cases consolidated by the Court as the *National Prohibition Cases* pitted an extraordinary array of legal talent against one another, including half the state attorneys general in the Union. The states of Rhode Island and New Jersey brought suit in the Supreme Court itself; the other five cases were appeals from applications for injunctions against enforcement of the Eighteenth Amendment and the Volstead Act. On June 1, 1920, the Supreme Court ruled both the Eighteenth Amendment and the Volstead Act constitutional. The result was unanimous, though several Justices submitted concurring opinions. The majority agreed with Justice Willis Van Devanter's holdings that the Amendment had been validly adopted, that the subject of Prohibition was within the scope of the amending process authorized by Article V, and that the Volstead Act was appropriate legislation to achieve an authorized constitutional objective.[18]

Historians disagree on how effectively Prohibition was enforced. In early 1921, in the wake of the ratification of the Nineteenth Amendment, President Warren G. Harding appointed Mabel Walker Willebrandt as an assistant attorney general charged with overseeing enforcement of the Volstead Act.[19] Acclaimed as a tireless enforcer and damned as a "dry" zealot, Willebrandt vainly tried to combat the two leading obstacles to successful prohibition: public indifference and competition between the Justice Department and the Treasury Department's inefficient, unprofessional Prohibition Unit. In 1929, after she left government, she explained to her parents:

> One hard thing about my service has been that so much of it
> is like the little boy who stood for hours with his arm in the hole
> in the dike. I've *prevented* floods of wrong things, but it's a wearing
> way to be a "hero"![20]

For every cask of beer or liquor axed into kindling or spilled down sewers, perhaps two or three found their way to eager customers. At the same time, critics of Prohibition enforcement focused on what they deemed widespread and blatant violations of civil liberties and individual rights.[21]

Prohibition received general lip-service in public—and was defied or ignored in private. Lawyers, judges, and scholars fretted that the gulf between theory and practice threatened the rule of law. The noted journalist H. L. Mencken observed that Southern voters would vote dry as long as they could stagger to the polls. Federal courts were inundated with thousands of cases growing out of the enforcement of Prohibition, including some, such as the wiretapping case *Olmstead v. United States,*[22] that were to have profound effects on such constitutional issues as the right of privacy.

At the beginning of the 1920s, Senator Sheppard grandly proclaimed, "There is as much chance of repealing the Eighteenth Amendment as there is for a hummingbird to fly to the planet Mars with the Washington Monument tied to its tail."[23] By 1929, however, thirty proposed repeal amendments had been introduced in Congress,[24] a countermovement spurred by changing political conditions. These included the growing shift of the nation's population to the cities, where Prohibition had always been unpopular; general recognition that enforcement of Prohibition had become a ghastly failure; the evils of the speakeasy (and of the Amendment's creation of a nation of lawbreakers); and the Great Depression's highlighting of the severe economic impact of Prohibition. By the 1932 Presidential election, it appeared likely that a nationwide repeal movement could succeed, especially after the Democratic party endorsed repeal in its national platform.

Again, the coalition that had sought to block the Eighteenth Amendment reassembled. This time, however, its prospects were rosy, and advocates of repeal knew it.[25] Led by the patrician Voluntary Committee of Lawyers organized by the noted Philadelphia attorney Joseph H. Choate, Jr., the coalition had spent years softening up Representatives and Senators and orchestrating public, professional, and academic opinion to support a repeal amendment.[26] Even the Wickersham Commission Report (1931), which opposed repeal of either the Eighteenth Amendment or the Volstead Act, provided repeal advocates with a detailed and devastating analysis of the impossibilities of enforcement.[27]

The longest, most elaborate debates on the proposed repeal amendment took place in the Senate in January and February 1933. Senators contrasted the evils that Prohibition was intended to solve with the evils that it had brought in its wake. Senator Joseph W. Robinson (Democrat–Arkansas) fought repeal, prophesying "the return of the American saloon with all its evils." In response, Senator Millard Tydings (Democrat–Maryland) mocked the Eighteenth Amendment:

> Prohibition enforcement! Temperance! Morality! Where is it under the aegis of the eighteenth amendment? Where are the gains? Where are they—with the young? With the women? Elimination of the saloon and substitution of the speakeasy? The crime, the murder, the graft, the corruption, the hypocrisy of men who occupy the highest legislative positions in the gift of this Republic? Are there any Senators in this Chamber who have violated the eighteenth amendment or the Volstead Act? Are there any Representatives in the other Chamber who have violated the eighteenth amendment? I do not say there are. Senators themselves know the answer to my question; and if this law cannot be observed in those places, in God's name, where can it be observed?[28]

A unique feature of the repeal movement was its change, for this occasion only, of the method by which states could ratify an amendment proposed by Congress. Recognizing that it might be political suicide for a "dry-state" legislator to vote for repeal, advocates of repeal urged that the Amendment be submitted (as Article V authorized) to specially elected ratifying conventions in each state. This shift in strategy represented a turnabout in amendment politics. Opponents of the Eighteenth and Nineteenth Amendments had sought without success to have them submitted to state ratifying conventions precisely because they believed such conventions *less* likely than the state legislatures to ratify proposed amendments. In this case, however, proponents of repeal believed that it would be easier to get special conventions to approve the Amendment—and they were right. The Twenty-first Amendment, proposed on February 20, 1933, was ratified less than a year later, on December 5. Attempts by "dry" forces to use litigation to stall or block the Amendment were as unavailing as attempts by the "wet" forces to use litigation to impede the progress of the Eighteenth Amendment had been, thirteen years earlier.[29]

The tactics used by supporters and opponents of the Eighteenth and Twenty-first Amendments would recur, time and again, in later amendment fights, most notably those over amendments designed to mold individuals' moral values and private conduct. In addition, both advocates and opponents of "morality" amendments would seek to draw appropriate and useful conclusions from the nation's experience with Prohibition. Those favoring "morality" amendments invoked an honorable strand of American political argument. Maintaining that private morality is closely linked to public virtue, which is vital to the preservation of American liberty and democracy, they concluded that such "noble experiments" as Prohibition are not only desirable but necessary. Their adversaries cited the dismal failure of the Eighteenth Amendment's attempt to write an enforceable rule of moral conduct into the Constitution, stressing the Amendment's serious and lasting damage to public willingness to obey the law; they prophesied that any comparable effort to enlist the Constitution in a moral crusade was likewise doomed to fail.

THE ORPHANS OF THE AMENDING PROCESS

IN ADDITION TO THE FOUR unratified amendments already discussed,* Congress has proposed two other amendments that failed the test of ratification by the states. The first was designed to strengthen and extend a statement of principle already present in the Constitution, the second to overturn a decision of the United States Supreme Court blocking federal and state legislation to combat a serious social problem.

The 1810 proposal would have supplemented Article I, section 9, clause 8 of the Constitution, which provides:

> No Title of Nobility shall be granted by the United States: And no Person holding any Office of Profit or Trust under them, shall, without the Consent of the Congress, accept of any present, Emolument, Office, or Title, of any kind whatever, from any King, Prince, or foreign State.

Although the people were committed to the principles of republicanism and the rejection of European ideas of aristocracy and nobility,[30] nervous lawmakers believed that ideas of nobility exercised a pernicious, seductive power. In 1788, the ratifying conventions of four states demanded amendments either forbidding Congress from granting consent to a citizen's acceptance of a title of nobility or striking the phrase "without the Consent of the Congress." Attempts to revive these proposals during the First Congress's discussion of the Bill of Rights failed to gather any support.[31]

---

*The 1789 Reapportionment Amendment, the 1861 Corwin Amendment, the 1972 Equal Rights Amendment, and the 1978 D.C. Statehood Amendment.

But, on May 1, 1810, Congress proposed an amendment strengthening the ban on titles of nobility, with only five Senators and three Representatives voting against the proposal:[32]

> If any citizen of the United States shall accept, claim, receive or retain any title of nobility or honour or shall, without the consent of Congress, accept and retain any present, pension, office or emolument of any kind whatever, from any emperor, king, prince or foreign power, such person shall cease to be a citizen of the United States, and shall be incapable of holding any office of trust or profit under them, or either of them.

The origins of this proposal are a minor mystery of American constitutional history. Neither the record of debates in Congress nor the major newspapers of the period cast any light on its purposes or the motives of its supporters. Historians have suggested two possible explanations:

First, apprehension was widespread, especially in Federalist-dominated New England, that the French empire of Napoleon I might exert a dangerously corrupting influence on American life. Jérôme Bonaparte, a brother of Napoleon, had come to the United States and conducted a liaison with a Baltimore prostitute named Betsy Patterson, whom he made pregnant. Federalists, seizing on the scandal of the Bonaparte-Patterson relationship, charged that Bonaparte would attempt to secure the election of his illegitimate son to the Presidency. Although Federalists in Congress offered the amendment to embarrass Republican President James Madison, the Republicans endorsed it, declaring, "It can do no harm."[33] Second, the amendment was another manifestation of American nativism and resentment against foreigners and foreign countries—feelings that achieved special virulence during the Napoleonic Wars in Europe and just before the War of 1812.[34]

Whether a political maneuver or a powerful expression of nativist prejudice, the amendment fell only one state short of ratification. Ironically, in a mirror-image of the problems plaguing the Eleventh Amendment (which was adopted in fact three years before it was declared adopted in law), Congress and the American people erroneously assumed that the "titles" amendment had been ratified. The manual prepared for the Fifteenth Congress (1817–1819) listed it as part of the Constitution. Confusion over the listing sparked a congressional investigation, which confirmed that the upper house of South Carolina's legislature had rejected the proposal as unnecessary. Even so, in some nineteenth-century histories of the United States and editions of the Constitution, this "Article XIII" appeared as a valid part of the Constitution.[35]

The other failed amendment—known as the Child Labor Amendment—was offered in 1924 to deal with a practice that nobody in 1787–1788 would have defined as a pressing national problem. Throughout the late nineteenth and early twentieth centuries, Progressive reformers agitated for national, state, and local action to protect the rights of children employed in factories and mines. Often laboring under nightmarish working conditions, paid minimal wages, and subject to serious risks of maiming and disfigurement, children were the invisible work force. Although the practice of child labor originated in New England, it spread after the Civil War to the South and the West, with the growth of industrialization.

Opponents of child labor charged that allowing children to work blighted their lives, wrested jobs from adult workers, seriously depressed the scale of wages paid in many industries, and conferred an unfair economic advantage on states that permitted child labor over states that rejected it. Defenders of the practice maintained, first, that if children did not work, their families would be deprived of valuable extra income; and, second, that work strengthened children's character and self-reliance. Defenders of child labor denounced government measures prohibiting the practice as a paternalistic or even socialistic infringement on familial privacy.[36]

In 1906, Progressives organized a National Committee on Child Labor to combat the practice, securing widespread support in Congress. The influential Senator Albert Beveridge (Republican–Indiana) spent several days in 1906 reading into the *Congressional Record* reports of conditions under which children were forced to work, supporting statistics and other data, and statutory proposals to outlaw the practice. Ten years later, on September 1, 1916, Congress enacted a measure proposed by Representative Edward Keating (Democrat–Colorado) and Senator Robert Owen (Democrat–Oklahoma) that barred from interstate commerce goods manufactured by children.

The day before the statute was to take effect, the U.S. District Court for the Western District of North Carolina enjoined its enforcement. In 1918, the Supreme Court upheld the injunction; by a vote of 5 to 4, *Hammer v. Dagenhart* invalidated the federal statute as a violation of the limits on the congressional power to regulate interstate commerce.[37] Shaken by this decision, Congress and the reformers tried a different tactic: imposing a federal tax on the profits of industries employing child labor. But the Court struck down this statute as well, by a vote of 8 to 1.[38] The Court's decisions posed the issue in its starkest form: either Congress must give up its attempts to outlaw or penalize child labor or it must use the amending process to establish an unambiguous power to do so.

On June 2, 1924, Congress answered the challenge, proposing a constitutional amendment to overturn the Court's decisions:

Section 1. The Congress shall have power to limit, regulate, and prohibit the labor of persons under eighteen years of age.

Section 2. The power of the several States is unimpaired by this article except that the operation of State laws shall be suspended to the extent necessary to give effect to legislation enacted by the Congress.

This Amendment was the culmination of six years of agitation within Congress and without, including sixty attempts to introduce amendments to the Constitution to set aside *Hammer v. Dagenhart.*[39] Supporters of the Amendment cited 1920 census figures showing that there were over one million children between ten and fifteen years of age working in the United States. Opponents charged that the number was half what it had been in 1910; because the practice was swiftly dying out, they declared, there was no need to amend the Constitution to prohibit it. Supporters disputed their claims, retorting that the 1920 census reflected the effects of the tax on industrial profits from child labor (which had not yet been invalidated by the Court); the number of children working in 1924 probably would be much larger.

Senators opposing the proposal railed against the prospect of "an imperial government at Washington, whose territory will be divided into what might be termed Provinces, instead of what we have known as sovereign states." They also cited lists of notable citizens who opposed the Amendment—including the remarkable alliance of James Cardinal O'Connell, Archbishop of Boston, and President A. Lawrence Lowell of Harvard University. Still other arguments deployed against the Amendment focused on the experience of Prohibition— which dramatized to the nation the dismaying spectacle (or so the Amendment's opponents charged) of fundamentalist Protestants fastening narrow, parochial views on the rest of the nation.[40] Finally, opponents demanded that the Amendment be submitted not to the state legislatures (as was the case with all previous amendments) but to popularly elected ratifying conventions, which supposedly would be free from political influence—an ironic position, considering the political clout they were able to mobilize against the Amendment within the state legislatures.

Despite ratification by twenty-eight states, the combination of arguments and the powerful alliance of otherwise disparate groups—Southern mill owners, the National Association of Manufacturers, patriotic organizations, and leading members of the Roman Catholic hierarchy—derailed the Child Labor Amendment. By February 1, 1925, thirteen states had declined to adopt the Amendment, making ratification impossible unless one of those states changed its vote. In 1938, five years after the rise of the New Deal, Congress turned back to using the lawmaking process to regulate conditions of labor, adopting the Fair Labor Standards Act (1938), which the Supreme Court upheld in 1941,[41] thereby overturning *Hammer v. Dagenhart.* The Amendment proposed so hopefully in 1924 had become irrelevant.

No OTHER AMENDMENT HAS YET emerged from Congress. But examining the most noteworthy of the more than ten thousand amendments proposed since 1789 enables us to chart how different groups have sought to reshape the nation through Article V—whether by remodeling the nation's government, by revising or expanding the codified ideals of the republic, or by using the amending process to overturn a particularly unpopular or controversial interpretation of the Constitution by the Supreme Court.

Recently, politicians at all levels have shown increasing willingness to invoke the amending process to solve pressing problems beyond the reach of the normal political process. Opponents denounce such attempts as cynical evasions of hard political choices. The most noteworthy of these are the campaigns for amendments to require a balanced federal budget and to impose term limits on members of Congress.

BIDS TO MAKE GOVERNMENT "RESPONSIBLE"

ON JUNE 11, 1992, THE House of Representatives faced the latest, and perhaps the most serious, eruption of a perennial constitutional issue: the Balanced Budget Amendment. Of the alternatives before the Representatives, that framed by Representative Charles W. Stenholm (Democrat–Texas) had amassed 277 sponsors and seemed most likely to be adopted.

Stenholm's amendment did not let the President or Congress off the hook, recognizing that both the executive and legislative branches had to assume responsibility for the budgetary process. The proposal bristled with technicalities and terms of art, reflecting its author's ingenious attempts to cover all contingencies. Whatever escape hatches the proposal included were themselves hedged about with provisos and threshold requirements:

> Section 1. Total outlays for any fiscal year shall not exceed total receipts for that fiscal year, unless three-fifths of the whole number of each House of Congress shall provide by law for a specific excess of outlays over expenditures by a rollcall vote.
>
> Section 2. The limit on the debt of the United States held by the public shall not be increased, unless three-fifths of the whole

number of each House shall provide by law for such an increase by a rollcall vote.

Section 3. Prior to each fiscal year, the President shall transmit to the Congress a proposed budget for the United States Government for that fiscal year, in which total outlays do not exceed total receipts.

Section 4. No bill to increase revenues shall become law unless approved by a majority of the whole number of each House by a rollcall vote.

Section 5. The Congress may waive the provisions of this article for any fiscal year in which a declaration of war is in effect. The provisions of this article may be waived for any fiscal year in which the United States is engaged in military conflict which causes an imminent and serious threat to national security and is so declared by a joint resolution, adopted by a majority of the whole number of each House, which becomes law.

Section 6. The Congress shall enforce and implement this article by appropriate legislation, which may rely on estimates and outlays.

Section 7. Total receipts shall include all receipts of the United States Government except those derived from borrowing. Total outlays shall include all outlays of the United States Government except those for repayment of debt principal.

Section 8. This article shall take effect beginning with fiscal year 1998 or with the second fiscal year beginning after its ratification, whichever is later.

President George Bush lobbied Congress vigorously to support the amendment, building on the eight-year campaign of his predecessor, Ronald Reagan, who emerged from retirement to endorse the measure yet again. They and their allies, such as the House minority whip, Representative Newt Gingrich (Republican–Georgia), insisted that it was necessary to write the principle of a balanced budget into the nation's fundamental law.

On the day of the vote, Representative Robin Tallon (Democrat–South Carolina) paced back and forth outside the House chamber, his head down, studying two statements he and his aides had prepared for that day's debate. One statement endorsed the Stenholm proposal—the other denounced it. Other Representatives, including at least one cosponsor of the amendment, had switched their stands two or three times in the week preceding the vote. As one complained: "I've been all over the place. I can't count how many times I've changed my mind in the past couple of days."[42]

As the House agonized over the amendment, a fierce lobbying campaign for and against it raged in the corridors of the Capitol and the House and Senate Office Buildings. Representatives from such organizations as the National Taxpayers Union, supporting the amendment to ease the burden on middle-class and working-class taxpayers, crossed rhetorical swords with the AFL-CIO, public employees' unions, the American Association of Retired Persons, and Common Cause, who were intent on preserving public services from major reductions. The lines seemed to be clear, but not always: the National Association of Manufacturers and the National Association of Small Businesses, which had long campaigned for the amendment, discovered that their longtime ally the U.S. Chamber of Commerce had just come out against it, on the grounds that it might result in higher taxes on business.[43]

Proponents drew analogies between deficit spending and alcoholism, suggesting that only a constitutional amendment could bring the spending-drunk federal government to its senses.[44] They also pointed out that forty-three states had constitutional provisions limiting the growth of their debts and that thirty-nine state constitutions mandated balanced budgets.[45] Furthermore, they argued, the amendment would eliminate what they deemed an unfair congressional advantage over the President in the budgetary process.

Constitutional scholars and economists had reached a consensus that the amendment would do no good and could do much harm.[46] Nonetheless, Stenholm and his allies pointed out, more than three-fourths of the American people favored adding a balanced-budget amendment to the Constitution.[47]

ALTHOUGH PROPONENTS OF A BALANCED-BUDGET amendment have claimed antecedents dating back to Thomas Jefferson,[48] the controversy truly began in the twentieth century, once the United States had become a world power. In 1921, Congress and the executive branch created an independent government agency, the Bureau of the Budget, entrusted with the task of preparing the federal budget. This institution evolved into the Office of Management and Budget (OMB), the principal organ of the executive branch that deals with Congress in framing each year's federal budget. Although the OMB was supposed to professionalize the budgetary process and keep it under nonpolitical control, the record of the past twenty-five years tells a different story.[49]

The federal deficit has become a commonplace of American public life. The last time the United States had no budget deficit was Fiscal Year 1969, when the federal government had a $3.2 billion surplus. Since then, deficits have burgeoned into the hundreds of billions of dollars. At the same time, balanced-budget amendment proposals have proliferated, especially among Republicans, who see them as a means to rein in the federal government's expenditures on what they deem wasteful programs.

Observers of the budgetary process agree that, because political benefits from supporting specific spending programs are so high, and political risks of tolerating deficit spending are so low, there has been no strong political incentive to assume responsibility for the budget process. Balancing the budget thus becomes "a visible, but unrealized, second priority." As a result, support for a requirement that the budget be balanced has grown side by side with exponential growth of federal deficits.[50]

Would a balanced-budget amendment work? Those who support it point out that congressional attempts to solve the problem through a statute have failed. In 1978, Congress enacted a bill offered by Senator Harry F. Byrd, Jr. (Republican–Virginia) that declared: "Beginning with fiscal year 1981, the total budget outlays of the Federal Government shall not exceed its receipts."[51] Byrd's statute had no effect on the deficit problem. Seven years later, Congress enacted the Balanced Budget and Emergency Deficit Reduction Act, known as the Gramm-Rudman-Hollings law after its sponsors, Representative Phil Gramm (Republican–Texas), Senator Warren Rudman (Republican–New Hampshire), and Senator Ernest F. Hollings (Democrat–South Carolina). This statute established an elaborate system of automatic budget-cutting procedures and devices to achieve a balanced budget.[52] But in *Bowsher v. Synar* (1986),[53] the Supreme Court declared these procedures unconstitutional. Despite further tinkering by Congress, the statute has not met its authors' goals.

In 1982, 1986, and again in 1990, Congress attempted to write a balanced-budget amendment or to begin the process to authorize its framing, but each time the vote fell short of the two-thirds requirement specified in Article V.[54] Congress's repeated failure to meet the supermajority requirement provides an ironic echo of the argument that the balanced-budget amendment would be undemocratic. One sharp battle has focused on where the balance between the President and Congress in the budgetary process should be. Opponents of an amendment argue that the proposed supermajority requirements for tax increases, deficit increases, and deficit spending would give the President and two-fifths plus one of either chamber of Congress a lock on the budgetary process, frustrating democratic decision-making.

The greatest risk seen by critics of the proposals before Congress (more than thirty versions were introduced in the One Hundredth Congress alone) is that a balanced-budget amendment would embroil federal courts in the budgetary process, which is supposed to be the province of Congress and the Presidency. Members of Congress doubt that the courts should assume this role, and federal judges are skeptical that the courts could do so. Former Judge Robert H. Bork has predicted that "hundreds, if not thousands, of lawsuits" would arise from such an amendment, "many of them on inconsistent theories and providing inconsistent results." And, Bork has added, the Supreme Court's resolution of the first crop of lawsuits would take so long that dozens more lawsuits, challenging subsequent budgets, would continue to clog the judicial system.[55]

In June 1992, Stanley Collender, director of federal budget policy for Price Waterhouse, pointed out another problem with enforcing the amendment: under present federal law, no person would have "standing" to bring suit to compel Congress to obey the amendment. If the courts could not enforce it, then the amendment would have no teeth, and its failure would breed contempt for the Constitution and the rule of law—again echoing the disaster of constitutional Prohibition. Collender concluded, "This whole effort is nothing but a scam."[56]

As DEBATE DRONED ON IN the House, the Senate leadership made clear its readiness to oppose the amendment. Senate President *pro tempore* Robert C. Byrd (Democrat–West Virginia), who vowed to fight the 1992 Stenholm amendment, observed, "What we really need is a constitutional amendment that says, 'There shall be some spine in our national leaders.' "[57] (Some Senators worried privately that Byrd's stand would persuade some undecided Representatives to support the Stenholm proposal; this politically advantageous, guilt-free vote would saddle the Senate with the politically unpopular task of defeating the measure.)

Across the Capitol, as Representative Tallon struggled to make up his mind, he recalled a conversation he had had with President Bush: "I told the President we both need to know what needs to be done to balance the budget and asked him what he was going to do about entitlements." The President's sole answer was a note that read, "Robin, do the right thing." Tallon exclaimed in frustration: "[T]here was not the wisp of a plan between the President and Congress to actually make the hard choices, to do the heavy lifting, to balance the budget."[58]

When the House voted, 433 Representatives were on the floor, only one short of perfect attendance. (The Speaker, by custom, does not vote except to break a tie.) The vote was 280 to 153, a sizable majority but 9 votes short of the two-thirds required by Article V. Shaking his head, Representative Tallon was among those voting no.

Once the House failed to approve the balanced-budget amendment, public interest subsided. But the failure of the Stenholm proposal took place against a background of increasing public disgust with the doings of their elected officials—and, perhaps, declining public confidence in the constitutional system.[59] The deficit issue continued to cast an ominous shadow over American politics, and supporters of the balanced-budget amendment vowed to revive it.

IN THE EARLY YEARS OF Congress, the turnover rate was high; for example, James Madison's retirement from the House in 1797 after four two-year terms marked the close of one of the most durable legislative careers in the early republic. By the standards of the 1990s, Madison's eight years in the House would barely have given him time to get his feet wet.[60]

As an increasing number of Senators and Representatives racked up careers of two, three, or even four decades of service, and as Democratic control of the House stretched unbroken over more than thirty years, Republicans cast about for ways to break the Democratic stranglehold on the national legislature. At the same time, congressional scandals in the 1970s and 1980s provoked an increasing number of citizens to wonder whether the nation's legislators were too removed from their constituents, too comfortable in their secure incumbency, too cozy with the capital's teeming corps of lobbyists and influence-peddlers, and too prone to view their posts in Congress as theirs by right.[61] Moreover, controversial decisions of the Supreme Court reminded Americans that federal judges held their posts "during good behavior"—which, because of the difficulty of the impeachment process, meant that judges could serve for life. With the Twenty-second Amendment limiting Presidential terms of office as a useful model, critics of the federal government began to drum up support for a constitutional amendment setting term limits for federal legislators and judges.

Public discontent with elected officials exploded when, on September 18, 1991, a miniscandal exposed the sloppy management of the "bank" maintained by the House of Representatives for its members. Over two hundred Representatives had "bounced" checks drawn on the House credit union. Some had blundered only a few times for small amounts, as a result of the inefficiency of the bank's administrators, but others had written hundreds of overdrafts, equaling or exceeding their annual salaries. The scandal touched off a full-scale spasm of public anger at "the people's branch." Political commentators such as George F. Will prophesied that the House bank scandal would spur a popular movement to amend the Constitution to impose term limits on Senators and Representatives, and the Bush Administration swiftly pointed out that the President and Vice President supported the proposal.[62]

The furor over the House bank scandal fed a widespread anger with government that cut across all points of view, party loyalties, racial lines, and classes:

> [O]fficeholders comprise a career elite whose lifetime political preoccupation has separated them from most people. . . . There is something about the image of the entrenched congressional incumbent, immersed in politics as his life's work and impregnable in an elected office that pays $125,000 a year, that challenges some fundamental American notions of democracy and fairness.[63]

Opponents of the measure pointed out that, just as the balanced-budget amendment represented an attempt by Congress to evade its responsibility, voters were seduced by term-limit proposals into evading theirs. The surest cure for an incumbent staying in office too long, they argued, was for the voters to throw him or her out. In a complex system which took years to understand, what point was there in forcing a legislator to retire just as he or she mastered the job? Even if the problem is that professional politicians are out of touch with their constituents, it is no solution to "exchange one crew of professionals for another." In response, term-limit advocates reject their opponents' emphasis on the complexities of modern government—and the need for experienced political professionals to cope with them—as smokescreens designed to dissuade ordinary citizens from meeting the challenge of self-government. Term limits, they insist, actually would increase voters' responsibility by breaking the insidious cycle of incumbency and political careerism that removes government from the control of the electorate. Citizen-legislators (who, they maintain, would be fostered by term limits) would be immune from the pressures of lobbyists for special interests, the tyranny of unelected legislative staffers, and the seductive pleasures and perquisites of incumbency. Finally, they cite the principle of rotation in office, a basic tenet of constitutional thought in the era of the American Revolution, as the theoretical grounding for a term-limit amendment.[64]

Yet again, however, the record of the modern term-limit controversy bears out an important principle at the heart of the amending process: a successful amendment campaign requires a sustained consensus that a problem exists which is not readily fixed by anything short of an amendment. As the 1992 Congressional primaries weeded out many of the most vulnerable check-writing Representatives, and as dozens of Senators and Representatives announced their retirements from politics or sought other offices, the impetus of the movement for a term-limit amendment seemed to abate. Its advocates and opponents watched anxiously as the 1992 campaign unfolded, knowing that the debate would continue in 1993 and beyond.

ABORTION

ROE V. WADE (1973),[65] THE SUPREME Court's decision extending the constitutional right of privacy to protect a woman's decision whether or not to terminate her pregnancy, touched off a constitutional firestorm that continues to rage throughout the nation. The byproducts of the controversy include repeated proposals to amend the Constitution to overturn the decision. Between 1969 and 1984, nearly two hundred proposed amendments were introduced in Congress to prohibit abortion, protect human life from the moment of conception, or both; many of these amendments granted both Congress and the states concurrent powers of enforcement.[66]

Most frequently, advocates of an amendment strategy to overturn *Roe v. Wade* have favored a Human Life Amendment—one defining the constitutional right of life protected by the Fifth and Fourteenth Amendments' due process clauses as beginning at the moment of conception. This choice of strategy is a response to critics who argue that attempts to use the Constitution against abortion are just as destined to fail as was the attempt to use it against alcohol. Rather than a "morality" amendment, the Human Life Amendment is framed as a rights-protecting amendment analogous to the Thirteenth. Its advocates analogize abortion to slavery, the unborn to the slaves, and the crusade against abortion to the abolitionists' battles against the "peculiar institution."

None of these proposed amendments has ever emerged from committee—in part because advocates of human life amendments have come to hope that the Supreme Court will overturn *Roe v. Wade* and thus remove the offending case from the nation's constitutional law without the need for an amendment. In *Webster v. Reproductive Health Services* (1989), *Ohio v. Akron Center for Reproductive Health* (1990), *Rust v. Sullivan* (1991), and *Planned Parenthood of Southeast Pennsylvania v. Casey* (1992), the Justices have chipped and trimmed *Roe v. Wade,* but they have not yet moved against the core of the 1973 decision.[67]

Concurrent with the Court's gradual retreat from *Roe v. Wade* is legal scholars' and political thinkers' struggle to find a middle ground on the issue on which a consensus could unite—one that rejects the present formulation of the conflict as a clash between a woman's fundamental right to control her own body and an unborn child's fundamental right to life.[68] The confluence of these legal, political, and intellectual developments makes it less likely that an amendment will muster the broad-based consensus needed to surmount the amending process.[69]

WHAT IT MEANS TO BE AN AMERICAN

DISAGREEMENTS OVER THE CHARACTER OF America's culture also have made their presence felt in the amending process. In 1863, for example, representatives of eleven Protestant Christian denominations met at Xenia, Ohio, to discuss the significance of the Civil War. Concluding that the war was divine retribution on a godless nation, they organized the National Reform Association to secure a constitutional amendment recognizing "Almighty God" as "the Author of National Existence and the source of all power and authority in Civil Government, Jesus Christ as the Ruler of Nations, and the Bible as the foundation of law and supreme rule for the conduct of nations." The National Reform Association had a brisk but short-lived run of success, amassing a distinguished list of supporters both in and out of government, but it also provoked the organization of a rival association, the National Liberal League.

The brainchild of Francis E. Abbot, a liberal Unitarian clergyman, the National Liberal League countered the "Christian nation" amendment with a "Religious Freedom Amendment," which would have added a new clause to the First Amendment's religion clauses:

> Congress shall make no law respecting an establishment of religion, *or favoring any particular form of religion,* or prohibiting the free exercise thereof . . . [emphasis added]

The efforts of the National Reform Association and the National Liberal League canceled each other out, but they presaged subsequent attempts to use the Constitution to define key elements of the national identity.[70]

In recent decades, proposals to amend the Constitution to protect what are deemed key elements of the national identity—the English language and the American flag—have generated more controversy than any proposal except the Equal Rights Amendment.

By casting a spotlight on the connections between language and national identity, the official-language controversy raises deep and troubling questions of American nationalism.[71] At the heart of the debate is the conflict between the majority and government interest in a shared language for public and official purposes and the individual's right not to be forced into political, legal, or social ostracism because he or she does not speak the majority's language. This conflict has been present since the settlement of North America by European peoples; examples include the difficulties experienced by the English in conquering and governing Dutch New York in the late 1600s, the problems generated by the British conquest of French-speaking Quebec in 1763, and the controversies between English-speaking and Spanish-speaking communities throughout the United States.

Amendment advocates stress the role played by a common language in binding the nation together. In a statement circulated by proponents of an English Language Amendment (ELA), Representative Bill Emerson (Republican–Missouri) declared:

> Official English does not mean English is "better" than any other language, nor does it mean that English would be the only language spoken in our country. That would be ridiculous. Official English means simply that our government will continue to function in English.
>
> Our Nation's motto says *E Pluribus Unum.* Out of many, one.

We owe much of that unity to our common language. Many Americans already believe English is our official language. It is time to make it so.[72]

In 1981, Senator S. I. Hayakawa (Republican–California), a scholar of semantics and linguistics before his election, first proposed an ELA, and others have introduced later versions regularly. The most recent version reads:

Section 1. The English language shall be the official language of the United States.

Section 2. Neither the United States nor any State shall require, by law, ordinance, regulation, order, decree, program, or policy, the use in the United States of any language other than English.

Section 3. This article shall not prohibit any law, ordinance, regulation, order, decree, program, or policy—

(1) to provide educational instruction in a language other than English for the purpose of making students who use a language other than English proficient in English,

(2) to teach a foreign language to students who already are proficient in English,

(3) to protect public health and safety, or

(4) to allow translators for litigants, defendants, or witnesses in court cases.

Section 4. The Congress and the States may enforce this article by appropriate legislation.[73]

On May 11, 1988, the House Judiciary Committee's Subcommittee on Civil and Constitutional Rights held hearings on the ELA which generated much heat but little light. All who testified were members of Congress; no expert witnesses on the legal, linguistic, or educational aspects of the controversy appeared before the subcommittee. Supporters of the measure stressed the desirability and necessity of a common official language to American unity; opponents argued that the amendment would exacerbate tensions between different language communities and could lead to discrimination against those who did not speak English. Congress has taken no action since.[74]

U.S. English, an organization founded by Hayakawa in 1983 to coordinate the campaign to make English the official language of the United States on both national and state levels, switched its emphasis from the ELA to a bill that would achieve the same goals without having to brave the obstacle course of Article V. In 1992, the proposed Language of Government Act boasted more than twice as many cosponsors as the proposed amendment. Kyle Rogers of U.S. English attributed the bill's greater popularity to a desire by Representatives and Senators "not to be seen as amendment fanatics."[75]

Attempts to write an amendment conferring constitutional protection on the American flag have also miscarried—though, in 1989–1990, the issue threatened to swamp the ordinary business of national politics. The flag controversy began with a little-noticed protest at the 1984 Republican National Convention in Dallas. Gregory Lee Johnson and several others set fire to an American flag and danced around the burning banner, chanting, "Red, white, and blue, we spit on you." They were charged with violating a Texas law prohibiting the desecration of the flag. Five years later, in a 5-to-4 decision, the U.S. Supreme Court held that the act of burning an American flag was symbolic speech protected by the First Amendment and rejected the Texas statute as unconstitutional.[76]

Texas v. Johnson, coming a week after Flag Day 1989 and a year after the 1988 Presidential campaign, galvanized its foes. President George Bush had won his office in 1988 in part by capitalizing on issues of patriotism symbolized by the flag.[77] *Texas v. Johnson* thus became a rallying point for conservatives seeking to enforce national loyalty and allegiance.

Congress turned first to a statutory solution, enacting the Flag Protection Act of 1989. (At the same time, the Senate approved the resolution calling for an amendment by only a three-vote margin, far short of the two-thirds majority needed under Article V.) Although President Bush insisted that an amendment was the only solution he found acceptable, he signed the bill into law. Within minutes of its becoming law, however, the statute was violated throughout the nation by activists such as Sara Eichman, who sought to launch a test case to bring the new law before the courts. In *United States v. Eichman* (1990),[78] the Court rejected the federal statute as unconstitutional, again by a vote of 5 to 4, reasserting its commitment to *Texas v. Johnson.* Supporters of a flag amendment again launched a vigorous campaign, but the public's attention had turned elsewhere.[79] Congress has not reopened the question of amending the Constitution to protect the flag.[80]

Opponents of a flag amendment have expressed concern that it would be the first to revise or limit the First Amendment. They also note that the proposal seems to revive the old common-law crime of seditious libel, under which an individual could be punished for criticizing the government or government officials, whether or not the criticism is true. Finally, echoing the reasoning of Justice Antonin Scalia (a member of the Court majority in *Texas v. Johnson* and *United States v. Eichman*), opponents reject the idea that the flag should be treated as being outside the scope of the First Amendment. Such an amendment would elevate the symbol over the values it is supposed to symbolize and thereby damage those values. They deemed the proposal an effort at "legislating patriotism"—which was doomed to fail.

Steve Short, of the Americanism Office at the American Legion's national headquarters in Indianapolis, explained the Legion's support for an amendment: "The Legion does not like to horse around with the Constitution, but the Supreme Court decision has forced the matter. The amending process is the only thing that's left."[81] Steve Robertson, deputy director of the American Legion's Legislative Division, agreed:

> Our Constitution is a living Constitution; it was designed to meet the changing needs of our society. That's why the Constitution was made the way it was, and that's why the amending process is there. . . . When Congress proposed an amendment, they're just giving the people a chance to say whether or not it's a good idea. If the people disagree, the amendment dies. We want the people to have the final say on this critical issue. That's all we've been saying since day one.[82]

Robertson denied that the flag amendment would damage the freedom of speech protected by the First Amendment:

> [T]here is no absolute freedom under the First Amendment. There are specific acts that the government recognizes are not protected, and the disgusting act of burning a flag should be one of those acts. Nobody's rights and freedoms are injured by banning the desecration of the flag. I can't fire off an M-16 on the Mall to get people's attention; you shouldn't be allowed to burn a flag to get attention. When you burn a flag, when you desecrate a synagogue or burn a cross, all you express is hatred. Nothing good comes out of burning.[83]

As Professor Alan Brinkley of Columbia University has noted, "Battles over the flag have almost always been battles over how to define patriotism and, by implication, how to define America."[84] And, when some Americans attempt to define the national character, identity, or values, they often run head-on into constitutional safeguards of liberty that other Americans regard as being at the core of the American ideals that the flag merely symbolizes.

The history of the flag salute cases of the 1940s provides confirmation of this phenomenon.[85] When in 1940 the Supreme Court permitted school boards to punish Jehovah's Witness schoolchildren for their refusal (based on their religion) to say the Pledge of Allegiance,[86] the controversy divided the nation and led the Justices, within three years, to reverse themselves. In *West Virginia Board of Education v. Barnette* (1943),[87] the Court upheld individual liberty for these schoolchildren even in the face of the strong national interest in encouraging patriotism in time of war by honoring national symbols.

Nearly forty years later, however, many defenders of the Court's decision in the flag-burning cases found it disturbing that the consensus of American public opinion had turned so sharply—from defending the rights of individuals dissenting from patriotic values to attacking those rights. Part of the difference, of course, is the contrast between schoolchildren who simply did not wish to salute the flag and radical protesters whose burning of the flag most Americans found a blatant and offensive rejection of their cherished values. Professor Brinkley concluded:

> Democracies secure in their identities and confident of their principles—as the United States was through much of its history—do not usually feel the need to define patriotism by law. But given the conspicuous absence of either security or confidence in contemporary American culture, no one should assume that the flag issue has been put to rest for good.[88]

A POTPOURRI OF PROPOSALS

SINCE 1789, MEMBERS OF CONGRESS have proposed thousands of amendments, displaying an extraordinary ingenuity as well as an insistence that the Constitution is the appropriate repository for remedies to any or all national problems.

Proposals to restructure the government make up the largest category of amendment proposals. Some focus on the Presidency—on its mode of election, duration in office, terms of office, reeligibility, and alternate methods of impeachment or removal. Others would take an ax to the federal judiciary, abolishing the lower federal courts, restructuring the Supreme Court, or stripping the Court of its power to hear specific kinds of cases (as with the Eleventh Amendment) or to exercise the power of judicial review. Few amendments have focused on the structure of Congress; proponents of amendments prefer to tinker, as we have seen, with methods of election and terms of office, or to expand or contract the Constitution's grant of lawmaking powers.

On March 1, 1791, in the last week of the First Congress, Representative Egbert Benson (Federalist–New York) introduced a remarkable set of fifteen amendments. The knowledgeable and politically astute Benson sought to use Article V to defuse a nasty controversy brewing over the federal court system— in particular, the problem of drawing boundaries between federal and state courts. In late 1790, Attorney General Edmund Randolph caused more trouble than he bargained for when, in response to a request by Congress, he prepared a report urging the drawing of precise boundaries between federal and state judicial power. Federalists were appalled, seeing in the ambiguous and overlapping jurisdictions of federal and state courts a valuable opportunity to vindicate federal supremacy. Benson sought to short-circuit this unpalatable boundary-drawing by proposing amendments that would designate the highest court of each state as the lowest federal court in that state. These new courts would thus be joint artifacts of Congress and the individual states and answerable to both. Opponents predicted that Benson's circuit courts would tilt irretrievably toward the federal government, damaging the independence of state judiciaries. Benson's amendments and Randolph's report were held over till the Second Congress, in which, after some parliamentary maneuvering, they vanished from sight. By elevating the issue to a constitutional level, Benson succeeded in killing it.[89]

Other proponents of amending the Constitution have sought to set aside its core principles of federalism and diversity. Although most Americans would agree with Justice Louis D. Brandeis that it is valuable to permit states to serve as laboratories of reform,[90] others demand the establishment of uniform national rules, standards, or requirements in areas they consider vital to American life. Such "uniformity" amendments would revise Article I, section 8 of the Constitution, adding specific grants of power to permit Congress to address issues that might not fall within federal legislative authority. Uniformity amendments have become less common during the twentieth century, for the nation is more closely bound together than ever before by improvements in transportation and communications. Further, in recognition of the growing interconnectedness of American life, the American bar has drafted and secured the enactment of "uniform state laws," such as the Uniform Commercial Code, across the nation.

One famous uniformity amendment is that proposed in Congress in 1828 and revived ten years later to give Congress the authority to outlaw dueling.[91] Introduced to the United States by French and British officers during the American Revolution, dueling was a controversial practice in the early republic. At times, individuals' efforts to defend and vindicate their honor could pose serious threats to the public good. In 1789, for example, after Representative Aedanus Burke of South Carolina made comments on the floor of the House offensive to Treasury Secretary Alexander Hamilton, a committee of the House arbitrated the personal dispute to avoid the risk of two of the nation's highest officials slaughtering each other over points of honor.[92] In 1804, Vice President Aaron Burr shot Hamilton dead in the most notorious duel in American history.

The tragedy led to revulsion against the practice throughout the nation—except in the Southern states. In 1838, two members of the House, Jonathan Cilley of Maine and William J. Graves of Kentucky, fought a duel on the grounds of the Capitol; Graves shot Cilley dead. In the resulting furor, amendments were introduced to permit Congress to abolish dueling throughout the United States, but nothing came of the attempts.[93]

Similarly, in the late nineteenth and early twentieth centuries, several members of Congress sought to persuade their colleagues to consider amendments concerning divorce. At the root of these proposals were widespread concerns about differing state standards for recognizing marriages and divorces as legitimate. In some states, a person could be divorced and legally remarry under circumstances that in other states would render him or her liable for prosecution for bigamy. Some states permitted divorce freely, some permitted divorce under limited circumstances, and some barred divorce altogether.[94]

Sixty proposals, introduced in Congress between 1884 and 1929, would have empowered Congress to establish a uniform national rule governing marriages and divorces.[95] Nearly one-third aimed to limit the availability of divorce or to abolish it altogether—for example, a 1914 proposal to prohibit "absolute divorce with the right to remarry" and to permit Congress to enact "uniform laws with regard to marriage and to separation from bed and board without permission to remarry."[96] None of these proposals could garner enough support even to come to a vote.

In 1875, President Ulysses S. Grant made the first formal suggestion of an amendment prohibiting polygamy throughout the United States; over the next fifty-four years, fifty-three such amendments were introduced. These were responses to the controversy between the United States government and adherents of the Mormon faith (most of whom lived in the Utah Territory), who insisted that polygamy was a commandment of their religion protected by the First Amendment's free exercise clause.[97] The Mormons officially renounced the doctrine of polygamy in 1890, removing the last obstacle to the admission of Mormon-dominated Utah to the Union—but in 1899 controversy exploded in the House of Representatives over the presence in that body of Brigham H. Roberts, an "avowed polygamist" from Utah. The House voted the following year to expel Roberts, and his irate colleagues introduced a flurry of proposals to amend the Constitution to bar any polygamist from Congress, to bar any polygamist from holding federal or state office, and to outlaw the practice altogether. Social pressures, however, were sufficient to render any amendment unnecessary.[98]

Three proposals in the late nineteenth and early twentieth centuries sought to give Congress the authority to outlaw intermarriage between people of different races, their supporters fearing that the Fourteenth Amendment deprived states of the power to prohibit miscegenation.[99] Again, these proposals were unable to garner sufficient support in Congress to come to a vote; it was not until 1967 that the Supreme Court fully extended the Fourteenth Amendment's equal protection clause to strike down state miscegenation laws as unconstitutional.[100]

Still other nineteenth-century proposals would have required the federal government to establish a national university (a proposal rejected by the Federal Convention in 1787), to direct states to provide free public schools, to acknowledge the sovereignty of Jesus Christ, and to prohibit the teaching of any religious tenets in the public schools. This last proposal, also endorsed by President Grant in 1875, stands in stark contrast to proposals made since 1962 to overturn the Supreme Court's decisions outlawing compulsory prayer and Bible-reading in public schools.[101]

Amendments have been proposed as well to limit individuals' economic power in order to avoid extremes of wealth and inequity. In 1914 and 1916, three proposed amendments would have prohibited any one American from possessing wealth in excess of ten million dollars and given the federal government power to confiscate any such surplus. Another would have empowered the individual states and the United States to dispossess any citizen or combination of citizens of all "wealth, property, power, influence, or honor" gained through dishonesty. This proposal resurfaced in 1919, along with another denying the Supreme Court the power to declare any law unconstitutional.[102]

The strangest proposed amendments, however, have had to do with changing the name of the United States. In 1866, the House received a proposal to rename the United States "America." Its author insisted that the name "the United States of America" was "not sufficiently comprehensive and significant to indicate the real unity and destiny of the American people as the eventual, paramount power of this hemisphere."[103] In 1893, a far more sweeping proposal was introduced (by a constituent's request): "The name of this Republic is hereby changed from the United States of America to the United States of the Earth." As the historian Michael A. Musmanno observed, "[T]his amendment contains many whimsical features, and . . . the sponsor may not have been responsible for any of its erratic provisions." These included a proposal to abolish the Army and Navy, "including the Army and Navy schools of organized murder"; a clause requiring the House and the Senate to "vote by electricity"; and a clause providing, "No law shall go into effect or remain in effect that is not at all times demanded and sustained by a majority of the people whom it affects."[104]

THE RECORD OF "ROADS NOT TAKEN" enables us to trace the changing conceptions of the amending process in American constitutional history.

Neither the Federalists nor the Anti-Federalists were willing to present a detailed and impartial explanation of the scope and limits of Article V. The amending process, as they saw it, was supposed to correct defects in the Constitution—but it is not easy to pin down the meaning of that phrase. After all, the Federalists insisted that the Constitution conferred no power to injure individual rights but concurred in the proposing and ratification of the Bill of Rights—the lack of which, Anti-Federalists insisted, was the foremost defect of the constitutional system.

Within five years of the ratification of the Constitution, *Chisholm v. Georgia* (1793) spurred the American people to identify a new use for Article V. The Eleventh Amendment illustrated how Article V could function as a mechanism to overturn decisions of the United States Supreme Court that presented unacceptable interpretations of the Constitution—whether unacceptable to the great majority of the people or merely offensive to a powerful minority that the majority was obliged to placate.

The bewildering variety of proposed amendments that surfaced throughout the nineteenth century identified still another use for Article V: as a means to give Congress the power to impose uniform national rules that were not feasible within the unamended constitutional framework. The grants of federal legislative power codified in Article I, section 8 did not extend to authorizing Congress to enact a nationwide ban on dueling or a uniform national set of rules for divorce. That Congress proposed only two amendments between the Twelfth Amendment in 1804 and the Thirteenth Amendment in 1865, and that neither the "Titles of Nobility" Amendment nor the Corwin Amendment (see Chapter 5) succeeded, suggests that the amending process served as an effective barrier to all but the most essential or desirable amendments.

The ratification of the Thirteenth, Fourteenth, and Fifteenth Amendments after the Civil War expanded the scope of Article V and prompted further experiments with this new power. During the latter half of the nineteenth century and the first third of the twentieth century, advocates of amendments treated Article V as a grant of superlegislative power. Measures that normally might have been considered through the ordinary lawmaking process were now proposed as constitutional amendments so that they could not be disturbed, limited, or revoked by the ordinary political process. The confluence of the superlegislative conception of the amending process and the use of Article V to create uniform national rules led to the Eighteenth Amendment, as well as to its repeal fourteen years later.

The disastrous experience of Prohibition worked another transformation in the amending process. Both legislators and the people retreated from viewing Article V as a grant of superlegislative power. They scaled it back to the dimensions marked out by previous successful uses of the amending process: engrafting principles of democratization on, and adjusting defects in, the constitutional system.

The products of the amending process, successful and unsuccessful alike, have shaped the development of the nation in unanticipated ways. Though we revere James Madison today as the father of the Bill of Rights, his initial skepticism about the amending process was right: unless independent means exist to enforce constitutional safeguards, whether provisions of the original Constitution or amendments added later, they are little more than parchment barriers. Constitutional amendments are not self-executing, nor are their seemingly clear and direct commands free from ambiguity. The American people have "amended America" twenty-seven times, but most of these Amendments sowed the seeds of new controversies in the process of putting old ones to rest. Using Article V is only the beginning of the process of reshaping the Constitution to meet our changing needs—and of reshaping our hopes and expectations to adapt to the new constitutional framework.

CHAPTER 11

THE NATION
THE AMENDING PROCESS MADE

All eyes are opened, or opening to the rights of man. The general spread of the light of science has already laid open to every view the palpable truth that the mass of mankind has not been born, with saddles on their backs, nor a favored few booted and spurred, ready to ride them legitimately, by the grace of god.

THOMAS JEFFERSON
letter to Mayor Roger C. Weightman
June 24, 1826[1]

ONCE AN AMENDMENT IS PROPOSED and ratified, it subtly alters all that has gone before. The Constitution has expanded—whether to include new areas of federal authority, to recognize individual rights previously unprotected, or to enlarge the basic principles of American public life. As we live under the Constitution and its new amendment, we gradually reorient ourselves to the changed legal and political landscape. The people and the Constitution continue to amend each other.

THE PARADOX OF RIGHTS IN A DEMOCRATIC REPUBLIC

THE HISTORY OF THE BILL of Rights records American efforts to resolve a paradox: how to protect the rights of the people against the powers of government of, by, and for the people.[2] In 1943, the historian Henry Steele Commager summed up that history in the arresting phrase "majority rule and minority rights."[3]

Before the American Revolution, peoples and their rulers coexisted in a wary relationship. The conventional wisdom of government dictated that the people were only one segment of the society, having one body of interests distinct from and hostile to the interests of the monarchy, the nobility, or the established church. Even in Great Britain, whose people prided themselves on the ancient and honorable traditions of British liberty dating back to Magna Carta and beyond,[4] individual rights were products of immemorial custom governing the relationship between two distinct entities—the sovereign and the people. Similarly, written declarations of rights found in state constitutions and in the United States Constitution were products of the traditional view that rights are concessions made, willingly or reluctantly, by government to the people.[5]

The Revolutionary generation of Americans believed that their revolution had established that the people could and should govern themselves—in other words, that the people are sovereign (that is, they possess the society's ultimate political authority). At the same time, the Americans had only begun to work out the consequences of the Revolution for the theory and practice of popular government. James Madison identified one such consequence with epigrammatic terseness: "In Europe, charters of liberty have been granted by power. America has set the example . . . of charters of power granted by liberty."[6]

The conceptual reversal of the relationship between liberty and power so deftly sketched by Madison undercut the conventional understanding of the purpose of a declaration of rights: if such guarantees of rights previously were extracted from grudging sovereigns who were adverse to the people, what function do these guarantees have when the people are their own sovereigns? What need is there for a bill of rights, for is it not illogical that the people would take away their own liberties? Federalists opposing the demand for a bill of rights during the ratification of the Constitution made frequent use of these arguments, but they did not prevail. The majority of the nation's politicians agreed with Thomas Jefferson that "a bill of rights is what the people are entitled to against any government on earth, general or particular, and what no government should refuse, or rest on inference."[7]

Jefferson also pointed out to Madison a powerful argument for a bill of rights: "the legal check which it puts into the hands of the judiciary."[8] A bill of rights would enable one branch of the people's government (in this case, the judiciary) to protect the people against violations or abuses by other branches, thus resolving the paradox of protecting the people's rights against the people's government.[9] In a rare instance of agreement with Jefferson, Alexander Hamilton wrote in *The Federalist No. 78* (1788):

> The complete independence of the courts is peculiarly essential in a limited Constitution. By a limited Constitution, I understand one which contains certain specified exceptions to the legislative authority; such, for instance, as that it shall pass no bill of attainder, no *ex post facto* laws, and the like. Limitations of this kind can be preserved in practice no other way than through the medium of courts of justice, whose duty it must be to declare all acts

contrary to the manifest tenor of the Constitution void. Without this, all the reservations of particular rights or privileges would amount to nothing.[10]

Once the first ten amendments became part of the Constitution, however, they lost much of the hold they had on the public mind. Even the scattered attempts to invoke the federal Bill of Rights in its first decades did not win general support—in part because issues of rights were not as clear-cut to the contending parties as they seem to posterity, in part because they were entangled with other issues (such as the division and balancing of powers between the states and the federal government) obscuring the issues of rights. The Sedition Act of 1798, whose terms would provoke countless First Amendment lawsuits today, was challenged at the time on the issue of whether the federal government had overstepped its limited grants of power under a Constitution that created a system of divided sovereignty between federal and state governments.[11]

The neglect of the Bill of Rights during this period also was a result of its still-problematic character: there was no firm consensus whether it was merely a codification of maxims of free government that citizens were to use to evaluate the conduct of their elected officials, or whether it was a set of judicially enforceable safeguards of individual rights.[12]

Its position in the American mind was further diminished by the United States Supreme Court's decision in *Barron v. Mayor and City Council of Baltimore* (1833).[13] John Barron, a Baltimore businessman, sued the city for ruining his wharf by diverting creeks near the city harbor to build paved streets. Barron claimed that the city had caused sand and gravel to build up around his dock, leaving it useless because ships could no longer tie up there. In so doing, he argued, Baltimore had violated his Fifth Amendment rights by taking his property for public use without just compensation. Barron won in the Maryland trial court, but the state's highest court reversed in favor of Baltimore, whereupon Barron took his case to the United States Supreme Court. In his last major constitutional opinion, Chief Justice John Marshall held for the Court that the federal Bill of Rights did not apply to state or local governments. (Marshall's argument rested, in part, on the rejection by the First Congress of Madison's proposed amendment limiting the powers of state governments to infringe individual rights.)

Barron provoked little comment and less surprise. At that time, most citizens had little contact of any sort with government; what contacts they had nearly always were with state and local governments, whose actions were guided and limited by state constitutions. The federal Bill of Rights thus had little actual effect on American legal and political life, except as a symbol of rights and as a pattern for bills of rights included in new or revised state constitutions.[14]

By contrast, the twentieth century has witnessed a major transformation in popular and legal understandings of the Bill of Rights. As Anthony Lewis observed in *The New York Times* in 1991, "More than any other society, we have a rights culture. Prick an American, and he reaches for his constitutional rights."[15] The growth of the law and culture of American rights exemplifies the creative interchange between the people and the Constitution:

First, the suffrage Amendments—the Fifteenth, Nineteenth, Twenty-third, Twenty-fourth, and Twenty-sixth—not only have expanded the "political population"[16] but have also encouraged those previously excluded groups to demand recognition and protection of their rights. The civil rights, civil liberties, and women's rights movements have exemplified the continuing diversification and democratization of American society and public life, particularly through their devising of legal strategies to define, expand, and protect rights.[17]

Second, the Fourteenth, Sixteenth, Eighteenth, and Twenty-first Amendments have reinforced and expanded the federal government's role in regulating interstate commerce and overseeing state actions affecting individual citizens. These amendments, combined with nonconstitutional factors such as improvements in transportation and communications, have ensured that issues that once were regarded as local are now legitimate concerns of national politics and federal law. These separate sets of developments came together to prompt and authorize such federal rights-protecting measures as the Civil Rights Act of 1964 and the Public Accommodations Act of 1964. Similarly, the rise of a national news media to serve a national political community has ensured that free speech and press, equal treatment, criminal procedure, and privacy receive national coverage and thus are confirmed as issues of national importance. Moreover, in a series of decisions beginning in 1925, the Supreme Court used the due process clause of the Fourteenth Amendment to impose selected guarantees of the Bill of Rights to limit state and local governments (a development discussed more fully later).[18]

Other historical forces have been at work as well—the growth of a national communications network, transportation system, and news media linking a huge populace into one community[19] and the effect of the national mobilization for democracy and against totalitarianism during the Second World War and the Cold War[20]—moving individual rights to a central position in the American consciousness.[21] And, as the government has grown in size, power, and responsibility since the 1930s, distrust of government has grown as well. The venerable belief that government is the enemy of the people, and that rights are the people's defense against government, has persisted and strengthened with increases in the scope of governmental activities and responsibilities, and in the distance (real or perceived) between the people and their government. Thus, even as the Bill of Rights enters its third century, the paradox of the people's government *versus* the people's rights is alive and well.

POLICING THE PARADOX:
THE JUDICIARY AND THE PROTECTION OF RIGHTS

TWELVE OF THE TWENTY-SEVEN AMENDMENTS to the Constitution (the Bill of Rights and the Thirteenth and Fourteenth Amendments) have to do with rights—more than with any other subject.[22] In addition to their substantive and procedural effects, these amendments have had a profound cultural effect on the American nation: they have fostered a democratic culture characterized by a remarkable diversity of religious beliefs and practices, philosophical systems, political arguments, and methods of self-expression.

The place of the American judiciary in the history of the rights-protecting amendments ties these strands together. More than in virtually any other democratic culture, the American judiciary plays a vital role in the interpretation and protection of individual rights. If the story of rights in American history is one of nested paradoxes, then the judiciary—especially in the twentieth century—has helped to police those paradoxes in its role as interpreter and enforcer of the Constitution's rights-protecting Amendments.

By laying the legal foundation of the American democratic culture, these Amendments help to shape the assumptions on which participants in that culture think and act.[23] Through constitutional interpretation, the courts have spun an intricate, ever-growing web of doctrines, rules, exceptions, tests, and benchmarks. Such terms of legal art as "pleading the Fifth" (invoking the Fifth Amendment's self-incrimination clause, prohibiting government from compelling anyone to be a witness against himself or herself), "unreasonable searches and seizures," "establishment of religion," "wall of separation," and "cruel and unusual punishments" are shorthand for an extraordinary profusion of case law and precedent, legal and historical scholarship, in the continuing effort to determine what they mean and how they apply to concrete cases.

Quarrels over rights and their limits mold and disclose deeper cultural questions—for example, the boundaries of acceptable academic, political, literary, and artistic expression; the range of protections for beliefs on religious matters; and the scope of the "zone of privacy" to which every person is entitled.[24] That the Amendments composing the Bill of Rights continue to spark controversy shows that the mere existence of an amendment protecting rights is no guarantee of a shared consensus on the dimensions of that protection. Polemical riptides surrounding disputes at the borders of constitutional rights give a distorted picture of the nature and purposes of those rights. Focusing public interest where disagreement exists blurs or obscures those areas of liberty on which a public consensus has emerged and opens gulfs between most Americans and those who must invoke the protection of the Bill of Rights because their rights are not protected by the sympathy of the majority.

We can see most clearly how rights suffer in the public mind because they are invoked by individuals and groups who "offend" the majority or "threaten shared values" in the context of the criminal justice Amendments. The Fourth, Fifth, Sixth, and Eighth Amendments (and the due process clause of the Fourteenth Amendment) are increasingly the target of those who characterize the rights they protect as "criminals' rights." Claiming that the law is indifferent to the interests of society or the rights of crime victims, critics of these rights overlook one vital fact: these rights belong to all Americans, not just those who most frequently invoke them.

The rights-protecting Amendments have shaped constitutional law, political argument, and law enforcement so extensively that they have entered American popular culture. Perhaps the most famous Bill of Rights case is *Miranda v. Arizona* (1966), which codified a set of warnings (rooted in the Fifth and Sixth Amendments) that police officers must give to arrestees or suspects before questioning; television "cop shows" have parroted these warnings for a generation.[25] And, over the past half century, Americans have displayed a remarkable tendency to use the Bill of Rights as a model for lesser codifications of relationships between individuals and government or between individuals and businesses. Examples (arranged in order from most to least significant) include the G.I. Bill of Rights, adopted in the years following the Second World War to aid returning veterans and their families;[26] the Hospital Bill of Rights, which New York State codified to govern rights and responsibilities of hospitals and patients; the Bottle Bill of Rights, which businesses that redeem deposit-return containers post on their walls; and credit-card billing companies' "billing rights summaries" printed on the backs of their statements.

But we cannot fully grasp the impact of the Bill of Rights without examining how it has been supplemented and extended by the Thirteenth and Fourteenth Amendments. Though they lay dormant for generations after their ratification, their revival in the twentieth century is perhaps the single most dramatic development in modern constitutional law.

In 1883, the United States Supreme Court heard a group of cases consolidated as the *Civil Rights Cases*.[27] At issue were the enforcement sections of the Thirteenth and Fourteenth Amendments—specifically, whether these sections authorized the Civil Rights Act of 1875. In a major setback for federal civil rights enforcement,[28] the Court limited the Amendments' reach sharply—in particular, the extent of congressional enforcement authority. The Justices declared that the Thirteenth Amendment protected

> only . . . those fundamental rights which appertain to the essence
> of citizenship, and the enjoyment of which constitutes the essen-
> tial distinction between freedom and slavery.[29]

They warned against expanding the reach of the prohibition of the "badges and incidents of slavery"[30] to a broad range of private discriminatory acts:[31]

> It would be running the slavery argument into the ground to make it apply to every act of discrimination which a person may see fit to make as to the guests he will entertain, or as to the people he will take into his coach or cab or car, or admit to his concert or theatre, or deal with in other matters of intercourse or business.

Such a crabbed reading of the Thirteenth Amendment has not survived to the present day. Recent decisions of the Supreme Court have relied on that Amendment as authority for congressional power to outlaw "badges and incidents of slavery" such as racial discrimination in the sale or rental of private property.[32] Such decisions, however, have come under biting criticism from conservative constitutional scholars, who argue that the Court abused the history of the amendment and impermissibly applied it to purely private dealings between individuals.[33]

The twentieth-century growth of the scope and meaning of the Fourteenth Amendment has wrought a revolutionary expansion of the protection of individual rights, most powerfully through what has become known as the "incorporation doctrine." Section 1 of the Fourteenth Amendment states, in part, that "[n]o State shall . . . deprive any person of life, liberty, or property, without due process of law." In its modern applications, section 1 has become the central problem of modern constitutional law, because the Supreme Court has held that its provisions "incorporate" various provisions of the United States Bill of Rights as restrictions on state and local governments.

Section 1 established a constitutional definition of citizenship of the United States, conferring that status on "[a]ll persons born or naturalized in the United States and subject to the jurisdiction thereof." It elevated citizenship of the United States to a constitutional status above that accorded state citizenship. Section 1 also invalidated the old view, championed by Southern politicians from Thomas Jefferson through John C. Calhoun to Jefferson Davis, that the Union is the creation of the states and that an individual's first loyalty is to his or her state.

Why should it be a significant change to impose federal constitutional limits on state and local governments? The answer is rooted in the origins of the Bill of Rights. In the early years of the republic, most Americans did not regard state governments as posing significant threats to individual liberty. They felt that they had closer ties with their state government, for they could effectively punish state officials who had abused the public trust by turning them out of office. Furthermore, most of the states had constitutions including declarations of rights or equivalent provisions that set limits on their powers. By contrast, the government created by the Constitution possessed almost as much power as Great Britain had claimed over the American colonies before the Revolution. Americans remembered that the British had invaded their rights and were fearful that the new federal government (which would include strangers from other states) might do the same.[34]

Thus, the principal purpose of the first ten Amendments was to defuse the fear that the federal government might violate individual liberties. We find evidence of this narrow scope in the language of such provisions as the First Amendment ("*Congress* shall make no law . . .") and the Tenth Amendment ("The powers not delegated to the United States by the Constitution, nor prohibited by it to the States, are reserved to the States respectively, or to the people"). Indeed, in 1789 the House of Representatives rejected an amendment proposed by James Madison—one he regarded as "the most important of the lot"—that would have barred state governments as well from infringing freedom of religion or of the press. The decision of the House that the Bill of Rights would bind only the federal government was, as we have seen, confirmed more than forty years later by the Supreme Court in *Barron v. Mayor of Baltimore.*[35]

After the Civil War, however, Congress perceived that the principal threat to the liberties of the freed slaves came from state laws and policies that already were limiting the civil and legal rights of blacks across the South. The Fourteenth Amendment was framed, in part, to address this concern. Today, the due process clause of the Fourteenth Amendment applies guarantees in the United States Bill of Rights to protect persons against infringements by state and local governments—although it is still a matter of bitter historical and jurisprudential controversy whether the framers of the amendment intended the clause to have that effect. Until the 1920s, however, blacks received few of the benefits of this Amendment, for the only "persons" who successfully claimed federal protection against state authority were corporations (and their stockholders and officials).[36] Under Anglo-American common law, a corporation is an artificial person, distinct from its owners, which can sue and be sued.

After the Civil War, many states passed statutes regulating various kinds of corporations, often railroad corporations. They based these measures on the "public interest" doctrine (the principle that the public has an interest, protectable by government, in any enterprise that affects it) and on the state's "police powers"—its authority to protect the health, safety, welfare, and morals of its inhabitants. At first, the Supreme Court upheld these laws, accepting the "public interest" and "police powers" rationales.[37] But lawyers for corporations claimed that some regulations deprived a corporation "of the lawful use of its property and thus, in substance and effect, of the property itself." In other words, state regulatory legislation took corporate property without compensation—a violation of due process of law. In the period between 1868 and 1933, states and localities were far more likely than the national government to enact laws that limited corporations, and the doctrine of "substantive due process" thus threatened to render invalid nearly all state laws regulating business.

Federal courts also struck down laws designed to protect individuals in the workplace, on the grounds that such measures deprived "persons"—that is, corporations—of property interests without due process and of constitutional liberty of contract. Employers claimed that state laws setting minimum wages and maximum hours, and regulating working conditions violated their own and their employees' "freedom of contract"—a liberty protected by Article I, section 10 of the Constitution and by the Fourteenth Amendment's due process clause. The courts accepted these arguments, most sweepingly in *Lochner v. New York* (1906),[38] in which a nearly unanimous Supreme Court struck down a New York state law limiting a baker's workday to ten hours. In lonely and eloquent dissent, Justice Oliver Wendell Holmes, Jr., argued that, whether the statute was sound public policy or not, the legislature had the discretion to adopt it and was not barred from doing so by the Constitution or by abstract notions of liberty of contract.

In the 1920s, the Justices began to rethink the meaning of the Fourteenth Amendment. *Gitlow v. New York* (1925)[39] upheld the conviction of Benjamin Gitlow, a Communist leader, under a New York statute outlawing criminal anarchy. Although the Justices rejected on the merits Gitlow's claim that he was protected under the First Amendment, they did agree that the First Amendment bound state and local governments:

> We may and do assume that freedom of speech and of the press—which are protected by the First Amendment from abridgement by Congress—are among the fundamental personal rights and "liberties" protected by the due process clause of the Fourteenth Amendment from impairment by the States.

Gitlow began the process by which the Court incorporated clauses of the Bill of Rights into the due process clause of the Fourteenth Amendment. The Court incorporated the balance of the First Amendment, clause by clause and case by case:

> • *Near v. Minnesota* (1931)[40] applied the free press clause of the First Amendment to the states, striking down an attempt by the Minnesota attorney general to enjoin publication of Jay Near's vicious scandal sheet, the *Saturday Press*.

- *De Jonge v. Oregon* (1937)[41] incorporated the freedom of assembly clause. The Justices invalidated Oregon's criminal syndicalism law after local police, acting on the basis of that statute, had broken up a peaceful demonstration sponsored by Communist organizations.

- *Cantwell v. Connecticut* (1940)[42] incorporated the free exercise clause in a suit brought by Jehovah's Witnesses, who had been the victims of religious discrimination and persecution throughout the nation. The Justices held that, although a state could adopt licensing requirements for those who sought to solicit money for charitable or religious causes, Connecticut's statute violated the First Amendment because it gave the secretary of the state's public welfare council sole discretion to determine whether a solicitor's cause was legitimate.

- *Everson v. Board of Education* (1947)[43] incorporated the establishment clause. In the "New Jersey school bus case," the Court ruled that a state may provide transportation for students attending parochial schools— so long as the program's primary purpose was to benefit the children rather than to advance the cause of the religious denomination operating the schools.

In 1947, impatient with what lawyers had come to call piecemeal incorporation, Justice Hugo L. Black began a campaign to incorporate the entire Bill of Rights. His point of departure was a racially charged murder case, *Adamson v. California,* which reached the Supreme Court on appeal.[44] Admiral Dewey Adamson, a poor black man with a record of petty crime, was arrested for the murder of a white woman. On advice of counsel, who was convinced that the prosecution's case was weak, Adamson refused to take the stand—as was his right under the Fifth Amendment. Even so, the prosecutor cited Adamson's refusal as an indication of his guilt, relying on a California rule permitting comments on a defendant's refusal to take the stand. Adamson appealed his conviction for murder on this ground, but the Supreme Court rejected his argument. On the basis of *Twining v. New Jersey* (1908), a decision on the same issue,[45] the Justices held (i) that the prosecutor's comments did not violate the "fundamental fairness" that the Fourteenth Amendment's due process clause was supposed to protect, and (ii) that the Fifth Amendment's self-incrimination clause did not control state criminal law.

Justice Black filed an outraged dissent that amassed historical evidence for his position that the Fourteenth Amendment incorporated the entire Bill of Rights, including the Fifth Amendment's self-incrimination clause. In his opinion concurring with the majority, Justice Felix Frankfurter disputed Black's historical arguments, igniting a long and bitter argument between his and Black's intellectual allies and heirs.

Although Black persisted in his views until his death in 1971, the Court continued the process of piecemeal incorporation. Today, most key provisions of the Bill of Rights are binding on the states. In the 1960s, for example, the Justices began to incorporate the criminal procedure guarantees:

• *Mapp v. Ohio* (1961)[46] incorporated the Fourth Amendment. The Supreme Court overturned the conviction of Dollree Mapp, a landlady who had been convicted of possessing pornography that local police had seized during an illegal, warrantless search seeking a former boarder of Mapp's. The pornography was found among the former boarder's belongings, which Mapp had placed in her basement for safekeeping.

• *Gideon v. Wainwright* (1963)[47] incorporated the right to counsel protected by the Sixth Amendment. Clarence Earl Gideon, a Florida drifter, was tried for breaking into a poolroom. The state rejected his demands under the Sixth Amendment for a court-appointed lawyer; Gideon was forced to act as his own defense lawyer and was convicted. He filed a handwritten petition with the United States Supreme Court for a writ of *certiorari* (a legal order requiring a lower court to forward the record of a case to the Supreme Court for review of the merits of the decision). The Court granted Gideon's application and named the noted Washington attorney (and future Supreme Court Justice) Abe Fortas to represent him. Gideon won his case, establishing a landmark of federal constitutional law.

• Two cases, *Malloy v. Hogan* (1964)[48] and *Escobedo v. Illinois* (1964),[49] tied together the Fifth Amendment privilege against self-incrimination and the Sixth Amendment right to counsel, and applied both to the states. The Court confirmed this linkage in *Miranda v. Arizona* (1966),[50] overturning Ernesto Miranda's murder conviction because of police misconduct in extracting a confession from him without having granted him access to an attorney.

• *In re Gault* (1967)[51] extended to juveniles the criminal procedure rights of adults and thus applied the incorporation doctrine to impose federal constitutional guarantees on state juvenile justice systems. Arizona juvenile authorities apprehended fifteen-year-old Gerald Gault with a friend after a neighbor complained that the two boys had made an obscene telephone call to her. Gault was held for several days and otherwise deprived of his constitutional rights, and was sentenced to a youth facility until his twenty-first birthday (effectively, a six-year sentence). Justice Fortas held for the Court that juveniles are entitled to the criminal justice rights guaranteed by the Fifth and Sixth Amendments, including the rights to notice of charges, to counsel, to the opportunity to confront and cross-examine witnesses, and to the privilege against self-incrimination. *Gault* thus transformed the juvenile justice systems of the fifty states.[52]

• *Furman v. Georgia* (1972)[53] incorporated the Eighth Amendment's prohibition of cruel and unusual punishments, invalidating state death penalty statutes. Though the Court reversed *Furman* only four years later,[54] the Justices upheld the principle that the Eighth Amendment applies to the states as a criterion for approving new state laws and procedures designed to ensure fairness in imposing the death penalty. (The death penalty continues to create headaches for the Justices, as proponents and opponents try to bring each new case before the Court.)

The few exceptions to piecemeal incorporation include the right to jury trial in civil cases (Seventh Amendment), the right to be held answerable for a crime only through a grand jury indictment (Fifth Amendment), and the right to bear arms (Second Amendment). Although in the past decade the Supreme Court has cut back on the extent to which it will protect certain incorporated rights, the Justices have not rejected the basic principle of incorporation, which is one of the amending process's most enduring legacies.

All these cases were controversial at the time the Court decided them—in the field of criminal procedure, in particular. Such decisions as *Miranda* were enormously unpopular; law enforcement officials and conservative politicians charged that the Justices were hampering the fight on crime by being too tender of the rights of criminals.

Some constitutional scholars and judges, arguing that the incorporation doctrine has no basis in the "original understanding" of the framers of the Fourteenth Amendment, conclude that the doctrine is therefore bad law—an invalid "usurpation" by unelected judges of powers properly left in the hands of democratically elected officials. Although the Justices are unlikely to reject the incorporation doctrine, conservative theorists continue to advance arguments for abolishing it, and liberal scholars continue to man the barricades in its defense.[55]

SECTION 1 OF THE FOURTEENTH AMENDMENT also forbids states from denying "to any person within [their] jurisdiction the equal protection of the laws." The Justices first dealt with issues arising under the equal protection clause in *Plessy v. Ferguson* (1896).[56] The Court rejected Homer Plessy's challenge to a Louisiana law that required segregation of the races on railroads passing through the state. Justice Henry B. Brown held for the majority that "separate but equal" public facilities were permissible under the Fourteenth Amendment. Justice John Marshall Harlan, a former slaveowner, filed a lone dissent in *Plessy,* maintaining in vain that "[o]ur Constitution is color-blind" and pointing to the Fourteenth Amendment to substantiate his view.

On its face, *Plessy* seemed a victory for segregationists, who wanted to prevent the mixing of blacks and whites. Yet in the 1930s and 1940s, civil rights advocates used the "separate but equal" doctrine as a powerful legal weapon *against* racist policies:

> • In *Sipuel v. Board of Regents of the University of Oklahoma* (1948),[57] the Justices ordered the state of Oklahoma to provide Ada Sipuel, a black woman, with a legal education equivalent to that given at the all-white University of Oklahoma Law School; however, they declined to determine whether a "law school" consisting of three professors teaching in a roped-off area of the Oklahoma state capitol was an "equal" facility.

> • In *McLaurin v. Oklahoma State Regents* (1950),[58] the Justices rejected a similar attempt by Oklahoma authorities to discriminate against George McLaurin, a sixty-eight-year-old graduate student, holding that the state was imposing inequalities on him (including such degrading tactics as building a railing around his seat in the classroom bearing the sign "Reserved for Colored").

> • In *Sweatt v. Painter* (1950),[59] the Court required Texas either to found a law school for black students or to integrate the University of Texas Law School. The Justices found unanimously that the "law school" the state had opened for black students at Prairie View University had none of the facilities necessary to a law school. In this instance, the Court declared, "separate but equal" required either that the state provide separate facilities that truly were equal or that it integrate its all-white facility to permit equal access by blacks.

Despite such victories, the "separate but equal" doctrine still shielded segregation. Enforced separation of the races, most advocates of civil rights argued, is inherently unequal—even in the unlikely prospect that the facilities provided are exactly equal.

Responding to these arguments, in the 1950s the Justices, led by Chief Justice Earl Warren,[60] began to experiment with the equal protection clause of the Fourteenth Amendment. In *Brown v. Board of Education* (1954)[61] (which has become the touchstone of modern constitutional law), the parents of eight-year-old Lisa Brown sued the board of education of Topeka, Kansas, to invalidate its segregation policies. The Browns felt that it was outrageous for their daughter to have to travel across town to attend a blacks-only school when she lived just a few blocks from a whites-only school. The Justices ordered *Brown* consolidated for review with five other appeals from similar decisions throughout the United States. All six cases presented the same question—the constitutionality of segregated schools.

On May 17, 1954, Chief Justice Warren announced the decision of a unanimous Court outlawing segregation in public schools. Holding that separation is inherently unequal, the Court overturned the principles of *Plessy*, without formally overruling the precedent. The NAACP Legal Defense Fund attorneys (led by future Supreme Court Justice Thurgood Marshall) who took *Brown* up the legal system had won a great victory, capping decades of patient legal work to make the promise of the Civil War Amendments a reality. The scope of the equal protection clause continued to grow in the coming years, particularly through such landmark cases as *Baker v. Carr* (1962),[62] which Chief Justice Warren later declared was the most important decision handed down during his tenure on the Court, and *Craig v. Boren* (1976).[63] In *Baker* the Court applied the clause to overturn Tennessee's system of legislative districting and to establish the principle of "one man, one vote." In *Craig,* the Court ruled state statutes classifying persons based on gender invalid unless they serve "important governmental objectives" and are "substantially related to achievement of those objectives." (At issue was an Oklahoma statute that allowed the purchase of 3.2 beer by women when they reached the age of eighteen but required male would-be purchasers to be at least twenty-one.)

But the most controversial issue arising under the equal protection clause has been "affirmative action"—the practice of establishing preferences in favor of those who have suffered previous discrimination based on race, ethnicity, or sex.[64] The most famous (and troublesome) case involving an affirmative action program reached the Court in 1977.[65] Allan Bakke had been turned down by the University of California, Davis, medical school. Because his academic record apparently was better than those of black and minority students admitted under an affirmative action program that set aside a specified number of places in the entering class, Bakke filed suit against the university, arguing that it had violated his rights under the equal protection clause. (To pose the issue in its starkest form, Bakke and the university stipulated that only the affirmative action plan was at issue in the case, discarding as irrelevant the other reasons he was denied admission.)

After two oral arguments, a divided Court handed down *Regents of the University of California v. Bakke* (1978).[66] All nine Justices wrote opinions, resulting in a decision over one hundred pages long. Four Justices held that the university's plan was invalid under the 1964 Civil Rights Act, making it unnecessary to reach the constitutional question. Four Justices held the opposite—that the plan was constitutional under the equal protection clause and legal under the statute. Justice Lewis F. Powell, known to most observers of the Court as the "swing vote" because he so often decided closely divided cases, filed the crucial opinion. Agreeing with one group of four Justices, he held that it was necessary to address the constitutional question, and that affirmative action in general is constitutional under the equal protection clause, but he agreed with the other four Justices that the Davis plan violated the equal protection clause because it made race the sole factor governing admissions decisions. Because all the parts of Justice Powell's opinion could command a majority of five Justices, it became the opinion of the Court—even though no other Justice agreed with the entirety of his reasoning.

The lack of consensus in *Bakke* has exacerbated the controversy over affirmative action, especially in employment cases. Perhaps the single most painful affirmative action issue is the question of layoffs, in which the traditional rule of "last hired, first fired" has been challenged as gutting the positive effects of affirmative action policies in public and private employment. At this writing, the Justices have refused to require affirmative action in layoffs.[67] Moreover, the Court's increasing rightward drift poses the threat that the Justices will abandon affirmative action.

DEMOCRATIC AND RESPONSIBLE GOVERNMENT

ANOTHER PRINCIPAL THEME OF THE history of Article V has been the American people's continuing efforts to secure democratic, responsible government. Amendments have reshaped much of the democratic content of American government—by expanding constitutional protection of the franchise, by democratizing institutions such as the Senate, and by increasing the responsibility and accountability of government to the citizenry.

Though generally referred to as the "right to vote," the suffrage is actually a privilege to take part in the governance of the polity—one hedged about with restrictions and qualifications. The Framers of the Constitution decided not to establish a uniform national voting standard because they recognized the remarkable diversity—in economics, ethnicity, religion, political viewpoints, and cultures—of the American states. Moreover, the attempt to craft such a standard would have set off a political firestorm that might have destroyed the new plan of government. The Framers therefore agreed to leave the regulation of the franchise to the state governments—a decision that became a key component of constitutional federalism between 1787 and 1870.

In 1870, the Fifteenth Amendment injected national power into the regulation of access to the polls. Although states still established basic qualifications for the suffrage, the federal government now had the authority to bar certain kinds of qualifications. The first qualification ruled out of bounds was race. As we have seen, the Fifteenth Amendment served as a model for the later suffrage Amendments.

The suffrage Amendments have unquestionably changed our nation. Anyone comparing the United States at the beginning of this century with the nation today would recognize that a major transformation had taken place:

> • Whereas in 1901 American society was rigidly segregated according to race, the nation has closed a significant part of the gap between reality and the ideals codified in the Constitution; indeed, two African-Americans, Thurgood Marshall and Clarence Thomas, have served on the Supreme Court. Nonetheless, segregation and its consequences continue to plague our nation's neighborhoods and schools, even if they no longer carry the imprimatur of the state.[68]

> • Whereas in 1901 the women of the nation were clamoring in vain for inclusion in the political population and for recognition of their equality with men, today women have entered the nation's public life at virtually all levels of government. In 1984, Geraldine Ferraro became the first woman to receive a major party's Vice Presidential nomination; women have served in the Cabinet, in the Congress, and in the diplomatic corps; women have won governorships, mayoralties, and state legislative seats; and in 1981 Sandra Day O'Connor became the first woman to sit on the Supreme Court.

But constitutional guarantees do not ensure the success of the newly enfranchised in American politics. The history of voting and voting rights in America is more clouded than the clear, unambiguous guarantees of the suffrage amendments would suggest.

Although the Fifteenth Amendment was celebrated in engravings and public gatherings, and although at first it sheltered political activity by the freed slaves, its promise was short-lived. From the end of Reconstruction in 1877, when the federal government withdrew its last occupation forces from the Southern states, white populations reasserted their supposed right to rule and effectively disenfranchised their black fellow citizens. State governments used such devices as literacy tests, "grandfather clauses," and property qualifications to erect insurmountable barriers to the freed slaves and their descendants. (A grandfather clause automatically enfranchised any person whose grandfather had been entitled to vote, thus discriminating against the freed slaves, whose grandfathers had not been permitted to vote. By disenfranchising freed slaves, the grandfather clause also operated to deprive their descendants of the franchise.) As a result, the Fifteenth Amendment went into constitutional cold storage for nearly a century.

Beginning in the 1930s, the federal courts insisted that state and local governments conform to the requirements of the Fifteenth Amendment. Beginning in 1965, Congress followed suit, enacting and renewing Voting Rights Acts to protect the voters enfranchised by the Amendment.[69] The effects of the statutes have been dramatic: whereas in 1940 only 5 percent of eligible blacks were registered to vote, by 1960 the figure had grown to 28 percent, and by 1976 it reached 63 percent, narrowing the gap between black and white registrations from 44 percent to 5 percent. Growth in the number of registered black voters helped to spur comparable growth in the number of black elected officials in the South—from fewer than one hundred to more than a thousand.[70]

But the history of black Americans' struggle to remove obstacles to the franchise is just as much a history of white politicians' cynical ingenuity in crafting those obstacles.[71] And that history continues to this day. For example, some states and localities have stripped key powers from local governmental bodies, such as county legislatures, at the same time that black candidates have been poised to take control of those institutions. As a result, black candidates win the battle of the polls, only to find themselves stripped of any real power to serve those who elected them. In January 1992, the Supreme Court held that such maneuvers do not violate the Voting Rights Acts.[72] The Court's decision raises a troubling question: what good is access to the polls if those elected by newly enfranchised voters are deprived of power to solve the problems they were elected to address?

Once the Nineteenth Amendment became part of the Constitution, in 1920, white women did not experience the delays and difficulties that studded black Americans' path to full voting equality. With its adoption, women's place in politics was assured—though much remained to be done to establish as a practical matter women's capacity to campaign for and hold elective office at all levels of government. For example, in the One Hundred Third Congress (elected in 1992), only six out of the one hundred United States Senators were women, as were only a few dozen of the 435 members of the House of Representatives—numbers much smaller than women's proportion (52 percent) of the population at large.

Further, one unfortunate aftereffect of the women's suffrage movement was that its single-minded emphasis on securing the right to vote seemed to constrict the political activity of American women thereafter. One authority on the history of American women has observed:

> Without a unifying social agenda beyond the ballot, the postsuf-
> frage feminist movement foundered, splintered, and for the next
> half century, largely dissolved. During that period, women did not
> vote as a block on women's issues, support women candidates, or,
> with few exceptions, agitate for women's rights.[73]

In our own day, the failure of the Equal Rights Amendment, seen by many women and men as a necessary counterpoint to the Nineteenth Amendment, only underscored the many other setbacks for women's rights during the 1980s. Feminist scholars and activists insist that intolerance and bigotry against women has, if anything, grown stronger in the 1980s and 1990s.[74]

At first, these setbacks discouraged many women from making the effort to go to the polls. However, the 1991 controversy over Professor Anita Hill's charges of sexual harassment against Supreme Court nominee (and former director of the Equal Employment Opportunity Commission) Clarence Thomas galvanized women candidates, activists, and voters in 1992. An early indication that women would exercise their political power was the defeat in the Illinois Democratic primary of Senator Alan J. Dixon, who had voted for Thomas's confirmation, by Carol Moseley Braun, recorder of deeds in Cook County and an African-American woman. (In November, Braun became the first African-American woman to become a United States Senator.) Increasingly, the setbacks of the 1980s and the early 1990s stimulated women to organize to oppose efforts to damage or curtail their rights.[75]

The Twenty-third Amendment's partial enfranchising of residents of the District of Columbia has only whetted the appetite of the people of the nation's capital city for full political equality with their fellow citizens. However, the various attempts to pressure Congress and the nation to end the quasi-colonial status of the District have had only partial success.[76] Even the measure of home rule given to District residents continues at the pleasure or sufferance of Congress, which may repeal its grant of power at any time. The failure of the D.C. Statehood Amendment (discussed in Chapter 8) also has left the future of the District's governance in doubt.

Even the successes of the Twenty-fourth and Twenty-sixth Amendments, removing poverty and youth as bars to the suffrage, have not met their framers' ambitions. To this day, those citizens living below the poverty line and those aged eighteen to twenty-one show the lowest levels of registration and participation in elections.[77]

In sum, the amended Constitution can remove the barriers, but it cannot force an apathetic public to exercise its democratic rights.

Overlapping the suffrage Amendments are institutional Amendments (the Twelfth, Sixteenth, Seventeenth, Twentieth, and Twenty-fifth), which also have served to increase the responsibility and accountability of democratic institutions.

By removing the ambiguities that arose from the clash between the original, nonpartisan design of the Electoral College and the rise of national political parties in the 1790s, the Twelfth Amendment has brought a measure of order and certainty to the Presidential election process. The Electoral College system may well have helped to preserve the centrist bias of American politics by making it difficult for radical fringe parties to contest Presidential elections and thus upset the balance between the center-left Democrats and the center-right Republicans.

The democratizing effects of the Sixteenth Amendment, which shifted to the shoulders of the American people the direct burden of financing the federal government, have been at once the most widespread and the least noticed. Ever since its adoption in 1913, the Amendment has continued undisturbed—although Representatives and Senators occasionally demand its repeal.[78] The Internal Revenue Code enacted under its authority (now Title 26 of the United States Code) is still the most controversial federal statute. Repeatedly revised, as with the Tax Reform Act of 1986,[79] it has been a major campaign issue in every Presidential election—in particular, since 1972. Presidential candidacies have been made and broken by pledges to increase or not to increase taxes,[80] and more and more candidates have grappled with alternatives to the existing Code. In 1992, for example, Democrat Jerry Brown proposed a 13 percent "flat tax" supplemented by a consumption tax, and H. Ross Perot floated the suggestion that the Constitution be amended to transfer the federal taxing power from Congress to the American people, who would exercise it in an "electronic town hall."

The Code and the agency created to enforce it, the Internal Revenue Service, have been damned as oppressive by critics on the right and the left. In 1962, the noted literary critic Edmund Wilson published a scathing denunciation of the income tax as the principal financial engine of the military-industrial complex,[81] and the right wing has spawned tax-resistance movements throughout the Far West. Even mainstream political journalists have joined the chorus of criticism aimed at the IRS.[82]

Each time it debates a revision of the Internal Revenue Code, Congress must make decisions about whom to tax, what to tax, at what rate, and by what method. In the 1960s, Stanley S. Surrey (a Kennedy Administration expert on tax policy and a longtime professor of tax law at Harvard Law School) developed the theory of "tax expenditures."[83] Under this now influential theory, government makes decisions on tax policy for purposes having as much to do with substantive policy goals as with the task of raising revenue; for example, decisions not to tax certain sources of income (such as municipal bonds) have the goal of encouraging that form of private investment. Framing and revising the tax laws thus brings a huge body of regulatory issues, enforcement problems, and policy questions to the forefront of domestic politics.

The Seventeenth Amendment, transferring control of the membership of the Senate from state legislatures to the people of the states, transformed the Senate into a quasi-democratic branch of the national legislature. Even though the people of Vermont may have greater proportional influence over the Senate than do the people of California, the entire electorate now has more direct access to the Senate and can shape Senators' consideration of such institutional responsi-bilities as ratification of treaties and confirmation of executive and judicial appointments.[84]

The Amendment also affected the Senate in an immediate and practical way. Because its members have to campaign for election and reelection, Senators are of necessity more responsive—or must cultivate the appearance of being more responsive—to the needs of all the people of their states. Senators have had to develop the campaign and governing skills of democratic politicians, further altering the institution's character.

At the same time, however, the growing expense of political campaigning has made the raising of campaign funds a central part of a Senator's life—and one far greater, both proportionately and in absolute terms, than had been the case before 1913. This unintended effect of the Seventeenth Amendment has im-posed on incumbents, by one modern estimate, the necessity to raise fifteen thousand dollars each and every week of a Senator's six-year term to have a sufficient supply of funds to finance a reelection campaign; it has also imprisoned Senators in a tightening network of obligations to campaign donors.[85]

The Twentieth Amendment was designed to reinforce elected officials' re-sponsibility to their constituents by reducing (from four months to two-and-one-half months) the interregnum between departing and new Presidents and by eliminating the sessions in which lame-duck Presidents and Congresses could make laws without having to answer to the people. The Amendment has in-creased Presidential and Congressional accountability and responsibility, and its recognition and accommodation of the need for full-time government have hauled the federal government into the twentieth century.

Similarly, the Twenty-fifth Amendment was designed to answer a recurring question afflicting the institution at the focus of the modern constitutional system. What happens when a President dies, resigns, or becomes so ill as to be unable to perform his or her job? Democracy demands certainty and predictabil-ity in the resolution of questions afflicting the nation's highest office. Although some citizens, politicians, and scholars were shaken by the first uses of the Amendment (in 1973–1974), its existence and the speed with which Congress and the executive branch adapted to its provisions outweighed its supposed drawbacks. However, the Amendment's history during the Reagan and Bush Administrations raises troubling questions about sections 3 and 4, governing Presidential illness and disability. It is now an open question whether, in the eyes of a President—or of a President's advisers—the short-term political costs of invoking the disability sections loom larger than the allegedly abstract considera-tions of legitimacy and authority.[86]

Finally, the amending process not only has altered the text and workings of the Constitution, but also has revised a key constitutional doctrine, federalism—both in the effects of particular Amendments on the structure of federalism and in the changing roles of the states as participants in the amending process.

The state-sovereignty version of federalism (which began under the Articles of Confederation, touched off the Civil War, and inspired the notorious Southern "massive resistance" to the civil rights revolution) has taken a major beating in American constitutional history, especially at the hands of the amending process. The Civil War Amendments have imposed significant federal limitations on state lawmaking and law enforcement. Moreover, the suffrage Amendments established the legitimacy of federal constitutional regulation of the suffrage, formerly a cherished prerogative of the states.

Even the Eleventh Amendment—the amendment most clearly designed to protect state sovereignty from the federal government and the most obvious legacy of state-sovereignty federalism in the Constitution—has not functioned as its framers may have intended it to work. It originally endorsed a complex and technical area of law, sovereign immunity, under which a state's government may not be sued without its consent. But the Amendment has spawned a large and complex array of substantive and procedural devices designed to circumvent the doctrine, which, along with its myriad of exceptions and escape hatches, has generated extensive case law and scholarship.[87]

However, another kind of federalism—developing at the same time as, but in ways significantly different from, the antebellum version—is alive and well. Under this brand of federalism, federal and state governments coexist in a relationship of mutual respect and fruitful tension, sometimes working concurrently to address complementary aspects of the same issue, sometimes allotting important governmental problems to one or the other level of the federal system.

The Seventeenth Amendment has had many beneficial effects on this category of federalism. Senators are today more effective representatives of their states than they were in the years before 1913. The need to secure a majority of the electorate to win election compels Senators to pay close attention to the needs and interests of their constituents. Senators have thus become increasingly important to the political lives of their states and of the nation as a whole.

The Seventeenth Amendment's transfer of the power to choose Senators from the legislature of each state to its people not only transformed the Senate but also took away from the state governments direct influence over the federal government. Senators no longer are ambassadors of the state governments (or, in practice, envoys of those able to "buy" a Senate seat by corrupting a state legislature). State governments today exert only indirect influence over such matters as ratification of treaties or confirmation of executive or judicial appointments. At the same time, the Amendment's lifting of a divisive responsibility that often clogged state governance improved the functioning of state legislatures, in turn rendering them more responsive to the needs of their constituents on interests of local concern.

The significant role of state governments as participants in the amending process is thriving. As James Madison pointed out in *The Federalist No. 39,* Article V, like the rest of the Constitution, is partly national and partly federal (in the old sense of the term—designating the sphere of responsibility of the states). Amendment advocates may find it comparatively easy to urge one legislature—Congress—to propose an amendment, but the true challenge of the amending process is to persuade thirty-eight state legislatures to ratify a proposed amendment. The advocates of ERA discovered this, to their cost; their national organization was polished and effective, whereas they had few effective organized efforts at the state level. The pro-ERA forces were mirror images of their opponents, who had not succeeded in blocking ERA in Congress but were brilliantly effective in stopping it in the states.[88]

Federalism helps us to identify what is truly fundamental in our nation's identity. The need to gain majorities in legislatures speaks to the solemnity of the amending process. Americans look to the Constitution as the place for implanting universal concerns only; those that address issues of a particular era do not belong in the federal constitutional text—as we learned through our experience with Prohibition. The Eighteenth Amendment failed not only because it failed to embody a shared national consensus but also because its concerns—right or wrong—were not timeless and universal. The Twenty-first Amendment, which returned to the states the discretion to determine whether they were to be "wet" or "dry," recognized the limitations of amending the Constitution.

IT IS NOT POSSIBLE TO determine what kind of nation the United States would have become had the twenty-seven Amendments not been adopted, for essential elements of the national character—of the shared set of assumptions, beliefs, and principles that govern American public and private life—are embedded in the Amendments to the Constitution.

The Bill of Rights, the Thirteenth Amendment, and the Fourteenth Amendment have transformed the nature and purpose of constitutional provisions protecting rights. They have provided a legal shield for unpopular persons and groups against the awesome weight of government power, especially when that power is in the hands of a hostile, intolerant majority. In the process, they have raised the profound question of the nationalization of rights in the context of constitutional federalism. In this way, they have served as an important unifying force, continuing the forging of the United States into a true Union, albeit one with a vigorous and healthy federal system.

Furthermore, the democratizing Amendments, both on their own and interacting with the rights-protecting Amendments, have transformed the nation's public life—though perhaps not to the extent, or with the speed, envisioned by their advocates. The federal and state governments are, at least in theory, responsible and responsive to the citizenry—even though observers of American politics repeatedly have pointed out the growing dissatisfaction of the American people with all levels of government.

Even when these Amendments have not succeeded in protecting rights and democratic ideals, they have performed an important symbolic function, defining the goals of the nation's public life and providing a standard by which the citizenry can test the policies and actions of their elected and appointed officials. Thus, they have played vital roles in shaping the American culture of rights and democracy.

Chapter 12

"WITH ALL THE COOLNESS OF PHILOSOPHERS": PROPOSALS TO REWRITE THE CONSTITUTION

Happily for us, that when we find our constitutions defective and insufficient to secure the happiness of our people, we can assemble with all the coolness of philosophers, and set them to rights, while every other nation on earth must have recourse to arms to amend or to restore their constitutions.

THOMAS JEFFERSON
Letter to C. W. F. Dumas
September 1787[1]

THE HISTORY OF THE AMENDING process consists, for the most part, of targeted attempts to modify the Constitution in response to specific problems of the constitutional system—patching a clause here, grafting a new principle there. But incremental revision is only one part of the amending process. Article V also can trigger a thorough reworking of the entire Constitution.

At times when public displeasure with almost every public and private institution reaches high levels, it would seem natural for Americans to say, "Let's start over and rewrite the Constitution from scratch." Some members of the Revolutionary generation expected such overhauls to take place frequently. For example, Thomas Jefferson argued in 1788 that "the earth belongs always to the living generation" and therefore that the life of a constitution should be limited to one generation, which he set at nineteen years. As he saw it, no generation should be bound by any obligations contracted by its predecessors.

To the end of his life Jefferson held fast to his beliefs. In 1816, when he was seventy-three, he instructed his friend Samuel Kercheval on the strengths and limits of the political structures built by his own generation:

> Some men look at constitutions with sanctimonious reverence, and deem them like the ark of the covenant, too sacred to be touched. They ascribe to the men of the preceding age a wisdom more than human, and suppose what they did to be beyond amendment. I know that age well; I belonged to it, and labored

with it. It deserved well of its country. It was very like the present, but without the experience of the present; and forty years of experience in government is worth a century of book-reading; and this they would say themselves, were they to rise from the dead.[2]

Jefferson concluded:

> [L]aws and institutions must go hand in hand with the progress of the human mind. We might as well require a man to wear still the coat which fitted him when a boy, as civilized society to remain ever under the regimen of their barbarous ancestors.[3]

Opposed to Jefferson were those who feared that too-frequent constitutional revision and replacement would undermine the stability of free government. For example, the more cautious James Madison offered a series of gentle but pointed demurrers from Jefferson's theory, stressing the linkages between generations and the need for political and social stability as a bulwark of liberty.[4]

Though Jefferson's ideas have been adopted on the state level, where frequent constitutional overhauls and reframings have been the general practice since independence,[5] the United States still governs itself according to a constitution adopted in 1788 and only partly and infrequently revised thereafter.[6] The Constitution's growing symbolic and cultural importance, coupled with its flexibility over two centuries and the development of adjudication as a more responsive means of constitutional change than Article V, stifled most calls for a return to the constitutional drawing-board, and a second convention has never taken place.

Yet some Americans have not been willing to practice "Constitution-worship." Ever since the closing days of the Federal Convention, and with increasing frequency in the past century, scores of would-be framers have tried their hand at schemes of constitutional renovation.[7] Modern advocates of rewriting the Constitution invoke Jefferson as a guiding spirit of their endeavor and present themselves as deliberating the matter "with all the coolness of philosophers" rather than with the self-interest of politicians.

IN SEPTEMBER OF 1787, two men dipped quill pens in inkwells in the service of the Federal Convention. As the German-born clerk Jacob Shallus prepared the engrossed copy of the Constitution for signing by the Convention, Alexander Hamilton of New York scribbled an alternate version for the edification of his colleagues and posterity.[8]

More than any other member of the Revolutionary generation, Hamilton deserves credit for organizing the political movement that culminated in the Convention. But he had better success in bringing the meeting about than in making major contributions to its labors—even though he was a key member of the committee assigned to draft the Convention's rules for conducting business. One of three New York delegates to the Convention, Hamilton—an unabashed nationalist and an advocate of energetic government—found himself outvoted within his own delegation; moreover, he realized, he was far outside the boundaries of the consensus emerging among the delegates.

Like several other ambitious delegates—among them James Madison, Charles Pinckney of South Carolina, William Paterson of New Jersey, and James Wilson of Pennsylvania—Hamilton hoped to become the architect of the American commonwealth and to achieve the lasting fame that was the chief desire of so many American statesmen.[9] On June 18, 1787, he attempted to persuade his colleagues to abandon Madison's Virginia Plan and Paterson's New Jersey Plan. Denouncing both as inadequate to the needs of the Union, he expounded his own design of government in a brilliant oratorical performance—a speech estimated (by fellow delegates and by historians) to have been between three and six hours in length.[10]

Under Hamilton's plan, the chief executive and Senators would be elected indirectly to serve during good behavior (that is, for life unless removed from office by impeachment), with Representatives elected by the people to serve three years. The states would be reduced to administrative districts firmly under the control of the general government, which would appoint state governors and have the power to veto all state legislation inconsistent with national objectives. At the close of his epic performance, Hamilton waved aside the Virginia Plan as "pork still, with a change of sauce."

Hamilton impressed his colleagues but persuaded none to back his radically centralizing plan of government for an American nation. Disconsolate and frustrated, he returned to New York City at the end of June to prop up his law practice. The other New York delegates, Robert Yates and John Lansing, Jr., left Philadelphia two weeks later, to attend the sessions of the state's courts—and also to protest the nationalist tendencies exhibited by the Convention.

In August, Hamilton decided to return to Philadelphia and extended to his Anti-Federal colleagues a halfhearted invitation to join him, which they did not even answer.[11] He found himself in an embarrassing position—as the sole New York delegate present, he had no power to cast his state's vote. On September 10, however, the Convention elected him to the vital Committee on Style and Arrangement, charged with preparing the final draft of the Constitution. (The other members of the committee were Madison, Rufus King of Massachusetts, William Samuel Johnson of Connecticut, and Gouverneur Morris of Pennsylvania, who prepared the final draft.)

Hamilton still believed that his cherished plan of government was superior to anything else that had been placed before the delegates. Working from the outline of his June 18 speech, he recast the Constitution to bring it into conformity with what he believed the nation would someday need. Hamilton lent his version to Madison, who copied it into his notes of the Convention's work and returned it, thus gratifying Hamilton's desire that his prescription be preserved for posterity.[12]

Nothing came of the Hamilton plan; it was never presented to the Convention, and only a few delegates knew of its existence. Even Hamilton seemed not to have entertained any feelings for it beyond intellectual pride; on the Convention's last day he endorsed the Constitution, pledged to work for its adoption, and signed on behalf of New York though he lacked authority to do so.[13] Beginning in 1789, when he became the first Secretary of the Treasury, Hamilton determined that the best way to achieve his goals for the nation was to administer the government created by the Constitution to establish its independence and authority beyond challenge.[14] In this way he helped to bring about the strong central government that he was convinced the nation needed.[15]

The hundreds of amendments recommended between 1787 and 1790 by the Anti-Federalists and the state ratifying conventions amounted to a demand for sweeping constitutional revision—though for objectives diametrically opposed to those of Hamilton's draft. The Anti-Federalists' goal was to strip down the government limned in the Constitution to little more than what the Confederation had been—a loose network of sovereign states held together by a fragile general government. Although these recommendations carried widespread support in the country, they never emerged from Congress. In the spring of 1789, to the consternation of the Anti-Federalists, James Madison checkmated their plans by offering for consideration by the First Congress only those amendments that were designed to protect individual rights, leaving the structure and powers of the general government untouched. For generations, the Anti-Federalists' critique of the Constitution remained the only full-scale set of proposals for rewriting the document (however internally inconsistent and uncoordinated they might appear to modern observers).[16]

AS THE CONSTITUTION'S PRIMACY IN American public life grew in the first decades of its operation, pressures to rewrite the document eased. Recommendations for formal constitutional change between 1790 and 1860 focused on such specific institutional "defects" as the scope of federal judicial power and the workings of the Electoral College, or on problems emerging from the conflicts over slavery and federalism. Not until 1861 was there a comprehensive proposal to rewrite the Constitution.

Periodically, as outlined in Chapter 5, sectional crises of increasing seriousness and delicacy bedeviled American politics. The growth of constitutional strains and sectional tensions kindled several proposals to call a convention to propose a constitutional formula to preserve the Union. All these calls represented a desperate undercurrent of constitutional politics—implying that the normal mechanisms of the political system could not meet the problems confronting the nation. Equally significant, all these proposals collapsed, because of impracticability, the press of events, or the resolution of sectional controversies at the level of ordinary politics. These demands for a second convention served in the end to help restore sectional peace by resolving disputes between the states and the federal government.[17]

In 1799, James Madison (writing for the Virginia legislature) urged the propriety of an "explanatory amendment" to the Constitution explaining the rights of freedom of speech and of the press violated by the Sedition Act of 1798—and suggesting that such an amendment could be obtained through the convention procedure if Congress were not willing to act. Fifteen years later, from the other end of the political spectrum, the New England states organized the Hartford Convention of 1814–1815 to frame, among other things, a set of amendments that would have strengthened the region's influence vis-à-vis the South and the West on issues of war, peace, and foreign policy. However, news of the Treaty of Ghent of 1815, which ended the War of 1812, and of the victory of Andrew Jackson at the Battle of New Orleans, which sparked a surge of patriotism across the nation, derailing the convention's constitutional formula for sectional peace and reducing it to a timorous, defeatist laughingstock.[18]

Responding to the fierce argument over nullification waged between Senators Daniel Webster (Whig–Massachusetts) and Robert Y. Hayne (Democrat–South Carolina), in 1830 the aged James Madison recalled his position of 1799 on the desirability of a convention as a means to resolve sectional crises that reached the constitutional level,[19] a course of action adopted by several states in the wake of the 1832–1833 nullification crisis. South Carolina, Georgia, and Alabama demanded a convention to air the issues raised by the "Tariff of Abominations," which they felt violated the Constitution. The Georgia legislature proposed amendments to be submitted to the convention that would have gutted the power of the federal government to force a state to comply with federal law.[20] But, in the end, a sectional compromise brokered by Henry Clay of Kentucky rendered these demands irrelevant, and no convention assembled.

In the "secession winter" of 1860–1861, the likelihood that a convention was the only way to preserve the Union hung over both the Washington Peace Conference and the last days of the Thirty-sixth Congress (described in Chapter 5). The "session of amendments" witnessed the greatest single outpouring of proposed amendments since the adoption of the Constitution and the Bill of Rights seven decades before, but the hundreds of proposals never added up to a coherent basis for reworking the Constitution.

Such a reworking, however, was simultaneously taking place several hundred miles away, in Montgomery, Alabama. Invoking the principles of the Declaration of Independence, the politicians gathered in that city in February 1861 sought not to rewrite the Constitution within the confines of Article V but to create a new nation—the Confederate States of America.

In the Alabama state capitol, twelve delegates from the seven states that had voted to secede from the Union labored to frame a constitution for the Confederacy. They spurned the Lincoln Administration as a government bent on depriving the Southern states of their constitutional prerogatives, seeking instead to return to what they viewed as the original intent of the Framers. They deliberately used the 1787 document as the basis for their new charter of government, removing ambiguities and "correcting" the real and perceived "defects" of the original Constitution.[21]

Promulgated on March 11, 1861, the Confederate Constitution was swiftly ratified. At first glance, it closely resembles its 1787 progenitor in form and in most of its language.[22] Many of its provisions are taken unchanged from the earlier document, while most of the clauses that were altered incorporated the twelve amendments adopted between 1791 and 1804.[23] Many changes simply modernized spelling, punctuation, and capitalization.

Examined more closely, however, the Confederate Constitution displays notable differences from its model. Its Preamble fixed the doctrines of state sovereignty at the core of the new document and omitted the original Preamble's references to the common defense and the general welfare, suppressing these phrases' centralizing implications:

> We, the people of the Confederate States, *each State acting in its sovereign and independent character,* in order to form a *permanent federal government,* establish justice, insure domestic tranquility, and secure the blessings of liberty to ourselves and our posterity—invoking the favor and guidance of Almighty God—do ordain and establish this Constitution for the Confederate States of America. [emphasis added]

The Confederate Constitution assigned the power of impeachment to the Congress of the Confederate States *and* to the legislature of any member state over "any judicial or other federal officer resident and acting solely within the limits of [that] state" (Art. I, § 5). Similarly, it forbade Congress from carrying out any internal improvement projects (that is, roads, bridges, or canals) except coastal lights (Art. I, § 8, cl. 3) and reserved to the states the authority to appoint officers in the Army and Navy (Art. I, § 8, cl. 16). Only a convention to be called by Congress at the instance of the several states could propose amendments, thereby stripping the Confederate Congress of any role in the amending process

(Art. V).[24] The Confederate Constitution's doctrines of state sovereignty coexisted uneasily, however, with the idea of a permanent federal government called for in the Preamble and with the supremacy clause (Art. VI, § 2, cl. 1), which was identical to that of the original Constitution.

The Confederate Constitution established beyond challenge the legitimacy of the institution of slavery. It explicitly protected slaveowners' right to travel with their slaves free from any threat that they might lose their property rights (Art. IV, § 2, cl. 2) and directed that any new territory acquired by the Confederacy would be open to slavery (Art. IV, § 3, cl. 3). The Confederate framers' fealty to their 1787 model resulted in such oddities as the preservation of the three-fifths clause for apportioning representation and taxation (Art. I, § 2, cl. 3), even though every state was a slave state. Finally, Congress was required to forbid the importation of slaves from overseas or from any state or territory not included within the Confederacy (Art. I, § 9, cl. 1, 2).[25]

At the same time, the Confederate Constitution incorporated interesting institutional revisions.[26] Its framers elevated to constitutional status some practices that had evolved through custom and usage—for example, the power of the President to remove the heads of departments, though he could not remove lesser officials except for specified reasons of "dishonesty, incapacity, inefficiency, misconduct, or neglect of duty" (Art. II, § 2, cl. 3).

Other revisions presaged demands for constitutional change that continue to this day. A two-thirds vote in both houses of Congress was necessary to appropriate funds, but this requirement did not apply to bills initiated by the executive (Art. I, § 9). The provision's purpose was to curb appropriations by Congress enacted without consultation with the executive departments. The President was to serve only one six-year term (Art. II, § 1, cl. 1) and was given the power to exercise a line-item veto over appropriations (Art. I, § 7, cl. 2). And the Confederate Congress could "grant to the principal officer in each of the Executive Departments a seat upon the floor of either House, with the privilege of discussing any measure appertaining to his department" (Art. I, § 6, cl. 2).

Many of the Confederate Constitution's revisions of the legislative and executive branches were based on distrust of partisan politics, particularly as it had manifested itself in free-wheeling legislatures. The prescriptions that the document's framers sought to establish were echoed by many postwar observers and critics of federal and state government.[27]

We cannot adequately judge the Confederate Constitution as an alternative charter of government, because it lasted only four years. Nonetheless, the brief history of the Confederacy confirms that the weakness of the general government created by the 1861 document contributed to the eventual defeat of the Confederacy in 1865.[28]

. . .

IN THE YEARS FOLLOWING APPOMATTOX, the workings of government under the Constitution gradually subsided into patterns familiar from the antebellum period. The executive branch, its wings clipped as a result of the disastrous experience of Andrew Johnson, took a largely subsidiary place in policy-making and administration. Congress at the same time reasserted itself as the primary institution of the government, yet made sparing use of its legislative powers.[29]

As the Constitution approached its centennial in 1887, scholars, politicians, and controversialists began, for the first time in American history, to call for its thorough revision, or even replacement.[30] The strongest influence on these advocates of rewriting the Constitution was the growing popularity of the British form of government. The British parliamentary system (democratized in part by the Reform Bills of 1832 and 1867), which was complemented by centralized administration, seemed to promote government efficiency, responsibility, and accountability. The British constitution posed a stark contrast to American public life—which, critics believed, was tainted beyond repair by petty politics, the demands of selfish interests, corruption, and ruinous inefficiency.

This inchoate movement for constitutional change found its champion in a young professor at Bryn Mawr College, Woodrow Wilson.[31] His 1885 book *Congressional Government*[32] aspired to be the American equivalent of Walter Bagehot's landmark 1867 study, *The English Constitution,*[33] which Wilson deeply admired. Wilson offered no specific formula for change, but one strong theme ran throughout the pages of *Congressional Government*: a demand to replace the divided government so familiar to Americans with a unified, parliamentary system.

Though Wilson had no experience of government when he wrote (a fact for which he is often derided today), his slashing diagnosis of the problems afflicting the American polity was sound. He emphasized the legislative process's subservience to vested interests, the emasculation of the Presidency after 1868, and the general government's inability to formulate and enforce coherent, uniform public policies.[34]

Congressional Government set the pattern for virtually every later proposal for full-scale rewriting of the Constitution. A long parade of would-be framers in the twentieth century—political scientists, lawyers, jurists, public servants, and cranks—have looked with longing to the British constitution and dismissed American ideas of separation of powers and checks and balances with attitudes ranging from amiable contempt to bitter asperity. The great danger they have seen in the Constitution is that the dispersion of authority among three federal branches, and the sharing of power between the federal and state governments, make it all but impossible to frame, adopt, and enforce rational, consistent government policies absent a crisis of the direst sort.[35]

Most of these would-be framers have emphasized the superior efficiency and responsibility of the parliamentary system, especially at times when efficiency, centralized authority, and speedy response to crisis were deemed the highest priority (for example, the Depression and the Second World War).*[36] Just as important to Wilson's intellectual heirs was the parliamentary system's exorcism of the specter of divided party government. Under a parliamentary constitution, no longer would Republicans be pitted against Democrats, one party holding the Presidency, the other dominating Congress.

Such demands united politicians of the Right and the Left at a time when they could agree on little else. During the Second World War, the noted conservative economic journalist Henry Hazlitt, the moderate attorney Alexander Hehmeyer, and the liberal political scientist and New Dealer Thomas K. Finletter separately called for sweeping constitutional reform.[37] All three men wanted to rework American government into a parliamentary system, to ensure the concentration of government power and the elimination of divided party government. Systematization, centralization, and efficiency were vital, they argued, to the nation's economic recovery and military survival. None of these proposals garnered more than amusement or bemusement; none found a prominent advocate within the political system.

IN 1970, THE MAGAZINE OF a respected liberal think tank, the Center for the Study of Democratic Institutions, published a startling article by a senior fellow at the Center, Rexford G. Tugwell, who wrote as a spokesman for a Center project nearly a decade in preparation. Tugwell declared that the Constitution is inadequate to the needs of a modern industrial democracy and set forth his draft of a proposed "Constitution for a United Republics of America." The published version, he announced proudly, was his thirty-seventh draft.[38]

Tugwell's emergence as a would-be constitution-maker capped a remarkable career, which had begun at Columbia University, where he gained fame as an expert on agricultural policy and public administration. A New Deal "Brain Truster," he had served as assistant secretary of agriculture and as governor of the Commonwealth of Puerto Rico. Leaving the government in 1945 after the

---

*Not all would-be constitution-makers who admired British government favored its modern incarnation as a parliamentary democracy. In the 1930s, the noted church architect and medieval enthusiast Ralph Adams Cram sought to remove what he saw as the corruptions and secularism of modern America and to help restore the calm, generous spirituality of the High Middle Ages. He wanted, among other things, to abolish universal suffrage, to establish social and political institutions that would promote agrarianism, to recast the Senate as an American House of Lords and the Presidency as a constitutional monarchy, and to foster the development of the "natural aristocracy" that he believed necessary for a healthy nation.

death of his hero, Franklin D. Roosevelt, Tugwell taught at the University of Chicago. In 1966, he became a Senior Fellow at the headquarters of the Center for the Study of Democratic Institutions in Santa Barbara, California, writing books defending Franklin D. Roosevelt, the programs of the New Deal, and the conception of an activist Presidency modeled on Roosevelt's example.[39]

Tugwell found little cause for reassurance about the health of the Constitution as he reflected on the lessons of midcentury American government. An ardent proponent of centralized government and executive initiative, in the 1930s Tugwell had been consumed by agony and bitterness as the Supreme Court struck down many of his cherished legislative programs. He observed how Roosevelt had dissipated energy and concentration in his frequent battles to get legislative programs through Congress. In particular, Tugwell recalled Roosevelt's bitter and ineffective campaign in the 1938 midterm election, in which he failed to persuade the electorate to oust his bitterest congressional critics.

Tugwell's experience of politics and government brought forth a gloomy verdict on the American constitutional system:

> Because it has, in essentials, not been amended and has fallen, in certain respects, into irrelevance; because it has been warped by the aggressions of the branches; and because it has been extended in such ways that its original organic nature has been broken up, the Constitution cannot be taken as the prototype meant by those who would argue that some such instrument as was originally intended is necessary.[40]

With the full encouragement and support of the Center, he assumed the task of rethinking the entire structure of the American political and constitutional system. The project became a major focus of the Center's activities in the late 1960s. Tugwell's 1970 article in the *Center Magazine* only began his labors. Four years later, he published an elaborate treatise, *The Emerging Constitution,* which set forth the fortieth draft of his proposed constitution.

Tugwell argued for a massive restructuring of the American political system. He deemed judicial review and divided government to be dangerous luxuries that a modern nation no longer could afford—reflecting, in part, his lingering resentment of the Supreme Court's constitutional massacre of New Deal programs. Disapproving of the prevailing structure of federalism, he sought to reorganize the federal system into twenty "newstates" which would be more securely under the thumb of the general government, permitting greater coordination and consistency between levels of government.

Tugwell also favored a thorough overhaul of the Presidency. He wanted the President to serve a single nine-year term (with the possibility of recall by a 60 percent vote after three years). Two Vice Presidents would assist the President, one for "general" and one for "internal" affairs. The President would have the power to name Senators for life (as would the Principal Justice of the federal judiciary and the House of Representatives). Tugwell reassigned the power to name federal judges from the President to the Principal Justice of a radically revised and constricted federal judiciary. He proposed not one but two supreme federal courts—a Supreme Court and a High Court of Appeal—each with a different sphere of authority. In addition, a Judicial Assembly would meet each year to review the workings of the judiciary, to nominate candidates for the Principal Justiceship (from which the Senate would pick the new Principal Justice), and to share some powers with a Judicial Council, a body appointed by the Principal Justice to oversee the courts and to prepare codes of ethics.

In Tugwell's redesigned Congress, half the members of the House would represent individual states and districts, and half would be members-at-large representing (unspecified) national constituencies with terms of office coterminous with the President's. The Senate, whose members would serve for life, would include former Presidents and other major public officials.

Three new branches of government—of planning, regulation, and elections—would function alongside the familiar executive, legislative, and judicial branches. In addition, Tugwell presented a revised Bill of Rights and a Bill of Responsibilities. A sample provision from each will give a flavor of the whole:

> Freedom of expression, of communication, of movement, of assembly, or of petition shall not be abridged except in declared emergency.
>
> Each freedom of the citizen shall prescribe a corresponding responsibility not to diminish that of the others: of speech, communication, assembly, and petition, to grant the same freedom to others; of religion, to respect that of others; of privacy, not to invade that of others; of the holding and disposal of property, the obligation to extend the same privilege to others.[41]

His purpose was to clarify and systematize individual rights while protecting the government's efforts to define and carry out measures in the public interest without having to worry about interference by those claiming violations of individual rights.

Tugwell proposed a new, complex scheme of constitutional amendment; the Judicial Council and the Senate would share the power to propose amendments, which would be adopted or rejected by popular referendum. Every twenty-five years, a referendum would determine whether the people were satisfied with the constitution; if the people voted that the current constitution was unsatisfactory, they could authorize the Judicial Council to prepare a new one. This feature echoed the methods of constitutional revision found in the Pennsylvania constitution of 1776 and the Massachusetts constitution of 1780.

Tugwell's constitution bore little resemblance to the present structure of American public life—or, as has been pointed out, to any other form of government on the face of the Earth—which is precisely why it stood so small a chance of popular acceptance.[42] To American eyes, his proposal was innovative in some ways, grotesque in others. Born of his own academic career and political experience, it reflected his hostility to certain features of the constitutional system, such as judicial review, and his inability to appreciate the role of the judiciary as the guardian of individual liberties.

The Emerging Constitution prompted puzzlement and sharp criticism, rather than interest in its prescription of reform. Robert M. Hutchins, the pioneering educator who was director of the Center, was deeply disappointed that this venture into constitution-making did not spark the serious, wide-ranging public discussion he had hoped for when he and Tugwell had launched the project.[43] Perhaps the unkindest reaction to Tugwell's proposal was scholarly and public indifference; when he died in 1979, his obituary in *The New York Times* omitted all mention of his decades-long quest to recast the Constitution.

In November 1971, Professor Henry Steele Commager of Amherst College delivered a sobering verdict on most attempts to frame a new constitution, and on the general challenge of constitution-making:

> Now there are two ways of going about this. One is to do what Tugwell has done—a kind of playing games. You pretend that you are just writing a constitution in a vacuum, an IDEAL constitution, with no thought whatever of getting it adopted by the people. That seems to me playing games. If you are interested in getting a constitution which has some chance of being accepted—and working—then I think you must start with the present one and go on from there.[44]

Speaking for the vast majority of Americans who have resisted comprehensive redraftings of the Constitution, Commager observed, "Actually I don't think our trouble is the Constitution, but the rules and habits that have grown up under it and that make it so difficult to get anything done."[45]

PERHAPS THE MOST IRONIC ASPECT of Tugwell's failure was that his book was published in the midst of what may have been the single most serious constitutional crisis since the Great Depression—Watergate.[46] The Watergate scandals and the resignations of Vice President Spiro T. Agnew and President Richard M. Nixon induced widespread alarm over whether the Constitution was working as a system of government. In the aftermath of Watergate, scholars, judges, and political officials suggested that the time had come to reexamine the Constitution—perhaps even to revise or replace it. Most proposals focused on the Presidency, seeking to remedy what an increasing number of observers agreed was the office's tendency to isolate the President from disagreement or bad news or to make it easier to remove from office a President in whom the electorate and the Congress had no confidence.[47]

None of the proposals for reform got beyond academic discussion, in part because of the Constitution's weathering of the Watergate crisis and the failure of the more apocalyptic prophecies of constitutional breakdown. But they prompted what some scholars and officials hoped would be a movement for reform comparable, in the distinction of its membership and the urgency of its calls for action, to the Federalists of 1787.

If any one group today can be said to represent the political, intellectual, and cultural "establishment" in the United States, it is the Committee on the Constitutional System (CCS). Founded in 1982, the CCS numbers among its members present and former Senators and Representatives, members of the Cabinet and White House staff, officials of the national and state political parties, state governors, university and college presidents, journalists, lawyers, historians, political scientists, labor officials, business and financial leaders, and other interested citizens across the nation.[48] At its founding, the co-chairs of the CCS were Senator Nancy Landon Kassebaum (Republican–Kansas), former White House counsel Lloyd Cutler, and former Treasury Secretary C. Douglas Dillon.

In 1974, Professor Charles M. Hardin of the University of California, Davis, set in motion the process of discussion and consultation that led to the founding of the CCS. A noted political scientist who (like Rexford Tugwell) was an authority on agricultural policy, Hardin charged that the "imperial Presidency" had drawn most of its swollen power from the constitutional system of separation of powers. In his 1974 book, *Presidential Power and Accountability: Toward a New Constitution,* Hardin argued that the constitutional gulfs separating the executive, legislative, and judicial branches fostered executive independence and crippled any attempts to render the President accountable to the nation.[49] Only a constitutional upheaval on the order of the Watergate crisis (entering its final stages as he published his book) was sufficient to bring the rogue-elephant Presidency under control.

Having stated his diagnosis of the American constitutional system's defects, Hardin was bold about his prescription: the system should be rebuilt around party government, on the model of European parliamentary democracies. While conceding the need for a strong executive, Hardin declared:

[A] measure of control over the president can be provided by subjecting him to the criticism of an organized, focused opposition with leadership centered in one person who will be continuously visible and vocal as the alternative to the president. As the presidency is unified, so should the opposition be unified.[50]

His main proposals were that the President and Congress should be elected for simultaneous four-year terms, and that each defeated major-party candidate for the Presidency should be granted a seat in the House of Representatives, priority in committees and on the floor, and a staff, offices, and other perquisites suitable to his position as leader of the opposition.[51] Prescriptions like these were designed to augment the electorate's sense of political responsibility; to bring coherence, structure, and order to national politics; and to combat what Hardin deemed the dangerous tendencies that had grown out of the separation of powers and the system of checks and balances.

Hardin's book had little immediate effect, but many of his colleagues in political science and notable figures in public affairs found its message congenial.[52] In 1980–1981, Hardin and C. Douglas Dillon began discussions that led to the organization of the Committee on the Constitutional System, whose name was the brainchild of the historian and political scientist James MacGregor Burns. A biographer of Franklin D. Roosevelt and the author of influential books on politics and leadership, Burns pointed out that the CCS should "embrace not only the Constitution but also the institutions and governmental processes that flesh it out and try to make it work, especially political parties."[53]

The members of the CCS are the modern custodians of the Wilsonian tradition, particularly in their admiration for parliamentary democracy as promoting governmental efficiency and responsibility.[54] At the Constitution's bicentennial in 1987, the CCS issued a report, which declared:

> If aspects of the system framed in 1787 prevent the national government from meeting its present responsibilities, we must identify the outmoded features, separate them from the good and durable parts of the system . . . and make the necessary modifications.
>
> To do so is not to reject the great work of our forebears. It honors their spirit in the most sincere way: by seeking to emulate it.[55]

Though the CCS praised the constitutional doctrines of separation of powers and checks and balances as important guards against tyranny, it declared that in practice the system has functioned by "encouraging confrontation, indecision

and deadlock, and by diffusing accountability for the results."[56] The group
identified five major problems:

> 1. "brief honeymoons," providing only a short period for deci-
> sive action on domestic problems
>
> 2. divided government, leading to "inconsistency, incoherence,
> and even stagnation in national policy"
>
> 3. lack of party cohesion in Congress
>
> 4. loss of accountability
>
> 5. lack of a mechanism for replacing failed or deadlocked govern-
> ment.[57]

The array of proposals commanding majority support within the CCS included several that would require only party rules changes or new federal
statutes—for instance, new rules permitting party candidates for House and
Senate seats to serve as superdelegates in Presidential nominating conventions
to improve cohesion and working relations between the President and Congress;
a federal statute requiring states to provide voters the option of voting the
straight party ticket; and public financing of Congressional campaigns.[58]

The CCS proposals requiring amendments would (i) extend terms of Representatives from two to four years and terms of Senators from six to eight years,
eliminating off-year elections and again linking the Presidential and Congressional candidates' fortunes at the polls to increase the likelihood that the majority
party would control both the executive and legislative branches; (ii) permit
members of Congress to serve in the President's Cabinet; (iii) reduce the supermajority needed in the Senate to ratify treaties from two-thirds to three-fifths;
and (iv) amend the First Amendment to provide Congress authority to set
campaign spending limits (overturning the Supreme Court's 1976 decision in
Buckley v. Valeo).[59]

Members of the CCS proposed other reforms that did not win a majority vote
but were included in the 1987 report to stimulate further discussion. Some called
for requiring additional Presidential appearances before Congress and for creating a "shadow cabinet" among the opposition party in the legislature. Others
demanded a constitutional amendment making straight-ticket voting compulsory, another calling for Congressional elections to take place two to four weeks
after the Presidential elections, and yet another establishing a procedure for
requiring a new election in the event of governmental deadlock or failure. Some
members also suggested a periodic convocation of federal, state, and local
government officials to review the functioning of the federal system and to
suggest ways to improve coordination among the levels of government.[60]

Finally, the CCS faced the question of which amending procedure authorized by Article V should be used to give effect to its proposed amendments. It endorsed the standard Congress-driven amending process, calling it "a proven way to insure thoughtful consideration for proposed reforms." But the CCS did not reject a second convention out of hand nor did it state clearly the drawbacks of the convention process.

Given the eminence of the members of the CCS, the urgency of their diagnosis of impending constitutional crisis, the clarity of their proposals, and the energy with which they sought to lay their ideas before the American public, it is surprising how little reaction they generated, showing clearly how attached Americans are to the Constitution even as they express dissatisfaction with some of its workings. The most detailed response came from Mark P. Petracca, a political scientist at the University of California, Irvine.[61] Unpersuaded by the background, experience, and professed disinterestedness of the CCS's membership, Petracca perceived that many of the major CCS proposals

> are based on an incorrect diagnosis of a political problem while other reforms do not effectively match the political need. . . . Most disturbing of all, the CCS fails to fulfill its weighty burden of justifying these reforms by attempting to persuade the analyst or reader that such reforms would actually be good for the nation.

Perhaps the most important function of the CCS thought experiment, he wrote, was to "crystalliz[e] hope in the possibility of constitutional reform."[62]

Despite the urgency of their calls for reform, the members of the CCS seemed resigned to the lack of support for their specific proposals, expressing instead their hope for continuing reflection on the weaknesses of the constitutional system.[63] As one scholar has suggested, the bicentennial of the Constitution in 1987 may have been one of the most serious obstacles to an effective hearing for the CCS: "While bicentennial celebrations might be a good time for constitutional reflection, they might not be as conducive to real constitutional reform."[64]

In 1992, as this book was nearing completion, Barry Krusch published what may well be the most thoughtful and thorough reframing of the Constitution yet attempted. His study, *The 21st Century Constitution: A New America for a New Millenium*,[65] is the first proposed rewriting of the Constitution to take account of the twentieth-century revolutions in information and communications technologies; it is also noteworthy for its intellectual grounding in the American Revolution's series of experiments in government.

Krusch, a 34-year-old computer consultant living in New York City, began his labors in 1987, prompted by the commemoration of the Constitution's bicentennial. Struck by the contrast between the political creativity of the Revolutionary generation and the increasing ineffectiveness of their modern counterparts,

Krusch pursued two complementary lines of research. He steeped himself in the primary sources produced by the framing and ratification of the Constitution in 1787–1788, and he traced the divergences between the Constitution as written and the Constitution as administered (the "Empirical Constitution").[66] In 1990, Krusch opened a file on rewriting the Constitution on GENIE, a national computer bulletin board. He posted draft revisions of selected constitutional provisions and solicited comments from other users of GENIE, using the accumulating drafts and comments as the raw material for his first comprehensive presentation of a clause-by-clause revision of the Constitution.

Four major themes shape Krusch's proposals. First, emphasizing the vital role that access to information must play in democratic governance, he proposes that modern information and communications technologies be the core of a new constitutional framework. Technological constitutionalism of this type, he maintains, could make it possible for all Americans to take part in government. Second, he seeks to close the gap between the written Constitution and the Empirical Constitution, so that divergences between theory and practice in constitutional government no longer would sap the legitimacy of the constitutional system. Third, Krusch urges the reworking of constitutional doctrines of separation of powers and checks and balances, and the recasting of key institutions such as the Senate, to improve government's responsiveness and efficiency while incorporating added protections for individual rights. Fourth, Krusch stresses the dangers to democracy posed by professional politicians and the major political parties and the need to restore ordinary citizens as the true sources of sovereign power. His proposals therefore would, for example, exclude members of the major parties from holding federal legislative, executive, or judicial posts.

Krusch's plan of revision differs in several notable ways from all previous attempts to rewrite the Constitution. His plan is distinct from the parliamentary tradition (though it shares that tradition's dissatisfaction with separation of powers) and from Tugwell's executive-centered model (though, like Tugwell, Krusch seeks to bridge the gap between the theoretical and actual operation of American government). While retaining the structure and much of the original language of the 1787 Constitution, Krusch hopes to construct a form of government in which ordinary citizens retain and exercise power to set national goals and objectives and to monitor effectively the doings of their elected and appointed officials. Finally, thanks to his familiarity with modern computer technology, Krusch has helped to advance the theory of electronic governance beyond the model of the "electronic town hall" familiar to most Americans from the tantalizing 1992 Presidential initiative of H. Ross Perot.[67]

The next step in Krusch's efforts to persuade Americans to consider rewriting the Constitution along the lines marked out in his book is the organizing of a mock constitutional convention. His purpose is to demonstrate that constitutional revision is both necessary and within the capabilities of ordinary Americans.

IN 1885, WOODROW WILSON ENDED his first book with the following eloquent call to arms for would-be framers:

> The Constitution is not honored by blind worship. The more open-eyed we become as a nation, to its defects, and the prompter we grow in applying with the unhesitating courage of conviction all thoroughly-tested or well-considered expedients necessary to make self-government among us a straightforward thing of simple method, single, unstinted power, and clear responsibility, the nearer will we approach to the sound sense and practical genius of the great and honorable statesmen of 1787.[68]

Twenty-four years later, Herbert D. Croly, a founder of *The New Republic* and one of the architects of Progressive thought, offered his own verdict on projects of constitutional revision. Though they differed in personality and in their perceptions of public life, Wilson and Croly shared a vaulting intellectual ambition. Croly's diffidence and shyness made it all but impossible for him to take part in modern politics, but he was not shy about publishing his ideas, or in his often stern and skeptical views of his fellow reformers. It was precisely this habit of thought that animated Croly's concerns about rewriting the Constitution:

> [Although] a political theorist may be interested in some ideal plan of American national organization, it will be of little benefit under existing conditions to enter into such a discussion. Let it wait until the Americans have come to think seriously and consistently about fundamental political problems. The Federal Constitution is not all it should be, but it is better than any substitute upon which American public opinion could now agree. Modifications may and should somehow be made in details, but for the present not in fundamentals.[69]

Between them, Wilson and Croly indicate the poles and the contours of the debate about rewriting the Constitution. Wilson embodied the quest for order, rationality, and coordination that has driven virtually every plan for constitutional redesign since Reconstruction.[70] Rexford G. Tugwell and the CCS had the same targets in view, rejecting the principal features of the Constitution of 1787—checks and balances, separation of powers, and federalism—on the basis that these features have been rendered obsolete by the growth in the size and complexity of government. (Some, such as Charles Hardin, have even argued that these doctrines have threatened the success of constitutional government from their inception.) The would-be reformers concluded that the principles of the 1787 Constitution must go, or must be radically reconceptualized so that they do not obstruct the workings of efficient and responsive government.

Despite the survival of the Wilsonian model of rethinking the nation's constitutional arrangements, and whatever the virtues of Wilson's constitutional call to arms, Croly's estimate of the feasibility and desirability of rewriting the Constitution remains valid. No matter how well-informed and intelligent advocates of rewriting the Constitution may be, they are powerless to write their prescriptions into the nation's fundamental law unless they can garner the popular support and the political forces needed to satisfy the "supermajority" requirements of Article V. If constitutional revision is to succeed, the American people must be prepared to engage in a profound and far-reaching discussion of fundamental principles, driven by an equally powerful conviction of the need for constitutional change[71] and neither condition has been met.

However sincere and well-intentioned the would-be framers are, their proposals have failed precisely because they have not been able to convince the public that serious constitutional problems exist, or that the solution for these problems is a sweeping revision of the Constitution by a new convention. Indeed, opening up the nation's fundamental charter to wholesale alterations is often viewed as a frightening prospect. This does not mean, however, that we could not get to such a point—perhaps by an unexpected route.

Part III

IMPLICATIONS OF THE AMENDING PROCESS

CHAPTER 13

RIDDLES WITHOUT ANSWERS: ISSUES OF THE AMENDING PROCESS

Difficulties . . . as to the form, the quorum, &c. . . . in Constitutional regulations ought to be as much as possible avoided.

JAMES MADISON
Speech at Federal Convention
September 15, 1787

FEW AMERICANS POSSESS GREATER HANDS-ON knowledge of the workings of the amending process than Gregory D. Watson, a legislative aide to Texas State Representative Ric Williamson. On May 7, 1992, Watson saw the triumph of his ten-year quest to add to the Constitution an Amendment that James Madison had proposed in 1789. The long, tangled story of the Twenty-seventh Amendment is unique in the history of Article V.[1]

In 1982, while a sophomore majoring in economics at the University of Texas–Austin, Watson was looking for a paper topic. Observing that the Bill of Rights had been sent to the states as a package of twelve proposed Amendments, he concluded that the two unratified proposals might yet be before the states. The second of these seemed to Watson to have abiding relevance:

> No law, varying the compensation for the services of the Senators and Representatives, shall take effect, until an election of Representatives shall have intervened.

Only six states had ratified that proposed Amendment by 1791,[2] when the Bill of Rights was added to the Constitution. But, Watson discovered, Ohio had ratified the Amendment nearly a century later, on May 6, 1873. Ohio acted to protest the "salary grab" act of 1873, which authorized a massive salary increase (retroactive to the beginning of the year) throughout the federal government. As the Ohio General Assembly declared in its ratification resolution,

> the action of the last Congress . . . was unnecessary, uncalled for, and distasteful to the people of Ohio, and it is believed of the

whole Union, and its speedy repeal earnestly demanded by the people.[3]

Although Ohio succeeded in its effort to shame Congress into repealing the measure, no other state ratified the amendment at that time.

Watson concluded that the 1789 Amendment was still validly before the states—principally because, unlike most recent proposed amendments, the Compensation Amendment had no internal time limit. Intrigued, he wrote a paper reporting and analyzing his discovery and urging that the amendment be adopted. But Watson received only a C from his instructor, who told him that the Amendment was a dead letter and never would become part of the Constitution. Ten years later, Watson proved his instructor wrong—and confounded Congress, legal scholars, and historians throughout the nation.

Watson pursued his quest to revive the Congressional Compensation Amendment, encouraging state legislators throughout the Union to introduce it in their legislatures and work for its ratification. Starting with Maine in 1983 and Colorado in 1984, the states gradually responded to his arguments, and many of those legislatures that did ratify the Amendment cited his point that the lack of a time limit confirmed the Amendment's "live" status.

Soon after the Maine and Colorado ratifications, Watson discovered that Wyoming had ratified the 1789 Amendment six years earlier. Reviving the Ohio strategy in response to a 1977 Congressional pay increase, the Wyoming legislature had acted on March 3, 1978, resolving that

> the percentage increase in direct compensation and benefits was at such a high level, as to set a bad example to the general population at a time when there is a prospect of a renewal of double-digit inflation; and . . . increases in compensation and benefits to most citizens of the United States are far behind these increases to their elected Representatives.[4]

No other state had followed Wyoming's lead, and it was only because of the coverage of the Maine and Colorado ratifications in the magazine *State Legislatures* that a Wyoming resident reported his state's action on the Amendment. Meanwhile, as Watson's crusade gathered momentum, conservative and liberal activists of national reputation tried to jump on the bandwagon.[5]

As grounds for reviving a nearly two-hundred-year-old proposal, Watson and his allies cited the public's general and growing anger with the mechanisms by which Congress has sought to raise its salaries without going on record. They also invoked the authority of the original authors and supporters of the Amendment, particularly James Madison, arguing that history had borne out their concerns. For example, the Colorado legislature declared as part of its resolution of ratification:

> Whereas, The General Assembly of the State of Colorado finds that the proposed amendment is still meaningful and needed as part of the United States Constitution and that the present political, social, and economic conditions are the same or even more demanding today than they were when the proposed amendment was submitted for its adoption . . .[6]

Most scholars had dismissed the 1789 Amendment as a trivial backwater of constitutional law. For example, Professor Walter Dellinger of Duke University Law School commented in 1989:

> I think it's clearly dead. It was proposed without any time deadline. There's no rule in the Constitution saying an amendment proposed by Congress expires if not ratified by a certain time. But the Supreme Court has held that the adoption of an amendment is to reflect a 'contemporary consensus.' Therefore an amendment dormant for 200 years is no longer viable.[7]

Yet the parade of state ratifications continued:

1984 1	1987 4	1990 2
1985 5	1988 3	1991 1
1986 3	1989 7	1992 6

The ratification of the Compensation Amendment spawned several constitutional oddities of its own. For example, in only one state (for the only time in the history of the amending process) did the people have the chance to decide the Amendment's fate themselves. In 1978, Idaho's legislature had adopted a resolution requiring that any proposed amendment to the Constitution be approved by a statewide referendum before the legislature could ratify it. In 1986, the state's attorney general issued an opinion declaring that the 1978 requirement was a violation of Article V, but in 1988 the state legislature directed the holding of a referendum on the Compensation Amendment. Once it was overwhelmingly approved by the voters, on November 8, 1988, the Idaho legislature ratified it.[8]

On May 7, 1992, the legislatures of Michigan and New Jersey raced to supply the needed thirty-eighth ratification. Michigan acted first; New Jersey's legislators, disappointed that they had missed the honor of putting the Amendment into the Constitution, nonetheless ratified. Five days later, Illinois also ratified, bringing the total number of states approving the amendment to forty. As of December, forty-one states have ratified.[9]

Members of Congress and constitutional scholars reacted with confusion to the news. Some made a quick check to see if there were any other "unexploded time bombs" lurking in the amending process; others insisted that the Amendment had become a dead letter sometime between September 26, 1789, when Congress proposed it to the states, and May 7, 1992.

Attention focused on Don W. Wilson, the Archivist of the United States, who since 1984 has had the statutory responsibility for certifying amendments.*[10] The task of certifying an amendment extends only to determining whether the state certificates of ratification meet the requirements of Article V and whether the certificates set forth congruent texts of the amendment. With these requirements met, Wilson ruled the Twenty-seventh Amendment ratified, on May 18. A day later, it was published in the *Federal Register,* the official repository of statutes, regulations, and constitutional Amendments.[11] Wilson's action persuaded most constitutional scholars to accept the Amendment. For example, Professor Dellinger declared, "My own view is that Congress has no formal role to play. The amendment process is completed by act of the last necessary state."[12]

Stunned by the adoption of the Amendment, the leadership of the House and the Senate seesawed. Speaker of the House Thomas S. Foley (Democrat–Washington), who at first was dubious about the validity of the Amendment, declared that, if the Archivist was willing to certify it, that was good enough for him. At the same time, however, he publicly toyed with the possibility of holding hearings on the amending process—which in the end never took place.

The Senate's President *pro tempore,* Robert C. Byrd (Democrat–West Virginia), maintained that Congress retained its prerogative to determine whether and when an amendment is validly ratified, even though most scholars believed that the Archivist's decision to certify settled the matter. Senator Charles E. Grassley (Republican–Iowa) agreed with Byrd, insisting that "there is reason that the Senate needs to act . . . to ward off any legal attacks that might come on the issue of timeliness."[13] Byrd and Grassley reproved the Archivist for not following the former custom of sending notification to the House and the Senate and allowing Congress a brief time to review the documents related to the Amendment in

---

*From 1791 through 1818, the Secretary of State carried out the duty of certifying amendments as a matter of course; in 1818, Congress enacted a statute officially assigning the Secretary that responsibility. In 1951, Congress amended the statute to transfer the responsibility to the Administrator of General Services, who supervised the publication of the *Federal Register,* and in 1984, yet another statute transferred both tasks to the Archivist of the United States.

question before certifying it; this procedure, they maintained, had been followed with previous Amendments, particularly the Fourteenth, which had been beset by the problem of state legislatures' attempts to rescind their ratifications.[14]

While praising the Twenty-seventh Amendment, Senator William V. Roth, Jr. (Republican–Delaware) pointed out that "some issues are left unanswered." Noting the existence of four other unratified amendments lacking time limits (the 1789 Reapportionment Amendment, the 1810 "Titles of Nobility" Amendment, the 1861 Corwin Amendment, and the 1924 Child Labor Amendment), Roth asked that Congress adopt Byrd's proposed resolution declaring these proposals to have lapsed. If Congress could declare ratified an amendment that most scholars had assumed was a dead letter for two centuries, Roth demanded, "why cannot the States ratify even the expired amendments—those which failed ratification before a congressionally imposed deadline—in the hope that Congress would later extend the deadline?"[15]

At the same time, Representative William Clay (Democrat–Missouri) reminded his colleagues that since 1989 Congress had by statute followed the procedure that the 1789 Amendment mandated; the 1989 Ethics Reform Act, passed in response to the public outcry against the latest Congressional pay raises, seemed to make the Twenty-seventh Amendment unnecessary. Clay also asked whether the Amendment would outlaw for members of Congress the automatic cost-of-living adjustments (COLAs) that federal law provided to every federal employee.[16] (When asked about this issue, Professor Laurence H. Tribe of Harvard Law School was uncertain, suggesting that he could come up with plausible arguments either way but doubting whether it would be "politically wise" for any member of Congress to bring the issue to court. Gregory Watson concluded that the amendment would bar annual COLAs but not a statute permitting a COLA at the beginning of each Congress.)[17]

Whatever the merits of these issues and problems, political realities dictated speedy endorsement of the Twenty-seventh Amendment. On May 20, Congress confirmed the Archivist's decision by overwhelming margins in both houses. The Senate vote was 99 to 0 (Lloyd Bentsen, Democrat–Texas, missed the vote because of illness); the House approved the Amendment (after brief discussion) by a vote of 414 to 3, with 18 Representatives either absent or not voting. The 3 Representatives voting "No" were Neal Smith (Democrat–Iowa), Carl C. (Chris) Perkins (Democrat–Kentucky), and Craig Washington (Democrat–Texas). Smith explained that, while he had no problem with the substance of the Amendment, "it's short-term political pandering without regard to long-term consequences to the Constitution."[18] Washington, inexplicably, cast his ballot against the Amendment despite having voted for ratification as a Texas state senator in 1989. (Still awaiting a vote are resolutions introduced by Senators Byrd and Grassley declaring the other four unratified Amendments expired.)

Though some journalists have characterized the campaign to resurrect the Compensation Amendment as a right-wing attack on Congress, Gregory Watson has rejected the charge: "That's pure nonsense. The state legislators who voted to ratify the amendment formed bipartisan coalitions, from both political parties, and those few who opposed the amendment also came from both parties. It transcended party; it transcended 'liberal versus conservative.' It was truly bipartisan." He declares the adoption of the Twenty-seventh Amendment to be "the greatest thing in my thirty-year life."[19]

UNRESOLVED ISSUES

THE STRANGE GENESIS OF THE Twenty-seventh Amendment suggests just some of the unresolved issues that haunt the Constitution's amending process. Ironically, at the time the Constitution was framed, only a few of the delegates to the Federal Convention were willing to confront and resolve these questions. As we saw in Chapter 2, the delegates were weary of their long, drawn-out summer of constitution-making; eager to finish their work and return home, they were impatient with those who would have them devote more time to the details of the amending process. On September 15, 1787, James Madison protested to his colleagues in the Convention, "Difficulties . . . as to the form, the quorum, &c. . . . in Constitutional regulations ought to be as much as possible avoided."[20] On this subject, as on so many others, Madison knew what he was talking about.

The procedures outlined in Article V pose a host of unresolved difficulties. For example: does a proposed amendment have a "shelf life"—that is, a period after which it may be deemed to have expired? (This issue is posed most starkly by the 202 years of the Twenty-seventh Amendment's birth pangs.) May a state rescind its ratification of an amendment? May Congress abolish a time limit on a proposed amendment's ratification?

What, if any, standards govern the convention procedure authorized by Article V—a procedure that has never been used? May Congress set conditions for determining when the constitutional prerequisites for calling a convention have been met? Do the terms of the Constitution control the organization and administration of a convention? May Congress impose enforceable limits or mandates on a convention? Is there any recourse if such a convention casts aside its mandate and limitations? May the convention set aside the requirements of Article V?

Because they fear the minefield of unresolved issues surrounding Article V, many scholars and politicians are reluctant to contemplate formal constitutional change, viewing the amending process in general, and specific proposed amendments, with suspicion and dread.[21] In part, they are all too aware of the intimidating practical obstacles posed by the process.

But something more is going on here. Article V induces constitutional vertigo. Invoking the amending process is as threatening to modern politicians and scholars, and as fraught with risk, as calling up demons would have been to medieval alchemists. The question is not, "But what if we fail?"—it is, "But what if we *succeed?*"

For this reason, many observers have found especially alarming the willingness of right-wing politicians to reach for Article V as if it were a fire-ax on the wall.[22] The 1980s let loose a flood of suggested amendments to the Constitution. Would-be framers proposed to give the President a line-item veto over appropriations measures; to require a balanced budget; to define human life as beginning at the moment of conception (thereby outlawing abortion as a matter of federal constitutional law); to authorize Congress and the states to prohibit the burning of the American flag (thereby overturning recent Supreme Court decisions); and to impose a limit on the number of terms that a Representative or Senator can serve in Congress or on the number of years that a federal judge can hold office. President Ronald Reagan and other officials of his Administration endorsed many of these proposals and encouraged their underlying assumption—that the constitutional system, unable to function to their liking as now organized, requires overhaul through the amending process. President George Bush was at least as assiduous as his predecessor in championing amendments, including on his shopping-list school-prayer, line-item veto, balanced-budget, flag-burning, term-limit, and human life amendments, and Vice President Dan Quayle loyally supported the Bush Administration's constitutional agenda.*[23]

Article V's newfound popularity in American politics was fueled by the remarkable success rate of amendments proposed between 1960 and 1971.[24] Right-wing partisans increasingly came to believe that they, too, were entitled to make use of Article V after the Amendment successes garnered by the Left

---

*When he was a Republican Representative from Texas, George Bush proposed three amendments—one in 1969 to permit prayer in public buildings, another in 1969 to establish mandatory retirement ages for members of Congress and federal judges, and a third in 1970 on equal rights for women. During his years as a Republican Representative from Indiana, Dan Quayle proposed five amendments—one in 1977 establishing term limits for President, Vice President, members of Congress, and federal judges (reintroduced in two different versions in 1979), one in 1979 to require a balanced budget, and another in 1980 to command a balanced budget with a three-fifths supermajority needed to raise taxes.

during those years (the Twenty-third, adding the District of Columbia to the Electoral College for Presidential elections; the Twenty-fourth, abolishing the poll tax in federal elections; and the Twenty-sixth, lowering the voting age to eighteen).

The victory of the "Stop ERA" campaign between 1978 and 1982, which blocked ratification of the proposed Equal Rights Amendment even after Congress had extended its built-in time limit, reinforced the growing appeal of amendment politics among right-wing groups. "Stop ERA" gave right-wing activists a crash course in the workings of Article V. The hands-on familiarity they thus acquired instilled in them a renewed appreciation of its potential as an instrument to achieve their constitutional agenda.[25] The "Stop ERA" campaign helped to catalyze the Reagan Administration's affinity for demanding constitutional change when the processes of "normal politics" did not yield the results they and their ideological allies desired.

In a development paralleling the multiplication of specific proposed amendments, talk of a second convention—more often to propose a specific amendment than to rewrite the entire document—resurfaced for the first time in a generation.[26] By October 1989, thirty-two states—only two short of the thirty-four required under Article V's convention method—had adopted calls for a second convention; meanwhile, however, several states had rescinded their applications.[27] Again, President Reagan and other government officials embraced calls for a second convention; they argued that the normal processes of government were incapable of responding to the needs of the nation.

Thus, the increasing tendency to propose formal changes in the Constitution to solve political problems has conferred new importance on issues of the amending process left unsettled by the constitutional text.

"ORDINARY" ISSUES OF THE AMENDING process have erupted in disputes over the framing and adoption of specific amendments, and most of them arose for the first time in 1787–1788, during the ratification of the original Constitution. These issues fall into two categories: (i) the status of proposed amendments, and (ii) the states' actions in ratifying or rejecting amendments.

Only two decisions of the Supreme Court have addressed such issues: *Dillon v. Gloss*,[28] addressing issues raised by the Eighteenth Amendment, and *Coleman v. Miller*,[29] establishing the modern doctrinal framework for deciding issues arising under Article V.

Dillon v. Gloss addressed the validity of time limits imposed by Congress on proposed amendments. When Congress proposed the Eighteenth Amendment (authorizing Prohibition), it imposed a time limit of seven years within which the Amendment had to be ratified; if the time limit passed without the Amendment receiving a sufficient number of ratifications, then it expired. All but one of the Amendments following the Eighteenth have incorporated a time limit, either in the text or in the authorizing resolution adopted by Congress. (The Child Labor Amendment, proposed in 1924, did not contain a time limit because the House and the Senate could not agree on how long that limit should be.)[30] In *Dillon,* Justice Willis Van Devanter held for the Court that Congress could impose a reasonable time limit, and that the seven-year limit chosen was reasonable:

> We do not find anything in [Article V] which suggests that an amendment once proposed is to be open to ratification for all time, or that ratification in some of the states may be separated from that in others by many years and yet be effective. We do find that which strongly suggests the contrary.[31]

First, Van Devanter declared, proposal and ratification are succeeding steps in a single process, "the natural inference being that they are not to be widely separated in time." Second, amendments are proposed when they are deemed necessary, and necessity implies that ratification should be accomplished with speed. Third, because ratification is the approval of an amendment by the people in three-fourths of the states, it ought to be "sufficiently contemporaneous . . . to reflect the will of the people in all sections at relatively the same period."[32] In pursuing his reasoning, Van Devanter commented on the unratified amendments in words sadly ironic seven decades later:

> [F]our amendments proposed long ago—two in 1789, one in 1810 and one in 1861—are still pending and in a situation where their ratification in some of the States many years since by representatives of generations now largely forgotten may be effectively supplemented in enough more States to make three-fourths by representatives of the present or some future generation. To that view few would be able to subscribe, and in our opinion it is quite untenable.[33]

Time limits again became an issue when, in 1979, Congress adopted a three-year extension of the deadline for the Equal Rights Amendment—a limit specified in the authorizing resolution but not in the Amendment's text. Some charged that Congress had illegally changed the rules in the middle of the process. Defenders of the extension maintained that Congress only lacked the power to adjust time limits incorporated in the text of proposed amendments. Although a federal district court in Idaho ruled that Congress had erred in extending the time limit, the case did not reach the Supreme Court until after the Amendment's extended deadline had elapsed, and the Justices vacated the lower court's decision as moot.[34]

Coleman v. Miller, decided in 1939, established the principle that issues having to do with the ratification of amendments are political questions best left to the determination of Congress. At issue in *Coleman* was the ratification of the Child Labor Amendment by the Kansas legislature, which in 1925 had rejected the Amendment but reconsidered it in 1937, thirteen years after Congress had sent it to the states. Although the Kansas house of representatives voted to ratify, the state senate divided equally, 20 to 20. The lieutenant governor, who presided over the senate, cast the tie-breaking vote in favor of ratification. Twenty-one state senators and three state representatives then sued for an order directing the Kansas secretary of state not to authenticate the resolution. They cited three grounds: (1) as an executive officer, the lieutenant governor should have no role in the ratification process; (2) the 1925 vote to reject the Amendment had ended Kansas's discussion of ratification and could not be set aside by a later legislative vote; and (3) the Amendment had lapsed, not having been ratified within a reasonable time. The state supreme court rejected all three arguments.[35]

The United States Supreme Court heard the legislators' appeal and held (5 to 4) that the legislators had standing to bring the suit.[36] As to the issue of the power of the lieutenant governor to break a legislative tie vote on a proposed amendment, Chief Justice Charles Evans Hughes reported that the Court was equally divided and therefore "expresses no opinion upon that point."[37]

Lumping together the issues of the effect of the 1925 vote to reject and of timeliness, Chief Justice Hughes (joined by Justices Harlan Fiske Stone and Stanley F. Reed) disposed of each in turn. Citing the precedents established in 1868 by the adoption of the Fourteenth Amendment (in which the Secretary of State referred the question of rescinded ratifications to Congress, which in turn ignored the rescissions and declared the Amendment ratified), Hughes wrote the following cloudy paragraph, which has dominated Congressional views on the amending process for over half a century:

> We think that in accordance with this historic precedent the question of the efficacy of ratifications by state legislatures, in the light of previous rejection or attempted withdrawal, should be regarded as a political question pertaining to the political departments, with the ultimate authority in the Congress in the exercise of its control over the promulgation of the adoption of the amendment.[38]

Turning to the timeliness issue, Hughes acknowledged that *Dillon* had accepted the power of Congress to set a time limit on a proposed amendment but rejected the petitioners' contention "that, in the absence of a limitation by the Congress, the Court can and should decide what is a reasonable period within which ratification may be had."[39] Pointing out that there was no source from which criteria of timeliness could be derived, Hughes declared that the congressional power to set a time limit was part of a broader congressional prerogative to determine whether such a limit was necessary and appropriate.

Justices Hugo L. Black, Owen J. Roberts, Felix Frankfurter, and William O. Douglas reached the same conclusion as did Chief Justice Hughes, but by a slightly different route, which recognized an even wider scope for congressional discretion:

> The [amending] process itself is "political" in its entirety, from submission until an amendment becomes part of the Constitution, and is not subject to judicial guidance, control or interference at any point. . . . Congress, possessing exclusive power over the amending process, cannot be bound by and is under no duty to accept the pronouncements upon that exclusive power by this Court or by the Kansas courts.[40]

Justices Pierce Butler and James C. McReynolds dissented, arguing in vain that the Amendment had expired because "more than a reasonable time had elapsed." Noting that in *Dillon* the Court had held that the seven-year time limit set by Congress was reasonable, Butler and McReynolds charged that the majority had brushed aside the holding and reasoning of the earlier case. They concluded that the Child Labor Amendment had lapsed.[41]

Congress has relied ever since on *Coleman v. Miller* as authority for its exclusive prerogative to decide whether to recognize proposed amendments as validly ratified. For example, in the May 1992 Senate debate on the Twenty-seventh Amendment, Senator Byrd invoked *Coleman*, a position with which Gregory Watson agreed: "Had Congress rejected the amendment, it would have been within their powers to do so under the doctrines of *Coleman v. Miller*. That's why, in many of the state resolutions of ratification, I made sure that *Coleman v. Miller* was cited and recognized."[42] As Watson rightly perceived, *Coleman* has established the context within which issues of the amending process, including the following three, are played out:

> • *Contemporaneity:* We can keep a bottle of milk in our refrigerator indefinitely, but at some point it will spoil and become undrinkable. By analogy, even in cases where Congress has not set a specific time limit on a proposed amendment, and despite the holding of *Coleman*, many scholars point to *Dillon* and maintain that there must be some point in the life of the

proposal when it is no longer "live." In 1873, as we have seen, Ohio ratified an amendment proposed in 1789, leading Congress to impose a time limit on most subsequent proposed amendments.[43] But is an amendment lacking a time limit still valid? Or does Congress simply "make assurance double sure" by including time limits in proposed amendments even though they may not be needed?

• *Rescission:* May a state rescind its decision to ratify a constitutional amendment? Or may a state that has rejected an amendment reverse itself and ratify the amendment? These issues are most famous in connection with the Equal Rights Amendment, but (as noted in Chapter 6) they first arose in connection with the Civil War Amendments.

Although most courts seek to avert such questions by citing the "political questions" doctrine, the prevailing view is that the amending process may be understood as working in only one direction. Once a state rejects an amendment, it is free to reconsider and ratify it; however, once a state ratifies an amendment, it may not rescind that ratification. Why should this be the case? A state's decision to adopt an amendment forms the basis for later states' decisions to adopt or to reject. To permit rescission of a ratification would be to confuse and perhaps derail the amending process's orderly functioning.[44] By contrast, if a state reconsiders its rejection of an amendment, its action does not undercut the basis for later states' decisions. A state should be free to change its mind about rejecting an amendment if other states' actions demonstrate that the amendment has general popular support.[45]

• *Constitutionality:* Is it possible to invalidate a constitutional amendment, even one otherwise validly ratified, as unconstitutional? The conventional and commonsense answer to this question is No. For example, in the mid-1980s the Moral Majority movement demanded a constitutional amendment overturning the Supreme Court's decisions forbidding mandatory school prayer under the First Amendment's establishment clause. In an informal televised debate between the Reverend Jerry Falwell and Professor (now Dean) John E. Sexton of New York University Law School, the moderator asked Professor Sexton if the amendment were constitutional. Astonished, he responded, "Before an amendment is ratified, it is just a proposal—nothing more and nothing less. If it is ratified, then it is part of the Constitution, and becomes constitutional by definition."

This commonsensical approach has been challenged by several legal scholars, who have suggested that certain amendments could be so threatening to the fabric of the constitutional system that they might well be deemed unconstitutional.[46] They note that in other nations, such as India, it is possible to invalidate a constitutional amendment if it would subvert the constitution's "basic structure."[47]

To be sure, Article V sets forth one limitation on the *kinds* of amendments that may be proposed: "that no State, without its Consent, shall be deprived of it's equal Suffrage in the Senate." But even this limitation could be overcome by a two-step process: an amendment repealing the last clause of Article V, followed by an amendment restructuring the Senate's system of representation.

Questions about implicit constitutional limitations on Article V arose for the first time in reaction to the Civil War Amendments of 1865–1870. Opponents of the Thirteenth Amendment, which abolished slavery, and the Fifteenth Amendment, which outlawed racial discrimination in access to the franchise, asserted that these amendments radically expanded the power of the general government beyond the confines set by the framers in 1787–1788 and thus exceeded the boundaries set to the amending process. These arguments failed, but opponents of proposed amendments excluding issues of school prayer and reapportionment from the jurisdiction of the federal courts have tried to make a similar case.

Consider, for example, an amendment that establishes the Judeo-Christian tradition as the nation's official set of religious values. Such an amendment, being directly contrary to the commands of the First Amendment's free exercise and establishment clauses and the extraordinary religious diversity of American life,[48] might be an unconstitutional amendment that could not be adopted as a matter of constitutional law. Or suppose Congress decided to adopt the amendment (proposed in 1985 by a lawyer practicing in California) repealing the Civil War Amendments and limiting citizenship to white people of European descent.[49] Would this proposed amendment do such violence to the settled system of constitutional law and governance, and the long-established network of individual rights, that it should be deemed unconstitutional and unadoptable, even in the face of popular demand for it?

A major stumbling block for the argument is that under these criteria the Thirteenth Amendment can be deemed unconstitutional, for it was an extraordinary reversal of constitutional doctrines having to do with the institution of slavery and the question of racial equality. Arguments against the constitutionality of proposed amendments revive the arguments by border-state Senators and Representatives in 1865 that the Thirteenth Amendment was unconstitutional because it exceeded the permissible scope of the amending power recognized by Article V and struck at central components of the compromises undergirding the original Constitution.

Can these issues be resolved, whether by Congress or by the federal courts? One obstacle is the principle underlying the "political questions" doctrine: because the people can and should govern themselves, the institutions of a representative democracy entrusted with the operation of the amending process ought to assume the responsibility of dealing with such questions, rather than handing them off to an unelected judiciary. Another obstacle is practical: the courts do not wish to inject themselves into disputes between political institutions, or between the people and their elected officials. Whatever the reason, these questions are unlikely to be resolved in the foreseeable future.

Citing such problems as these, Gregory Watson favors amending Article V. After enduring a lonely, decade-long struggle to get the compensation amendment adopted by the states, his assessment is that "it's a terrible process. It's sloppy, extremely unprofessional, and terribly haphazard." Recalling his unexpected discovery of Wyoming's ratification of the Amendment more than six years after the event, he asked, "Is it possible that there are state ratifications that nobody knows about? I think it is. This amendment may have been ratified a long time ago, and nobody knew it. There still may be ratifications floating around out there that nobody knows about."[50]

Watson's proposed amendment to Article V would require that any amendment be proposed "by a two-thirds vote of the *entire membership* of the House and of the *entire membership* of the Senate," thereby eliminating the present practice of using two-thirds of those present and voting. Once proposed, the amendment would be put before a national popular referendum, to take place on Election Day in the next even-numbered year, to coincide with Presidential elections or midterm Congressional elections. An amendment would be declared adopted if it amassed "an absolute majority—at least 51 percent—in two-thirds of the House districts through the entire nation." Watson maintains that this revision would preserve the requirement of a contemporaneous national consensus in support of a successful amendment, and it would bring order, professionalism, and certainty to this "terrible process." Pointing out that forty-nine of the fifty states submit state constitutional amendments to a popular vote (Delaware being the only exception), Watson concludes:

> I would take state legislatures out of the amending process. They shut out the majority of the American people. Amending the Constitution should be a matter between the U.S. government and the American people.[51]

SECOND-CONVENTION MOVEMENTS

EVEN BEFORE THE FEDERAL CONVENTION had finished its work, delegate Edmund Randolph of Virginia urged that a second convention be called to review and revise the proposed Constitution. Randolph's demand became an Anti-Federalist rallying cry, but the second-convention movement never acquired the momentum it needed and was put to rest by James Madison's leadership in proposing the amendments that became the Bill of Rights.

But since that time there have been three serious attempts to call a second convention, all of them in the twentieth century:[52]

> • Between 1893 and 1929, thirty-five states filed applications with Congress for a second convention—some seeking specific amendments (in particular, amendments requiring the direct election of Senators), others seeking a convention with no mandate or limitation. In 1929, the thirty-fifth state, Wisconsin, insisted that Congress had to call a convention because it had received three more than the then-required number of applications (thirty-two, two-thirds of the forty-eight states). The applications, however, covered a potpourri of purposes, some were twenty and thirty years old, and at least eleven sought the direct election of Senators, a goal achieved in 1913 by the Seventeenth Amendment. The second-convention movement had been useful in forcing the Senate to accede to the Seventeenth Amendment, but its usefulness was at an end. Subtracting those applications proposing direct election of Senators from the thirty-five, Congress determined that it was under no obligation to call a convention.

> • From 1941 through the mid-1950s, over twenty-five states applied for a convention to consider an amendment to limit the rate on federal income, inheritance, and gift taxes to 25 percent, but the movement ran out of steam.

> • In 1967, after a concerted effort championed by Senator Everett McKinley Dirksen (Republican–Illinois), Congress received applications from thirty-two states, two short of the thirty-four needed (with the admission in 1959 of Alaska and Hawaii) for a convention to consider amendments to reverse the Supreme Court's reapportionment decisions. The two final applications never materialized, and Congress set aside the applications already received.

In the late 1960s and 1970s, three conservative Senators—Samuel J. Ervin, Jr. (Democrat–North Carolina), Orrin Hatch (Republican–Utah), and Jesse Helms

(Republican–North Carolina)—introduced legislation either specifying procedures for Congress to follow in the event of a second convention or requiring Congress to adopt procedures to govern a convention. None of these proposals has emerged from Congress,[53] and several have drawn extensive scholarly criticism.[54]

However, as many constitutional scholars have pointed out, in the early 1990s we are once again approaching the critical number of applications from two-thirds of the states. Recent estimates indicate that thirty-two of the needed thirty-four states have submitted applications to Congress calling for a convention to propose a balanced-budget amendment. The June 1992 failure in the House of the Stenholm balanced-budget amendment may also spur advocates of a second convention to secure the additional applications.

If thirty-four applications for a second convention do land on the Congressional doorstep, and if they all clear the hurdles of consistency and contemporaneousness on which Congress has relied in the past, the nation will confront several thorny issues in organizing the gathering that reporters are almost certain to dub ConCon II:

(i) In the Federal Convention of 1787, each state, large or small, had one vote. Is such a voting system acceptable for ConCon II in the era of "one person, one vote"?

(ii) The state legislatures chose delegates in 1787 without reference to formal national political parties, equal districting, or any other matters of federal constitutional law in regulating state elections; at that time, such issues were matters neither of federal constitutional principle nor of state electoral procedure. Would the delegate-selection process for ConCon II be exempt from these considerations? Or would the states have to hold elections?

(iii) The original Convention and the Confederation Congress maintained a discreet "arm's-length" relationship; this was the case with the state governments as well. What relationship, if any, should the governments of the nation and of the fifty states have with ConCon II? In particular, the original Convention included a large number of delegates from the Confederation Congress. Would the provision of the Constitution forbidding Senators and Representatives from holding any other posts during their term of office disqualify them from serving in ConCon II? Political operatives also speculate on what effect ConCon II might have on any intervening Congressional elections.

(iv) Questions of sheer size emerge as well, each having larger substantive and theoretical consequences. If ConCon II were as big as the

House of Representatives, it would number 435 delegates. The entire group of delegates selected for the 1787 Convention amounted to 74; 55 delegates attended at least some sessions, 41 gathered at the largest single session, and no more than a few dozen attended most sessions. How could so large a gathering debate and resolve complex political issues without risking chaos?

(v) ConCon II would lack internal structure or a sense of institutional continuity, both of which are of great value in enabling such a body to carry out its assigned tasks. It would be composed largely of members new to the task before them and to the means by which it is to be completed. Would such a convention be able to function at all, let alone as well as the 1787 Convention? For example, the delegates in Philadelphia made use of the full range of parliamentary procedure, a matter of shared knowledge among educated gentlemen of the late eighteenth century but far removed from the experience of most Americans in the 1990s. Further, these procedures included a rule permitting the delegates to revise and reconsider their work. Would abrupt reversals of the sort common in the 1787 Convention be tolerated by—or even comprehensible to—the national electorate watching ConCon II? Or would the citizenry denounce delegates' attempts at compromise as betrayals of principle and abandonment of their constituents?

(vi) The original Convention's deliberations were kept secret—a near-impossible prospect today. The "public's right to know" was in its infancy in 1787; there were no aggressive, well-organized news-gathering organizations, nor did the delegates in 1787 leak information in order to embarrass or discredit their colleagues.[55] Even if ConCon II took place behind closed doors, would not leaks to the media thwart the original purpose of holding such deliberations in secret?

(vii) How would ConCon II's proposals be considered for adoption, and by whom? After all, there is venerable precedent for proposing a new ratification procedure: in 1787, the Federal Convention redesigned the process of amendment set forth in the Articles of Confederation. Suppose that ConCon II declared that its amendments would be added to the Constitution if they were approved in a nationwide referendum,[56] to take place in all fifty states and the District of Columbia. (The inclusion of the District in the ratification procedure would touch off its own controversy, for its residents have never had a chance to have their say on a proposed amendment.)[57] How should Congress choose between Article V of the Constitution and the resolutions of ConCon II? Should Congress accept the report and send it to the states? Should Congress reject the report if it exceeded the convention's original mandate? Could Congress rewrite the report? Even if Congress followed Article V, how would the states function in that process? Would the elections for delegates to ratifying conventions have to conform to the principle of one person, one vote? Would the political parties become embroiled in, or be excluded from, the elections of delegates and the conventions? Would issues arising from the ratification process go to the courts for ultimate resolution?

Lurking behind all the controversies over whether to call a "limited constitutional convention" is one large question—that of the convention's mandate and its obligation to adhere to it. Constitutional scholars have dubbed this the "runaway convention" issue. After all, in 1787 the Confederation Congress had authorized the Federal Convention to consider only amendments to the Articles of Confederation. Four days after achieving a quorum, however, the delegates in Philadelphia abandoned that mandate for a broader goal: writing an entirely new constitution. Given this result, and its general acceptance for more than two centuries, would a second convention feel any more restraint or obligation to follow its mandate than did Madison, Wilson, Morris, Washington, Hamilton, Franklin, and their colleagues?

In the 1980s, right-wing politicians and legal theorists added a second constitutional convention to their jurisprudential shopping list. They saw the second-convention mechanism as the ultimate weapon in their revolt against the constitutional orthodoxies of the previous half-century—settled law that many conservative federal judges seemed unable or unwilling to undo. The Reagan Administration adopted the second-convention movement as a recurring sub-theme of its constitutional agenda, and Attorney General Edwin Meese III led an effort to prepare the institutional and procedural groundwork for such a gathering. Between 1986 and 1988, the Office of Legal Policy of the Department of Justice issued a series of studies outlining the Reagan Administration's agenda for the development of American constitutional law, including a monograph focusing on procedural and other issues for a second constitutional convention.[58]

Russell L. Caplan's 1988 monograph *Constitutional Brinkmanship*[59] paralleled, with far more extensive historical and legal documentation and analysis, the arguments of the 1987 Justice Department document. Caplan, who was a staff attorney for the Department of Justice at the time he wrote his book, maintained that Congress may and should establish procedures governing the calling and operation of a convention, provided that those procedures are consistent with the terms of the Constitution, with the state applications seeking a convention, and with the rules and procedures that governed the 1787 Federal Convention. Caplan maintained, specifically, that it is possible to convene a limited constitutional convention. Citing the views of Justice Antonin Scalia (who, when he expressed them, was a law professor at the University of Chicago), Caplan declared that those who stress the dangers of a convention do so to keep control of the amending process in the hands of an ossified Congress. Caplan and his intellectual allies regarded a limited convention as the constitutional equivalent of a battering-ram or fire hose, useful for applying pressure to problems that do not yield to the methods of ordinary politics.

But Caplan offered little more than wishful thinking and confident assertion to justify the hope of controlling a "limited" convention. He assumed that states could bring suit in federal courts to compel Congress to do certain things, or to compel the convention to abide by its mandate; if it turned out that courts in such lawsuits deemed the complex and labyrinthine rules of standing not to have been satisfied, and thus threw out the lawsuits, Caplan further assumed that the legal rulings or refusals to rule would doom the proposed amendments.

In a useful discussion of the history of attempts to call a second convention,[60] Caplan pointed out that such movements begin slowly, quietly, and largely out of the public view. They gather steam until twenty or more states have adopted resolutions applying to Congress for a convention; then the general public, the scholarly community, and Congress begin to pay attention. At that point, opponents of the convention urge all the arguments against it that have been sketched in the preceding discussion and, somewhere short of the goal of two-thirds of the states, the movement runs out of steam.

Caplan offered this summary of the rise and fall of a second-convention movement as reassurance that it would not succeed unless its desirability were generally recognized. At the same time, throughout his study he criticized as disingenuous those scholars and politicians who raise questions of risk and danger; they seek to discourage conventions, he claimed, only because they are satisfied with the constitutional orthodoxy as it is and want to preserve it from change at the hands of an infuriated populace using the convention mechanism. Reaching the same conclusion by slightly different reasoning, Paul J. Weber and Barbara A. Perry have argued that the many political safety valves built into the Article V procedures and American public life would slow down any mad rush toward a scrapping of the Constitution for a quasi-tyrannical alternative.[61] To bear out their argument, they cite the record of state constitutional conventions, which occur far more frequently than most Americans would suppose but with few, if any, of the deleterious effects ascribed to a second constitutional convention at the federal level.[62]

Hovering over all of Caplan's cheery assumptions is a precedent—the assumption of the Confederation Congress on February 21, 1787, that it had set a carefully defined limit on the mandate of the Federal Convention. History proved that assumption invalid.

. . .

THE CALLS FOR A SECOND convention are premised on the belief that the processes of normal politics are not generating the "needed," "right," or "desired" answers. The growing popularity of amendment politics suggests that the people—or those who purport to speak for them—are increasingly dissatisfied with the course of normal politics.

Three key questions persist as various partisans continue to demand a second convention, or seek to manipulate the unresolved questions of the amending process. First, is it accurate or alarmist to posit that the difficulties afflicting the constitutional system are so severe that a second convention is warranted? Second, does the polity as a whole share this belief? Third, what response is warranted should this belief be both an accurate diagnosis of the nation's political ills and a widely held view?

As noted in Chapter 12, the success of a movement to call a convention or rewrite the Constitution requires that the American people be prepared to engage in a discussion of fundamental principles, driven by an equally powerful conviction of the need for constitutional change. The people's readiness for such a discussion in turn depends on their recognition of its necessity. Despite the profusion of proposals for specific amendments, and the advocacy of a second convention by many in the right wing, the electorate has not yet shown itself to be convinced of the need for a second convention.

CHAPTER 14

AMENDING AMERICA

To insert essential principles only; lest the operations of government should be clogged by rendering those provisions permanent and unalterable, which ought to be accommodated to times and events . . .

EDMUND RANDOLPH
"Draught of a Constitution"
July 26, 1787

THE CONSTITUTION OF THE UNITED States has entered its third century as the organizing charter of the American nation. The oldest written constitution in continuous operation anywhere in the world, it has survived far longer than even the most optimistic of the men who framed and adopted it would have believed possible.[1] A charter of government originally designed for a fragile young republic, and for a population of about four million Americans scattered along the eastern coast of North America, now performs the same functions for the world's most powerful democratic republic and only surviving superpower, whose population has grown to more than two hundred fifty million.

Many Americans act as if the Constitution's remarkable longevity is cause for uncritical celebration. They maintain that the duration of the Constitution is somehow a warrant of American virtue, forethought, and moral superiority.[2] But just as many Americans are dubious of these sweeping claims for the success of the American experiment. For them, the important questions are: "How has the Constitution persisted? Does it truly live up to its aspirations—and ours?"

Indeed, one can make the case that the Constitution—at least the version framed in 1787 and adopted in 1788—failed. The emblems of that failure are scattered across the American landscape: the battlefields of the Civil War of 1861–1865, the cemeteries sheltering the dead of that war, the sites of bloody struggles for the rights of black Americans in both North and South. The antebellum Constitution is no more, and only those who would reject one hundred twenty-five years and more of American history and development mourn its passing.

Even though the antebellum Constitution is long gone, the document on public display in the National Archives is still the mainspring of our public life.

One of the principal reasons for the duration—and the continuing fascination—of the American constitutional experiment is the intricate network of methods that we have developed to reshape the Constitution to meet the nation's changing needs.

The persistence of "Constitution-worship" is a popular theme of constitutional scholarship.[3] But the long history of veneration of the Constitution contrasts oddly with the stories recounted in these pages of the twenty-seven times we have added provisions to the Constitution, the more than ten thousand times that we have tried to amend the document, or the dozens of suggestions for replacing the Constitution altogether. Indeed, if we love the Constitution so much, it is natural to ask why we keep trying to change it.

One reason for the unceasing ferment of amendment proposals is that the handiwork of the Federal Convention was not perfect, as one of its principal members was quick to acknowledge. On September 17, 1787, Benjamin Franklin (aided by James Wilson, who read the speech for him) pleaded with his colleagues to "doubt a little of [their] own infallibility" and agree to the Constitution:

> I doubt . . . whether any other Convention we can obtain may be able to make a better Constitution. For when you assemble a number of men to have the advantage of their joint wisdom, you inevitably assemble with those men, all their prejudices, their passions, their errors of opinion, their local interests, and their selfish views. From such an assembly can a perfect production be expected? It therefore astonishes me, Sir, to find this system approaching as near to perfection as it does; and I think it will astonish our enemies.[4]

A second reason for so many proposed alterations is the remarkable changes experienced by the American people in the more than two centuries since the United States declared its independence from Great Britain. The nation has undergone demographic, social, sexual, cultural, technological, religious, and political upheavals at an increasingly dizzying pace.[5] It is only natural that those who see an imperfect fit between the nation and its Constitution should invoke Article V to correct the problem.

A third reason is, paradoxically, the same public reverence for the Constitution that the recurring pressure for amendments seems to contradict. That the Constitution is the core of the national identity suggests to many that it should embody specific and clear statements of principles that either do not appear in the constitutional text or are not stated with sufficient clarity for those who want to remove all doubt.

A fourth—perhaps the most alarming—reason is *amendment politics,* the growing tendency to use the amending process either as an alibi for not seeking to solve major political problems through the ordinary political process or as a means to distract the electorate from more pressing issues.

The prime example of "Article V as alibi" is the campaign by the Reagan and Bush Administrations—and by Senators and Representatives of both parties— to add a balanced-budget amendment to the Constitution (discussed in Chapter 10). Some of those who seek such an amendment sincerely believe that it is the only means to compel the federal government to break its addiction to deficit spending. As their critics point out, however, using the amending process, with its inherent delays and supermajority requirements, only postpones the day of reckoning should the amendment ever become part of the Constitution. Moreover, the proposals for a balanced-budget amendment all delay the effective date of the constitutional requirement for several years, further putting off the eventual budgetary crisis to a time so far in the future that virtually all present incumbents will have safely retired. Most disturbing of all, invoking the amending process creates the comforting but illusory impression that the government is grappling with the problem, rather than sealing it in a constitutional time vault which will only defer the reaping of the budgetary whirlwind.

The prime example of "Article V as distraction" is the flurry of excitement in 1989 and 1990 over an amendment to protect the American flag from "desecration" and thus to overturn the Supreme Court's decisions in *Texas v. Johnson* and *United States v. Eichman* (also discussed in Chapter 10). Again, many advocates of a flag protection amendment acted out of a genuine reverence for the flag and an equally forthright belief that the amending process was the only way to nullify objectionable Supreme Court decisions. However, the amending furor provided politicians of all parties a useful distraction from dealing with the serious issues confronting the nation, including (yet again) the budget deficit.

Americans therefore should be alert to the political temptations of using the amending process to deflect political heat or to avoid institutional and personal responsibility. They ought to be wary when urged to add yet another amendment to the Constitution. Yet, as the pace of change in American life continues to accelerate, and as American legal and political ingenuity spurs the raising of new issues arising under the Constitution for which the document provides no clear solutions, the pressure to amend the Constitution will continue.

THE PERSISTENCE OF CHANGE

WHEN WE TALK ABOUT CONSTITUTIONAL change, we actually are grappling with a process that operates on three distinct yet connected levels.[6] Article V, which occupies the highest level of that process, establishes a method of formal constitutional change: the amending process is a means to add new language to the Constitution having equal status with the original document through a procedure emphasizing the seriousness of the step being taken. As we saw in Chapters 1 and 2, the Revolutionary generation of Americans believed the act of framing and adopting a written constitution to be an exercise of the people's power to constitute their government. The exercise of this constituent power, they maintained, requires procedural formalities and difficulty beyond that of ordinary lawmaking. Because amending a written constitution is just as much an exercise of constituent power as framing and adopting one, Americans of that era also believed that the act of revising a written constitution requires corresponding formality and difficulty.

Therefore, when we employ the amending process, the entire American political community assumes the collective mask of "We the People of the United States."[7] Only the same authority who adopted the Constitution—the People of the United States—may rework the document. The amending process is both *popular,* in that it is in the hands of the people and their elected representatives at the national and state levels, and *formal,* in that it actually changes the text of the Constitution by a means more elaborate and solemn than ordinary lawmaking.

As noted in Chapter 2, the Constitution's inclusion of a workable amending process, combined with the Federalists' promise to add a declaration of rights to it, ensured the Constitution's adoption by the American people. And, as the intervening chapters have shown, the Amendments that the American people have adopted through Article V have played vital roles in adapting the Constitution to changing times and circumstances.

The Amendments actually adopted fall into two categories (with occasional overlap): (i) defining—or redefining—the fundamental principles and relationships at the heart of the nation's constitutional system, and (ii) correcting defects in the mechanism of government established by the Constitution. The best-known and most controversial provisions of the Constitution, the ten Amendments composing the Bill of Rights, were the first offspring of Article V. Other provisions added to the original document—in particular, the equal protection and due process clauses of the Fourteenth Amendment—gave Americans of all races and creeds and both sexes powerful tools to make the nation's law correspond more closely to its professed ideals of liberty and equality. Finally, the existence of the Civil War Amendments and the suffrage Amendments as components of the nation's fundamental law has weighty symbolic power beyond the provisions' utility as the direct basis for governmental or private enforcement.

When Amendments succeed, we rarely hear from them again. Even though a few Amendments—notably the Bill of Rights and the Civil War Amendments—have received extensive scholarly and jurisprudential discussion, most have not, except for examinations of narrow technical issues.

Ironically, many Amendments are neglected precisely because they solved the problems they were designed to solve. Scholarly focus on an Amendment's meaning and applications is often a symptom of unresolved tensions in the constitutional system. By contrast, lack of scholarly interest in an Amendment confirms the usefulness of Article V as a tool for constitutional problem-solving. Even when an Amendment spawns technical controversies (such as the disputes over the nature of the states' sovereign immunity under the Eleventh Amendment), the disputes take their shape from the terms of the Amendment begetting them; the larger problem the Amendment was designed to solve has been removed from the board.

Most Amendments deal with issues not readily resolved through what has become the principal American method for solving constitutional problems—the judicial process. Legal and constitutional scholarship tends to concentrate on those questions regularly appearing or likely to be brought before the judiciary. For this reason, litigators pore over constitutional scholarship, hoping to find useful arguments and strategies; judges also read widely and deeply, hoping to discover creative means to resolve troublesome cases. The work of lawyers and judges in turn feeds the scholarly gristmill, and the cycle continues.

But political questions rooted in specific constitutional language or in the problems that language may cause—for example, whether to repair the Electoral College, how to elect Senators, how to deal with issues of Presidential succession and disability—are beyond the competence of the courts or the ordinary legislative powers of Congress. As a result, these issues tend not to arise in constitutional scholarship unless and until they beget major *political* problems demanding solution, whereupon it becomes necessary to activate the amending process. Once Congress identifies a solution and codifies it as a proposed amendment, and once the state legislatures agree to add the proposal to the Constitution, the problem usually ceases to have more than historical interest.

The amending process, however, is not the driving force of constitutional change. First, it is slow-moving and cumbersome, and was designed to be that way to guard against too-frequent alteration of the nation's fundamental law. As a result, we have used the amending process only in a comparative handful of cases. Second, like the original Constitution, Amendments depend for their effectiveness on the actions of government officials, lawyers, and ordinary citizens. Amendments develop as provisions of the original Constitution do—through the accumulation of legislative enactments, executive branch actions, and lawsuits and court decisions interpreting and applying them. These efforts—often undertaken without any higher aim to contribute to the evolution of constitutional government—develop and refine the framework of law within which the nation governs itself.

The Constitution and its Amendments thus depend for their effectiveness on the other two levels of constitutional change—interpretation (whether by Congress, the executive branch, or the courts) and custom and usage. These levels of change work more gradually, more subtly, and more frequently than the amending process does.

Just as we break in a new car or a new pair of shoes through use, so, too, we break in new constitutional provisions. New Amendments are wellsprings of federal legislative and executive power, opening new fields for the exercise of federal authority. The process of enacting and administering what the Constitution calls "appropriate legislation" is a vital part of adapting the amended Constitution to changing problems and new challenges. For example, a remarkable expansion of government power, especially federal power, took place during the Civil War and again in the twentieth century in response to war, social upheaval, and economic crisis. An equally notable spectrum of agencies and instrumentalities evolved without the formal sanctions of the amending process, but under the aegis of the Constitution's "necessary and proper" clause and the Amendments' "appropriate legislation" clauses.[8] Such creative uses of government, which reinvigorate constitutional provisions such as the Fourteenth Amendment, have reshaped the American political landscape.

Sometimes, unwritten customs and usages develop without any formal exercise of authority—for example, institutions (the Cabinet, political parties, the congressional committee system); practices (senatorial courtesy, executive privilege); and principles (separation of powers, the presumption of innocence). Either we foster their growth under the authority of the Constitution or we find niches for them within the "blank spaces" in the Constitution's outline of government.[9]

On occasion, customs and usages create more problems than they solve, as in the clashes during the Watergate crisis of 1973–1974 between claims of executive privilege and the demands of Congressional investigations of executive misconduct. Or a government statute or policy in support of one important constitutional interest collides head-on with other, apparently equally important principles, as with President Harry S Truman's order seizing strike-bound steel mills during the Korean Conflict.[10] Executive or legislative attempts to interpret the Constitution to support their positions do not always command general approval or agreement. Such instances of constitutional gear-stripping often land before the courts for resolution.

Successful uses of the amending process augment the importance of the other means of constitutional change. Once an Amendment becomes part of the Constitution, interpretation, custom, and usage assimilate the new constitutional text and adapt the constitutional system to the new rights and responsibilities growing out of that text.

Interpretation, custom, and usage often give new life to provisions previously neglected, as with the Fifteenth Amendment or the due process and equal protection clauses of the Fourteenth Amendment. Just as often, however, they can render constitutional provisions or doctrines rooted in them irrelevant to modern legal problems—as the Supreme Court's decisions of the 1870s and 1880s did to the Civil War Amendments. They also can short-circuit attempts by litigants and other individuals to take shelter under a given provision; for example, ideologues of the Second Amendment charge the federal courts with having interpreted the right to keep and bear arms so narrowly as to destroy it.[11]

Sometimes, however, none of these lesser methods of constitutional change will suffice to resolve an enduring problem. Or a broad consensus emerges in favor of adding new language to the Constitution to make both explicit and enforceable a principle (such as equality of rights) that is not clearly spelled out in the document as it stands. In such cases, the people have recourse to the process defined by Article V.

Again, we must recall that constitutional provisions are not self-executing. They depend for their enforcement on the will, ingenuity, and authority of those who seek to invoke them. We have seen, for example, how the Civil War Amendments languished, all but neglected, for generations while those whom they were supposed to protect lived at the mercy of hostile state and local authorities and the indifference of the federal government. Amendments to the Constitution thus are as much objects or targets of change as sources of change.

GOVERNMENT AS TALK: CONSTITUTIONAL DISCOURSE

EVEN IN A SOCIETY POSSESSING a written constitution, constitutional government encompasses more than that charter, the cluster of institutions and officeholders it authorizes, and the constellation of legal doctrines and supplementary practices rooted in its provisions. It also includes a vital factor—constitutional discourse—that enables it to function as the form of government of a democratic society. As Professor Alexander Bickel of Yale Law School astutely observed, "The rule of principle in our society is . . . evolved conversationally not perfected unilaterally."[12]

Constitutional discourse is the continuing conversation about the Constitution's origins, principles, meaning, and applications that takes place among politicians, lawyers, judges, scholars, and the public. Constitutional discourse has its own history, which complements and enriches the formal history of constitutional government.[13]

American constitutional discourse began with the debate over the Revolution and flowered during the dispute over the proposed Constitution, which provided a new core around which the argument could continue.[14] Politics-as-conversation has continued uninterrupted since the adoption of the Constitution,[15] although the cast of characters taking part in it has grown over time.

Article V is a key reason for the expansion of the cast of characters of American constitutional discourse. Amendments barring various forms of discrimination in access to the suffrage have brought within the nation's "political population"[16] African-Americans, women, those too poor to pay poll taxes or to satisfy other "means tests," residents of the District of Columbia (at least in Presidential elections), and those between eighteen and twenty-one years of age. This expansion has accelerated because of those provisions of the Fourteenth Amendment that courts have used to apply the guarantees of the federal Bill of Rights against state and local governments.[17]

The shared conversation about the Constitution is sustained and usually dominated by institutions (such as the courts) and communities (such as the legal and academic professions) whose principal concerns are law, politics, and government. Nonetheless, at key moments in the nation's history, constitutional discourse expands beyond these groups and institutions to bring citizens from all walks of life into the conversation. These moments represent the revival of a kind of politics—"constitutional politics"—that emphasizes the core principles of the American constitutional system and is conducted in the spirit of "Publius," the pseudonym used by the authors of *The Federalist*. As the leading theorist of constitutional politics, Professor Bruce Ackerman of Yale Law School, has observed:

> [C]onstitutional politics . . . is characterized by Publian appeals to the common good, ratified by a mobilized mass of American citizens expressing their assent through extraordinary institutional forms.[18]

Constitutional politics requires the full participation of the People of the United States, who adopted the original Constitution, in the efforts to resolve these great crises.

Such moments of constitutional politics may result in full-blown constitutional creation (e.g., the framing and adoption of the Constitution in 1787–1788), formal constitutional amendments (e.g., the Civil War Amendments in 1865–1870), or "structural amendments"—fundamental shifts in constitutional interpretation having the *effect* of changing the Constitution rather than formal additions of text to the document itself through the processes set forth in Article V (e.g., the New Deal "constitutional revolution" of the 1930s).

Periods when constitutional politics prevails are the exception rather than the rule. American politics usually takes place at the level that Ackerman designates as "normal politics"—when "factions try to manipulate the constitutional forms of political life to pursue their own narrow interests."[19]

While the shared conversation about the Constitution continues as a vital adjunct of the processes of government, it too unfolds on two levels. At times of constitutional politics, that conversation becomes the stage on which the People discuss the issues, explore the options, and hammer out the solutions. At times of normal politics, during which most individuals pursue the pressing needs of their daily lives rather than concern themselves in an ongoing manner with the maintenance of government and the formulation and enforcement of policy, that conversation takes place only among those individuals who make questions of governance, law, and constitutionalism their principal concerns.

As the history of Article V demonstrates, the amending process depends on this continuing conversation. When the political system confronts serious proposals to amend the Constitution, the American people and their elected representatives stand in the shoes of the Constitution's Framers and ratifiers. They shoulder what Benjamin Franklin called the task of "political building," with all its responsibilities and dangers. As they take up this burden, their shared arguments and discussions frame the issues and suggest possible solutions.

Rarely is constitutional discourse more energetic than when the nation confronts the challenge of amending the Constitution. This is true at every stage of the controversy over framing and adopting an amendment.

Before the activation of the amending process, politicians, scholars, and citizens engage in extensive discussion of the issues posed by the question of whether it is necessary to set that mechanism in motion. The issues they grapple with include the following:

- *What is the problem to be solved through the amending process?* Identifying the problem helps to determine the level at which it can be solved—whether administrative, statutory, judicial, or, at the highest level, through the use of Article V. In the case of the Eleventh Amendment, for example, the problem facing the nation was whether the Supreme Court's decision in *Chisholm v. Georgia* had exceeded the authority of the federal courts—or, at least, the people's understanding of that authority and its limits as expressed during the debate over the ratification of the Constitution. A simple statute divesting the federal courts of jurisdiction over suits against a state government by citizens of another state or of a foreign nation might have solved the problem, insofar as the federal courts were concerned. After all, such a statute clearly would have been a constitutional exercise of the Congressional power to regulate and limit the federal courts' jurisdiction. But, realizing that statutes can be repealed as easily as they can be enacted, the states and the people were alarmed by what they saw as the potential dangers of the *Chisholm* precedent, the rash of lawsuits threatening to take advantage of the holding in *Chisholm,* and the implicit breach by the federal courts of numerous assurances given by the Constitution's supporters during the ratification campaign. Nothing short of an amendment, therefore, would dissipate the menace represented by *Chisholm.*

• *What significance would the use of Article V have beyond the remedy of the perceived defect?* That is, might an amendment designed to solve a specific problem also incorporate new principles or subjects into the Constitution? If so, would the advantages of this expansion of the set of constitutional principles outweigh any of its perceived drawbacks? The Thirteenth Amendment resulted in a major redefinition and broadening of the scope of Article V, as well as the dismantling of perhaps the single most divisive and reprehensible American domestic institution. The framing and adoption of the Fifteenth and Nineteenth Amendments raised the larger issue of including blacks and women, respectively, within the voting population as a matter of federal constitutional law, as well as the surface question of whether to extend federal authority to regulate the suffrage, formerly a matter left to the states.

• *If the solution to the perceived difficulty is a constitutional amendment, how should it be worded?* Should it contain a statement of principle, as with the Second Amendment's opening clause ("A well-regulated militia being necessary to the security of a free state . . .")? Should it be expressed as a grant of power to government (as in the Sixteenth Amendment), a prohibition of public or private action (as in the Thirteenth and Eighteenth Amendments), a definition of individual rights coupled with a limitation of government power (as in the Bill of Rights), or an "explanatory" amendment, guiding the interpretation of the Constitution (as with the Eleventh Amendment)? Those impatient with the details of drafting constitutional or statutory language might dismiss this inquiry as a "mere technicality." Like law, however, constitutionalism is shot through with "mere technicalities" having far-reaching significance—for example, as already mentioned, the "appropriate legislation" enforcement clauses that we find in eight of the twenty-seven Amendments, which operate to expand federal lawmaking and enforcement powers.[20]

The discussion intensifies—at federal and state levels, in formal and informal arenas—once the amending process cranks into motion. The task of framing an amendment sharpens and focuses issues implicated in the debate over triggering Article V. Once the proposed text passes from Congress to the state legislatures, it further fixes the boundaries of debate. Adversaries of the proposal attack, and supporters defend, the drafting decisions of Congress. Just as important, advocates and opponents alike scrutinize the proposed amendment to determine its probable effects—not only on the specific subject with which it is to deal but on the rest of the constitutional system as well. How will the proposed amendment expand or restrict the powers of the federal government? What new subjects might it bring within federal purview? How will the proposed amendment affect the system of federalism? How will it alter the separation of powers or checks and balances? How will it influence the people's expectations of what government should do—or their fears of what it might do? What problems might follow in its wake?

Even if the amendment is ratified, the argument over it continues, but within an altered framework. Now the question becomes how to interpret and apply the new constitutional language—whether only to issues it was intended to resolve or to problems not within the contemplation of its framers or adopters. The possibility of unexploded time bombs lurks under the surface of a new constitutional provision, as when the Twenty-fifth Amendment made possible the complicated Nixon-Agnew-Ford-Rockefeller shuffle of 1973–1974.[21]

The Article V process replays the original argument over the Constitution. Although translated into modern idiom, applied to modern issues and problems, and refracted through a vastly altered society, that process puts into issue the terms of the nation's fundamental law. By asking whether and how to change the form of the Constitution, the Article V process has the potential to trigger a reconsideration of the entire constitutional system. The success or failure of a specific use of Article V in turn renders it more or less likely for others to use it to achieve *their* goals to solve different problems. The proposing of an amendment thus is an occasion for the broadest form of constitutional discourse.

DEFINING STANDARDS FOR ARTICLE V?

THE REVOLUTIONARY GENERATION OF AMERICANS offered little guidance for future uses of Article V. Defenders of the Constitution in 1787–1788 were particularly vague on this matter—a result of their obvious reluctance to admit defects of the document in the midst of their struggles to secure its adoption. Opponents of the Constitution tended to exaggerate its flaws and dangers in an effort not to guide future uses of the amending process but to prevent the adoption of the Constitution in the first place.

We know only that the Revolutionary generation believed that Article V should be used to correct future defects of the Constitution as they became apparent or to adapt it to changing circumstances. Later uses of the amending process rarely posed the question of identifying standards to guide the use of Article V. Each debate focused on the merits of the particular Amendment under discussion. When debate over an Amendment raised the question of the appropriateness of using the amending process, the results were predictable. Opponents of the proposal argued that it lay outside the power conferred by Article V; supporters insisted that the amending power was broad enough to permit the Amendment. Examples of such debates include those over the Thirteenth Amendment's abolition of slavery, the Fifteenth Amendment's application of limited federal constitutional protection to the suffrage, and the Seventeenth Amendment's reshaping of federalism by establishing direct election of Senators.[22]

Especially with the rash of proposed amendments that threatened to clog the arteries of American politics in the 1980s (and may do so in the 1990s), it may be more necessary than ever to question when and how we should activate the mechanisms of Article V.[23]

Moreover, advocates of a second convention—albeit for a host of purposes—have renewed their efforts to require Congress to call one under Article V. The latest calls for a second convention are premised on the belief that the processes of "normal politics" are not generating the needed, desired, or "right" answers to national problems. Advocates of such proposals as those limiting the terms of members of Congress or requiring a balanced budget argue that the present configuration of American government may well prevent its smooth and proper functioning. The fluctuating popularity of calls for a second convention suggests that the people are increasingly dissatisfied with the course of normal politics, but whether they are ready for a full systemic overhaul has not been proven.

The lack of criteria for "amending America" is comparable to what Professor Samuel Estreicher and Dean John Sexton of New York University School of

Law have identified as the Supreme Court's want of articulable criteria for selecting cases for review.[24] The Estreicher-Sexton project's success in defining criteria to govern the Court's case-selection process might suggest pursuing a similar effort for the amending and second-convention processes. Yet, if the history of Article V teaches anything, it teaches that amendments are too closely linked to the particular problems they are intended to solve, or to the particular objectives they are designed to serve, to provide a basis for formulating general criteria.

In her monograph questioning the validity and necessity of the 1978 D.C. Statehood Amendment, Professor Judith Best suggested five criteria to guide the use of Article V:

1. The language of an amendment must be precise.

2. The goal of an amendment must be to remedy a fundamental injustice or to fulfill a fundamental institution or power.

3. The means selected [must] be capable of achieving the designated goal and only that goal.

4. There [must] be no other way to achieve this goal.

5. The proposal must be compatible with our constitutional system as a whole.[25]

On superficial examination, these criteria seem rational and useful. Lurking beneath their surface, however, is a bias against the type of broad, principled amendment that would include most of the provisions of the United States Bill of Rights, the due process and equal protection clauses of the Fourteenth Amendment, or the unsuccessful Equal Rights Amendment. Indeed, it is questionable whether any constitutional provision could survive this scrutiny. It is instructive, therefore, to recall a memorandum written by Governor Edmund Randolph of Virginia in July 1787 to guide his preparation of the first committee draft of the Constitution. Randolph reminded himself "[t]o insert essential principles only; lest the operations of government should be clogged by rendering those provisions permanent and unalterable, which ought to be accommodated to times and events . . ."[26]

Further, there may be good reasons to resist the temptation to establish a yardstick for the amending and second-convention processes. The formulation of criteria implies a willingness to accept regular or even frequent resorts to formal constitutional change. Establishing criteria for Article V, or mechanisms for its regular use, might result in a sweeping alteration of the balance among the several processes of constitutional change. It also might bring about a radical transformation of the status and functions, both real and symbolic, of the Constitution itself. Students of the evolution of state constitutions have long recognized that the more frequently a constitutional text is amended or revised, the less authoritative it becomes.[27]

Advocates of criteria for Article V and mechanisms to supplement the constitutional text present their arguments as attempts to restore the original understanding of constitutional change. Closer examination suggests that they have a clear political agenda in mind—one focused less on reviving an original intent of dubious clarity and authority than on doing away with, or circumventing, processes of constitutional change and development that have produced results not to their liking. Their principal target is what they call "judicial activism"; their aim is to restrain the authority of judges to make creative use of their power to interpret and apply the Constitution to changing circumstances. They seem not to recognize the potential of their proposed reforms to set precedents for later changes antithetical to their cherished values. If, for example, one movement manages to win acceptance of a constitutional amendment permitting prayer in public schools or outlawing abortion, a later movement, from the other end of the ideological spectrum, may secure an amendment providing sweeping protection for a right of privacy in all sexual matters. The result would be a wholesale politicization of the Constitution, eviscerating whatever nonpolitical authority the document has in American life.

BEYOND ARTICLE V

THERE ARE STILL OTHER WAYS to change the Constitution—ways not covered by Article V or by the levels of constitutional change just discussed. Though such "structural amendments" may not produce new constitutional provisions, they transform how the Constitution operates.

For example, such episodes in American history as the "constitutional revolution" produced by the New Deal and the bitter controversy over President Franklin D. Roosevelt's Court-packing plan led to a complex reexamination and reformulation of constitutional law. Congress, the President, the Supreme Court, and the American people took part in one inclusive, wide-ranging discussion of how their government should function. The old Constitution—that of *laissez-faire*, economic substantive due process, and freedom of contract—was replaced by a "New Deal Constitution" authorizing energetic and creative uses of government power to regulate the economy and to respond to social problems, and legitimating vigorous judicial enforcement of individual liberties against the power of government—whether federal, state, or local.[28]

Structural amendments are not so easily perceived, articulated, or applied as are formal Amendments generated by the processes of Article V. They do, however, reshape the constitutional system—redirecting its initiatives and energies, foreclosing some policy options and displaying a range of others.

Another kind of structural amendment—the "technological amendment"—does not rely on explicit action by one or more branches of government. Its effects are more subtle than those of either the formal amending process or political structural amendments; indeed, technological amendments often are imperceptible until after they have taken hold.

Improvements in transportation, communications, medicine, weaponry, and other forms of technological development affect, and sometimes revolutionize, the constitutional and legal arrangements by which we govern ourselves.[29] Some technological advances affect the framework of assumptions undergirding basic constitutional principles. One example is the impact of technology on the constitutional conduct of foreign policy and war. One official, the President, can launch a nuclear attack having consequences more devastating than all the world's wars put together. Moreover, the President can act without putting the question of war or peace before the full Congress—a possibility that, many Americans would agree, seems inconsistent with the commands of the Constitution. Although there are statutory and informal arrangements for filling the gap between the commands of the Constitution and the realities of modern warfare, these procedures never have been tested (and, if we are lucky, never will be). But there is nothing to prevent a President from disregarding them, and there is no way to call a President to account after he or she brushes them aside.[30]

Another, less apocalyptic example is that of television, the source from which most Americans get their information about world and national events, politics and politicians, and the issues affecting their lives.[31] The mass media enable the Presidency to dominate the nation's politics, setting the national agenda and marking out the range of responses to issues identified as vital to the nation. The Presidency has become the only institution of government that can speak with one voice, giving an assurance of coherence, certainty, energy, and command.[32] As a result, other institutions of government (particularly, Congress) take the initiative on national policy only when the President does not or cannot act, accompanying these initiatives with complaints about the ineffectiveness of the President. The electronic mass media and the Presidency rose to preeminence together and assisted each other in their ascendancies.

A second consequence of the mass media for constitutional governance is what critics have labeled the shortening of the nation's attention span—the supposed inability of the public to concentrate on complex issues and intricate proposals to deal with national problems. The Constitution's founders based their handiwork on the premise that the nation's politics would proceed slowly enough to permit reasoned deliberation and discussion of national problems, as well as full examination of the ramifications of a problem and its proposed solutions. We are still struggling with the consequences for this assumption, and for the system of government on which it is based, of a national public discourse that eschews patient, reasoned deliberation.[33]

Still other technological amendments raise familiar constitutional questions in new settings—for example, whether and how the Constitution will apply to American outposts in space, on the Moon, or on other planets.[34] Other technological amendments create new issues that the nation must resolve within the constitutional matrix—for example, questions of life and death raised by advances in modern medical technology.[35] Still others give rise to questions that are unprecedented even in so freewheeling a sphere as moral philosophy—for example, the debate over whether a life-form can be patented. Genetic engineering and biotechnology bring up hundreds of such questions.[36]

However the issues present themselves, the amending of national life by technology requires regular reexamination of the fit between the nation's constitutional principles and the condition of American society. Moreover, they challenge the prevailing complacent faith that the Constitution is "a machine that would go of itself"[37] and that it will continue to be adaptable to changing conditions without full-scale revision.[38] It remains to be seen how far the American people can trust to their continuing capacity for political adaptability. In an ever-changing political and technological world, the task of amending America may yet lie before us.

THE CONSTITUTION
OF THE UNITED STATES

(Literal Text, with Amendments through 1992)

We the People of the United States, in Order to
form a more perfect Union, establish Justice, insure domestic Tranquility, provide for the common defence, promote the general Welfare, and
secure the Blessings of Liberty to ourselves and
our Posterity, do ordain and establish this Constitution for the United States of America.

Article. I.

Section. 1. All legislative Powers herein granted shall be vested in a Congress
of the United States, which shall consist of a Senate and House of Representatives.

Section. 2. The House of Representatives shall be composed of Members
chosen every second Year by the People of the several States, and the Electors
in each State shall have the Qualifications requisite for Electors of the most
numerous Branch of the State Legislature.

No Person shall be a Representative who shall not have attained to the Age
of twenty five Years, and been seven Years a Citizen of the United States, and
who shall not, when elected, be an Inhabitant of that State in which he shall be
chosen.

[Representatives and direct Taxes shall be apportioned among the several
States which may be included within this Union, according to their respective
Numbers, which shall be determined by adding to the whole Number of free
Persons, including those bound to Service for a Term of Years, and excluding
Indians not taxed, three fifths of all other Persons.]* The actual Enumeration
shall be made within three Years after the first Meeting of the Congress of the
United States, and within every subsequent Term of ten Years, in such Manner

---

*Changed by section 2 of the Fourteenth Amendment.

as they shall by Law direct. The number of Representatives shall not exceed one for every thirty Thousand, but each State shall have at Least one Representative; and until such enumeration shall be made, the State of New Hampshire shall be entitled to chuse three, Massachusetts eight, Rhode-Island and Providence Plantations one, Connecticut five, New-York six, New Jersey four, Pennsylvania eight, Delaware one, Maryland six, Virginia ten, North Carolina five, South Carolina five, and Georgia three.

When vacancies happen in the Representation from any State, the Executive Authority thereof shall issue Writs of Election to fill such Vacancies.

The House of Representatives shall chuse their Speaker and other Officers; and shall have the sole Power of Impeachment.

Section. 3. The Senate of the United States shall be composed of two Senators from each State, [chosen by the Legislature thereof,]* for six Years; and each Senator shall have one Vote.

Immediately after they shall be assembled in Consequence of the first Election, they shall be divided as equally as may be into three Classes. The Seats of the Senators of the first Class shall be vacated at the Expiration of the second Year, of the second Class at the Expiration of the fourth Year, and of the third Class at the Expiration of the sixth Year, so that one third may be chosen every second Year; [and if Vacancies happen by Resignation, or otherwise, during the Recess of the Legislature of any State, the Executive thereof may make temporary Appointments until the next Meeting of the Legislature, which shall then fill such Vacancies.]**

No Person shall be a Senator who shall not have attained to the Age of thirty Years, and been nine Years a Citizen of the United States, and who shall not, when elected, be an Inhabitant of that State for which he shall be chosen.

The Vice President of the United States shall be President of the Senate, but shall have no Vote, unless they be equally divided.

The Senate shall chuse their other Officers, and also a President pro tempore, in the Absence of the Vice President, or when he shall exercise the Office of President of the United States.

The Senate shall have the sole Power to try all Impeachments. When sitting for that Purpose, they shall be on Oath or Affirmation. When the President of the United States is tried, the Chief Justice shall preside: And no Person shall be convicted without the Concurrence of two thirds of the Members present.

Judgment in Cases of Impeachment shall not extend further than to removal

---

*Changed by the Seventeenth Amendment.

**Changed by the Seventeenth Amendment.

from Office, and disqualification to hold and enjoy any Office of honor, Trust or Profit under the United States: but the Party convicted shall nevertheless be liable and subject to Indictment, Trial, Judgment and Punishment, according to Law.

Section. 4. The Times, Places and Manner of holding Elections for Senators and Representatives, shall be prescribed in each State by the Legislature thereof; but the Congress may at any time by Law make or alter such Regulations, except as to the Places of chusing Senators.

The Congress shall assemble at least once in every Year, and such Meeting shall be [on the first Monday in December,]* unless they shall by Law appoint a different Day.

Section. 5. Each House shall be the Judge of the Elections, Returns and Qualifications of its own Members, and a Majority of each shall constitute a Quorum to do Business; but a smaller Number may adjourn from day to day, and may be authorized to compel the Attendance of absent Members, in such Manner, and under such Penalties as each House may provide.

Each House may determine the Rules of its Proceedings, punish its Members for disorderly Behaviour, and, with the Concurrence of two thirds, expel a Member.

Each House shall keep a Journal of its Proceedings, and from time to time publish the same, excepting such Parts as may in their Judgment require Secrecy; and the Yeas and Nays of the Members of either House on any question shall, at the Desire of one fifth of those Present, be entered on the Journal.

Neither House, during the Session of Congress, shall, without the Consent of the other, adjourn for more than three days, nor to any other Place than that in which the two Houses shall be sitting.

Section. 6. The Senators and Representatives shall receive a Compensation for their Services, to be ascertained by Law, and paid out of the Treasury of the United States. They shall in all Cases, except Treason, Felony and Breach of the Peace, be privileged from Arrest during their Attendance at the Session of their respective Houses, and in going to and returning from the same; and for any Speech or Debate in either House, they shall not be questioned in any other Place.

No Senator or Representative shall, during the Time for which he was elected, be appointed to any civil Office under the Authority of the United States, which shall have been created, or the Emoluments whereof shall have been encreased during such time; and no Person holding any Office under the United States, shall be a Member of either House during his Continuance in Office.

---

*Changed by section 2 of the Twentieth Amendment.

Section. 7. All Bills for raising Revenue shall originate in the House of Representatives; but the Senate may propose or concur with Amendments as on other Bills.

Every Bill which shall have passed the House of Representatives and the Senate, shall, before it becomes a Law, be presented to the President of the United States; If he approve he shall sign it, but if not he shall return it, with his Objections to that House in which it shall have originated, who shall enter the Objections at large on their Journal, and proceed to reconsider it. If after such Reconsideration two thirds of that House shall agree to pass the Bill, it shall be sent, together with the Objections, to the other House, by which it shall likewise be reconsidered, and if approved by two thirds of that House, it shall become a Law. But in all such Cases the Votes of both Houses shall be determined by yeas and Nays, and the Names of the Persons voting for and against the Bill shall be entered on the Journal of each House respectively. If any Bill shall not be returned by the President within ten Days (Sundays excepted) after it shall have been presented to him, the Same shall be a Law, in like Manner as if he had signed it, unless the Congress by their Adjournment prevent its Return, in which Case it shall not be a Law.

Every Order, Resolution, or Vote to which the Concurrence of the Senate and House of Representatives may be necessary (except on a question of Adjournment) shall be presented to the President of the United States; and before the Same shall take Effect, shall be approved by him, or being disapproved by him, shall be repassed by two thirds of the Senate and House of Representatives, according to the Rules and Limitations prescribed in the Case of a Bill.

Section. 8. The Congress shall have Power To lay and collect Taxes, Duties, Imposts and Excises, to pay the Debts and provide for the common Defence and general Welfare of the United States; but all Duties, Imposts and Excises shall be uniform throughout the United States;

To borrow Money on the credit of the United States;

To regulate Commerce with foreign Nations, and among the several States, and with the Indian Tribes;

To establish an uniform Rule of Naturalization, and uniform Laws on the subject of Bankruptcies throughout the United States;

To coin Money, regulate the Value thereof, and of foreign Coin, and fix the Standard of Weights and Measures;

To provide for the Punishment of counterfeiting the Securities and current Coin of the United States;

To establish Post Offices and post Roads;

To promote the Progress of Science and useful Arts, by securing for limited Times to Authors and Inventors the exclusive Right to their respective Writings and Discoveries;

To constitute Tribunals inferior to the supreme Court;

To define and punish Piracies and Felonies committed on the high Seas, and Offenses against the Law of Nations;

To declare War, grant Letters of Marque and Reprisal, and make Rules concerning Captures on Land and Water;

To raise and support Armies, but no Appropriation of Money to that Use shall be for a longer Term than two Years;

To provide and maintain a Navy;

To make Rules for the Government and Regulation of the land and naval Forces;

To provide for calling forth the Militia to execute the Laws of the Union, suppress Insurrections and repel Invasions;

To provide for organizing, arming, and disciplining, the Militia, and for governing such Part of them as may be employed in the Service of the United States, reserving to the States respectively, the Appointment of the Officers, and the Authority of training the Militia according to the discipline prescribed by Congress;

To exercise exclusive Legislation in all Cases whatsoever, over such District (not exceeding ten Miles square) as may, by Cession of particular States, and the Acceptance of Congress, become the Seat of the Government of the United States, and to exercise like Authority over all Places purchased by the Consent of the Legislature of the State in which the Same shall be, for the Erection of Forts, Magazines, Arsenals, dock-Yards and other needful Buildings;—And

To make all Laws which shall be necessary and proper for carrying into Execution the foregoing Powers, and all other Powers vested by this Constitution in the Government of the United States, or in any Department or Officer thereof.

Section. 9. The Migration or Importation of such Persons as any of the States now existing shall think proper to admit, shall not be prohibited by the Congress prior to the Year one thousand eight hundred and eight, but a Tax or duty may be imposed on such Importation, not exceeding ten dollars for each Person.

The Privilege of the Writ of Habeas Corpus shall not be suspended, unless when in Cases of Rebellion or Invasion the public Safety may require it.

No Bill of Attainder or ex post facto Law shall be passed.

[No Capitation, or other direct, Tax shall be laid, unless in Proportion to the Census or Enumeration herein before directed to be taken.]*

No Tax or Duty shall be laid on Articles exported from any State.

No Preference shall be given by any Regulation of Commerce or Revenue to

---

*Changed by the Sixteenth Amendment.

the Ports of one State over those of another: nor shall Vessels bound to, or from, one State, be obliged to enter, clear, or pay Duties in another.

No Money shall be drawn from the Treasury, but in Consequence of Appropriations made by Law; and a regular Statement and Account of the Receipts and Expenditures of all public Money shall be published from time to time.

No Title of Nobility shall be granted by the United States: And no Person holding any Office of Profit or Trust under them, shall, without the Consent of the Congress, accept of any present, Emolument, Office, or Title, of any kind whatever, from any King, Prince, or foreign State.

Section. 10. No State shall enter into any Treaty, Alliance, or Confederation; grant Letters of Marque and Reprisal; coin Money; emit Bills of Credit; make any Thing but gold and silver Coin a Tender in Payment of Debts; pass any Bill of Attainder, ex post facto Law, or Law impairing the Obligation of Contracts, or grant any Title of Nobility.

No State shall, without the Consent of the Congress, lay any Imposts or Duties on Imports or Exports, except what may be absolutely necessary for executing it's inspection Laws: and the net Produce of all Duties and Imposts, laid by any State on Imports or Exports, shall be for the Use of the Treasury of the United States; and all such Laws shall be subject to the Revision and Controul of the Congress.

No State shall, without the Consent of Congress, lay any Duty of Tonnage, keep Troops, or Ships of War in time of Peace, enter into any Agreement or Compact with another State, or with a foreign Power, or engage in War, unless actually invaded, or in such imminent Danger as will not admit of delay.

Article. II.

Section. 1. The executive Power shall be vested in a President of the United States of America. He shall hold his Office during the Term of four Years, and, together with the Vice President, chosen for the same Term, be elected, as follows

Each State shall appoint, in such Manner as the Legislature thereof may direct, a Number of Electors, equal to the whole Number of Senators and Representatives to which the State may be entitled in the Congress: but no Senator or Representative, or Person holding an Office of Trust or Profit under the United States, shall be appointed an Elector.

[The Electors shall meet in their respective States, and vote by Ballot for two Persons, of whom one at least shall not be an Inhabitant of the same State with themselves. And they shall make a List of all the Persons voted for, and of the

Number of Votes for each; which List they shall sign and certify, and transmit sealed to the Seat of the Government of the United States, directed to the President of the Senate. The President of the Senate shall, in the Presence of the Senate and House of Representatives, open all the Certificates, and the Votes shall then be counted. The Person having the greatest Number of Votes shall be the President, if such Number be a Majority of the whole Number of Electors appointed; and if there be more than one who have such Majority, and have an equal Number of Votes, then the House of Representatives shall immediately chuse by Ballot one of them for President; and if no Person have a Majority, then from the five highest on the List the said House shall in like Manner chuse the President. But in chusing the President, the Votes shall be taken by States, the Representation from each State having one Vote; A quorum for this Purpose shall consist of a Member or Members from two thirds of the States, and a Majority of all the States shall be necessary to a Choice. In every Case, after the Choice of the President, the Person having the greatest Number of Votes of the Electors shall be the Vice President. But if there should remain two or more who have equal Votes, the Senate shall chuse from them by Ballot the Vice President.]*

The Congress may determine the Time of chusing the Electors, and the Day on which they shall give their Votes; which Day shall be the same throughout the United States.

No Person except a natural born Citizen, or a Citizen of the United States, at the time of the Adoption of this Constitution, shall be eligible to the Office of the President; neither shall any person be eligible to that Office who shall not have attained to the Age of thirty five Years, and been fourteen Years a Resident within the United States.

[In Case of the Removal of the President from Office, or of his Death, Resignation, or Inability to discharge the Powers and Duties of the said Office, the Same shall devolve on the Vice President, and the Congress may by Law provide for the Case of Removal, Death, Resignation or Inability, both of the President and Vice President, declaring what Officer shall then act as President, and such Officer shall act accordingly, until the Disability be removed, or a President shall be elected.]**

The President shall, at stated Times, receive for his Services, a Compensation, which shall neither be increased nor diminished during the Period for which he shall have been elected, and he shall not receive within that Period any other Emolument from the United States, or any of them.

---

*Changed by the Twelfth Amendment.

**Changed by the Twenty-fifth Amendment.

Before he enter on the Execution of his Office, he shall take the following Oath or Affirmation:—"I do solemnly swear (or affirm) that I will faithfully execute the Office of President of the United States, and will to the best of my Ability, preserve, protect and defend the Constitution of the United States."

Section. 2. The President shall be Commander in Chief of the Army and Navy of the United States, and of the Militia of the several States, when called into the actual Service of the United States; he may require the Opinion, in writing, of the principal Officer in each of the executive Departments, upon any Subject relating to the Duties of their respective Offices, and he shall have Power to grant Reprieves and Pardons for Offenses against the United States, except in Cases of Impeachment.

He shall have Power, by and with the Advice and Consent of the Senate, to make Treaties, provided two thirds of the Senators present concur; and he shall nominate, and by and with the Advice and Consent of the Senate, shall appoint Ambassadors, other public Ministers and Consuls, Judges of the supreme Court, and all other Officers of the United States, whose Appointments are not herein otherwise provided for, and which shall be established by Law: but the Congress may by Law vest the Appointment of such inferior Officers, as they think proper, in the President alone, in the Courts of Law, or in the Heads of Departments.

The President shall have Power to fill up all Vacancies that may happen during the Recess of the Senate, by granting Commissions which shall expire at the End of their next Session.

Section. 3. He shall from time to time give to the Congress Information of the State of the Union, and recommend to their Consideration such Measures as he shall judge necessary and expedient; he may, on extraordinary Occasions, convene both Houses, or either of them, and in Case of Disagreement between them, with Respect to the Time of Adjournment, he may adjourn them to such Time as he shall think proper; he shall receive Ambassadors and other public Ministers; he shall take Care that the Laws be faithfully executed, and shall Commission all the Officers of the United States.

Section. 4. The President, Vice President and all civil Officers of the United States, shall be removed from Office on Impeachment for, and Conviction of, Treason, Bribery, or other high Crimes and Misdemeanors.

Article. III.

Section. 1. The judicial Power of the United States, shall be vested in one supreme Court, and in such inferior Courts as the Congress may from time to time ordain and establish. The Judges, both of the supreme and inferior Courts, shall hold their Offices during good Behaviour, and shall, at stated Times, receive for their Services, a Compensation, which shall not be diminished during their Continuance in Office.

Section. 2. The judicial Power shall extend to all Cases, in Law and Equity, arising under this Constitution, the Laws of the United States, and Treaties made, or which shall be made, under their Authority;—to all Cases affecting Ambassadors, other public Ministers and Consuls;—to all Cases of admiralty and maritime Jurisdiction;—to Controversies to which the United States shall be a Party;—to Controversies between two or more States; [between a State and Citizens of another State;—]* between Citizens of different States—between Citizens of the same State claiming Lands under Grants of different States, [and between a State, or the Citizens thereof, and foreign States, Citizens or Subjects.]**

In all Cases affecting Ambassadors, other public Ministers and Consuls, and those in which a State shall be Party, the supreme Court shall have original Jurisdiction. In all the other Cases before mentioned, the supreme Court shall have appellate Jurisdiction, both as to Law and Fact, with such Exceptions, and under such Regulations as the Congress shall make.

The Trial of all Crimes, except in Cases of Impeachment; shall be by Jury; and such Trial shall be held in the State where the said Crimes shall have been committed; but when not committed within any State, the Trial shall be at such Place or Places as the Congress may by Law have directed.

Section. 3. Treason against the United States, shall consist only in levying War against them, or in adhering to their Enemies, giving them Aid and Comfort. No Person shall be convicted of Treason unless on the Testimony of two Witnesses to the same overt Act, or on Confession in open Court.

The Congress shall have Power to declare the Punishment of Treason, but no Attainder of Treason shall work Corruption of Blood, or Forfeiture except during the Life of the Person attainted.

Article. IV.

Section. 1. Full Faith and Credit shall be given in each State to the public Acts, Records, and judicial Proceedings of every other State; And the Congress may

---

*Changed by the Eleventh Amendment.

**Changed by the Eleventh Amendment.

by general Laws prescribe the Manner in which such Acts, Records and Proceedings shall be proved, and the Effect thereof.

Section. 2. The Citizens of each State shall be entitled to all Privileges and Immunities of Citizens in the several States.

A Person charged in any State with Treason, Felony, or other Crime, who shall flee from Justice, and be found in another State, shall on Demand of the executive Authority of the State from which he fled, be delivered up, to be removed to the State having Jurisdiction of the Crime.

[No Person held to Service or Labour in one State, under the Laws thereof, escaping into another, shall, in Consequence of any Law or Regulation therein, be discharged from such Service or Labour, but shall be delivered up on Claim of the Party to whom such Service or Labour may be due.]*

Section. 3. New States may be admitted by the Congress into this Union; but no new State shall be formed or erected within the Jurisdiction of any other State; nor any State be formed by the Junction of two or more States, or Parts of States, without the Consent of the Legislatures of the States concerned as well as of the Congress.

The Congress shall have Power to dispose of and make all needful Rules and Regulations respecting the Territory or other Property belonging to the United States; and nothing in this Constitution shall be so construed as to Prejudice any Claims of the United States, or of any particular State.

Section. 4. The United States shall guarantee to every State in this Union a Republican Form of Government, and shall protect each of them against Invasion; and on Application of the Legislature, or of the Executive (when the Legislature cannot be convened) against domestic Violence.

Article. V.

The Congress, whenever two thirds of both Houses shall deem it necessary, shall propose Amendments to this Constitution, or, on the Application of the Legislatures of two thirds of the several States, shall call a Convention for proposing Amendments, which, in either Case, shall be valid to all Intents and Purposes, as Part of this Constitution, when ratified by the Legislatures of three fourths of the several States, or by Conventions in three fourths thereof, as the one or the other Mode of Ratification may be proposed by the Congress; Provided that no Amendment which may be made prior to the Year One

---

*Changed by the Thirteenth Amendment.

thousand eight hundred and eight shall in any Manner affect the first and fourth Clauses in the Ninth Section of the first Article; and that no State, without its Consent, shall be deprived of it's equal Suffrage in the Senate.

Article. VI.

All Debts contracted and Engagements entered into, before the Adoption of this Constitution, shall be as valid against the United States under this Constitution, as under the Confederation.

This Constitution, and the Laws of the United States which shall be made in Pursuance thereof; and all Treaties made, or which shall be made, under the Authority of the United States, shall be the supreme Law of the Land; and the Judges in every State shall be bound thereby, any Thing in the Constitution or Laws of any State to the Contrary notwithstanding.

The Senators and Representatives before mentioned, and the Members of the several State Legislatures, and all executive and judicial Officers, both of the United States and of the several States, shall be bound by Oath or Affirmation, to support this Constitution; but no religious Test shall ever be required as a Qualification to any Office or public Trust under the United States.

Article. VII.

The Ratification of the Conventions of nine States, shall be sufficient for the Establishment of this Constitution between the States so ratifying the Same.

done in Convention by the Unanimous Consent of the States present the Seventeenth Day of September in the Year of our Lord one thousand seven hundred and Eighty seven and of the Independence of the United States of America the Twelfth In Witness whereof We have hereunto subscribed our Names,

G°. Washington—Presidᵗ.
and deputy from Virginia

New Hampshire John Langdon
Nicholas Gilman
Massachusetts Nathaniel Gorham
Rufus King

Connecticut Wm: Saml. Johnson
            Roger Sherman
New York Alexander Hamilton
New Jersey Wil: Livingston
            David Brearley
            Wm. Paterson.
            Jona: Dayton
Pensylvania B Franklin
            Thomas Mifflin
            Robt Morris
            Geo. Clymer
            Thos. FitzSimons
            Jared Ingersoll
            James Wilson
            Gouv. Morris
Delaware Geo: Read
            Gunning Bedford jun
            John Dickinson
            Richard Bassett
            Jaco: Broom
Maryland James McHenry
            Dan of St Thos. Jenifer
            Danl Carroll
Virginia John Blair—
            James Madison Jr.
North Carolina Wm. Blount
            Richd. Dobbs Spaight.
            Hu Williamson
South Carolina J. Rutledge
            Charles Cotesworth Pinckney
            Charles Pinckney
            Pierce Butler
Georgia William Few
            Abr Baldwin

Attest William Jackson Secretary

IN CONVENTION MONDAY
SEPTEMBER 17TH 1787.

Present The States of New Hampshire, Massachusetts, Connecticut, Mr. Hamilton from New York, New Jersey, Pennsylvania, Delaware, Maryland, Virginia, North Carolina, South Carolina and Georgia.

RESOLVED,

That the preceeding Constitution be laid before the United States in Congress assembled, and that it is the Opinion of this Convention, that it should afterwards be submitted to a Convention of Delegates, chosen in each State by the People thereof, under the Recommendation of its Legislature, for their Assent and Ratification; and that each Convention assenting to, and ratifying the Same, should give Notice thereof to the United States in Congress assembled. Resolved, That it is the Opinion of this Convention, that as soon as the Conventions of nine States shall have ratified this Constitution, the United States in Congress assembled should fix a Day on which Electors should be appointed by the States which shall have ratified the same, and a Day on which the Electors should assemble to vote for the President, and the Time and Place for commencing Proceedings under this Constitution.

That after such Publication the Electors should be appointed, and the Senators and Representatives elected: That the Electors should meet on the Day fixed for the Election of the President, and should transmit their Votes certified, signed, sealed and directed, as the Constitution requires, to the Secretary of the United States in Congress assembled, that the Senators and Representatives should convene at the Time and Place assigned; that the Senators should appoint a President of the Senate, for the sole Purpose of receiving, opening and counting the Votes for President; and, that after he shall be chosen, the Congress, together with the President, should, without Delay, proceed to execute this Constitution.

By the unanimous Order of the Convention

G°. Washington—Presid'.

W. Jackson Secretary.

AMENDMENTS TO THE CONSTITUTION
OF THE UNITED STATES OF AMERICA

ARTICLES IN ADDITION TO, AND Amendment of, the Constitution of the United States of America, Proposed by Congress, and Ratified by the Several States, Pursuant to the Fifth Article of the Original Constitution.

Amendment I.

Congress shall make no law respecting an establishment of religion, or prohibiting the free exercise thereof; or abridging the freedom of speech, or of the press, or the right of the people peaceably to assemble, and to petition the Government for a redress of grievances.

Amendment II.

A well regulated Militia, being necessary to the security of a free State, the right of the people to keep and bear Arms, shall not be infringed.

Amendment III.

No Soldier shall, in time of peace be quartered in any house, without the consent of the Owner, nor in time of war, but in a manner to be prescribed by law.

Amendment IV.

The right of the people to be secure in their persons, houses, papers, and effects, against unreasonable searches and seizures, shall not be violated, and no Warrants shall issue, but upon probable cause, supported by Oath or affirmation, and particularly describing the place to be searched, and the persons or things to be seized.

Amendment V.

No person shall be held to answer for a capital, or otherwise infamous crime, unless on a presentment or indictment of a Grand Jury, except in cases arising in the land or naval forces, or in the Militia, when in actual service in time of War or public danger; nor shall any person be subject for the same offence to be twice put in jeopardy of life or limb, nor shall be compelled in any criminal case to be a witness against himself, nor be deprived of life, liberty, or property, without due process of law; nor shall private property be taken for public use without just compensation.

Amendment VI.

In all criminal prosecutions, the accused shall enjoy the right to a speedy and public trial, by an impartial jury of the State and district wherein the crime shall have been committed; which district shall have been previously ascertained by law, and to be informed of the nature and cause of the accusation; to be confronted with the witnesses against him; to have compulsory process for obtaining witnesses in his favor, and to have the assistance of counsel for his defence.

Amendment VII.

In Suits at common law, where the value in controversy shall exceed twenty dollars, the right of trial by jury shall be preserved, and no fact tried by a jury shall be otherwise re-examined in any Court of the United States, than according to the rules of the common law.

Amendment VIII.

Excessive bail shall not be required, nor excessive fines imposed, nor cruel and unusual punishments inflicted.

Amendment IX.

The enumeration in the Constitution of certain rights shall not be construed to deny or disparage others retained by the people.

Amendment X.

The powers not delegated to the United States by the Constitution, nor prohibited by it to the States, are reserved to the States respectively, or to the people.

Amendment XI.

The Judicial power of the United States shall not be construed to extend to any suit in law or equity, commenced or prosecuted against one of the United States by Citizens of another State, or by Citizens or Subjects of any Foreign State.

Amendment XII.

The Electors shall meet in their respective states, and vote by ballot for President and Vice President, one of whom, at least, shall not be an inhabitant of the same state with themselves; they shall name in their ballots the person voted for as President, and in distinct ballots the person voted for as Vice-President, and they shall make distinct lists of all persons voted for as President, and of all persons voted for as Vice-President, and of the number of votes for each, which lists they shall sign and certify, and transmit sealed to the seat of the government of the United States, directed to the President of the Senate;—The President of the Senate shall, in the presence of the Senate and House of Representatives, open all the certificates and the votes shall then be counted;— The person having the greatest number of votes for President, shall be the President, if such number be a majority of the whole number of Electors appointed; and if no person have such majority, then from the persons having the highest numbers not exceeding three on the list of those voted for as President, the House of Representatives shall choose immediately, by ballot, the President. But in choosing the President, the votes shall be taken by states, the representation from each state having one vote; a quorum for this purpose shall consist of a member or members from two-thirds of the states, and a majority of all the states shall be necessary to a choice. [And if the House of Representatives shall not choose a President whenever the right of choice shall devolve upon them, before the fourth day of March next following, then the Vice-President shall act as President, as in the case of the death or other constitutional disability of the President—]* The person having the greatest number of votes as Vice-President, shall be the Vice-President, if such number be a majority of the whole number of Electors appointed, and if no person have a majority, then from the two highest numbers on the list, the Senate shall choose the Vice-President; a quorum for the purpose shall consist of two-thirds of the whole number of Senators, and a majority of the whole number shall be necessary to a choice. But no person constitutionally ineligible to the office of President shall be eligible to that of Vice-President of the United States.

Amendment XIII.

Section 1. Neither slavery nor involuntary servitude, except as a punishment for crime whereof the party shall have been duly convicted, shall exist within the United States, or any place subject to their jurisdiction.

Section 2. Congress shall have power to enforce this article by appropriate legislation.

Amendment XIV.

Section 1. All persons born or naturalized in the United States and subject to the jurisdiction thereof, are citizens of the United States and of the State wherein they reside. No State shall make or enforce any law which shall abridge the

---

*Superseded by section 3 of the Twentieth Amendment.

privileges or immunities of citizens of the United States; nor shall any State deprive any person of life, liberty, or property, without due process of law; nor deny to any person within its jurisdiction the equal protection of the laws.

Section 2. Representatives shall be apportioned among the several States according to their respective numbers, counting the whole number of persons in each State, excluding Indians not taxed. But when the right to vote at any election for the choice of electors for President and Vice President of the United States, Representatives in Congress, the Executive and Judicial officers of a State, or the members of the Legislature thereof, is denied to any of the male inhabitants of such State, being twenty-one years of age, and citizens of the United States, or in any way abridged, except for participation in rebellion, or other crime, the basis of representation therein shall be reduced in the proportion which the number of such male citizens shall bear to the whole number of male citizens twenty-one years of age in such State.

Section 3. No person shall be a Senator or Representative in Congress, or elector of President and Vice President, or hold any office, civil or military, under the United States, or under any State, who, having previously taken an oath, as a member of Congress, or as an officer of the United States, or as a member of any State legislature, or as an executive or judicial officer of any State, to support the Constitution of the United States, shall have engaged in insurrection or rebellion against the same, or given aid or comfort to the enemies thereof. But Congress may by a vote of two-thirds of each House, remove such disability.

Section 4. The validity of the public debt of the United States, authorized by law, including debts incurred for payment of pensions and bounties for services in suppressing insurrection or rebellion, shall not be questioned. But neither the United States nor any State shall assume or pay any debt or obligation incurred in aid of insurrection or rebellion against the United States, or any claim for the loss or emancipation of any slave; but all such debts, obligations and claims shall be held illegal and void.

Section 5. The Congress shall have power to enforce, by appropriate legislation, the provisions of this article.

Amendment XV.

Section 1. The right of citizens of the United States to vote shall not be denied or abridged by the United States or by any State on account of race, color, or previous condition of servitude.

Section 2. The Congress shall have power to enforce this article by appropriate legislation.

Amendment XVI.

The Congress shall have power to lay and collect taxes on incomes, from whatever source derived, without apportionment among the several States, and without regard to any census or enumeration.

Amendment XVII.

The Senate of the United States shall be composed of two Senators from each State, elected by the people thereof, for six years; and each Senator shall have one vote. The electors in each State shall have the qualifications requisite for electors of the most numerous branch of the State legislatures.

When vacancies happen in the representation of any State in the Senate, the executive authority of such State shall issue writs of election to fill such vacancies: *Provided,* That the legislature of any State may empower the executive thereof to make temporary appointments until the people fill the vacancies by election as the legislature may direct.

This amendment shall not be so construed as to affect the election or term of any Senator chosen before it becomes valid as part of the Constitution.

Amendment XVIII.

[Section 1. After one year from the ratification of this article the manufacture, sale, or transportation of intoxicating liquors within, the importation thereof into, or the exportation thereof from the United States and all territory subject to the jurisdiction thereof for beverage purposes is hereby prohibited.

Section 2. The Congress and the several States shall have concurrent power to enforce this article by appropriate legislation.

Section 3. This article shall be inoperative unless it shall have been ratified as an amendment to the Constitution by the legislatures of the several States, as provided in the Constitution, within seven years from the date of the submission hereof to the States by the Congress.]*

Amendment XIX.

The right of citizens of the United States to vote shall not be denied or abridged by the United States or by any State on account of sex.

Congress shall have power to enforce this article by appropriate legislation.

---

*The Eighteenth Amendment was repealed by the Twenty-first Amendment.

Amendment XX.

Section 1. The terms of the President and Vice President shall end at noon on the 20th day of January, and the terms of Senators and Representatives at noon on the 3d day of January, of the years in which such terms would have ended if this article had not been ratified; and the terms of their successors shall then begin.

Section 2. The Congress shall assemble at least once in every year, and such meeting shall begin at noon on the 3d day of January, unless they shall by law appoint a different day.

Section 3. If, at the time fixed for the beginning of the term of the President, the President elect shall have died, the Vice President elect shall become President. If a President shall not have been chosen before the time fixed for the beginning of his term, or if the President elect shall have failed to qualify, then the Vice President elect shall act as President until a President shall have qualified; and the Congress may by law provide for the case wherein neither a President elect nor a Vice President elect shall have qualified, declaring who shall then act as President, or the manner in which one who is to act shall be selected, and such person shall act accordingly until a President or Vice President shall have qualified.

Section 4. The Congress may by law provide for the case of the death of any of the persons from whom the House of Representatives may choose a President whenever the right of choice shall have devolved upon them, and for the case of the death of any of the persons from whom the Senate may choose a Vice President whenever the right of choice shall have devolved upon them.

Section 5. Sections 1 and 2 shall take effect on the 15th day of October following the ratification of this article.

Section 6. This article shall be inoperative unless it shall have been ratified as an amendment to the Constitution by the legislatures of three-fourths of the several States within seven years from the date of its submission.

Amendment XXI.

Section 1. The eighteenth article of amendment to the Constitution of the United States is hereby repealed.

Section 2. The transportation or importation into any State, Territory, or possession of the United States for delivery or use therein of intoxicating liquors, in violation of the laws thereof, is hereby prohibited.

Section 3. This article shall be inoperative unless it shall have been ratified as an amendment to the Constitution by conventions in the several States, as provided in the Constitution, within seven years from the date of the submission hereof to the States by the Congress.

Amendment XXII.

Section 1. No person shall be elected to the office of the President more than twice, and no person who has held the office of President, or acted as President, for more than two years of a term to which some other person was elected President shall be elected to the office of the President more than once. But this Article shall not apply to any person holding the office of President when this Article was proposed by the Congress, and shall not prevent any person who may be holding the office of President, or acting as President, during the term within which this Article becomes operative from holding the office of President or acting as President during the remainder of such term.

Section 2. This article shall be inoperative unless it shall have been ratified as an amendment to the Constitution by the legislatures of three-fourths of the several States within seven years from the date of its submission to the States by the Congress.

Amendment XXIII.

Section 1. The District constituting the seat of Government of the United States shall appoint in such manner as the Congress may direct:

A number of electors of President and Vice President equal to the whole number of Senators and Representatives in Congress to which the District would be entitled if it were a State, but in no event more than the least populous State; they shall be in addition to those appointed by the States, but they shall be considered, for the purposes of the election of President and Vice President, to be electors appointed by a State; and they shall meet in the District and perform such duties as provided by the twelfth article of amendment.

Section 2. The Congress shall have power to enforce this article by appropriate legislation.

Amendment XXIV.

Section 1. The right of citizens of the United States to vote in any primary or other election for President or Vice President, for electors for President or Vice President, or for Senator or Representative in Congress, shall not be denied or abridged by the United States or any State by reason of failure to pay any poll tax or other tax.

Section 2. The Congress shall have power to enforce this article by appropriate legislation.

Amendment XXV.

Section 1. In case of the removal of the President from office or of his death or resignation, the Vice President shall become President.

Section 2. Whenever there is a vacancy in the office of the Vice President, the President shall nominate a Vice President who shall take office upon confirmation by a majority vote of both Houses of Congress.

Section 3. Whenever the President transmits to the President pro tempore of the Senate and the Speaker of the House of Representatives his written declaration that he is unable to discharge the powers and duties of his office, and until he transmits to them a written declaration to the contrary, such powers and duties shall be discharged by the Vice President as Acting President.

Section 4. Whenever the Vice President and a majority of either the principal officers of the executive departments or of such other body as Congress may by law provide, transmit to the President pro tempore of the Senate and the Speaker of the House of Representatives their written declaration that the President is unable to discharge the powers and duties of his office, the Vice President shall immediately assume the powers and duties of the office as Acting President.

Thereafter, when the President transmits to the President pro tempore of the Senate and the Speaker of the House of Representatives his written declaration that no inability exists, he shall resume the powers and duties of his office unless the Vice President and a majority of either the principal officers of the executive department or of such other body as Congress may by law provide, transmit within four days to the President pro tempore of the Senate and the Speaker of the House of Representatives their written declaration that the President is unable to discharge the powers and duties of his office. Thereupon Congress shall decide the issue, assembling within forty-eight hours for that purpose if not in session. If the Congress, within twenty-one days after receipt of the latter written declaration, or, if Congress is not in session, within twenty-one days after Congress is required to assemble, determines by two-thirds vote of both Houses that the President is unable to discharge the powers and duties of his office, the Vice President shall continue to discharge the same as Acting President; otherwise, the President shall resume the powers and duties of his office.

Amendment XXVI.

Section 1. The right of citizens of the United States, who are eighteen years of age or older, to vote shall not be denied or abridged by the United States or by any State on account of age.

Section 2. The Congress shall have power to enforce this article by appropriate legislation.

Amendment XXVII

No law, varying the compensation for the services of the Senators and Representatives, shall take effect, until an election of Representatives shall have intervened.

AMENDMENTS PROPOSED BY CONGRESS BUT NOT RATIFIED BY THE STATES

REAPPORTIONMENT (1789)

After the first enumeration required by the first article of the Constitution, there shall be one Representative for every thirty thousand, until the number shall amount to one hundred, after which the proportion shall be so regulated by Congress, that there shall be not less than one hundred Representatives, nor less than one Representative for every forty thousand persons, until the number of Representatives shall amount to two hundred; after which the proportion shall be so regulated by Congress, that there shall not be less than two hundred Representatives, nor more than one Representative for every fifty thousand persons.

[This amendment was proposed by Congress on September 25, 1789, with the Bill of Rights and the amendment that became the Twenty-seventh Amendment in 1992.]

TITLES OF NOBILITY (1810)

If any citizen of the United States shall accept, claim, receive or retain any title of nobility or honour or shall, without the consent of Congress, accept and retain any present, pension, office or emolument of any kind whatever, from any emperor, king, prince or foreign power, such person shall cease to be a citizen of the United States, and shall be incapable of holding any office of trust or profit under them, or either of them.

[This amendment was proposed by Congress on May 1, 1810.]

CORWIN AMENDMENT (1861)
ARTICLE THIRTEEN

No amendment shall be made to the Constitution which will authorize or give to Congress the power to abolish or interfere, within any State, with the domestic institutions thereof, including that of persons held to labor or service by the laws of said State.

[This amendment was proposed by Congress on March 2, 1861.]

CHILD LABOR AMENDMENT (1924)

Section 1. The Congress shall have power to limit, regulate, and prohibit the labor of persons under eighteen years of age.

Sec. 2. The power of the several States is unimpaired by this article except that the operation of State laws shall be suspended to the extent necessary to give effect to legislation enacted by the Congress.

[This amendment was proposed by Congress on June 2, 1924.]

EQUAL RIGHTS AMENDMENT (1972)

Section 1. Equality of rights under the law shall not be denied or abridged by the United States or by any State on account of sex.

Sec. 2. The Congress shall have the power to enforce, by appropriate legislation, the provisions of this article.

Sec. 3. This amendment shall take effect two years after the date of ratification.

[This amendment was proposed by Congress on March 22, 1972. In 1978, Congress extended the seven-year deadline for ratification to June 30, 1982. The deadline elapsed before the amendment could be ratified by the needed three-fourths of the states.]

D. C. STATEHOOD AMENDMENT (1978)

Section 1. For purposes of representation in the Congress, election of the President and Vice President, and article V of this Constitution, the District constituting the seat of government of the United States shall be treated as though it were a State.

Sec. 2. The exercise of the rights and powers conferred under this article shall be by the people of the District constituting the seat of government, and as shall be provided by the Congress.

Sec. 3. The twenty-third article of amendment to the Constitution of the United States is hereby repealed.

Sec. 4. This article shall be inoperative, unless it shall have been ratified as an amendment to the Constitution by the legislatures of three-fourths of the several States within seven years from the date of its submission.

[This amendment was proposed by Congress on August 22, 1978. On August 22, 1985, the seven-year time limit elapsed.]

CHRONOLOGY OF THE AMENDMENTS

Frequent discrepancies in dates mar the available evidence of actions by Congress, the state legislatures, and the federal government in proposing, adopting, and certifying amendments. The information given here is derived from H.R. Doc. 100-94 (100th Cong., 1st Sess.), *The Constitution of the United States of America, as amended,* supplemented as needed by other sources. (Some states ratified some of these amendments, long after they became part of the Constitution, for symbolic reasons, chiefly to make amends for having previously rejected them.)

THE BILL OF RIGHTS (AMENDMENTS I–X): Proposed by Congress to the states on September 26, 1789. Ratified by eleven of the fourteen states by December 15, 1791. Proclaimed by the Secretary of State to be part of the Constitution on March 1, 1792. Massachusetts, Georgia, and Connecticut ratified the first ten Amendments on March 2, March 18, and April 19, 1939.

AMENDMENT XI: Proposed by Congress to the states on March 4, 1794. Ratified by twelve of the sixteen states by February 7, 1795, and by a thirteenth state on December 4, 1797. Proclaimed by the President and the Secretary of State to be part of the Constitution on January 23 (or January 8), 1798.

AMENDMENT XII: Proposed by Congress to the states on December 9 (or 12?), 1803. Ratified by thirteen of the seventeen states by June 15, 1804, and by a fourteenth state on July 27. Proclaimed by the Secretary of State to be part of the Constitution on September 25, 1804. Rejected and not subsequently ratified by Delaware, Massachusetts, and Connecticut.

AMENDMENT XIII: Proposed by Congress to the states on January 31 (or February 1), 1865. Ratified by twenty-seven of the thirty-six states by December 6, 1865, and by eight more states by March 18, 1976. Proclaimed by the Secretary of State to be part of the Constitution on December 18, 1865. Rejected and not subsequently ratified by Mississippi.

AMENDMENT XIV: Proposed by Congress to the states on June 13, 1866. Ratified by twenty-eight of the thirty-seven states by July 9, 1868, and by nine more states by March 18, 1976. Proclaimed by the Secretary of State to be part of the Constitution on July 18, 1868.

AMENDMENT XV: Proposed by Congress to the states on February 26, 1869. Ratified by twenty-nine of the thirty-seven states on February 3, 1870, and by six more states by March 18, 1976. Proclaimed by the Secretary of State to be part of the Constitution on March 30, 1870. Rejected and not subsequently ratified by Tennessee.

Amendment XVI: Proposed by Congress to the states on July 12, 1909. Ratified by thirty-six of the forty-eight states by February 3, 1913, and by two more states by March 7, 1913. Proclaimed by the Secretary of State to be part of the Constitution on February 25, 1913. Rejected and not subsequently ratified by Connecticut, Rhode Island, and Utah.

Amendment XVII: Proposed by Congress to the states on May 13, 1912. Ratified by thirty-six of the forty-eight states by April 8, 1913, and by one more state by June 11, 1914. Proclaimed by the Secretary of State to be part of the Constitution on May 31, 1913. Rejected and not subsequently ratified by Utah.

Amendment XVIII: Proposed by Congress on December 18, 1917. Ratified by thirty-six of the forty-eight states by January 16, 1919, and by nine more states by March 9, 1922. Proclaimed by the Secretary of State to be part of the Constitution on January 29, 1919. Effective date (by its own terms): January 16, 1920. Rejected and not subsequently ratified by Rhode Island.

Amendment XIX: Proposed by Congress to the states on June 4, 1919. Ratified by thirty-six of the forty-eight states by August 18, 1920, and by eleven more states by March 22, 1984. Proclaimed by the Secretary of State to be part of the Constitution on August 26, 1920.

Amendment XX: Proposed by Congress to the states on March 2, 1932. Ratified by thirty-six of the forty-eight states by January 23, 1933, and by eight more states by April 26, 1933. Proclaimed by the Secretary of State to be part of the Constitution on February 6, 1933.

Amendment XXI: Proposed by Congress to the states on February 20, 1933. Ratified by thirty-six of the forty-eight states by December 5, 1933, and by two more states by August 6, 1934. Proclaimed by the Secretary of State to be part of the Constitution on December 5, 1933. Rejected and not subsequently ratified by South Carolina.

Amendment XXII: Proposed by Congress to the states on March 21, 1947. Ratified by thirty-six of the forty-eight states by February 27, 1951, and by five more states by May 4, 1951. Declared by the Administrator of General Services to be part of the Constitution on March 1, 1951 (published in *Federal Register,* March 1, 1951). Rejected and not subsequently ratified by Oklahoma and Massachusetts.

Amendment XXIII: Proposed by Congress to the states on June 17, 1960. Ratified by thirty-eight of the fifty states by March 29, 1961, and by one more state on March 30, 1961. Declared by the Administrator of General Services to be part of the Constitution on April 3, 1961 (published in *Federal Register,* April 3, 1961). Rejected and not subsequently ratified by Arkansas.

Amendment XXIV: Proposed by Congress to the states on August 27, 1962. Ratified by thirty-eight of the fifty states by January 23, 1964, and by one more state by February 25, 1977. Declared by the Administrator of General Services to be part of the Constitution on February 4, 1964 (published in *Federal Register,* February 5, 1964). Rejected and not subsequently ratified by Mississippi.

AMENDMENT XXV: Proposed by Congress to the states on July 6, 1965. Ratified by thirty-nine of the fifty states by February 10, 1967, and by nine more states by May 25, 1967. Declared by the Administrator of General Services to be part of the Constitution on February 23, 1967 (published in *Federal Register,* February 25, 1967).

AMENDMENT XXVI: Proposed by Congress to the states on March 23, 1971. Ratified by thirty-eight of the fifty states by June 30, 1971, and by three more states by October 4, 1971. Declared by the Administrator of General Services to be part of the Constitution on July 5, 1971 (published in *Federal Register,* July 7, 1971).

AMENDMENT XXVII: Proposed by Congress to the states on September 25, 1789. Ratified by thirty-nine of the fifty states by May 7, 1992, and by two more states by June 26, 1992. Declared by the Archivist of the United States to be part of the Constitution on May 18, 1992 (published in *Federal Register,* May 19, 1992). Ratification and certification confirmed by Congress on May 20, 1992.

Notes

CHAPTER I
ANTECEDENTS OF ARTICLE V

1. Michael Kammen, *A Machine That Would Go of Itself: The Constitution in American Culture* (New York: Alfred A. Knopf, 1986), 72–73, 127, 153, 223–224; David C. Mearns and Verner W. Clapp, *The Constitution of the United States Together with an Account of Its Travels* (Washington, D.C.: U.S. Government Printing Office for the Library of Congress, 1952).

2. Charles Borgeaud's *Adoption and Amendment of Constitutions in Europe and America,* Charles D. Hazen, trans. (New York: Macmillan, 1895) presents an argument paralleling the one in the text; Borgeaud, too, stressed the significance of modes of constitutional amendment, both in particular and as illustrations of the great importance of the invention of the written constitution. John R. Vile, *The Constitutional Amending Process in American Political Thought* (New York: Praeger, 1992) came to hand too late to be used in the preparation of this book.

3. To be sure, the language of the Preamble was not universally admired during the ratification controversy of 1787–1788; many of the Constitution's opponents questioned the authority of the Federal Convention to speak for the "People of the United States." And, many constitutional historians agree, Gouverneur Morris of Pennsylvania, the author of the final version of the Constitution, used this phrasing as a clever device to avoid embarrassment should the usual list of states—as had been used in the Articles of Confederation—include a state that chose not to ratify the Constitution. Still, such proponents of the Constitution as James Madison were quick, in defending the authority of the Convention, to cite the language from the Declaration of Independence quoted in the next paragraph. See generally Bruce Ackerman, *We the People, I: Foundations,* vol. 1 of 3 projected (Cambridge, Mass.: Belknap Press of Harvard University Press, 1991).

4. On the Declaration, see Carl L. Becker, *The Declaration of Independence* (1922; New York: Vintage, 1944); Julian Boyd, *The Declaration of Independence* (Princeton: Princeton University Press, 1943); Daniel J. Elazar and John Kincaid, *The Declaration of Independence: The Founding Covenant of the American People* (Philadelphia, 1980); and Garry Wills, *Inventing America: Jefferson's Declaration of Independence* (New York: Anchor Press/Doubleday, 1978). Donald S. Lutz's commentary in Stephen L. Schechter, ed., and Richard B. Bernstein and Donald S. Lutz, contributing eds., *Roots of the Republic: American Founding Documents Interpreted*

(Madison: Madison House, 1990), 138–145, is a valuable brief discussion. On James Madison's use of the Declaration in *The Federalist No. 40,* see the discussion later in this chapter.

5. John Phillip Reid, "The Irrelevance of the Declaration," in Hendrik Hartog, ed., *Law in the American Revolution and the Revolution in the Law* (New York: New York University Press, 1981), 46–81, is a valuable corrective to the traditional argument (see, e.g., Becker, *Declaration of Independence*) that the Declaration's preamble is its most important part in the context of the constitutional controversy with Great Britain. The position taken in the text—that its preamble is nonetheless vitally important to the subsequent political, intellectual, and constitutional history of the American nation—shifts the focus to the influence of the Declaration.

6. On constitutionalism, see generally Donald S. Lutz, *The Origins of American Constitutionalism* (Baton Rouge: Louisiana State University Press, 1988); Charles H. McIlwain, *Constitutionalism: Ancient and Modern* (Ithaca: Cornell University Press, 1946); Francis D. Wormuth, *Origins of Modern Constitutionalism* (New York: Harper Brothers, 1947); and Don E. Fehrenbacher, *Constitutions and Constitutionalism in the Slaveholding South* (Athens: University of Georgia Press, 1989). For a challenging and lucid examination of the conventional distinction between written and unwritten constitutions, see generally Michael Foley, *The Silence of Constitutions: Gaps, "Abeyances," and Political Temperament in the Maintenance of Government* (London and New York: Routledge, 1989).

7. Foley, *Silence of Constitutions.* This book uses the term "British constitution" to describe the unwritten constitution of a nation that called itself Britain in the classical period, England during the medieval and early modern periods, and Great Britain with the unification of England, Scotland, Ireland, and Wales under the 1706 Act of Union. See generally J. H. Baker, *Introduction to English Legal History,* 3d ed. (London: Butterworths, 1990); P. P. Craig, *Public Law and Democracy in the United Kingdom and the United States of America* (Oxford: Clarendon Press of Oxford University Press, 1991) (Clarendon Law Series); Frederic W. Maitland, *The Constitutional History of England* (Cambridge: Cambridge University Press, 1906). It also includes certain historical understandings of that constitution having concrete political significance. The phrase is a deliberate anachronism—emphasizing the supposed continuity of the constitution from times immemorial, as described in the text—and was so used in the seventeenth and eighteenth centuries. But this usage was not consistent even in this period; for example, see Jean Louis de Lolme, *The Constitution of England,* 4th rev. ed. (Dublin, 1776). On all this, see, e.g., J. G. A. Pocock, *The Ancient Constitution and the Feudal Law: English Historical Thought in the Seventeenth Century* (Cambridge: Cambridge University Press, 1957; new ed., with afterword, 1987), and H. Trevor Colbourn, *The Lamp of Experience: Whig History and the Intellectual Origins of the American Revolution* (Chapel Hill: University of North Carolina Press for the Institute of Early American History and Culture, 1965).

Although many Americans use the words "British" and "English" interchangeably, the distinction between the two has immense political significance. Here, we will refer to the "British constitution" because one of the chief ideological props of that form of government is its antiquity, purportedly stretching back to a time before the British Isles were conquered, whether by the Norman French or the Romans, who designated the realm they had conquered as Britain. See Pocock, *Ancient Constitution,* and Colbourn, *Lamp of Experience.*

8. On this point, see generally Colbourn, *Lamp of Experience;* Trevor Colbourn, ed., *Fame and the Founding Fathers: Essays of Douglass Adair* (New York: W. W. Norton for the Institute of Early American History and Culture, 1974); Caroline Robbins, *The Eighteenth-century Commonwealthman* (Cambridge, Mass.: Harvard University Press, 1959); and Bernard Bailyn, *The Ideological Origins of the American Revolution* (Cambridge, Mass.: Belknap Press of Harvard University Press, 1967; expanded ed., 1992). John Phillip Reid agrees that the English—and British—constitutional experience is key to understanding the Americans' positions in their controversy with Great Britain, but he reads these arguments and their significance differently from Colbourn. See the works cited in note 12. Jack P. Greene's *Peripheries and Center* (Athens: University of Georgia Press, 1986) considers the influence of the British empire and its constitutional implications for the development of "extended polities," in particular the American federal republic.

9. Wormuth, *Origins of Modern Constitutionalism,* 98–111; and Derek Hirst, *Authority and Conflict: England, 1603–1658* (Cambridge, Mass.: Harvard University Press, 1986), 346–350. See also Foley, *Silence of Constitutions,* 15–34. For the most recent attempt to write a constitution for "the Commonwealth of Britain," see Bill no. 161, introduced in the House of Commons by the Rt. Hon. Tony Benn, M.P. (ordered to be printed, May 20, 1991).

10. R. C. Simmons, *The American Colonies* (New York: David McKay, 1976), is the best one-volume study of the American colonies' history, including their constitutional and political development; Bernard Bailyn, *The Origins of American Politics* (New York: Alfred A. Knopf, 1968), is another valuable and suggestive study. Lutz, *Origins of American Constitutionalism,* sets forth the clearest analysis of the colonial charters' influence on Anglo-American constitutionalism. See also Schechter, Bernstein, and Lutz, eds., *Roots of the Republic,* 17–105, 449–454, for examples of key colonial documents of political foundation with commentaries.

11. Compare David S. Lovejoy, *The Glorious Revolution in America* (New York: Harper & Row, 1972) (the best statement of the traditional view of the colonists' defense of their right to govern themselves under their old charters), with Stephen Saunders Webb, *1676: The Loss of American Independence* (New York: Alfred A. Knopf, 1985) (seeking to rehabilitate the claims of the architects of the Dominion of New England). See also Harry M. Ward, *"Unite or Die": Intercolony Relations, 1690–1763* (Port Washington: Kennikat, 1971).

12. The most notable statement of these problems and the impossibility of their solution within the British constitutional framework is the work of John Phillip Reid of New York University School of Law; e.g., John Phillip Reid, "Another Origin of Judicial Review: The Constitutional Crisis of 1776 and the Need for a Dernier Judge," *New York University Law Review* 64 (1989): 963–989; John Phillip Reid, *The Constitutional History of the American Revolution,* 3 vols. of 4 projected (Madison: University of Wisconsin Press, 1986–1991). The last volume, now in press, will discuss the failure of attempts to resolve the crisis within the British constitutional framework.

13. See generally Willi Paul Adams, *The First American Constitutions,* trans. Rita and Robert Kimber (Chapel Hill: University of North Carolina Press for the Institute of Early American History and Culture, 1980); Donald S. Lutz, *Popular Consent and Popular Control: Whig Political Theory in the Early State Constitutions* (Baton Rouge: Louisiana State University Press, 1980); Lutz, *Origins of American Constitutionalism;* and Richard B. Bernstein with Kym

S. Rice, *Are We to Be a Nation? The Making of the Constitution* (Cambridge, Mass.: Harvard University Press, 1987), ch. 3.

14. See Gordon S. Wood, *The Creation of the American Republic, 1776–1787* (Chapel Hill: University of North Carolina Press for the Institute of Early American History and Culture, 1969), 307–309.

15. See generally Ronald M. Peters, Jr., *The Massachusetts Constitution of 1780: A Social Compact* (Amherst: University of Massachusetts Press, 1978); Oscar Handlin and Mary F. Handlin, *The Popular Sources of Political Authority* (Cambridge, Mass.: Belknap Press of Harvard University Press, 1966); and Robert J. Taylor, ed., *Massachusetts from Colony to Commonwealth* (Chapel Hill: University of North Carolina Press for the Institute of Early American History and Culture, 1961). See also the commentary by Richard B. Bernstein in Schechter, Bernstein, and Lutz, eds., *Roots of the Republic,* 188–226.

16. Wood, *Creation,* 309.

17. See generally Robert Brunhouse, *The Counter-Revolution in Pennsylvania, 1776–1790* (Harrisburg: Pennsylvania State Manuscripts Commission, 1941).

18. Allan Nevins, *The American States During and After the Revolution, 1775–1783* (New York: Macmillan, 1926), is the standard account, but see also Merrill M. Jensen, *The New Nation: A History of the United States During the Confederation, 1781–1789* (New York: Alfred A. Knopf, 1950); Jackson Turner Main, *The Sovereign States, 1775–1783* (New York: New Directions, 1974); and Richard B. Morris, *The Forging of the Union, 1781–1789* (New York: Harper & Row, 1987). See also the documents usefully collected in J. R. Pole, ed., *The Revolution in America: 1754–1789* (Stanford: Stanford University Press, 1970).

19. Classic studies include Merrill M. Jensen, *The Articles of Confederation* (Madison: University of Wisconsin Press, 1940); Jensen, *New Nation;* Richard B. Morris, *The American Revolution Reconsidered* (New York: Harper & Row, 1967); Jack N. Rakove, *The Beginnings of National Politics: An Interpretive History of the Continental Congress* (New York: Alfred A. Knopf, 1979); and Morris, *Forging of the Union.* Jensen stresses the democratic, decentralizing beliefs of the architects of the Articles; Morris and Rakove emphasize their fear of consolidated government and the growing recognition by many of them that that fear had pushed them too far in the direction of a weak central government for the United States. Chapters 2 and 4 of Bernstein with Rice, *Are We to Be a Nation?* draw on and parallel the arguments of Morris and Rakove. See also the commentary on the Articles by Donald S. Lutz in Schechter, Bernstein, and Lutz, eds., *Roots of the Republic,* 227–248. Greene, *Peripheries and Center,* maintains convincingly that the question of resolving disputes between a central government and its peripheries dominated Anglo-American constitutional government from 1607 to 1787. The Americans evaded the issue, and thus postponed its ultimate resolution until the American Civil War of 1861–1865.

20. On this point, see Greene, *Peripheries and Center;* and Bernstein with Rice, *Are We to Be a Nation?,* ch. 4.

21. The best studies of Rhode Island in this period are Irwin Polishook, *Rhode Island and the Union, 1774–1791* (Evanston: Northwestern University Press, 1969); and Patrick T. Conley, *Democracy in Decline: Rhode Island's Constitutional Development, 1776–1841* (Providence: Rhode Island Historical Society, 1977).

22. Resolution of Confederation Congress, February 21, 1787, reprinted in Max Farrand, ed., *The Records of the Federal Convention of 1787,* rev. ed. in 4 vols. (New Haven: Yale University Press, 1937, 1966), 3: 13–14. [Hereafter cited as Farrand, *Records.*] A revised edition of vol. 4 was published in 1987: James H. Hutson, ed., *Supplement to Max Farrand's* The Records of the Federal Convention of 1787 (New Haven: Yale University Press, 1987).

23. The authorizing resolutions and delegates' credentials are reprinted in Farrand, *Records,* 3: 559–586. A letter dated May 11, 1787, to the Convention from Rhode Island merchants expressing distress at their state legislature's refusal to act is reprinted in ibid., 18–20; see also 47–48, 76–77.

CHAPTER 2
"AN EASY, REGULAR, AND CONSTITUTIONAL WAY"

1. Leonard Rapport, "Printing the Constitution: The Convention and Newspaper Imprints, August–November 1787," *Prologue* 2 (1970): 63–90. The September 19, 1787, issue of the *Pennsylvania Packet, and Daily Advertiser* is reproduced in Richard B. Bernstein with Kym S. Rice, *Are We to Be a Nation? The Making of the Constitution* (Cambridge, Mass.: Harvard University Press, 1987), 187–190. On the Constitution as a news story, see John T. Alexander, *The Selling of the Constitutional Convention: A History of News Coverage* (Madison: Madison House, 1990).

2. Rapport, "Printing the Constitution," recounts Claypoole's efforts, ultimately successful, to receive payment for his work.

3. For this phrase, see Morton White, *Philosophy,* The Federalist, *and the Constitution* (New York: Oxford University Press, 1987).

4. The phrase is James Madison's. Max Farrand, ed., *The Records of the Federal Convention of 1787,* rev. ed. in 4 vols. (New Haven: Yale University Press, 1937, 1966), 2: 630 (September 15, 1787). [Hereafter cited as Farrand, *Records;* all citations are to the notes kept by James Madison unless otherwise indicated.]

5. Charles Pinckney, "Observations on the Plan of Government submitted to the Federal Convention . . ." (1787), reprinted in Farrand, *Records,* 3: 106–123 (quote at 120). The extent of Pinckney's contributions to the framing of the Constitution is a matter of historical controversy; Pinckney's defenders claim that he was the true "Father of the Constitution," while his detractors maintain that he sought to steal credit for the work of the Convention. For Farrand's careful analysis of Pinckney's role, which rejects Pinckney's later claims, see ibid., 595–609.

6. Farrand, *Records,* 1: 22 (May 29, 1787).

7. Ibid., 121–122 (June 5, 1787).

8. Ibid., 202–203 (June 11, 1787).

9. Ibid.

10. Ibid., 2: 87 (July 23, 1787).

11. The best treatment of Wilson's ideas is Robert G. McCloskey, ed., *The Works of James Wilson*, 2 vols. (Cambridge, Mass.: Belknap Press of Harvard University Press, 1964) (John Harvard Library), "Introduction." See also Charles Page Smith, *James Wilson: Founding Father, 1742–1798* (Chapel Hill: University of North Carolina Press for the Institute of Early American History and Culture, 1956); and Jean Marc Pascal, *The Political Ideas of James Wilson* (Ph.D. diss., University of London, 1986; New York: Garland, 1991).

12. Undated memorandum by Wilson, reprinted in Farrand, *Records,* 2: 159–163 (quote at 159).

13. Committee of Detail draft, August 6, 1787, reprinted in Farrand, *Records,* 2: 188. (This provision is numbered XVIII in the printed draft, but Farrand points out that it should be numbered XIX; the printer made a numbering error.) This provision was also identical to paragraphs in the memorandum that Randolph prepared to jog his memory. See Memorandum in the handwriting of Edmund Randolph with emendations by John Rutledge, reprinted in Farrand, *Records,* 1: 137–150 (see esp. 148–149); corrected text in 4: 37–51 (see esp. 49–50), and in James H. Hutson, ed., *Supplement to Max Farrand's* The Records of the Federal Convention of 1787 (New Haven: Yale University Press, 1987), 183–193 (see esp. 191–192); hereafter cited as Hutson, *Supplement.*

14. Farrand, *Records,* 2: 468 (August 30, 1787).

15. Ibid., 557–558 (September 10, 1787).

16. Ibid., 558.

17. Ibid.

18. Ibid., 559.

19. Ibid.

20. Ibid., 602. Morris left the blanks because, even at this late date, it was not clear which provisions would go where in the final text of the Constitution.

21. George Mason, [Suggested revisions of Committee of Style report], September 13, 1787, reprinted in Hutson, *Supplement,* 269–271 (quote at 270). Originally reprinted in Farrand, *Records,* 4: 59–61 (quote at 61).

22. Farrand, *Records,* 2: 629–630 (September 15, 1787).

23. Ibid.

24. Ibid., 631.

25. The lone holdout, Rhode Island, elected a convention in 1790, only after the establishment of a national government under the Constitution and in the face of threats of punitive measures from the United States and her neighboring states. See generally Patrick T. Conley, *Democracy in Decline: Rhode Island's Constitutional Development, 1776–1841* (Providence: Rhode Island Historical Society, 1977); and Irwin Polishook, *Rhode Island and the Union, 1774–1791* (Evanston: Northwestern University Press, 1969).

26. See the important new study by Alexander, *Selling of the Constitutional Convention.*

27. On this point, see Bernstein with Rice, *Are We to Be a Nation?,* 201–202.

28. See Chapter 3. When Madison introduced his proposed amendments in June of 1789,

he explicitly avowed that he was fulfilling his own pledge to his constituents made during the Virginia ratifying convention in June of 1788 and during his campaign for the House of Representatives in February of 1789.

The pamphlet that Madison used—Augustine Davis, comp., *The Ratifications of the New Foederal Constitution, together with the Amendments, proposed by the several states* (Richmond, Va., 1788)—has been reprinted in Stephen L. Schechter and Richard B. Bernstein, eds., *Contexts of the Bill of Rights* (Albany: New York State Commission on the Bicentennial of the United States Constitution, 1990), 112–146. It does not include the proposed amendments adopted in the fall of 1789 by the second North Carolina ratifying convention or in June of 1790 by the Rhode Island ratifying convention, for these sets of amendments were proposed after Davis published his pamphlet.

29. Good discussions of the ratification controversy include Robert A. Rutland, *The Ordeal of the Constitution* (Norman: University of Oklahoma Press, 1966); and Patrick T. Conley and John P. Kaminski, eds., *The Constitution and the States* (Madison: Madison House, 1989). See the treatment in Bernstein with Rice, *Are We to Be a Nation?* ch. 7.

30. See, e.g., "Letters of Cato, No. II," *New York Journal,* September 1787–January 1788, reprinted in Herbert J. Storing, ed. (with the assistance of Murray Dry), *The Complete Anti-Federalist,* 7 vols. (Chicago: University of Chicago Press, 1981), 2.6.9. [All citations to documents reprinted in Storing use his suggested method of citation—to the volume, the document, and the paragraph.]

31. Luther Martin, *The Genuine Information Delivered to the Legislature of the State of Maryland Relative to the Proceedings of the General Convention Lately Held at Philadelphia* (1788), reprinted in Storing, ed., *Complete Anti-Federalist,* 2.4.110–114.

32. "Vox Populi, No. I," *Massachusetts Gazette,* October–November 1787, reprinted in Storing, ed., *Complete Anti-Federalist,* 4.4.13. Storing reports that the author, whose identity is not known, was believed at the time to be a member of the Massachusetts legislature.

33. [Alexander Hamilton,] *The Federalist No. 15,* in Alexander Hamilton, James Madison, and John Jay, *The Federalist Papers,* ed. Clinton Rossiter (New York: Mentor/New American Library, 1961), 107. Hamilton used the word "imbecility" to mean want of power, rather than the modern meaning of "want of intellectual power." See Richard B. Bernstein, "*The Federalist* on Energetic Government: *The Federalist Nos. 15, 70, and 78,*" in Stephen L. Schechter, ed., and Richard B. Bernstein and Donald S. Lutz, contributing eds., *Roots of the Republic: American Founding Documents Interpreted* (Madison: Madison House, 1990), 335–380.

34. Edmund Randolph, speech in Virginia ratifying convention, June 6, 1788, extract reprinted in John P. Kaminski and Richard Leffler, eds., *Federalists and Antifederalists: The Debate over the Ratification of the Constitution* (Madison: Madison House, 1989), 33. The most savage and convincing indictment is that of Alexander Hamilton in *The Federalist No. 15.* See Bernstein, "*The Federalist,*" 339–341.

35. Joseph Barrell to Nathaniel Barrell, December 20, 1787, reprinted in Merrill Jensen, John P. Kaminski, Gaspare J. Saladino, and Richard Leffler, eds., *The Documentary History of the Ratification of the Constitution and the Bill of Rights, 1787–1791,* 9 vols. of 17 projected

(Madison: State Historical Society of Wisconsin, 1976–), 15: 49–51 (quote at 50). (Volume 15 is the third of five volumes in a subseries within the project titled *Commentaries on the Constitution, Public and Private.*)

36. [James Madison,] *The Federalist No. 40,* in *The Federalist Papers,* 251.

37. See, e.g., [James Madison,] *The Federalist No. 40,* in *The Federalist Papers,* 251.

38. See ibid., 251–255.

39. Ibid., 253.

40. Ibid., 253–255.

41. Bernstein with Rice, *Are We to Be a Nation?* 210–211.

42. "An Old Whig, No. VIII," [Philadelphia] *Independent Gazeteer* (October 1787–February 1788), reprinted in Storing, ed., *Complete Anti-Federalist,* 3.3.50.

43. Ibid., 3.3.55–56.

44. "Observations . . . in a Number of Letters from the Federal Farmer to the Republican" (1787), reprinted in Storing, ed., *Complete Anti-Federalist,* 2.8.58. See also Edmund Randolph, "Letter from Edmund Randolph Giving His Reasons for Refusing His Signature To the Proposed Federal Constitution, 10 October 1787," reprinted in ibid., 2.5.37.

45. [Samuel Bryan,] "Letters of Centinel, No. II," [Philadelphia] *Freeman's Journal* (October 1787–April 1788), reprinted in Storing, ed., *Complete Anti-Federalist,* 2.7.56.

46. Consider Arms, Malichi Maynard, and Samuel Field, "Reasons for Dissent," *Hampshire Gazette,* April 9 and 16, 1788, reprinted in Storing, ed., *Complete Anti-Federalist,* 4.26.14–15.

47. [James Madison,] *The Federalist No. 39,* in *The Federalist Papers,* 246.

48. [James Madison,] *The Federalist No. 43,* in ibid., 278–279.

49. [Alexander Hamilton], *The Federalist No. 85,* in ibid., 524–526.

50. See the discussion of the alternatives in Sanford Levinson, "Accounting for Constitutional Change (Or, How Many Times Has the United States Constitution Been Amended? (a) < 26; (b) 26; (c) > 26; (d) all of the above)," *Constitutional Commentary* 8 (1991): 409–431. Conservative members of Congress revived this approach to the permissible scope of the amending process to block the Thirteenth, Fourteenth, and Fifteenth amendments. See Chapter 6.

51. Bruce Ackerman, *We the People, I: Foundations* (Cambridge, Mass.: Belknap Press of Harvard University Press, 1991), 165–229.

52. Akhil Reed Amar, "Philadelphia Revisited: Amending the Constitution Outside Article V," *University of Chicago Law Review* 55 (1988): 1043–1104.

53. E.g., Jeff Rosen, "Note: Was the Flag Burning Amendment Unconstitutional?" *Yale Law Journal* 100 (1991): 1073–1092.

54. Linda Grant DePauw, "The Anticlimax of Antifederalism: The Abortive Second Convention Movement, 1788–89," *Prologue* 2 (1970): 98–114; and Steven Boyd, *The Politics*

of Opposition: Antifederalists and the Acceptance of the Constitution (Millwood: KTO Press, 1979).

CHAPTER 3
THE FIRST FRUITS OF ARTICLE V: THE BILL OF RIGHTS

1. The best short account of the framing and adoption of the Bill of Rights is John P. Kaminski's "The Making of the Bill of Rights," in Stephen L. Schechter and Richard B. Bernstein, eds., *Contexts of the Bill of Rights* (Albany: New York State Commission on the Bicentennial of the United States Constitution, 1990), 18–64. Helen E. Veit, Kenneth R. Bowling, and Charlene Bangs Bickford, eds., *Creating the Bill of Rights: The Documentary Record from the First Federal Congress* (Baltimore: Johns Hopkins University Press, 1991), presents the surviving documentary evidence from the body that framed the Bill of Rights. See also Bernard Schwartz, *The Great Rights of Mankind* (1977; rev. ed., Madison: Madison House, 1991); Robert A. Rutland, *The Birth of the Bill of Rights, 1776–1791* (1955; rev. bicentennial ed., Boston: Northeastern University Press, 1991); Patrick T. Conley and John P. Kaminski, eds., *The Bill of Rights and the States* (Madison: Madison House, 1992); and the useful symposium volume, Michael J. Lacey and Knud Haakonssen, eds., *A Culture of Rights: The Bill of Rights in Philosophy, Politics, and Law—1791 and 1991* (Cambridge: Woodrow Wilson International Center for Scholars and Cambridge University Press, 1991).

2. See the suggestive essay by Donald S. Lutz, "The U.S. Bill of Rights in Historical Perspective," in Schechter and Bernstein, eds., *Contexts of the Bill of Rights*, 3–17. Lutz maintains that the principal influences on the American rights tradition as codified in the Bill of Rights were state constitutions and bills of rights and colonial charters.

3. The authoritative modern examination of this point is Kenneth R. Bowling, " 'A Tub to the Whale': The Founding Fathers and the Adoption of the Bill of Rights," *Journal of the Early Republic* 8 (1988): 223–251; see also, for an analysis that recapitulates many of Bowling's arguments, Paul Finkelman, "James Madison and the Bill of Rights: A Reluctant Paternity," *Supreme Court Review 1990:* 301–347.

4. These may be found most conveniently in Veit, Bowling, and Bickford, eds., *Creating the Bill of Rights,* 14–28, and in a 1788 pamphlet printed by Augustine Davis of Richmond, Virginia; Davis's pamphlet is reprinted in Schechter and Bernstein, eds., *Contexts of the Bill of Rights,* 112–146 (see also the brief biographical essay on Davis by Thomas E. Burke in ibid., 110–111). North Carolina and Rhode Island submitted their lists of recommendations in November 1789 and May 1790, respectively, once they ratified the Constitution; however, a few weeks after each state ratified the Constitution, its legislature also ratified the amendments proposed by Congress in 1789.

5. James Madison to Thomas Jefferson, October 17, 1788, in William M. Hutchinson, William M. E. Rachal, Robert A. Rutland, and J. C. A. Stagg, eds., *The Papers of James Madison,* 17 vols. to date (vols. 1–10, Chicago: University of Chicago Press, 1962–1977; vols. 11–, Charlottesville: University Press of Virginia, 1977–), 11: 295–300 (esp. 297–

300). [Hereafter *Madison Papers.*] See also Jack N. Rakove, "Parchment Barriers and the Politics of Rights," in Lacey and Haakonssen, eds., *Culture of Rights,* 98–143.

6. Donald S. Lutz, *The Origins of American Constitutionalism* (Baton Rouge: Louisiana State University Press, 1988); Lutz, "The U.S. Bill of Rights in Historical Perspective," in Schechter and Bernstein, eds., *Contexts of the Bill of Rights,* 3–17; Robert C. Palmer, "Liberties as Constitutional Provisions: 1776–1791," in William E. Nelson and Robert C. Palmer, *Liberty and Community: Constitution and Rights in the Early American Republic* (New York University School of Law Linden Studies in Legal History) (New York: Oceana Publications, 1987), 55–148.

7. *The Federalist No. 48* (Madison).

8. On Madison's "new science of politics" (the phrase is Alexis de Tocqueville's, from *Democracy in America*), see, e.g., Jack N. Rakove, *James Madison and the Creation of the American Republic* (Glenview: Little, Brown/Scott, Foresman, 1990); Gordon S. Wood, *The Creation of the American Republic, 1776–1787* (Chapel Hill: University of North Carolina Press for the Institute of Early American History and Culture, 1969), pt. 5; Trevor Colbourn, ed., *Fame and the Founding Fathers: Essays of Douglass Adair* (New York: W. W. Norton for the Institute of Early American History and Culture, 1974); Michael Foley, *Law, Men and Machines: Modern American Constitutionalism and the Appeal of Newtonian Mechanics* (London and New York: Routledge, 1990); and Bruce Ackerman, *We the People, I: Foundations,* vol. 1 of 3 projected (Cambridge, Mass.: Belknap Press of Harvard University Press, 1991), pt. 2.

9. See Madison's masterful analysis of the consequences of the imprecision and ambiguity of language in *The Federalist No. 37.*

10. See the following letters as published in *Madison Papers:* Jefferson to Madison, December 20, 1787, in 10: 335–339; Jefferson to Madison, February 6, 1788, in 10: 473–475; Jefferson to Madison, July 31, 1788, in 11: 210–214; Jefferson to Madison, November 13, 1788, in 11: 353–355; Jefferson to Madison, March 15, 1789, in 12: 13–16; and Jefferson to Madison, August 28, 1789, in 12: 360–365. See also Madison to Jefferson, October 17, 1788, in 11: 295–300; Madison to Jefferson, December 8, 1788, in 11: 381–384; Madison to Jefferson, May 27, 1789, in 12: 185–186; Madison to Jefferson, June 14, 1789, in 12: 217–218; and Madison to Jefferson, June 30, 1789, in 12: 267–272.

11. Thomas Jefferson to James Madison, December 20, 1787, reprinted in *Madison Papers,* 11: 335–339.

12. Thomas Jefferson to James Madison, March 15, 1789, in Veit, Bowling, and Bickford, eds., *Creating the Bill of Rights,* 219.

13. To be sure, however, even the best of the older scholarship—e.g., Adrienne Koch, *Jefferson and Madison: The Great Collaboration* (New York: Alfred A. Knopf, 1950)—adopts the Jeffersonian-influence view out of a sense of fitness and a tendency to assume the decisive role of personal relations between great men in historical events.

14. See note 4.

15. George Washington, Inaugural Address, April 30, 1789, extract reprinted in Veit, Bowling, and Bickford, eds., *Creating the Bill of Rights,* 233–234.

16. Reprinted in Veit, Bowling, and Bickford, eds., *Creating the Bill of Rights*, 11–14.

17. Madison's major speech of June 8, 1789, appears in the *Daily Advertiser,* June 9, 1789, the *Gazette of the United States,* June 10, 1789, and the *Congressional Register,* June 8, 1789. The reported debates from all three newspapers are reprinted in Veit, Bowling, and Bickford, eds., *Creating the Bill of Rights,* 63–95; Madison's principal speech of that date appears in ibid., at 63–64, 66–68, and 77–86, respectively. The amendments Madison offered appear in ibid., at 11–14. Most legal scholars cite to the version reprinted in 1 *Annals of Congress,* 448–459 (1st Cong., 1st sess., H.R.), which is based on the *Congressional Register* version.

18. George Washington to James Madison, May [31], 1789, in Veit, Bowling, and Bickford, eds., *Creating the Bill of Rights,* 242.

19. Joseph Jones to James Madison, June 24, 1789, in Veit, Bowling, and Bickford, eds., *Creating the Bill of Rights,* 253–254 (quote at 253).

20. The stark recitation of motions in the *House Journal* conveys little of the atmosphere of the House debate on Madison's amendments. It is very difficult, perhaps impossible, to recover that atmosphere or the exact structure and terms of the debates themselves. Even though three New York City newspapers published reports of the House debates (see the headnote in Veit, Bowling, and Bickford, eds., *Creating the Bill of Rights,* 55–56), the accounts are by no means complete or verbatim (despite the tendency of legal scholars to assume their completeness).

Legislative reporting was in its infancy in the early national period. Only in 1787–1788 (with widespread newspaper coverage of the ratification debates) had citizens, politicians, and the publisher-editor-reporter-printers who made up the "news media" of the time begun to appreciate the value and interest of newspaper coverage of legislative business. Even with the newfound public taste for political news, coverage of congressional proceedings was more of an oddity in 1789 than it might look to us; the Senate did not open its debates to the public and the press until the Gallatin election controversy of 1795, and Representatives made periodic protests against the perceived bias and inaccuracy of the reporters, and occasional requests to expel them. On the early history of the public's "right to know," see J. R. Pole, *The Gift of Government* (Athens: University of Georgia Press, 1983); and Daniel Hoffman, *Governmental Secrecy and the Founding Fathers: A Study in Constitutional Controls* (Westport: Greenwood Press, 1981).

These protests were rooted in a related problem that complicates historical investigation of the First Congress. Technical and practical obstacles—among them, the bad acoustics of the House chamber and the lack of a practiced, reliable system of shorthand reporting—prevented even the most assiduous and responsible reporter of debates from recording anything more than fragments of a typical legislative session. As we sift the surviving evidence of the work of the First Congress, we should keep these cautions firmly in mind.

For a useful article debunking *legal* scholars' assumptions about the character and reliability of both Madison's notes and the surviving records of debates in the First Congress, see James H. Hutson, "The Creation of the Constitution: The Integrity of the Documentary Record," *Texas Law Review* 65 (1986): 1–39; see also the introduction to James H. Hutson, ed., *Supplement to Max Farrand's* The Records of the Federal Convention of 1787 (New Haven: Yale University Press, 1987). Madison himself was perhaps the greatest American recorder of debates of his time, as evidenced by his notes of the debates in the Federal Convention. Yet he confided to contemporaries that the rigors of his self-assumed task almost killed him, and he never again made the attempt. Modern scholars have concluded that Madison managed to preserve only a fraction of the actual debates in the Convention (James H. Hutson of the Library of Congress has estimated the proportion as about 10 percent). Hutson's strictures on these sources do not impeach their credibility or usefulness for *historical* inquiry, though he does not acknowledge this point; indeed he seems unduly harsh on Thomas Lloyd, the journalist who compiled the most complete surviving record of the House debates in the First Congress. See the headnote in Veit, Bowling, and Bickford, eds., *Creating the Bill of Rights,* 55–56.

21. The legislative history of the Bill of Rights is traced in Linda Grant DePauw, Charlene Bangs Bickford, Kenneth R. Bowling, and Helen E. Veit, eds., *The Documentary History of the First Federal Congress, March 4, 1789 to March 3, 1791,* 9 vols. of 20 projected (Baltimore: Johns Hopkins University Press, 1972–), 4: 1–48. This section is reprinted in Veit, Bowling, and Bickford, eds., *Creating the Bill of Rights,* 1–53.

22. James Madison, speech of June 8, 1789, in Veit, Bowling, and Bickford, eds., *Creating the Bill of Rights,* 77–86 (quote at 77–78).

23. Ibid., 80.

24. Veit, Bowling, and Bickford, eds., *Creating the Bill of Rights,* 6, notes a motion on July 21 by Smith—probably William L. Smith of South Carolina rather than William Smith of Maryland—that the committee not be bound by the calls for amendments received from the state ratifying conventions.

25. The text of this report appears in Veit, Bowling, and Bickford, eds., *Creating the Bill of Rights,* 29–33, with annotation indicating subsequent changes made by the House in August.

26. The debate, from August 17, 1789, is reprinted (from the *Gazette of the United States* and the *Congressional Register*) in Veit, Bowling, and Bickford, eds., *Creating the Bill of Rights,* 181, 187–188.

27. Roger Sherman, quoted in *Congressional Register,* August 13, 1789, as reprinted in Veit, Bowling, and Bickford, eds., *Creating the Bill of Rights,* 117. See the discussion in Schwartz, *Great Rights of Mankind,* 173–174.

28. Roger Sherman, quoted in *Congressional Register,* August 13, 1789, as reprinted in Veit, Bowling, and Bickford, eds., *Creating the Bill of Rights,* 117.

29. These journals have since been published as volumes 1 and 2 of the *Documentary History of the First Federal Congress.*
   To the extent that we know anything of the Senate's debates, we are indebted to William Maclay of Pennsylvania. A hard-bitten veteran of his state's rough-and-tumble politics, Maclay was a moderate Federalist from the western part of his state, elected to counterbalance Philadelphia financier Robert Morris. He kept an acerbic and entertaining journal that is by far our finest contemporary account of the launching of the new government. Unfortunately, like so many middle-aged men of his day (Maclay was in his early fifties), the Pennsylvanian was a man of variable health and a hypochondriac. Just

as the Senate was about to begin debate on the amendments, Maclay experienced one of his periodic bouts of illness and missed the sessions at which the amendments were reviewed, clause by clause. On Maclay, see Kenneth R. Bowling and Helen E. Veit, eds., *The Diary of William Maclay, and Other Notes of Senate Debates, March 4, 1789 to March 3, 1791,* vol. 9 of *Documentary History of the First Federal Congress* (Baltimore: Johns Hopkins University Press, 1988).

30. Veit, Bowling, and Bickford, eds., *Creating the Bill of Rights,* 37–41.

31. Ibid., 47–49. The Senate also condensed the religious-liberty clauses with those clauses protecting freedom of speech, press, assembly, and petition; the House accepted this revision.

32. Roger Sherman to Samuel Huntington, September 17, 1789; Paine Wingate to John Langdon, September 17, 1789; and Fisher Ames to Caleb Strong, September 15, 1789— all reprinted in Veit, Bowling, and Bickford, eds., *Creating the Bill of Rights,* 297.

33. Eleven of these official engrossed copies survive in various public and private repositories, including state archives, the Library of Congress, and the New York Public Library. What lawyers would dub the "file copy" is on permanent display at the National Archives in Washington, D.C.

34. Those who are frustrated by the lack of reliable documentary evidence on the intent of the framers of the Bill of Rights will be even more put out by an examination of the scanty evidence of the intent of the ratifiers of the Amendments. For the best examination of the Amendments' adoption, see Conley and Kaminski, eds., *Bill of Rights and the States.*

35. There is no evidence that Georgia completed action to adopt the Bill of Rights—the result in part of the destruction of many of the state's early records during and after the Civil War. It was formerly thought that Federalists in Connecticut and Massachusetts blocked consideration of the Amendments or engineered their rejection, but some scholars now suggest that legislative inattention resulted in Massachusetts's failure to adopt a formal instrument of ratification even though both houses of the legislature approved the Bill of Rights in 1790. See Daniel A. Farber and Suzanna Sherry, *A History of the American Constitution* (Minneapolis: West Publishing, 1990), 244.

36. In 1939, to mark the sesquicentennial of the Bill of Rights, the legislatures of Massachusetts, Connecticut, and Georgia ratified the first ten amendments. See Kaminski, "Making of the Bill of Rights," 54–57.

37. Lutz, "Bill of Rights in Historical Perspective"; see also Palmer, "Liberties as Constitutional Provisions."

38. See, e.g., on the capital, Kenneth R. Bowling, *The Creation of Washington, D.C.: The Idea and the Location of the National Capital* (Fairfax, Va.: George Mason University Press, 1991); on fiscal policy, E. James Ferguson, *The Power of the Purse: A History of American Public Finance, 1776–1790* (Chapel Hill: University of North Carolina Press for the Institute of Early American History and Culture, 1961), and Broadus Mitchell, *Alexander Hamilton,* vol. 2 (New York: Macmillan, 1962); on foreign policy, Felix Gilbert, *To the Farewell Address* (Princeton: Princeton University Press, 1961), and Jerald A. Combs, *The Jay Treaty* (Berkeley: University of California Press, 1970).

39. Irving N. Brant, *The Bill of Rights: Its Origin and Meaning* (Indianapolis: Bobbs-Merrill, 1965); and Schwartz, *Great Rights of Mankind.* See generally Gaspare J. Saladino, "The Bill of Rights: A Bibliographic Essay," in Schechter and Bernstein, eds., *Contexts of the Bill of Rights,* 65–109, and Gaspare J. Saladino, "The Bill of Rights: A Bibliographical Essay," in Conley and Kaminski, eds., *The Bill of Rights and the States,* 461–514.

40. See James MacGregor Burns and Stewart Burns, *A People's Charter: The Pursuit of Rights in America* (New York: Knopf, 1991); Lawrence M. Friedman, *The Republic of Choice* (Cambridge, Mass.: Harvard University Press, 1990); and John Phillip Reid, *The Constitutional History of the American Revolution: The Authority of Rights* (Madison: University of Wisconsin Press, 1986).

CHAPTER 4
SETTING THE PATTERN: THE ELEVENTH AND TWELFTH AMENDMENTS

1. The leading discussions of the Eleventh Amendment are John V. Orth, *The Judicial Power of the United States: The Eleventh Amendment in American History* (New York: Oxford University Press, 1987); and Clyde E. Jacobs, *The Eleventh Amendment and Sovereign Immunity* (Westport: Greenwood Press, 1972).

2. Edwin J. Perkins, *The Economy of Colonial America,* 2d ed. (New York: Columbia University Press, 1988); John J. McCusker and Russell R. Menard, *The Economy of British America, 1607–1789,* rev. ed. (Chapel Hill: University of North Carolina Press for the Institute of Early American History and Culture, 1991); and Alice Hanson Jones, *The Wealth of a Nation to Be* (New York: Columbia University Press, 1980), are the best treatments of American economic history from settlement through the establishment of government under the Constitution.

3. See generally Robert McCluer Calhoon, *The Loyalists in Revolutionary America* (New York: Harcourt Brace Jovanovich, 1971); Claude H. Van Tyne, *The Loyalists in the American Revolution* (1902; Gloucester, Mass.: Peter Smith, 1959); Wallace Brown, *The King's Friends* (Providence: Brown University Press, 1965); William H. Nelson, *The American Tory* (Boston: Beacon Press, 1961); Mary Beth Norton, *The British-Americans: The Loyalist Exiles in England, 1774–1789* (Boston: Little, Brown, 1972); and Richard B. Bernstein with Kym S. Rice, *Are We to Be a Nation? The Making of the Constitution* (Cambridge, Mass.: Harvard University Press, 1987), 73–80. Perhaps the single finest biography of a Loyalist is Bernard Bailyn, *The Ordeal of Thomas Hutchinson* (Cambridge, Mass.: Belknap Press of Harvard University Press, 1974); see also the insightful essay by John Phillip Reid, "The Ordeal by Law of Thomas Hutchinson," *New York University Law Review* 49 (1974): 593–620, reprinted in Hendrik Hartog, ed., *Law in the American Revolution and the Revolution in the Law* (New York: New York University Press, 1981), 20–45.

4. On the issues of citizenship and treason posed by the Loyalist problem, see James H. Kettner, *The Development of American Citizenship, 1607–1870* (Chapel Hill: University of North Carolina Press for the Institute of Early American History and Culture, 1975), 173–209, 222–224; and Bradley F. Chapin, "Colonial and Revolutionary Origins of the American Law of Treason," *William and Mary Quarterly,* 3d ser., 15 (1958): 56–70.

5. Elbridge Gerry to Samuel B. Gerry, July 31, 1783, Emmet Coll. No. 508, New York Public Library, Rare Books and Manuscripts Division.

6. See generally Malcolm J. Rohrbaugh, *The Land Office Business* (New York: Oxford University Press, 1977).

7. Peter J. Coleman, *Debtor and Creditor in America* (Madison: State Historical Society of Wisconsin, 1974); Bernstein with Rice, *Are We to Be a Nation?*, 7–9, 91–97.

8. Richard B. Morris, *The Peacemakers: The Great Powers and American Independence* (New York: Harper & Row, 1967).

9. See the useful discussion in ibid., 364–373, 417–420.

10. On *Rutgers v. Waddington*, see Richard B. Morris, ed., *Select Cases of the Mayor's Court of New York City, 1674–1784* (1935; Millwood: Kraus, 1975), 57–59; and Julius Goebel, Jr., and Joseph H. Smith, eds., *The Law Practice of Alexander Hamilton*, 5 vols. (New York: Columbia University Press, 1964–1980), 3: 282–419.

11. See Coleman, *Debtor and Creditor;* Bernstein with Rice, *Are We to Be a Nation?*, 91–97; and sources cited.

12. See generally E. James Ferguson, *The Power of the Purse: A History of American Public Finance, 1776–1790* (Chapel Hill: University of North Carolina Press for the Institute of Early American History and Culture, 1961).

13. Jacobs, *Eleventh Amendment;* and Orth, *Judicial Power,* provide useful background on the common-law doctrine of sovereign immunity.

14. Quoted in Jacobs, *Eleventh Amendment,* 10.

15. Melancton Smith to Abraham Yates, Jr., January 17, 1788, in Abraham Yates, Jr., Papers, The New York Public Library, Rare Books and Manuscripts Division.

16. Ibid.

17. Hamilton's arguments on this point appear in *The Federalist No. 81;* Madison and Marshall delivered their assurances during the debates of the Virginia ratifying convention in June of 1788. On the framing of the Judiciary Act of 1789, see generally Wilfred J. Ritz, Wythe Holt, and L. H. LaRue, *Rewriting the History of the Judiciary Act of 1789* (Norman: University of Oklahoma Press, 1990). On the specific issues mentioned in the text, see Orth, *Judicial Power,* 13–14. Jacobs, *Eleventh Amendment,* 26–40, disputes the belief that the "prevailing understanding" of the judicial power of the United States in 1789 did not extend to suits against a state by citizens of another state or by foreign subjects.

18. Jacobs, *Eleventh Amendment,* 96.

19. Details and documentation of *De Blois v. Hawley* (U.S.C.Ct., Conn. 1790) (state law staying interest on debts owed to British and Loyalist creditors for duration of Revolutionary War set aside) and *Barnes v. West* (U.S.C.Ct., R.I. 1791) (state tender law requiring payment of all debts in inflated paper currency set aside) will appear in Richard B. Morris and Ene Sirvet, eds., *John Jay: Chief Justice and Federalist Statesman, 1789–1829* (forthcoming).

20. On *Van Staphorst v. Maryland,* see Jacobs, *Eleventh Amendment,* 43–44 (though Jacobs misspells the name as Stophorst); Julius Goebel, Jr., *Antecedents and Beginnings to 1801,* vol.

1 of *The Oliver Wendell Holmes Devise History of the Supreme Court of the United States* (New York: Macmillan, 1971), 724.

21. The best account is in a pathbreaking article by Doyle Mathis, *"Chisholm v. Georgia:* Background and Settlement," *Journal of American History* 54 (1967): 19–29.

22. See Charles Warren, *The Supreme Court in United States History,* rev. ed. in 2 vols. (Boston: Little, Brown, 1926), 1: 92–104.

23. 2 Dall. (2 U.S.) 419 (1793). On the decision, see Orth, *Judicial Power,* 12–29; Jacobs, *Eleventh Amendment,* 50–55; Goebel, *Antecedents,* 729–734; and Richard B. Morris, *John Jay, the Nation, and the Court* (Boston: Boston University Press, 1967), 48–70.

24. As a result, most of the scholarship surrounding *Chisholm* has focused on the question "Did the Justices err?" Beginning in 1890, the Supreme Court and the legal community adopted the view that Jay and his colleagues had flown in the face of the "original intent" of the framers and adopters of the Constitution. The case was *Hans v. Louisiana,* 134 U.S. 1 (1890), discussed in Orth, *Judicial Power,* 22–29. By contrast, in 1967, Richard B. Morris, editor of the *Papers of John Jay,* offered a vigorous defense of the *Chisholm* Court, a position reaffirmed in 1972 by an influential history of the Amendment. Morris, *John Jay,* ch. 2; Jacobs, *Eleventh Amendment,* 28–40. Most recently, Professor John V. Orth of the University of North Carolina declared the question to be beyond satisfactory resolution: "The search for the original understanding on state sovereign immunity bears this much resemblance to the quest for the Holy Grail: there is enough to be found so that the faithful of whatever persuasion can find their heart's desire. And, of course, the object of the search may prove equally illusory." Orth, *Judicial Power,* 28.

25. Alan P. Grimes, *Democracy and the Amendments to the Constitution* (1978; Lanham, Md.: University Press of America, 1988), 18.

26. See generally Jesse H. Carpenter, *The South as a Conscious Minority, 1776–1861* (1930; Columbia: University of South Carolina Press, 1990).

27. See the cases cited in Mathis, *"Chisholm,"* 25 n. 33.

28. Ibid., 25–26 and nn. 34–38; see also Jacobs, *Eleventh Amendment,* 66–67.

29. Orth, *Judicial Power,* 20–21.

30. 3 U.S. (3 Dallas) 378 (1798).

31. 3 U.S. at 382.

32. Orth, *Judicial Power,* 21–22.

33. See John P. Kaminski, *George Clinton* (Madison, Wis.: Madison House, 1992), ch. 5.

34. The correspondence between Adams and Jay is reprinted in Henry P. Johnston, ed., *The Correspondence and Public Papers of John Jay,* 4 vols. (New York: G. P. Putnam's Sons, 1890–1893), 4: 284–286 (Adams to Jay, December 19, 1800, and Jay to Adams, January 2, 1801).

35. See Thomas C. Cronin, ed., *Inventing the American Presidency* (Lawrence: University Press of Kansas, 1989); Charles C. Thach, *The Creation of the Presidency, 1774–1789* (Baltimore: Johns Hopkins University Press, 1922); and Bernstein with Rice, *Are We to Be a Nation?,* 171–174.

36. Arthur M. Schlesinger, Jr., *The Imperial Presidency*, rev. ed. (Boston: Houghton Mifflin, 1989), 479.

37. Alexander Hamilton to James A. Bayard, April 6, 1802, in Harold C. Syrett, Jacob E. Cooke, Barbara Chernow et al., eds., *The Papers of Alexander Hamilton*, 27 vols. (New York: Columbia University Press, 1961–1987), 25: 587–589 (quote at 588).

38. See the documents reproduced in volume 4 of Merrill M. Jensen, Robert A. Becker, and Gorden DenBoer, eds., *The Documentary History of the First Federal Elections, 1788–1790*, 4 vols. (Madison: University of Wisconsin Press, 1976–1989); and Richard B. Bernstein, "The First Federal Elections: Notes for a Sketch," *Wisconsin Magazine of History* 75 (1992): 141–144 (esp. 143).

39. Some extreme Federalists deemed the Constitution's bar against naturalized citizens becoming President to be insufficient because of the escape clause making eligible anyone who was a citizen at the time of adoption of the Constitution. Herman V. Ames, *The Proposed Amendments to the Constitution of the United States during the First Century of its History*, in *Annual Report of the American Historical Association for the Year 1896*, vol. 2 (Washington, D.C.: Government Printing Office, 1897), 73–75, 323–324. [Hereafter cited as Ames, *Proposed Amendments*.]

40. James Morton Smith, *Freedom's Fetters: The Alien and Sedition Acts and American Civil Liberties* (Ithaca: Cornell University Press, 1955; rev. ed., 1963).

41. Alexander Hamilton to John Jay, May 7, 1800, reprinted in Johnston, ed., *Correspondence and Papers of Jay*, 4: 270–272, and in Syrett et al., eds., *Papers of Hamilton*, 24: 464–467.

42. The pamphlet is reprinted in Syrett et al., eds., *Papers of Hamilton*, 25: 186–234; see the headnote in ibid., 169–185.

43. Richard B. Bernstein, "Aaron Burr (1756–1836)," in Stephen L. Schechter and Richard B. Bernstein, eds., *New York and the Union: Contributions to the American Constitutional Experience* (Albany: New York State Commission on the Bicentennial of the United States Constitution, 1990), 575–587.

44. For Jefferson's views of the contested election, see Dumas Malone, *Jefferson and the Ordeal of Liberty* (Boston: Little, Brown, 1962), 491–505, and Dumas Malone, *Jefferson the President: First Term, 1801–1805* (Boston: Little, Brown, 1970), 5–16.

45. Alexander Hamilton, "Draft of a Resolution for the Legislature of New York for the Amendment of the Constitution of the United States" [January 29, 1802], reprinted in Syrett et al., eds., *Papers of Hamilton*, 25: 512–513.

46. Syrett et al., eds., *Papers of Hamilton*, 25: 513 n. 1.

47. Richard P. McCormick, *The Presidential Game* (New York: Oxford University Press, 1982), 82–87.

48. Only Delaware, Massachusetts, New Hampshire, and Connecticut—all Federalist strongholds—rejected the Amendment. Tennessee ratified the Amendment on July 27, 1804, more than a month after it was added to the Constitution.

49. Joseph Winston, circular letter dated March 20, 1804, reprinted in Noble E. Cunningham, Jr., ed., *Circular Letters of Congressmen to Their Constituents, 1789–1829*, 3 vols. (Chapel

Hill: University of North Carolina Press for the Institute of Early American History and Culture, 1978), 1: 369–371 (quote at 370).

50. Until the publication of Joanne B. Freeman's forthcoming study of the Hamilton-Burr duel, readers should consult volume 26 of Syrett et al., eds., *Papers of Hamilton,* for the surviving documentation of the dispute that led to the duel. For the aftereffects on Burr's career, see Milton Lomask, *Aaron Burr,* 2 vols. (New York: Farrar, Straus & Giroux, 1979, 1982).

51. Ames, *Proposed Amendments,* 70–71.

52. Grimes, *Democracy and the Amendments,* 22–23.

53. McCormick, *Presidential Game,* 86–87.

CHAPTER 5
"TAKE CARE OF THE UNION"

1. Senator John J. Crittenden (Kentucky), in *Congressional Globe,* 36 Cong., 2d sess. (Senate), 1375–79 (March 2, 1861).

2. This description of the Washington Peace Conference, and of the "secession winter," derives from several sources, the most useful of which are Robert Gray Gunderson, *Old Gentlemen's Convention: The Washington Peace Conference of 1861* (Madison: University of Wisconsin Press, 1961); and David M. Potter (completed by Don E. Fehrenbacher), *The Impending Crisis, 1848–1861* (New York: Harper & Row, 1976), chs. 19–20.

3. Previous explicit threats of disunion included

> (i) the "Compromise of 1790"—not a seemingly minor squabble over where to locate the nation's permanent capital but the first great sectional contest under the Constitution. Kenneth R. Bowling, *The Creation of Washington, D.C.: The Idea and the Location of the National Capital* (Fairfax: George Mason University Press, 1991).

> (ii) 1798–1800—the Alien and Sedition Acts and the nation's undeclared naval war with France. John C. Miller, *Crisis in Freedom* (Boston: Little, Brown, 1952); and James Morton Smith, *Freedom's Fetters: The Alien and Sedition Acts and American Civil Liberties* (Ithaca: Cornell University Press for the Institute of Early American History and Culture, 1955; rev. ed., 1963).

> (iii) 1814–1815—the War of 1812 and the New England states' abortive schemes at the Hartford Convention. James M. Banner, Jr., *To the Hartford Convention* (New York: Alfred A. Knopf, 1970); and Samuel Eliot Morison, Frederick Merk, and Frank Freidel, *Dissent in Three American Wars* (Cambridge, Mass.: Harvard University Press, 1970), ch. 1.

> (iv) 1832–1833—South Carolina's threatened nullification of a federal tariff, pitting the federal government against the state until Henry Clay orchestrated a compromise. See generally Merrill D. Peterson, *Olive Branch and Sword* (Baton Rouge: Louisiana State University Press, 1983); and Richard E. Ellis, *The Union at Risk* (New York: Oxford University Press, 1987).

(v) 1850–1852—but this plot, engineered by radical slaveholders in the Southern states, came to nothing, thanks to the Compromise of 1850. William W. Freehling, *The Road to Disunion: Secessionists at Bay, 1776–1854*, vol. 1 of 2 projected (New York: Oxford University Press, 1990).

4. The states announcing their secession from the Union before the Washington Peace Conference were South Carolina, Mississippi, Florida, Alabama, Georgia, Louisiana, and Texas. The other seceding states, which acted after Lincoln's inauguration and the failure of all compromise efforts, were Virginia, Arkansas, Tennessee, and North Carolina.

5. For a vivid description of the inauguration of Confederate President Jefferson Davis, see Freehling, *Road to Disunion*, Prologue. For a fine short study of Davis, see Robert Penn Warren, *Jefferson Davis Gets His Citizenship Back* (Lexington: University Press of Kentucky, 1980). A new major biography is William C. Davis, *Jefferson Davis* (New York: HarperCollins, 1991).

6. Perhaps the most profound student of this period was David M. Potter. See David M. Potter, *Lincoln and His Party in the Secession Crisis* (New Haven: Yale University Press, 1942; rept. with new introduction, 1962); and Potter (completed by Fehrenbacher), *Impending Crisis*.

7. Andrew Delbanco identifies Lincoln's sensitivity to Southern political assumptions, beliefs, and practices as an important contributing factor to his success as President. See Delbanco, Introduction, in Andrew Delbanco, ed., *The Portable Abraham Lincoln* (New York: Viking Penguin, 1992), esp. xxvii–xxviii.

8. Stephen B. Oates, *With Malice Toward None: The Life of Abraham Lincoln* (New York: Harper & Row, 1977), 213–217.

9. The best modern study of the Great Triumvirate is Merrill D. Peterson, *The Great Triumvirate: Clay, Calhoun, Webster* (New York: Oxford University Press, 1987), which also presents a useful analysis of their posthumous reputations. See also the fine new study by Robert V. Remini, *Henry Clay: Statesman for the Union* (New York: W. W. Norton, 1991); and Stephen B. Knupfer, *The Union As It Is: Constitutional Unionism and Sectional Compromise, 1787–1861* (Chapel Hill: University of North Carolina Press, 1991).

10. On the intellectual history of compromise, see Knupfer, *Union As It Is.*

11. See Jack P. Greene, *Peripheries and Center* (Athens: University of Georgia Press, 1986). Greene argues that the studied ambiguity of the Articles of Confederation and the Constitution about the balance between the central government and the states was a strategic decision that, its architects hoped, would hold the Union together; just as too-insistent efforts to define the exact boundaries between imperial and colonial authority helped rupture the British empire in North America, the excessive insistence on defining the balance between federal and state authority would risk splitting the Union asunder.

12. The leading study of the Union in American thought is Paul C. Nagel, *One Nation Indivisible: The Union in American Thought, 1776–1861* (New York: Oxford University Press, 1964).

13. Harry M. Ward, *The United Colonies of New England* (New York: Vantage Press,

1964); Harry M. Ward, *"Unite or Die": Intercolony Relations, 1690–1763* (Port Washington: Kennikat, 1971); Robert C. Newbold, *The Albany Congress and Plan of Union of 1754* (New York: Vantage Press, 1955); and Richard B. Bernstein with Kym S. Rice, *Are We to Be a Nation? The Making of the Constitution* (Cambridge, Mass.: Harvard University Press, 1987), ch. 2.

14. Edmund S. Morgan and Helen M. Morgan, *Prologue to Revolution: The Stamp Act Congress of 1765* (Chapel Hill: University of North Carolina Press, 1955); Pauline G. Maier, *From Resistance to Revolution* (New York: Alfred A. Knopf, 1972); Jack N. Rakove, *The Beginnings of National Politics: An Interpretive History of the Continental Congress* (New York: Alfred A. Knopf, 1979); and Jerrilyn Greene Marston, *King and Congress: The Transfer of Political Legitimacy, 1774–1776* (Princeton: Princeton University Press, 1988).

15. Nagel, *One Nation Indivisible;* and Paul C. Nagel, *This Sacred Trust: American Nationality, 1798–1898* (New York: Oxford University Press, 1977). On Madison, see Irving N. Brant, *James Madison: Commander in Chief, 1812–1836* (Indianapolis: Bobbs-Merrill, 1961); Adrienne Koch, *Madison's "Advice to My Country"* (Princeton: Princeton University Press, 1965); and Drew R. McCoy, *The Last of the Fathers: James Madison and the Republican Legacy* (Cambridge: Cambridge University Press, 1989).

16. See generally Nagel, *One Nation Indivisible;* Freehling, *Road to Disunion;* and Kenneth M. Stampp, *The Imperiled Union* (New York: Oxford University Press, 1980).

17. The core of the theory, in its most finished form, may be found in *The Federalist Nos. 10, 14* (Madison); its predecessors include Madison's April 1787 memorandum, "On the Vices of the Political System of the U[nited] States," and Madison's speech in the Federal Convention of June 6, 1787. The literature is huge and diverse, and it continues to grow. Leading discussions in the scholarly literature include Charles A. Beard, *An Economic Interpretation of the Constitution of the United States* (1913; rev. ed., New York: Macmillan, 1935), 152–188, esp. 156–158; Trevor Colbourn, ed., *Fame and the Founding Fathers: Essays of Douglass Adair* (New York: W. W. Norton for the Institute of Early American History and Culture, 1974), 75–106; Garry Wills, *Explaining America: The Federalist* (New York: Doubleday, 1981); Theodore Draper, "Hume and Madison: The Secrets of Federalist Paper No. 10," *Encounter* 58 (February 1982): 34–47; Albert Furtwangler, *The Authority of Publius: A Reading of the Federalist Papers* (Ithaca: Cornell University Press, 1984), 112–146 (including citations to other analyses and a useful tracing of the evolution of Madison's theory, including Hamilton's contributions); John Patrick Diggins, *The Lost Soul of American Politics* (New York: Basic Books, 1984); David F. Epstein, *The Political Theory of* The Federalist (Chicago: University of Chicago Press, 1984); and Morton White, *Philosophy,* The Federalist, *and the Constitution* (New York: Oxford University Press, 1987).

18. For the charge, see, e.g., *The Federalist Nos. 1, 2, 5, and 14.* Anti-Federalists such as Samuel Bryan of Pennsylvania, writing as "Centinel," indignantly refuted charges that they sought to split up the Union. See, e.g., "Letters of Centinel" (1787–1788), reprinted in Herbert J. Storing, ed. (with the assistance of Murray Dry), *The Complete Anti-Federalist,* 7 vols. (Chicago: University of Chicago Press, 1981), 2.7.139–143. [All citations to documents reprinted in Storing use his suggested method of citation—to the volume, the document, and the paragraph.]

19. See generally Bernstein with Rice, *Are We to Be a Nation?*

20. Two excellent books on American colonial history provide a synoptic overview of the diversity that was the hallmark of American origins: Bernard Bailyn, *The Origins of American Politics* (New York: Alfred A. Knopf, 1968); and R. C. Simmons, *The American Colonies* (New York: David McKay, 1976).

21. See, e.g., Rakove, *Beginnings of National Politics;* Edmund Cody Burnett, *The Continental Congress* (New York: Macmillan, 1941); H. James Henderson, *Party Politics in the Continental Congress* (New York: McGraw-Hill, 1974); and Jackson Turner Main, *Political Parties Before the Constitution* (Chapel Hill: University of North Carolina Press for the Institute of Early American History and Culture, 1973).

22. Comprehensive discussions of the evolving relationship between Southern character and Southern politics and constitutional development include Jesse H. Carpenter, *The South as a Conscious Minority, 1776–1861* (1930; Columbia: University of South Carolina Press, 1990); W. J. Cash, *The Mind of the South* (New York: Alfred A. Knopf, 1941); John Hope Franklin, *The Militant South, 1800–1861* (Cambridge, Mass.: Belknap Press of Harvard University Press, 1956); Emory M. Thomas, *The Confederate Nation, 1861–1865* (New York: Harper & Row, 1979); Don E. Fehrenbacher, *Constitutions and Constitutionalism in the Slaveholding South* (Athens: University of Georgia Press, 1989); and Drew Gilpin Faust, *The Creation of Confederate Nationalism* (Baton Rouge: Louisiana State University Press, 1988). For legal history in particular, see Paul Finkelman, "Exploring Southern Legal History," *North Carolina Law Review* 64 (1985): 77–116.

23. On this phenomenon, see, e.g., Joseph L. Davis, *Sectionalism in American Politics, 1774–1787* (Madison: University of Wisconsin Press, 1977); David Hackett Fischer, *Albion's Seed* (New York: Oxford University Press, 1990); Robert Kelley, *The Cultural Patterns of American Politics* (New York: Alfred A. Knopf, 1978); Merrill M. Jensen, ed., *Sectionalism in America* (Madison: University of Wisconsin Press, 1962); and Frederick Jackson Turner, *The Significance of Sections in American History* (New York: Henry Holt, 1932). Turner was the first historian to pay close attention to sectional rivalries and to work out careful methodologies to elucidate them.

24. Charles C. Thach, *The Creation of the Presidency, 1774–1789* (Baltimore: Johns Hopkins University Press, 1922).

25. The historiography of slavery continues to grow at an extraordinary rate. For a reliable survey, see Peter J. Parish, *Slavery: History and Historians* (New York: Harper & Row, 1990). Parish is particularly good on the vast literature dealing with slavery as a social institution and cultural practice.

   On slavery as a political, constitutional, and intellectual issue, see, e.g., Duncan MacLeod, *Slavery, Race, and the American Revolution* (Cambridge: Cambridge University Press, 1974); Donald L. Robinson, *Slavery and the Structure of American Politics, 1765–1820* (New York: Harcourt Brace Jovanovich, 1971); Winthrop D. Jordan, *White over Black: American Attitudes Towards the Negro, 1550–1812* (Chapel Hill: University of North Carolina Press for the Institute of Early American History and Culture, 1968); David Brion Davis, *The Problem of Slavery in Western Culture* (Ithaca: Cornell University Press, 1966); David

Brion Davis, *The Problem of Slavery in the Age of Revolution, 1770–1823* (Ithaca: Cornell University Press, 1973); David Brion Davis, *Slavery and Human Progress* (New York: Oxford University Press, 1985); and the magisterial work by Richard Kluger, *Simple Justice* (New York: Alfred A. Knopf, 1975).

26. See generally A. Leon Higginbotham, Jr., *In the Matter of Color: Race and the American Legal Process—The Colonial Period* (New York: Oxford University Press, 1978), the first of a projected multivolume series; Mark Tushnet, *The American Law of Slavery, 1810–1860: Considerations of Property and Interest* (Princeton: Princeton University Press, 1978); Paul Finkelman, *An Imperfect Union: Slavery, Federalism, and Comity* (Chapel Hill: University of North Carolina Press, 1981); and Paul Finkelman, ed., *The Law of Freedom and Bondage: A Casebook* (New York: Oceana Publications, 1986).

27. The American Colonization Society, which flourished in the 1820s and 1830s, had as its objective the colonization of freed slaves and free African-Americans in what is now the republic of Liberia. Key members of this society included former Presidents James Madison and James Monroe and Chief Justice John Marshall. The question of colonization preoccupied many of Madison's successors in the Presidency, most notably Abraham Lincoln, who in the years before the Emancipation Proclamation often speculated publicly whether black and white Americans could share the nation in peace. For a deeply moving and sensitive examination of the contradictions that slavery stimulated in the political thought and actions of perhaps the nation's leading constitutional statesman, see McCoy, *Last of the Fathers.*

28. See Paul Finkelman, "Slavery and the Constitutional Convention: Making a Covenant with Death," in Richard R. Beeman, Stephen H. Botein, and Edward C. Carter II, *Beyond Confederation: Dimensions of the Constitution and American National Identity* (Chapel Hill: University of North Carolina Press for the Institute of Early American History and Culture, 1987), 188–225. *Contra,* Don E. Fehrenbacher, *The Federal Government and Slavery* (Claremont: Claremont Graduate School, 1984), and his address to the American Society for Legal History at its 1987 convention in Philadelphia. Fehrenbacher is preparing a history of federal relations to slavery in American constitutional law.

29. In 1808, the earliest moment it could do so under the Constitution, the federal government enacted a law prohibiting that trade.

30. See Peterson, *Great Triumvirate;* Potter, *Lincoln and His Party,* Potter (completed by Fehrenbacher), *Impending Crisis;* Don E. Fehrenbacher, *The Dred Scott Case: Its Significance in Law and Politics* (New York: Oxford University Press, 1978); Freehling, *Road to Secession;* Stampp, *Imperiled Union,* ch. 1, "The Idea of a Perpetual Union"; and Knupfer, *Union As It Is.*

31. See Paul Finkelman, "Prelude to the Fourteenth Amendment: Black Legal Rights in the Antebellum North," *Rutgers Law Journal* 17 (1986): 415–482, and sources cited therein.

32. See, e.g., Clement Eaton, *The Freedom-of-Thought Struggle in the Old South* (1940; New York: Harper & Row, 1962), which chronicles the struggle of proslavery forces to prevent abolitionist and antislavery speakers and publications from circulating in the South, including censorship of the federal mails to block antislavery newspapers such as William Lloyd Garrison's *Liberator.*

33. See Phillip S. Paludan, *A Covenant with Death* (Urbana: University of Illinois Press, 1975); William M. Wiecek, *The Sources of Antislavery Constitutionalism in the United States, 1790–1848* (Ithaca: Cornell University Press, 1974); Harold M. Hyman and William M. Wiecek, *Equal Justice Under Law: Constitutional Development, 1835–1875* (New York: Harper & Row, 1982); William E. Nelson, *The Roots of American Bureaucracy, 1830–1900* (Cambridge, Mass.: Harvard University Press, 1982); and William E. Nelson, *The Fourteenth Amendment: From Political Principle to Judicial Doctrine* (Cambridge, Mass.: Harvard University Press, 1988).

34. On Douglass, see William S. McFeely, *Frederick Douglass* (New York: W. W. Norton, 1991).

35. See generally Wiecek, *Sources of Antislavery Constitutionalism.*

36. See Dumas Malone, *Jefferson and the Ordeal of Liberty* (Boston: Little, Brown, 1962); and Smith, *Freedom's Fetters.*

37. See Morison, Merk, and Freidel, *Dissent in Three American Wars,* ch. 1; Donald R. Hickey, *The War of 1812* (Bloomington: Indiana University Press, 1990); J. C. A. Stagg, *Mr. Madison's War* (Princeton: Princeton University Press, 1983); and Banner, *To the Hartford Convention.*

38. See Peterson, *Olive Branch and Sword;* and Ellis, *Union at Risk.*

39. Paul Finkelman, "Slavery and the Northwest Ordinance: A Study in Ambiguity," *Journal of the Early Republic* 6 (1986): 343–370, presents a strong case for a revisionist interpretation of the Ordinance's "antislavery" provision, Article VI. See generally, Peter S. Onuf, *Statehood and Union: A History of the Northwest Ordinance* (Bloomington: Indiana University Press, 1987); and see Onuf's commentary on the Northwest Ordinance in Stephen L. Schechter, ed., and Richard B. Bernstein and Donald S. Lutz, contributing eds., *Roots of the Republic: American Founding Documents Interpreted* (Madison, Wis.: Madison House, 1990), 249–265.

40. On the war, see Robert M. Johannsen, *To the Halls of Montezuma* (New York: Oxford University Press, 1986); Potter (completed by Fehrenbacher), *Impending Crisis,* ch. 1; and Morison, Merk, and Freidel, *Dissent in Three American Wars,* ch. 2.

41. Herman V. Ames, *The Proposed Amendments to the Constitution of the United States during the First Century of its History,* in *Annual Report of the American Historical Association for the Year 1896,* vol. 2 (Washington, D.C.: Government Printing Office, 1897), 201–202, notes that the only amendments proposed concerning Congressional power over slavery in the territories were offered during the second session of the Thirty-sixth Congress. [Hereafter cited as Ames, *Proposed Amendments,* with page number.]

42. See, e.g., the discussion in Harry V. Jaffa, *The Crisis of the House Divided: An Interpretation of the Lincoln-Douglas Debates* (Garden City: Doubleday, 1958); for a more favorable view, see Robert M. Johannsen, *Stephen A. Douglas* (New York: Oxford University Press, 1973).

43. The best discussion is in Potter (completed by Fehrenbacher), *Impending Crisis.*

44. See generally Fehrenbacher, *Dred Scott Case.*

45. 19 Howard (60 U.S.) 393 (1857).

46. Fehrenbacher, *Dred Scott Case*, is the definitive study of this extraordinary case. Fehrenbacher has suggested that the suit was cobbled together by antislavery activists. The actual parties, Scott and his owner of record, John F. A. Sanford of New York, played almost no role in the litigation. By the time the Court acted, Sanford was an inmate of a mental hospital—driven mad, some wags assert, by his part in the litigation. A clerical error at the Supreme Court resulted in the misspelling of his name in the caption of the case.

47. It is ironic that Edwin Meese III (the second Attorney General in the Reagan Administration), in his exposition and defense of the "jurisprudence of original intention," sought to label *Dred Scott v. Sandford* as a clear example of the catastrophes that can result when judges write their own views into the Constitution. Even a cursory reading of Taney's opinion shows that the Chief Justice cloaked his own preferences in the language, reasoning, and citation to authority familiar from "original intent" jurisprudence.

48. The concept of the concurrent majority was invented by Calhoun. See Richard Hofstadter, *The American Political Tradition: And the Men Who Made It* (New York: Alfred A. Knopf, 1948), ch. 4, "John C. Calhoun: The Marx of the Master Class."

49. Ames, *Proposed Amendments*, 91, 103.

50. Ibid., 103–104.

51. Ibid., 45–49.

52. Ibid., 168–169 (quote at 168).

53. The previous versions, the doctrines of 1798 propounded by Thomas Jefferson and James Madison, differed from Calhounian nullification in that they required the citation of specific constitutional clauses violated by the challenged federal action, and in that the 1798 versions of nullification and interposition were designed as "early warning signals" to prompt the states to conduct a general examination of the action or policy in question. In the 1820s, Jefferson seemed to tilt more and more in the direction of Southern sectionalism and explicit commitment to state sovereignty. Dumas Malone, *Jefferson and His Time: The Sage of Monticello* (Boston: Little, Brown, 1981), 316–361. Madison, more moderate and circumspect, resisted any attempt by Southern state-sovereignty advocates to claim him or Jefferson as patron or progenitor. See McCoy, *Last of the Fathers;* Koch, *Madison's "Advice,"* ch. 3.

54. The best overall discussion is Michael Gienapp, *The Origins of the Republican Party: 1852–1856* (New York: Oxford University Press, 1986). Gienapp is completing a second volume, taking the story through the election of Abraham Lincoln. Don E. Fehrenbacher, *Prelude to Greatness: Lincoln in the 1850's* (Stanford: Stanford University Press, 1962), is a definitive study of the career, during the party's formative years, of the man who became the first Republican President.

55. Quoted in Harold M. Hyman, *A More Perfect Union: The Impact of the Civil War and Reconstruction on the Constitution* (New York: Alfred A. Knopf, 1971), 34.

56. Joseph Holt to James O. Harrison, January 14, 1861, quoted in Hyman, *More Perfect Union*, 36.

57. Quoted in Hyman and Wiecek, *Equal Justice Under Law*, 217.

58. Potter, *Lincoln and His Party*, 259–260. For a balanced view of Stanton's activities, which nonetheless criticizes his breaches of confidence and apparent conflicts of interest in 1860–1861, see Benjamin P. Thomas and Harold M. Hyman, *Stanton: The Life and Times of Lincoln's Secretary of War* (New York: Alfred A. Knopf, 1962), ch. 5. The letter is quoted at 102.

59. Potter, *Lincoln and His Party*, is still the classic study. See also Hyman and Wiecek, *Equal Justice Under Law*, 218–231.

60. Ames, *Proposed Amendments*, 194.

61. Potter, *Lincoln and His Party*, 307–308 (quote at 308).

62. Quoted by Potter, *Lincoln and His Party*, 21.

63. Ibid., 91; Corwin to Lincoln, January 18, 1861, quoted in Gunderson, *Old Gentlemen's Convention*, 14.

64. See the discussions in Potter, *Lincoln and His Party*, 104–105, 110–111, 170–174, 186; Hyman and Wiecek, *Equal Justice Under Law*, 221–222.

65. *Prigg v. Pennsylvania*, 41 U.S. (16 Peters) 539 (1842).

66. John J. Crittenden (Kentucky), in *Congressional Globe*, 36 Cong., 2d sess. (Senate), 1375–79 (March 2, 1861).

67. Potter, *Lincoln and His Party*, 290–294, 297–299; and Hyman and Wiecek, *Equal Justice Under Law*, 222–223.

68. Potter, *Lincoln and His Party*, 91.

69. 2 Devereux Law Reporter 263 (1829), reprinted in Finkelman, ed., *Law of Freedom and Bondage*, 217–220. The owner of the slave who was shot by Mann pressured the state to prosecute Mann for battery, presenting the ironic picture of one slaveowner apparently seeking to punish another for cruelty to slaves. Actually, the slaveowner in *Mann* was seeking to protect his own property rights in the slave wounded by Mann.

70. On Rives, see McCoy, *Last of the Fathers*, 323–369.

71. Thomas and Hyman, *Stanton*, 111 (quoting reports by Charles Sumner to Governor John A. Andrew of Massachusetts).

72. Quoted in Gunderson, *Old Gentlemen's Convention*, 107, from Lucius E. Chittenden, *Report of the Debates and Proceedings* . . . (New York, 1864), 440–449.

73. On the history of federal courts' power to apply "federal common law" distinct from, and at times in conflict with, common law in the states in which they sat, see Tony Freyer, *Harmony and Dissonance: The* Swift *and* Erie *Decisions and American Federalism* (Linden Studies in American Legal History) (New York: New York University Press, 1981).

74. Gunderson, *Old Gentlemen's Convention*, 93–94.

75. *Congressional Globe*, 36 Cong., 2d sess. (Senate), 1333 (February 27, 1861), quoted in Gunderson, *Old Gentlemen's Convention*, 94.

76. Alexandria *Virginia Sentinel,* March 7, 1861, quoted in Gunderson, *Old Gentlemen's Convention,* 95.

77. Compare Gunderson's favorable assessment, *Old Gentlemen's Convention,* 100–102, and Knupfer, *Union As It Is,* 208–211 (oddly, Knupfer does not mention the Peace Conference, focusing instead on Crittenden in the Senate), with the hostile view of Potter, *Lincoln and His Party,* 307–308, and the negative verdict of Hyman and Wiecek, *Equal Justice Under Law,* 223.

78. Potter, *Lincoln and His Party,* 302 (Potter uses the term "dilatory courtesy").

79. Abraham Lincoln, First Inaugural Address, March 4, 1861, in Don E. Fehrenbacher, ed., *Abraham Lincoln: Speeches and Writings, 1859–1865* (New York: Library of America, 1989), 222. (The word "opportunity" was spelled "oppertunity" in the original manuscript.)

80. Ibid.

81. See the discussion in Hyman, *More Perfect Union,* 47. On Illinois's questionable ratification, see Alan P. Grimes, *Democracy and the Amendments to the Constitution* (1978; Lanham: University Press of America, 1988), 60 n. 5.

82. Warren, *Davis Gets His Citizenship Back.*

83. Potter (completed by Fehrenbacher), *Impending Crisis,* chs. 19–20. On such issues as whether Lincoln goaded the 'Confederates' into firing the first shot and whether he fully appreciated the severity of the crisis, see Potter, *Lincoln and His Party;* on the historiography of the crisis, see Potter's new introduction to the 1962 edition of that book, and Don E. Fehrenbacher, *Lincoln in Text and Context: Selected Essays* (Stanford: Stanford University Press, 1987).

84. See David F. Allmendinger, Jr., *Ruffin: Family and Reform in the Old South* (New York: Oxford University Press, 1990).

CHAPTER 6

REDEFINING THE UNION: THE CIVIL WAR AMENDMENTS

1. Representative Ignatius Donnelly (Republican–Minnesota), *Congressional Globe,* 39th Cong., 1st sess. (H.R.), 586 (February 1, 1866), quoted in Harold M. Hyman and William M. Wiecek, *Equal Justice Under Law: Constitutional Development, 1835–1875* (New York: Harper & Row, 1982), 392.

2. Throughout, the source for Lincoln's words is Don E. Fehrenbacher, ed., *Abraham Lincoln: Speeches and Writings, 1859–1865* (New York: Library of America, 1989). [Hereafter quoted as Fehrenbacher, ed., *Lincoln: 1859–1865.*] On Lincoln as a public speaker, see Waldo Braden, *Abraham Lincoln: Public Speaker* (Baton Rouge: Louisiana State University Press, 1988); and the essays collected in Don E. Fehrenbacher, *Lincoln in Text and Context: Selected Essays* (Stanford: Stanford University Press, 1987). On Lincoln's efforts to win the rhetorical Civil War, see the brilliant study by Garry Wills, *Lincoln at Gettysburg: The Words That Remade America* (New York: Simon & Schuster, 1992).

3. Quoted in Eric S. Foner, *Reconstruction: America's Unfinished Revolution, 1863–1877* (New York: Harper & Row, 1988), 32.

4. *Congressional Globe*, 37th Cong., 1st sess. (Senate), 78, 433 (July 12, 1861). His motion to consider was defeated, 11 to 24. See Herman V. Ames, *The Proposed Amendments to the Constitution of the United States during the First Century of its History*, in *Annual Report of the American Historical Association for the Year 1896*, vol. 2 (Washington, D.C.: Government Printing Office, 1897), 197, 365. [Hereafter Ames, *Proposed Amendments*.]

5. The text of this document is reprinted in Fehrenbacher, ed., *Lincoln: 1859–1865*, 276–278.

6. His most famous such warning was his letter to Horace Greeley. Abraham Lincoln, Letter to Horace Greeley, August 22, 1862, in Fehrenbacher, ed., *Lincoln: 1859–1865*, 357–358. For documents tracing Lincoln's experimentation with compensated emancipation from November 1861 to February 1865, see ibid., 276–278, 307–308, 309, 310–311, 312, 316, 319, 340–342, 368, 370, 403, 406–407, 408, 409, 411, 413–414, 586, 671.

7. On the Emancipation Proclamation and the Thirteenth Amendment, see John Hope Franklin, *The Emancipation Proclamation* (New York: Doubleday, 1963) (reproducing texts of both the Preliminary and Final Proclamations); and Foner, *Reconstruction*, ch. 1. Neither Franklin nor Foner even mentions the Corwin Amendment of 1861, underlining its irrelevance once Confederate guns opened fire on Fort Sumter.

8. The Proclamation had another effect—one that almost nobody recognized: it scuttled the Corwin Amendment, which, though still before the nation, was a constitutional and political nullity. However, some members of Congress worried about its twilight existence. On February 8, 1864, a constitutional amendment to repeal the Corwin Amendment was referred to the Committee on the Judiciary, which buried the proposal. Herman V. Ames concluded that "it would seem to be extremely doubtful whether Congress could recall an amendment when it has once been submitted." Ames, *Proposed Amendments*, 197 and n. 2, 369.

9. See generally Franklin, *Emancipation Proclamation;* and Eric S. Foner, *Nothing but Freedom: Emancipation and Its Legacy* (Baton Rouge: Louisiana State University Press, 1982).

10. The text appears in Fehrenbacher, ed., *Lincoln: 1859–1865*, 371.

11. Fehrenbacher, *Lincoln in Text and Context*, 113–142, 157–163; James M. McPherson, *Abraham Lincoln and the Second American Revolution* (New York: Oxford University Press, 1990), 43–64 (esp. 58–59); Stephen B. Oates, *Abraham Lincoln: The Man Behind the Myths* (New York: Harper & Row, 1984), 120–126; and Gabor S. Boritt, *Abraham Lincoln: War Opponent and War President*, 1987 Fluhrer Lecture (Gettysburg: Gettysburg College, 1987).

12. Leading treatments include J. G. Randall, *Constitutional Problems Under Lincoln* (Urbana: University of Illinois Press, 1926; rev. ed., 1953); Harold M. Hyman, *A More Perfect Union: The Impact of the Civil War and Reconstruction on the Constitution* (New York: Alfred A. Knopf, 1971); Hyman and Wiecek, *Equal Justice Under Law;* Foner, *Reconstruction;* and Mark E. Neely, Jr., *The Fate of Liberty: Abraham Lincoln and Civil Liberties* (New York: Oxford University Press, 1990).

13. Abraham Lincoln, Special Message to Congress, July 4, 1861, in Fehrenbacher, ed., *Lincoln: 1859–1865*, 253.

14. Ames, *Proposed Amendments*, 365–366.

15. Abraham Lincoln, Second Annual Message, December 1, 1862, reprinted in Fehrenbacher, ed., *Lincoln: 1859–1865*, 393–415 (esp. 406–407).

16. Foner, *Reconstruction*, 1.

17. Franklin, *Emancipation Proclamation;* Foner, *Reconstruction*, ch. 1.

18. Ames, *Proposed Amendments*, 212–213.

19. See, e.g., Gabor S. Boritt, *Lincoln and the Economics of the American Dream* (Memphis: Memphis State University Press, 1978); Allan G. Bogue, *The Earnest Men: Republicans in the Civil War Senate* (Ithaca: Cornell University Press, 1981); and Allan G. Bogue, *The Congressman's Civil War* (Cambridge: Cambridge University Press, 1989).

20. Ames, *Proposed Amendments*, 214.

21. Ibid., 215–216, 367, 368; see also ibid., 100 n. 4, referring to Davis's proposal to create East New England and West New England, and another state comprising Maryland, Delaware, and the eastern shore of Virginia, "for Federal and national purposes only."

22. Foner, *Reconstruction*, 66.

23. Abraham Lincoln, Response to a Serenade at the White House, February 1, 1865, reprinted in Fehrenbacher, ed., *Lincoln: 1859–1865*, 670.

24. See, e.g., the copy preserved in the New York Public Library, Rare Books and Manuscripts Division.

25. Alan P. Grimes, *Democracy and the Amendments to the Constitution* (1978; Lanham, Md.: University Press of America, 1988), 40–41.

26. Melvin Urofsky, *A March of Liberty: A Constitutional History of the United States* (New York: Alfred A. Knopf, 1988), 420.

27. Stephen B. Knupfer, *The Union As It Is: Constitutional Unionism and Sectional Compromise, 1787–1861* (Chapel Hill: University of North Carolina Press, 1991), 211.

28. The date is variously given as December 6 and December 9.

29. Moncure Daniel Conway, "Sursum Corda," *The Radical* 1 (1866), 291–292, quoted in Hyman and Wiecek, *Equal Justice Under Law*, 401.

30. The leading studies are Eric L. McKitrick, *Andrew Johnson and Reconstruction* (Chicago: University of Chicago Press, 1960); Michael Les Benedict, *The Impeachment and Trial of Andrew Johnson* (New York: W. W. Norton, 1973); and Hans Trefousse, *Andrew Johnson* (New York: W. W. Norton, 1990), the most recent and thorough biography.

31. McKitrick, *Andrew Johnson and Reconstruction*, 85–92, is a fine brief sketch of Johnson's pre-1865 career. It is aptly entitled "Andrew Johnson, Outsider." See 3–14 for an equally valuable sketch of the historiography of Johnson to 1960. Trefousse, *Andrew Johnson*, is an excellent supplement for scholarship since 1960.

32. Quoted in William E. Nelson, *The Fourteenth Amendment: From Political Principle to Judicial Doctrine* (Cambridge, Mass.: Harvard University Press, 1988), 43.

33. Lyman Trumbull to Mrs. Gary, June 27, 1866, quoted in Nelson, *Fourteenth Amendment,* 42.

34. On the difficulties of the term "Radical Republicans," see Michael Les Benedict, *A Compromise of Principle* (New York: W. W. Norton, 1974).

35. Key works include Charles Fairman, "Does the Fourteenth Amendment Incorporate the Bill of Rights? The Original Understanding," *Stanford Law Review* 2 (1949): 5–139 (Amendment did not incorporate Bill of Rights); Alexander M. Bickel, "The Original Understanding and the Segregation Decisions," *Harvard Law Review* 69 (1955): 1–65 (original intent of framers cannot be ascertained and thus ought not bind the modern Court); Raoul Berger, *Government by Judiciary: The Transformation of the Fourteenth Amendment* (Cambridge, Mass.: Harvard University Press, 1977) (Amendment did not incorporate Bill of Rights or impose general principle of equal protection on government; intent binding); Chester J. Antieau, *The Original Understanding of the Fourteenth Amendment* (Tucson: Mid-America Press, 1981), (same); Judith A. Baer, *Equality under the Constitution: Reclaiming the Fourteenth Amendment* (Ithaca: Cornell University Press, 1983) (Amendment should now be interpreted to include sweeping authority in federal courts to enforce equality); Robert J. Kaczorowski, *The Politics of Judicial Interpretation: The Federal Courts, Department of Justice and Civil Rights, 1866–1876* (New York: Oceana Publications, 1985) (Amendment designed to protect fundamental rights against all levels of government); Michael Kent Curtis, *No State Shall Abridge: The Fourteenth Amendment and the Bill of Rights* (Durham, N.C.: Duke University Press, 1986) (Amendment intended to incorporate Bill of Rights); Nelson, *Fourteenth Amendment* (Amendment intended to be source of judicial power to ensure equal protection of the laws); Raoul Berger, *The Fourteenth Amendment and the States* (Norman: University of Oklahoma Press, 1989) (same as *Government by Judiciary*); and Earl M. Maltz, *Congress, the Courts, and Civil Rights, 1863–1869* (Lawrence: University Press of Kansas, 1990) (Civil War Amendments should be construed strictly, because only the narrowest understanding of their scope can be said to have commanded support throughout Congress). This list is far from exhaustive.

36. Nelson, *Fourteenth Amendment,* 62–63.

37. E.g., Kaczorowski, *Politics of Judicial Interpretation.*

38. Nelson, *Fourteenth Amendment.*

39. Berger, *Government by Judiciary.*

40. See, e.g., the history of the school segregation cases of the 1950s as recounted in Richard Kluger, *Simple Justice* (New York: Alfred A. Knopf, 1975). Indeed, one of the classic examinations of the question, Bickel, "Original Understanding," grew out of a request, after the first argument of *Brown v. Board of Education,* by Justice Felix Frankfurter to Bickel (then Frankfurter's clerk) to prepare an extensive memorandum on the legislative debates on the Fourteenth Amendment. Nelson, *Fourteenth Amendment,* ch. 1, presents a masterly examination of the historiographical and legal literature and the main contours of the modern debates over the Amendment.

41. Nelson, *Fourteenth Amendment,* 93–96.

42. *Congressional Globe,* 38th Cong., 1st sess. (Senate), 1490 (1864).

43. Nelson, *Fourteenth Amendment,* 113.

44. *Congressional Globe,* 39th Cong., 1st sess. (Senate), 2892 (1866), quoted in Nelson, *Fourteenth Amendment,* 114.

45. Governor's Message, *Mobile Daily Advertiser and Register,* November 13, 1866, quoted in Nelson, *Fourteenth Amendment,* 105.

46. *Congressional Globe,* 39th Cong., 1st sess. (H.R.), 3148 (June 13, 1866), quoted in Foner, *Reconstruction,* 254–255.

47. "Leo," in Charleston (S.C.) *Courier,* December 21, 1866, reprinted in December 22, 25, 1866, and January 5, 1867, all quoted and cited in McKitrick, *Andrew Johnson and Reconstruction,* 470–471.

48. On Johnson's role, see generally McKitrick, *Andrew Johnson and Reconstruction,* ch. 11 and 467–471; Foner, *Reconstruction,* 251–261.

49. Foner, *Reconstruction,* 228–280, esp. 251–261 on the Amendment and 261–280 on the results and aftermath of the 1866 elections. The now standard monograph on the ratification of the Amendment is Joseph B. James, *The Ratification of the Fourteenth Amendment* (Macon: Mercer University Press, 1984).

50. See Benedict, *Impeachment and Trial,* and Eleanore Bushnell, *Crimes, Follies, and Misfortunes: The Federal Impeachment Trials* (Urbana: University of Illinois Press, 1992), 127–164, for the most reliable and perceptive modern accounts. John F. Kennedy's *Profiles in Courage* (New York: Harper, 1956) includes a chapter on Senator Edmund G. Ross of Kansas, who provided the final vote needed to save Johnson; this famous chapter presents the more traditional understanding of the Johnson impeachment. See also William H. Rehnquist, *Grand Inquests* (New York: William Morrow, 1992), 143–261.

51. Grimes, *Democracy and the Amendments,* 50.

52. See generally Robert Penn Warren, *Jefferson Davis Gets His Citizenship Back* (Lexington: University Press of Kentucky, 1980).

53. On the origins of the Amendment, see generally William Gillette, *The Right to Vote: Politics and the Passage of the Fifteenth Amendment* (1965; rev. ed. with new epilogue, Baltimore: Johns Hopkins University Press, 1969).

54. On the antebellum history of the franchise, see Chilton Williamson, *American Suffrage from Property to Democracy, 1790–1860* (Princeton: Princeton University Press, 1960).

55. See generally Wendy Hamand Venet, *Neither Ballots nor Bullets: Women Abolitionists and the Civil War* (Charlottesville: University Press of Virginia, 1991), esp. 151–161.

56. Quoted in Dorothy Sterling, *Ahead of Her Time: Abby Kelley and the Politics of Antislavery* (New York: W. W. Norton, 1991), 348.

57. Lucy Stone to Abby Kelley, January 24, 1867, quoted in Sterling, *Ahead of Her Time,* 347.

58. Abby Kelley to Lucy Stone, February 10, 1867, quoted in Sterling, *Ahead of Her Time*, 347.

59. Data drawn from Gillette, *Right to Vote*, 84–85.

60. The term "political population" is derived from Henry Adams, *History of the United States during the Administrations of Thomas Jefferson, 1801–1809* (1889–1891; New York: Library of America, 1986), 5.

61. Charles Sumner (Mass.), in *Congressional Globe*, 38 Cong., 1st sess. (Senate), 1480 (March 28, 1864), quoted in Grimes, *Democracy and the Amendments*, 36.

CHAPTER 7
DEMOCRATIZING THE CONSTITUTION: THE PROGRESSIVE AMENDMENTS

1. For this argument, see Alan P. Grimes, *Democracy and the Amendments to the Constitution* (1978; Lanham: University Press of America, 1988), 65–66.

2. Herman V. Ames, *The Proposed Amendments to the Constitution of the United States during the First Century of its History*, in *Annual Report of the American Historical Association for 1896*, vol. 2 (Washington, D.C.: Government Printing Office, 1897), 23–25. [Hereafter Ames, *Proposed Amendments*.] These proposals are discussed in Chapter 10.

3. See Forrest McDonald, *Alexander Hamilton: A Biography* (New York: W. W. Norton, 1979); Broadus Mitchell, *Alexander Hamilton*, 2 vols. (New York: Macmillan, 1957–1962); and Joanne B. Freeman, " 'Very Busy and Not a Little Anxious': Alexander Hamilton, America's First Secretary of the Treasury," in Stephen L. Schechter and Richard B. Bernstein, eds., *Well Begun: Chronicles of the Early National Period* (Albany: New York State Commission on the Bicentennial of the United States Constitution, 1989), 71–79. Hamilton's *Reports* as Secretary of the Treasury are collected in Jacob E. Cooke, ed., *The Reports of Alexander Hamilton* (New York: Harper & Row, 1964), and in the appropriate volumes of Harold C. Syrett, Jacob E. Cooke, Barbara Chernow et al., eds., *The Papers of Alexander Hamilton*, 27 vols. (New York: Columbia University Press, 1961–1987).

4. Joseph Pechman, *Federal Tax Policy*, 3d ed. (Washington, D.C.: Brookings Institution, 1977), 288.

5. Ibid.; Margaret G. Myers, *A Financial History of the United States* (New York: Columbia University Press, 1970), 240–241; and Grimes, *Democracy and the Amendments*, 67–69.

6. For the figures on wealth distribution, see Grimes, *Democracy and the Amendments*, 67–68.

7. Quoted in ibid., 70–71.

8. Quoted in ibid., 72.

9. 157 U.S. 429 (1895); 158 U.S. 601 (1895).

10. [Michael A. Musmanno], *Proposed Amendments to the Constitution: A Monograph on the Resolutions Introduced in Congress proposing Amendments to the Constitution of the United States of*

America, House Doc. No. 551, 70th Cong., 2d sess. (1929; rept., Westport, Conn.: Greenwood Press, 1976), 212. [Hereafter Musmanno, *Proposed Amendments.*]

11. On the legislative maneuvering, see Grimes, *Democracy and the Amendments,* 73–74; Musmanno, *Proposed Amendments,* 213–215, is more tactful and thus less enlightening.

12. Grimes, *Democracy and the Amendments,* 74.

13. *The New York Times,* February 4, 1913, p. 5.

14. Myers, *Financial History,* 266–267.

15. Max Farrand, ed., *The Records of the Federal Convention of 1787,* rev. ed. in 4 vols. (New Haven: Yale University Press, 1937, 1966), 1: 4 (May 25, 1787); 3: 574–575 (text of Delaware's resolutions).

16. Clinton L. Rossiter, *1787: The Grand Convention* (New York: Macmillan, 1966; rept., New York: W. W. Norton, 1987), 191.

17. Ames, *Proposed Amendments,* 61 and n. 1.

18. See the instructions adopted in 1790 by the Virginia legislature for its Senators in the First Congress, Richard Henry Lee and James Monroe, demanding that the Senate open its deliberations to the public, as the House had done since April of 1789. James Monroe Papers, New York Public Library, Rare Books and Manuscripts Division.

19. On Adams, see John F. Kennedy, *Profiles in Courage* (New York: Harper & Brothers, 1956); on Tyler, see Ames, *Proposed Amendments,* 65.

20. On the general effects of the Civil War, see Robert Penn Warren, *The Legacy of the Civil War: Meditations on the Centennial* (New York: Random House, 1961); James M. McPherson, *Battle Cry of Freedom* (New York: Oxford University Press, 1988); James M. McPherson, *Abraham Lincoln and the Second American Revolution* (New York: Oxford University Press, 1990); and Eric S. Foner, *Reconstruction: America's Unfinished Revolution, 1863–1877* (New York: Harper & Row, 1988). On the war's effects on the Senate, see, e.g., Allan G. Bogue, *The Earnest Men: Republicans in the Civil War Senate* (Ithaca: Cornell University Press, 1981).

21. The leading student of the interaction between the economy and the law in American history is James Willard Hurst of the University of Wisconsin Law School. See, e.g., *The Growth of American Law: The Law Makers* (Boston: Little, Brown, 1950). Lawrence M. Friedman, *A History of American Law,* 2d ed. (New York: Simon & Schuster, 1985), is a valuable synthesis of its subject by Hurst's foremost adherent. Alfred D. Chandler, Jr., *The Visible Hand: The Managerial Revolution in American Business* (Cambridge, Mass.: Belknap Press of Harvard University Press, 1977); and Alfred D. Chandler, Jr., *Scale and Scope* (Cambridge, Mass.: Belknap Press of Harvard University Press, 1990), delineate this transformation of American economic life, the latter adding a valuable comparative dimension. Morton J. Horwitz, *The Transformation of American Law, 1870–1960* (New York: Oxford University Press, 1992), presents an account, imbued with the interpretative approach of critical legal studies, of the legal changes accompanying this economic transformation. G. Edward White, *Tort Law in America: An Intellectual History* (New York: Oxford University Press, 1980), examines the effects of changes in American society on the intellectual structure of American law.

22. The most famous of these exposés was David G. Phillips's inflammatory series of articles for the Hearst magazines (which were collected as a book) titled *The Treason of the Senate* (1906; rept., Chicago: Quadrangle, 1964).

23. George H. Haynes, *The Election of Senators* (New York: Henry Holt, 1906), 47. Haynes, in 1906 an instructor in political science, became the leading authority on the history of the Senate. See George H. Haynes, *The Senate of the United States*, 2 vols. (Boston: Houghton Mifflin, 1938).

24. As reported in Haynes, *Election of Senators*, 47–48.

25. As reported in ibid., 48–49.

26. Ibid., 63.

27. *Review of Reviews*, February 1897, quoted in Haynes, *Election of Senators*, 204 n. 22.

28. Boston *Herald*, January 14, 1897, quoted in Haynes, *Election of Senators*, 290.

29. Haynes, *Election of Senators*, 98–99.

30. Ames, *Proposed Amendments*, 61.

31. Ibid.

32. Harry V. Jaffa, *Crisis of the House Divided: An Interpretation of the Lincoln-Douglas Debates* (Garden City: Doubleday, 1958); and Don E. Fehrenbacher, *Prelude to Greatness: Lincoln in the 1850's* (Stanford: Stanford University Press, 1962).

33. Musmanno, *Proposed Amendments*, 217.

34. *Congressional Quarterly's Guide to Congress*, 3d ed. (Washington, D.C.: Congressional Quarterly, 1982), 96.

35. Ames, *Proposed Amendments*, 61.

36. Haynes, *Election of Senators*, 104; Ames, *Proposed Amendments*, 61–62.

37. See the discussion in Chapter 13.

38. Ames, *Proposed Amendments*, 62.

39. For those who tend to regard every constitutional provision as both legitimate and foreordained, it is instructive to read the fair-minded, impartial presentation of arguments for and against the election of Senators by the people in Haynes, *Election of Senators*, 153–258. See also Ames, *Proposed Amendments*, 62–63; and Musmanno, *Proposed Amendments*, 215–218.

40. Ames, *Proposed Amendments*, 63.

41. Musmanno, *Proposed Amendments*, 219–225; Grimes, *Democracy and the Amendments*, 82; and *Congressional Quarterly's Guide to Congress*, 96–97.

42. Henry Adams, *History of the United States during the Administrations of Thomas Jefferson, 1801–1809* (1889–1891; New York: Library of America, 1986), 5.

43. The phrase comes from Eleanor Flexner, *Century of Struggle: The Women's Rights Movement in the United States* (New York: Atheneum, 1968).

44. Abigail Adams to John Adams, March 31, 1776, and John Adams to Abigail Adams,

April 14, 1776, in L. H. Butterfield, ed., *Adams Family Correspondence* (Cambridge, Mass.: Belknap Press of Harvard University Press, 1963–), 1: 369–403. See Joan Hoff, *Law, Gender, and Injustice: A Legal History of U.S. Women* (New York: New York University Press, 1991), 59–66.

45. Hoff, *Law, Gender, and Injustice*, 98–102.

46. Marylynn Salmon, *Women and the Law of Property in Early America* (Chapel Hill: University of North Carolina Press, 1984).

47. Mercy Otis Warren (Lester H. Cohen, ed.), *The History of the Rise, Progress, and Termination of the American Rebellion* (1805; Indianapolis, Ind.: Liberty Press/Liberty Classics, 1989). See also Linda K. Kerber, *Women of the Republic: Intellect and Ideology in Revolutionary America* (Chapel Hill: University of North Carolina Press for the Institute of Early American History and Culture, 1980), 80–84, 227, 240, 246, 250–252, 256–258; Lester H. Cohen, "Explaining the Revolution: Ideology and Ethics in Mercy Otis Warren's Historical Theory," *William and Mary Quarterly*, 3d ser., 37 (1980): 200–218; and Maud M. Hutcheson, "Mercy Warren, 1728–1814," *William and Mary Quarterly*, 3d ser., 10 (1953): 378–402.

48. See generally Kerber, *Women of the Republic*.

49. Richard B. Morris, *Studies in the History of American Law* (New York: Columbia University Press, 1930); for a critique of the Morris thesis as overly optimistic, see Salmon, *Women and the Law of Property in Colonial America*.

50. Wendy Hamand Venet, *Neither Ballots nor Bullets: Women Abolitionists and the Civil War* (Charlottesville: University Press of Virginia, 1991).

51. Norma Basch, *In the Eyes of the Law: Women, Marriage, and Property in Nineteenth-Century New York* (Ithaca: Cornell University Press, 1982), is the leading study; see also Hoff, *Law, Gender, and Injustice*, 124–132.

52. Hoff, *Law, Gender, and Injustice*, 138.

53. Declaration of Sentiments, Seneca Falls, New York, July 19–20, 1848, reprinted in Hoff, *Law, Gender, and Injustice*, 383–387.

54. Ames, *Proposed Amendments*, 237.

55. Hoff, *Law, Gender, and Injustice*, 152–161.

56. 88 U.S. 162 (1875).

57. Hoff, *Law, Gender, and Injustice*, 170–174.

58. 1876 Declaration of Rights, reprinted in Hoff, *Law, Gender, and Injustice*, 388–392 (quotes at 388, 391).

59. Musmanno, *Proposed Amendments*, 244–245.

60. Ames, *Proposed Amendments*, 237–238.

61. See the list in Musmanno, *Proposed Amendments*, 245–246, and the map in Clement E. Vose, *Constitutional Change: Amendment Politics and Supreme Court Litigation Since 1900*, A Twentieth Century Fund Study (Lexington, Mass.: Lexington Books/D. C. Heath, 1972), 54.

62. Deborah L. Rhode, "Nineteenth Amendment," in Leonard W. Levy, Kenneth Karst, and Dennis Mahoney, eds., *Encyclopedia of the American Constitution*, 4 vols. (New York: Free Press/Macmillan, 1986), 3: 1315–1316 (quote at 1315).

63. Quoted in Musmanno, *Proposed Amendments*, 249.

64. Quoted in ibid., 250.

65. Grimes, *Democracy and the Amendments*, 93.

66. Flexner, *Century of Struggle*, 302.

67. Musmanno, *Proposed Amendments*, 251.

68. Anne F. Scott and Andrew M. Scott, *One Half the People: The Fight for Woman Suffrage* (Philadelphia: Lippincott, 1975), 46.

CHAPTER 8
TESTING THE LIMITS OF DEMOCRATIZATION

1. Jane J. Mansbridge, *Why We Lost the ERA* (Chicago: University of Chicago Press, 1986), 34.

2. Russell Baker, "District of Columbia Wins Vote by 23d Amendment," *The New York Times*, March 30, 1961, pp. 1, 16. For the term "political population," see Henry Adams, *History of the United States during the Administrations of Thomas Jefferson, 1801–1809 . . .* (1889–1891; New York: Library of America, 1986), 5.

3. Kenneth R. Bowling, *The Creation of Washington, D.C.: The Idea and the Location of the National Capital* (Fairfax: George Mason University Press, 1991). See also his earlier study, *Creating the Federal City: Potomac Fever* (Washington, D.C.: American Institute of Architects, 1988). By "Potomac fever," Bowling means the almost pathological belief that the Potomac River valley had limitless potential as the site of a new American metropolis.

4. The account in the following paragraphs draws on Alan P. Grimes, *Democracy and the Amendments to the Constitution* (1978; Lanham: University Press of America, 1988), 126–136.

5. Ibid., 126.

6. For an alarming recent study of the federal government's plans for governance following a nuclear conflict, see Edward Zuckerman, *The Day After World War III* (New York: Random House, 1985).

7. Kennedy quote from *The New York Times*, March 30, 1961, at 16.

8. Voting Rights Act of 1965, sec. 10, 79 Stat. 442, 42 U.S.C. sec. 1973h.

9. *Harper v. Virginia State Board of Elections*, 383 U.S. 663 (1966). *Harper* overturned earlier decisions upholding state poll taxes against federal constitutional challenge: *Breedlove v. Suttles*, 302 U.S. 277 (1937), *Saunders v. Wilkins*, 152 F.2d 235 (4th Cir. 1945), *cert. den.*, 328 U.S. 870; *Butler v. Thompson*, 97 F. Supp. 17 (E.D.Va.), *aff'd*, 341 U.S. 937 (1951).

10. The discussion in the text draws on Grimes, *Democracy and the Amendments*, 141–147.

11. 400 U.S. 112 (1970).

12. 403 U.S. 713 (1971). On the Pentagon Papers case, see Sanford J. Ungar, *The Papers and the Papers* (1972; New York: Columbia University Press, 1991).

13. See R. W. Apple, Jr., "The States Ratify Full Vote at 18," *The New York Times,* July 1, 1971, pp. 1, 43.

14. Quoted in Mansbridge, *Why We Lost the ERA,* 8. Mansbridge's study is the best examination of the history and politics of the ERA controversy. It is the basis for the next several paragraphs. See also Donald G. Mathews and Jane Herron De Hart, *Sex, Gender and the Politics of ERA: The State and the Nation* (New York: Oxford University Press, 1990), which focuses on the ERA's fate in North Carolina.

15. Mansbridge, *Why We Lost the ERA,* 8. [Michael A. Musmanno], *Proposed Amendments to the Constitution: A Monograph on the Resolutions Introduced in Congress proposing Amendments to the Constitution of the United States of America,* House Doc. No. 551, 70th Cong., 2d sess. (1929; rept., Westport: Greenwood Press, 1976), 253, reports that the amendment was introduced in Congress six times between 1923 and 1929. [Hereafter Musmanno, *Proposed Amendments.*]

16. 410 U.S. 113 (1973).

17. Mansbridge, *Why We Lost the ERA,* 13.

18. Richard A. Davis, *Proposed Amendments to the Constitution of the United States of America Introduced in Congress from the 91st Congress, 1st Session, Through the 98th Congress, 2nd Session, January 1969–December 1984,* Report No. 85-36 GOV (Washington, D.C.: Congressional Research Service of the Library of Congress, February 1, 1985), 264. On the vexed issue of rescission, which has not yet been resolved, see Congressional Research Service, *The Constitution of the United States of America: Analysis and Interpretation* (Washington, D.C.: U.S. Government Printing Office, 1982 and 1990 Supp.), 902–909.

19. House Joint Resolution 638, 95th Cong., adopted by a vote of 233 to 189 in the House and 60 to 36 in the Senate. Davis, *Proposed Amendments,* 223–226.

20. In *Idaho v. Freeman,* 529 F. Supp. 1107 (D. Idaho 1981), *prob. juris. noted,* 455 U.S. 918 (1982), *vacated and remanded to dismiss,* 459 U.S. 809 (1982), the United States district court in Idaho ruled the extension invalid, but the extended time limit expired, mooting the lawsuit, before the Supreme Court could resolve the question.

21. See the studies by Kenneth R. Bowling cited in note 3.

22. Bowling, *Creation of Washington, D.C.*

23. See, e.g., David Brinkley, *Washington Goes to War* (New York: Alfred A. Knopf, 1988).

24. [James Madison], *The Federalist No. 43,* in Alexander Hamilton, James Madison, and John Jay, *The Federalist,* Jacob E. Cooke, ed. (Middletown: Wesleyan University Press, 1961), 289.

25. The summary of the history of the District's governance is based on Philip G. Schrag, *Behind the Scenes: The Politics of a Constitutional Convention* (Washington, D.C.: Georgetown University Press, 1985), 10–15. Schrag's excellent history and personal

memoir of the D.C. Statehood Constitutional Convention of 1982, is, interestingly, silent on the D.C. Statehood Amendment.

26. Schrag, *Behind the Scenes,* 9–10, presents this analogy in stark and persuasive terms.

27. The text of this constitution appears in Schrag, *Behind the Scenes,* 259–297; for a discussion of its framing, see ibid.

28. Judith A. Best, *National Representation for the District of Columbia* (Frederick: University Publications of America, 1984), 1.

29. Best, *National Representation,* chs. 4 and 5.

30. Davis, *Proposed Amendments,* 266.

31. See, e.g., Clinton L. Rossiter, *The American Presidency* (1956; rev. ed., with new introduction by Michael Nelson, Baltimore: Johns Hopkins University Press, 1987); and Theodore H. White, *Breach of Faith: The Fall of Richard Nixon* (New York: Atheneum/ Reader's Digest Press, 1975).

CHAPTER 9
THE FIRST CITIZEN: ADJUSTING THE PRESIDENCY

1. Quoted in Clinton L. Rossiter, *1787: The Grand Convention* (1966; rept., New York: W. W. Norton, 1987), 191 and n. 31. This news item—which appeared in the (Philadelphia) *Pennsylvania Herald,* August 18, 1787; in the (Philadelphia) *Pennsylvania Journal,* August 22, 1787; in the *Boston Gazette,* August 27, 1787; and in the *Salem Mercury,* August 28, 1787—is the only deliberate leak we know of during the Convention. On the activities of journalists in 1787 to stimulate and organize public opinion in favor of the Constitution, see John T. Alexander, *The Selling of the Constitutional Convention: A History of News Coverage* (Madison: Madison House, 1990).

2. Leading works on the origins of the Presidency include Charles C. Thach, *The Creation of the Presidency, 1774–1789* (Baltimore: Johns Hopkins University Press, 1922); Arthur M. Schlesinger, Jr., *The Imperial Presidency* (Boston: Houghton Mifflin, 1973; rev. ed., 1989); and the essays collected in Thomas C. Cronin, ed., *Inventing the American Presidency* (Lawrence: University Press of Kansas, 1989). For a first-rate collection of Federalist and Anti-Federal arguments concerning the Presidency, see Gaspare J. Saladino and Charles Schoenleber, eds., *The Presidency* (Constitutional Heritage Series) (Madison: Madison House, forthcoming).

3. For this metaphor, see Richard B. Bernstein and Jerome Agel, *Into the Third Century: The Presidency* (New York: Walker, 1989), ch. 1.

4. See Adrienne Koch, *Jefferson and Madison: The Great Collaboration* (New York: Alfred A. Knopf, 1950), for Jefferson's comments to Madison; for Jefferson's epistolary discussions of the Constitution with John Adams, see Lester J. Cappon, ed., *The Adams-Jefferson Letters* (Chapel Hill: University of North Carolina Press, 1959).

5. Herman V. Ames, *The Proposed Amendments to the Constitution of the United States during the First Century of its History,* in *Annual Report of the American Historical Association for the Year*

1896, vol. 2 (Washington, D.C.: Government Printing Office, 1897), 308–310. [Hereafter cited as Ames, *Proposed Amendments,* with page number.]

6. Ibid., 315.

7. See generally Edward S. Corwin, *The President: Office and Powers,* 5th rev. ed. (New York: New York University Press, 1984); Richard M. Pious, *The American Presidency* (New York: Basic Books, 1980); and Harold Hongju Koh, *The National Security Constitution: Sharing Power After the Iran-Contra Affair* (New Haven: Yale University Press, 1990). On the Presidency's role as the rhetorical focus of American public life, see Jeffrey Tulis, *The Rhetorical Presidency* (Princeton: Princeton University Press, 1988); Roderick D. Hart, *The Sound of Leadership* (Chicago: University of Chicago Press, 1984); and three books by Kathleen Hall Jamieson: *Packaging the Presidency,* 2d rev. ed. (New York: Oxford University Press, 1992); *Eloquence in an Electronic Age: The Transformation of Political Speechmaking* (New York: Oxford University Press, 1988); and *Presidential Debates* (New York: Oxford University Press, 1988).

8. Ames, *Proposed Amendments,* ch. 3.

9. Walter Berns, ed., *After the People Vote: A Guide to the Electoral College,* rev. and exp. ed. (Washington, D.C.: American Enterprise Institute, 1992), is a crisp, indispensable monograph on the functioning of the institution and a calm, dispassionate defense of its legitimacy.

10. The most recent scholarly treatment of Clay's life and career, Robert V. Remini, *Henry Clay: Statesman for the Union* (New York: W. W. Norton, 1991), convincingly refutes the "corrupt bargain" charge.

11. David W. Abbott and James P. Levine, *Wrong Winner: The Coming Debacle in the Electoral College* (New York: Praeger, 1991).

12. Berns, ed., *After the People Vote,* 30, 35–43.

13. Lucius Wilmerding, Jr., *The Electoral College* (Princeton: Princeton University Press, 1958), presents a strong argument that electors should not exercise judgment independent of the popular will.

14. Berns, ed., *After the People Vote,* 10–14, and app. C at 86–88.

15. See the discussion in Chapter 4.

16. See Stanley I. Kutler, *The Wars of Watergate: The Last Crisis of Richard Nixon* (New York: Alfred A. Knopf, 1990); J. Anthony Lukas, *Nightmare: The Underside of the Nixon Years,* rev. ed. (New York: Viking Penguin, 1988); and Theodore H. White, *Breach of Faith: The Fall of Richard Nixon* (New York: Atheneum/Reader's Digest Press, 1975).

17. See generally Judith A. Best, *The Case Against Direct Election of the President* (Ithaca: Cornell University Press, 1975).

18. Best, *Case Against Direct Election,* makes this point effectively.

19. Schlesinger, *Imperial Presidency,* 481.

20. See the documents collected in volume 1 of Merrill M. Jensen, Robert A. Becker, and Gordon DenBoer, eds., *The Documentary History of the First Federal Elections, 1788–1790,* 4 vols. (Madison: University of Wisconsin Press, 1976–1989).

21. See Richard E. Ellis, *The Jeffersonian Crisis: Courts and Politics in the Young Republic* (New York: Oxford University Press, 1971); Julius Goebel, Jr., *Antecedents and Beginnings to 1801*, vol. 1 of Oliver Wendell Holmes Devise History of the Supreme Court of the United States (New York: Macmillan, 1971); George L. Haskins and Herbert A. Johnson, *Foundations of Judicial Power: John Marshall, 1801–1815*, vol. 2 of Oliver Wendell Holmes Devise History of the Supreme Court of the United States (New York: Macmillan, 1982); and [John D. Gordan III, ed.,] *Egbert Benson: First Chief Judge of the Second Circuit (1801–1802)* (New York: Second Circuit Commission on the Bicentennial of the United States Constitution, 1987).

22. See Ralph Ketcham, *Presidents Above Party: The First American Presidency, 1789–1829* (Chapel Hill: University of North Carolina Press for the Institute of Early American History and Culture, 1984); Leonard D. White, *The Federalists* (New York: Macmillan, 1948); James D. Hart, *The American Presidency in Action: 1789* (New York: Macmillan, 1948); and Richard B. Bernstein, " 'I Walk on Untrodden Ground': George Washington as President, 1789–1797," in Stephen L. Schechter and Richard B. Bernstein, eds., *Well Begun: Chronicles of the Early National Period* (Albany: New York State Commission on the Bicentennial of the United States Constitution, 1989), 53–60.

23. Ames, *Proposed Amendments*, 349–350.

24. William S. McFeely, *Grant* (New York: W. W. Norton, 1981), 440, 478–483.

25. The best study of the subject remains Herbert S. Parmet and Marie B. Hecht, *Never Again: A President Runs for a Third Term* (New York: Macmillan, 1968).

26. See generally Eugene W. Hickok, Jr., "Pique over Principle: Partisan Politics and the 22nd Amendment," in Ronald W. Reagan, Joseph M. Bessette, Bruce Buchanan, David K. Nichols, Eugene W. Hickok, Jr., Jeffrey Leigh Sedgwick, and Ralph A. Rossum, *Restoring the Presidency: Reconsidering the Twenty-second Amendment* (Washington, D.C.: National Legal Center for the Public Interest, November 1990), 33–42.

27. Quoted in Kenneth R. Crispell and Carlos F. Gomez, *Hidden Illness in the White House* (Durham: Duke University Press, 1988), 240. It may have been for this reason that some Democrats (including John F. Kennedy, then a first-term member of the House from Massachusetts) voted for the Amendment. Hickok, "Pique over Principle," 35.

28. This campaign's basic document is *Restoring the Presidency*, a valuable analysis of the controversy tilted in favor of repeal. We are indebted to James M. Sparling, Jr., for lending us his copy.

29. Note, for example, President Ronald W. Reagan's citation of Henry Steele Commager's 1947 attack on the Amendment: *Restoring the Presidency*, 3 and n. 2.

30. H. J. Res. 61, 102d Cong., 1st sess. By September of 1991, a bipartisan group of fourteen cosponsors had joined Representative Vander Jagt. Letter from James M. Sparling, Jr., chief of staff for Representative Vander Jagt, to Richard B. Bernstein, February 17, 1992.

31. Telephone interview with James M. Sparling, Jr., chief of staff to Rep. Guy Vander Jagt, February 13, 1992.

32. Bruce Buchanan, "The Six-year One Term Presidency: A New Look at an Old Proposal," in *Restoring the Presidency*, 91–106.

33. John D. Feerick, *The Twenty-fifth Amendment: Its Complete History and Earliest Applications* (New York: Fordham University Press, 1976), is the definitive treatment and a model for monographic histories of a specific Amendment; the findings and arguments of Feerick's earlier study, *From Failing Hands: The Story of Presidential Succession* (1965), are summarized in his 1976 monograph. See also Birch Bayh, *One Heartbeat Away* (Indianapolis and New York: Bobbs-Merrill, 1968), and Allan F. Sindler, *Unelected Presidents* (Berkeley: University of California Press, 1978).

34. Feerick, *Twenty-fifth Amendment,* 27–34, discusses vacancies in the Vice Presidency.

35. See Ames, *Proposed Amendments,* 350–351. Charles Dickens described the aristocratic but harassed Tyler in an affecting passage in his *American Notes for General Circulation* (1842; New York: Penguin Books, 1972), 172.

36. The most recent treatment is Jules Witcover, *Crapshoot* (New York: Crown, 1992).

37. Ames, *Proposed Amendments,* 70–71.

38. Feerick, *Twenty-fifth Amendment,* 3–25, discusses periods of Presidential illness and disability.

39. Crispell and Gomez, *Hidden Illness,* 204.

40. Ibid., 13–74.

41. Ibid., 75–120.

42. Ibid., 121–160; David S. McCullough, *Truman* (New York: Simon and Schuster, 1992), 332–404.

43. See generally Garry Wills, *Nixon Agonistes: The Crisis of the Self-made Man* (Boston: Houghton Mifflin, 1970).

44. Feerick, *Twenty-fifth Amendment,* 17–22.

45. See generally Robert Dallek, *Lone Star Rising* (New York: Oxford University Press, 1991), for an excellent biography of Lyndon B. Johnson from his birth in 1908 to his election to the Vice Presidency in 1960; Dallek is especially good on Johnson's medical history.

46. Conversation with Richard B. Morris, January 11, 1988.

47. See the evenhanded discussion in Crispell and Gomez, *Hidden Illness,* 160–202; and Joan Blair and Clay Blair, *The Search for JFK* (New York: Berkley Publishing, 1976).

48. See the thoughtful discussion in Crispell and Gomez, *Hidden Illness,* 203–241.

49. Feerick, *Twenty-fifth Amendment,* 51–58.

50. Ibid., 59–113; Bayh, *One Heartbeat Away,* is a useful "insider's account."

51. Quoted in Feerick, *Twenty-fifth Amendment,* 65.

52. Quoted in Crispell and Gomez, *Hidden Illness,* 239–240.

53. Richard M. Cohen and Jules Witcover, *A Heartbeat Away: The Investigation and Resignation of Vice President Spiro T. Agnew* (New York: Viking Press, 1974).

54. See Herbert L. Abrams's terrifying monograph, *"The President Has Been Shot"* (New York: W. W. Norton, 1992). Abrams recommends the restructuring of the Office of the

White House Physician and the inclusion of a board of medical professionals in any decision-making procedure on the health of the President. See also Crispell and Gomez, *Hidden Illness,* 213–216.

55. Jane Mayer and Doyle McManus, *Landslide: The Unmaking of the President, 1984–1988,* rev. ed. (Boston: Houghton Mifflin, 1989), ch. 1.

56. For a useful symposium demonstrating awareness of these shifting political and thus constitutional perspectives, see Charles Roberts, ed., *Has the President Too Much Power?* (New York: Harper's Magazine Press with Harper & Row, 1974); see also the definitive study by Louis Fisher, *Constitutional Controversies Between Congress and the President,* 3d ed. (Lawrence: University Press of Kansas, 1991).

57. The leading study is Duane Tananbaum, *The Bricker Amendment Controversy* (Ithaca: Cornell University Press, 1990). See also Schlesinger, *Imperial Presidency,* 151–152, 311–312, 529.

58. Ames, *Proposed Amendments,* 132–133, 143; Schlesinger, *Imperial Presidency,* 476–478.

59. William E. Leuchtenberg, *In the Shadow of FDR* (Ithaca: Cornell University Press, 1983; rev. ed., 1988); and White, *Breach of Faith.*

Chapter 10
Roads Not Taken: Proposed Amendments to the Constitution

1. Ruth Bader Ginsburg, "On Amending the Constitution: A Plea for Patience," *University of Arkansas at Little Rock Law Journal* 12 (1989–1990): 677–694, at 680 and n. 28, citing James Beck, *The Constitution of the United States, 1787–1927* (New York, 1927), 16–17.

2. According to the Subcommittee on the Constitution of the Senate Judiciary Committee, 9,984 proposals had been submitted in the House and the Senate by 1984. *Amendments to the Constitution: A Brief Legislative History,* Senate Report No. 87, 99th Cong., 1st sess., 95 (1985). Between January 1985 and December 1990, an additional 437 amendments were proposed. Daryl B. Harris, comp., CRS Report for Congress 92-555 GOV: *Proposed Amendments to the U.S. Constitution: 99th–101st Congresses (1985–1990)* (July 9, 1992).

3. For an intriguing inquiry into just how many times the Constitution has been amended, exploring such issues as the ambiguity inherent in the concept of "explanatory amendments," and the role of judicial interpretation in "amending" the Constitution, see Sanford Levinson, "Accounting for Constitutional Change (Or, How Many Times Has the United States Constitution Been Amended? (a) < 26; (b) 26; (c) > 26; (d) all of the above)," *Constitutional Commentary* 8 (1991): 409–431.

4. To be sure, the number of proposed amendments usually given is—to some extent—misleading. Proposals for amendments come in bursts, in fits and starts, usually spurred by a major constitutional crisis such as the Civil War, the Depression, or Watergate. These clusters often include dozens or even hundreds of variants on, or revisions of, proposals that actually emerge from Congress. Richard A. Davis, *Proposed Amendments to the Constitution of the United States of America Introduced in Congress from the 91st Congress, 1st Session, Through the 98th Congress, 2nd Session, January 1969–December 1984,* Report No. 85–36

GOV (Washington, D.C.: Congressional Research Service of the Library of Congress, February 1, 1985), 267–268, notes the difficulties of an accurate count of proposed amendments. [Hereafter Davis, *Proposed Amendments.*]

5. Matt Groening, "Life, Liberty, and the Pursuit of Hellishness: New, Improved Amendments to the Constitution," *Washington Post Magazine,* June 28, 1987, at 58.

6. Charlie Haas, "Bill of Improvements," *Washington Post Magazine,* June 28, 1987, at 59–60. For a serious compilation of proposed amendments by historians, legal scholars, and past Presidents, see "Taking Another Look at the Constitutional Blueprint," *American Heritage,* vol. 38, no. 4 (May–June 1987): 53–71.

7. Michael A. Musmanno, "The Difficulty of Amending Our Federal Constitution: Defect or Asset?" *American Bar Association Journal* 15 (1929): 505, 507. Musmanno's article draws on [Michael A. Musmanno], *Proposed Amendments to the Constitution: A Monograph on the Resolutions Introduced in Congress proposing Amendments to the Constitution of the United States of America,* House Doc. No. 551, 70th Cong., 2d sess. (1929; rept., Westport: Greenwood Press, 1976). [Hereafter Musmanno, *Proposed Amendments.*] The proposed "United States of the Earth" amendment is discussed at 185–186.

8. W. J. Rohrbaugh, *The Alcoholic Republic* (New York: Oxford University Press, 1985). American women frequently espoused the causes of temperance and prohibition in this period; see, e.g., Linda K. Kerber, *Women of the Republic: Intellect and Ideology in Revolutionary America* (Chapel Hill: University of North Carolina Press for the Institute of Early American History and Culture, 1980). An especially useful study is Norman H. Clark, *Deliver Us from Evil: An Interpretation of American Prohibition* (New York: W. W. Norton, 1976).

9. *American Museum,* 4 (Philadelphia: Mathew Carey, 1788), reproduced in Richard B. Bernstein with Kym S. Rice, *Are We to Be a Nation? The Making of the Constitution* (Cambridge, Mass.: Harvard University Press, 1987), 217 [fig. 7.12].

10. Quoted in John Sexton and Nat Brandt, *How Free Are We? What the Constitution Says We Can and Cannot Do* (New York: M. Evans, 1986), 60, and discussed in Clark, *Deliver Us from Evil,* 23–24.

11. Abraham Lincoln, "Temperance Address," February 22, 1842, reprinted in Roy P. Basler, ed., *The Collected Works of Abraham Lincoln,* 8 vols. (New Brunswick: Rutgers University Press, 1953), 1: 271–279.

12. Clark, *Deliver Us from Evil,* 35–90. On the Maine law, see also Clement E. Vose, *Constitutional Change: Amendment Politics and Supreme Court Litigation Since 1900,* A Twentieth Century Fund Study (Lexington, Mass.: Lexington Books/D. C. Heath, 1972), 71; and Musmanno, *Proposed Amendments,* 226.

13. See Clark, *Deliver Us from Evil,* 68–91.

14. Alan P. Grimes, *Democracy and the Amendments to the Constitution* (1978; Lanham: University Press of America, 1988), 84.

15. Vose, *Constitutional Change,* 70–85; Musmanno, *Proposed Amendments,* 227–228; Grimes, *Democracy and the Amendments,* 82–89. According to Grimes, the 1910 census was the last showing a majority of Americans living in rural areas. Ibid., 109.

16. Musmanno, *Proposed Amendments*, 230–231.

17. Clark, *Deliver Us from Evil*, 113–130. Of the forty-eight states, only Rhode Island refused to adopt the Amendment, and Connecticut took no action on it; New Jersey belatedly ratified it in 1922.

18. *National Prohibition Cases*, 253 U.S. 350 (1920). See the table of all Prohibition cases before the Court in Vose, *Constitutional Change*, 95–97.

19. Dorothy H. Brown, *Mabel Walker Willebrandt: A Study of Power, Loyalty, and Law* (Knoxville: University of Tennessee Press, 1984), esp. 49–80.

20. Mabel Walker Willebrandt to parents, March 31, 1929, quoted in Brown, *Willebrandt*, 80.

21. Paul L. Murphy, "Societal Morality and Individual Freedom," in David E. Kyvig, ed., *Law, Alcohol, and Order: Perspectives on National Prohibition* (Westport: Greenwood Press, 1985), 67–80.

22. 277 U.S. 438 (1928), overturned by *Katz v. United States*, 389 U.S. 347 (1967), on the basis of Justice Louis D. Brandeis's dissent in *Olmstead*.

23. Quoted in Brown, *Willebrandt*, 51.

24. Musmanno, *Proposed Amendments*, 237–242.

25. See generally David E. Kyvig, *Repealing National Prohibition* (Chicago: University of Chicago Press, 1979); and Clark, *Deliver Us from Evil*, 181–208.

26. Vose, *Constitutional Change*, 110–121.

27. Clark, *Deliver Us from Evil*, 193–194, 202–203.

28. Quoted in Grimes, *Democracy and the Amendments*, 111–112.

29. Vose, *Constitutional Change*, 243–256; on litigation, see ibid., 121–126.

30. See, e.g., Gordon S. Wood, *The Radicalism of the American Revolution* (New York: Alfred A. Knopf, 1992).

31. Though, in April of 1789, the United States Senate engaged in a lengthy and pointless debate, behind closed doors, on the propriety of adopting grand-sounding titles for the President. For the most thorough (and most entertaining) account of this controversy, see Kenneth R. Bowling and Helen E. Veit, eds., *The Diary of William Maclay and Other Notes of Senate Debates, March 4, 1789 to March 3, 1791* (Baltimore: Johns Hopkins University Press, 1988)—vol. 9 of Linda Grant DePauw, Charlene Bangs Bickford, Kenneth R. Bowling, and Helen E. Veit, eds., *The Documentary History of the First Federal Congress, March 4, 1789 to March 3, 1791*, 9 vols. of 20 projected (Baltimore: Johns Hopkins University Press, 1972–).

32. On the "Titles of Nobility" Amendment, see Herman V. Ames, *The Proposed Amendments to the Constitution of the United States during the First Century of its History*, in *Annual Report of the American Historical Association for the Year 1896*, vol. 2 (Washington, D.C.: Government Printing Office, 1897), 186–189. [Hereafter cited as Ames, *Proposed Amendments*, with page number.]

33. W. H. Earle, "The Phantom Amendment and the Duchess of Baltimore," *American*

History Illustrated, November 1987, at 33–39. We thank Gregory D. Watson for drawing our attention to this article. See also Ames, *Proposed Amendments,* 187 and nn. 4–5.

34. Ibid., 188 and n. 1.

35. Ibid., 188–189, 329–330.

36. Vose, *Constitutional Change,* 248–250; Grimes, *Democracy and the Amendments,* 101–104; and Musmanno, *Proposed Amendments,* 137–145.

37. 247 U.S. 251 (1918).

38. *Bailey v. Drexel Furniture Co.,* 259 U.S. 20 (1922).

39. Musmanno, *Proposed Amendments,* 139–140.

40. Vose, *Constitutional Change,* 248–249.

41. *United States v. Darby Lumber Co.,* 312 U.S. 100 (1941).

42. Michael Ross, "Amendment: Tough Choices for Lawmakers," *Los Angeles Times,* June 12, 1992, p. 1, col. 4. The amendment is H. J. Res. 290, 102d Cong., 1st Sess. (June 26, 1991).

43. Eric Pianin and Gary Lee, "Balanced-Budget Amendment Faces a Barrage," *Washington Post,* June 9, 1992, p. A6.

44. The analogy is made explicitly in Bob Deans, "House Mulls Big Fix on Budget," *Atlanta Journal and Constitution,* June 7, 1992, p. A1.

45. On state constitutional provisions limiting the growth of state debts, see James D. Savage, *Balanced Budgets and American Politics* (Ithaca: Cornell University Press, 1988), 117, quoting A. James Heins, *Constitutional Restrictions Against State Debt* (Madison: University of Wisconsin Press, 1963). On state constitutional provisions requiring balanced budgets, see Alvin Rabushka, "Fiscal Responsibility: Will Anything Less Than a Constitutional Amendment Do?" in Michael J. Boskin and Aaron Wildavsky, eds., *The Federal Budget: Economics and Politics* (San Francisco: Institute for Contemporary Studies, 1982), 333–352 (esp. 342).

46. Michael deCourcy Hinds, "Scholars Scorn Budget Proposal," *The New York Times,* June 11, 1992, p. A18, col. 1.

47. Pianin and Lee, "Barrage."

48. In 1798, Jefferson proposed an amendment "taking from the federal government the power of borrowing." Thomas Jefferson to John Taylor, November 26, 1798, quoted in Savage, *Balanced Budgets,* 106. As Savage points out, Jefferson never revived the suggestion once he became President; instead, he pioneered the federal borrowing of money to pay for the Louisiana Purchase. Ibid., 107.

49. Savage, *Balanced Budgets,* is the leading history and policy study. See also John B. Gilmour, *Reconcilable Differences? Congress, the Budget Process, and the Deficit* (Berkeley: University of California Press, 1990), and Joseph White and Aaron Wildavsky, *The Deficit and the Public Interest: The Search for Responsible Budgeting in the 1980s* (Berkeley: University of California Press, 1989).

50. James V. Saturno, *Congress and a Balanced Budget Amendment to the U.S. Constitution,*

Report No. 89-4 GOV (Washington, D.C.: Congressional Research Service of the Library of Congress, January 3, 1989), 3; see also Thomas J. Nicola, *Constitutional Amendments to Balance the Budget and Limit Federal Spending in the 100th Congress: A Table of Features,* Report No. 87-445 A (Washington, D.C.: Congressional Research Service of the Library of Congress, April 13, 1987). We are indebted to Timothy L. Hanford, Esq., assistant minority tax counsel to the Committee on Ways and Means of the United States House of Representatives, for making these studies available to us.

51. Public Law 95–435, § 7, quoted and discussed in Saturno, *Congress and a Balanced Budget Amendment,* 5.

52. Public Law 99-177, 99 Stat. 1037 (1985).

53. 106 S.Ct. 3181 (1986).

54. In 1982, the Senate approved a proposal but the House failed; in 1986, a proposal failed in the Senate, one vote short of a two-thirds majority; and in 1990, a proposal fell seven votes short of a two-thirds majority in the House. Eric Pianin, "A Balanced-Budget Amendment: The Dream and the Debate," *Washington Post,* June 2, 1992, p. A17. See also the discussion in Savage, *Balanced Budgets,* 203–204, 217–218.

55. Quoted in Saturno, *Congress and a Balanced Budget Amendment,* 9.

56. David R. Francis, "Budget Amendment: What Comes Next?" *Christian Science Monitor,* June 12, 1992, p. 8.

57. Helen Dewar, "Byrd v. Balanced-Budget Amendment," *Washington Post,* June 11, 1992, p. A8.

58. Ross, "Amendment."

59. Books chronicling the growing disgust of the American electorate with its politicians and its government include Alan Ehrenhalt, *The United States of Ambition: Politicians, Power, and the Pursuit of Office* (New York: Times Books/Random House, 1991; rev. ed., 1992); William Greider, *Who Will Tell the People? The Betrayal of American Democracy* (New York: Simon & Schuster, 1992); and E. J. Dionne, Jr., *Why Americans Hate Politics* (New York: Simon & Schuster, 1991; rev. ed., 1992).

60. See Nelson W. Polsby's pathbreaking article, "The Institutionalization of the U.S. House of Representatives," *American Political Science Review* 62 (1968): 144–168, reprinted in Mathew D. McCubbins and Terry Sullivan, eds., *Congress: Structure and Policy* (Cambridge: Cambridge University Press, 1987), 91–130.

61. Philip M. Stern, *The Best Congress Money Can Buy* (New York: Pantheon, 1988).

62. George F. Will, *Restoration: Congress, Term Limits, and the Renewal of Deliberative Democracy* (New York: Free Press, 1992); Americans to Limit Congressional Terms, *Kick the Bums Out! The Case for Term Limitations* (Washington, D.C.: National Press Books, 1992).

63. Ehrenhalt, *United States of Ambition,* xx.

64. Ibid., xxiii; Will, *Restoration;* and *Kick the Bums Out!* For a detailed and critical analysis, see Linda Cohen and Matthew Spitzer, "Term Limits," *Georgetown Law Journal* 80 (1992): 477–522.

65. 410 U.S. 113 (1973). On the case, see Laurence H. Tribe, *Abortion: The Clash of*

Absolutes (New York: W. W. Norton, 1990, rev. ed., 1992); Mary Ann Glendon, *Abortion and Divorce in Western Law* (Cambridge, Mass.: Harvard University Press, 1988); Roger Rosenblatt, *Life Itself* (New York: Random House, 1992); and Joan Hoff, *Law, Gender, and Injustice: A Legal History of U.S. Women* (New York: New York University Press, 1991), especially the discussion of the legal issues at 299–316.

66. Davis, *Proposed Amendments*, 287, 292, 302, 312, 313.

67. *Webster v. Reproductive Health Services*, 492 U.S. 490 (1989); *Ohio v. Akron Center for Reproductive Health*, 497 U.S. 502 (1990); *Rust v. Sullivan*, 111 S.Ct. 1759 (1991); and *Planned Parenthood of Southeast Pennsylvania v. Casey*, 60 U.S.L.W. 4795 (U.S., 1992).

68. See, e.g., Glendon, *Abortion;* Rosenblatt, *Life Itself.* Tribe, *Abortion*, while still espousing a woman's right to control her body, seeks common ground that would enable the nation to move beyond the constitutional dead end of the controversy.

69. See generally Hoff, *Law, Gender, and Injustice*, 313–316. One curiosity of this controversy is Sue Robinson's novel *The Amendment* (New York: Carroll & Graf, 1990), one of only a handful of novels devoted to a future constitutional amendment. Robinson's book postulates the ratification in 1998 of a Human Life Amendment and the growth of a huge and oppressive domestic security system designed to enforce its ban on abortion. In response, American women organize a clandestine network of abortion clinics modeled on the legendary "Underground Railroad."

70. Lawrence B. Goodheart, "The Ambiguity of Individualism: The National Liberal League's Challenges to the Comstock Law," in Richard O. Curry and Lawrence B. Goodheart, eds., *American Chameleon: Individualism in Trans-national Context* (Kent: Kent State University Press, 1991), 133–150 (see esp. 134–136 and sources cited).

71. Dennis Baron, *The English-Only Question: An Official Language for Americans?* (New Haven: Yale University Press, 1990); and James Crawford, ed., *Language Loyalties: A Source Book on the Official English Controversy* (Chicago: University of Chicago Press, 1992).

72. Quoted in "The English Language Amendment," in *U.S. English*, vol. 1, no. 2 (n.d.), p. 6.

73. H. J. Res. 81, 102d Cong., 1st sess., January 18, 1991.

74. Baron, *English-Only Question*, 188–191, analyzes the hearings.

75. Telephone interview with Kyle Rogers, February 3, 1992.

76. *Texas v. Johnson*, 109 S.Ct. 2533 (1989).

77. Sidney Blumenthal, *Pledging Allegiance: The Last Presidential Campaign of the Cold War* (New York: HarperCollins, 1990); and Richard Ben Cramer, *What It Takes* (New York: Random House, 1992).

78. 110 S.Ct. 2404 (1990).

79. See, e.g., *The American Legion Dispatch*, February 7, 1992, pp. 1–3.

80. Congressional Research Service, *The Constitution of the United States of America: Analysis and Interpretation* (Washington, D.C.: U.S. Government Printing Office, 1982 and 1990 Supp.), supp. at 125.

81. Telephone interview with Steve Short, February 4, 1992. See also "The American Legion's Flag Resolution Campaign—Clarifying Two Points of Confusion," undated press release supplied by the American Legion.

82. Telephone interview with Steve Robertson, February 4, 1992.

83. Ibid. Following their defeat in 1990, advocates of a flag amendment, adopting a change of strategy, have begun to collect memorial resolutions from state legislatures urging Congress to propose an amendment protecting the flag. As of February 1992, twenty-five states have adopted such resolutions. Steve Robertson, deputy director of the legislative division of the American Legion, in telephone interview, February 4, 1992. "If we get thirty-eight," Robertson said, "then we can go back to Congress, and if we show them that enough states [to satisfy Article V's requirement for ratifying an amendment] present a good case, then maybe we can provoke Congress to vote on the amendment." Ibid.

84. Alan Brinkley, "Old Glory: The Saga of a National Love Affair," *The New York Times,* July 1, 1990, sec. 4, p. 2.

85. On the flag salute cases, see David Mainwaring, *Render unto Caesar: The Flag Salute Cases* (Chicago: University of Chicago Press, 1962).

86. *Minersville School District v. Gobitis,* 310 U.S. 586 (1940).

87. 319 U.S. 624 (1943).

88. Brinkley, "Old Glory."

89. Wythe Holt, " 'Federal Courts as the Asylum to Federal Interests': Randolph's Report, the Benson Amendment, and the 'Original Understanding' of the Federal Judiciary," in [John D. Gordan III, ed.,] *Egbert Benson: First Chief Judge of the Second Circuit (1801–1802)* (New York: Second Circuit Commission on the Bicentennial of the United States Constitution, 1987), 41–52.

90. *New State Ice Co. v. Liebmann,* 285 U.S. 262, 311 (1932) (Brandeis, J., dissenting).

91. We are indebted to extensive discussions of the history of dueling with Joanne B. Freeman, who is preparing a major study of the subject in the early republic. See also V. G. Kiernan, *The Duel in European History* (Oxford: Clarendon Press of Oxford University Press, 1986).

92. John C. Meleney, *The Public Life of Aedanus Burke* (Columbia: University of South Carolina Press, 1990), 198–202, is the best account.

93. Ames, *Proposed Amendments,* 189.

94. This discussion is indebted to conversations with Professor Norma Basch of Rutgers University, Newark, who is writing a major history of divorce in nineteenth-century America.

95. Musmanno, *Proposed Amendments,* 104–108.

96. Ibid., 107.

97. See Richard A. Van Wagoner, *Mormon Polygamy: A History* (Salt Lake City: Signature, 1986); Sarah Barringer Gordon, *The Twin Relic of Barbarism* (in progress).

98. Musmanno, *Proposed Amendments*, 131–135; Ames, *Proposed Amendments*, 272.

99. Musmanno, *Proposed Amendments*, 108; see also Ames, *Proposed Amendments*, 190.

100. *Loving v. Virginia*, 388 U.S. 1 (1967).

101. Ames, *Proposed Amendments*, 274–278; *Engel v. Vitale*, 370 U.S. 421 (1962); *School District of Abington Township v. Schempp*, 374 U.S. 203 (1963); *Wallace v. Jaffree*, 105 S.Ct. 2479 (1985).

102. Musmanno, *Proposed Amendments*, 187–188.

103. Ames, *Proposed Amendments*, 279–280.

104. Musmanno, *Proposed Amendments*, 185–186.

CHAPTER 11
THE NATION THE AMENDING PROCESS MADE

1. Thomas Jefferson, Letter to Mayor Roger C. Weightman, June 24, 1826, reprinted in Stephen L. Schechter, ed., and Richard B. Bernstein and Donald S. Lutz, contributing eds., *Roots of the Republic: American Founding Documents Interpreted* (Madison: Madison House, 1990), 444–445 (quote at 445).

2. This section presents arguments examined at greater length in "Editors' Introduction: Restoring the Contexts of the Bill of Rights," in Stephen L. Schechter and Richard B. Bernstein, eds., *Contexts of the Bill of Rights* (Albany: New York State Commission on the Bicentennial of the United States Constitution, 1990), ix–xxii.

3. See Henry Steele Commager, *Majority Rule and Minority Rights* (New York: Oxford University Press, 1943).

4. See generally John Phillip Reid, *The Constitutional History of the American Revolution: The Authority of Rights* (Madison: University of Wisconsin Press, 1986); and John Phillip Reid, *The Concept of Liberty in the Age of the American Revolution* (Chicago: University of Chicago Press, 1988). Reid stresses the centrality of ancient and immemorial custom as an authority for rights and a safeguard of liberty.

5. See A. E. Dick Howard, *The Road from Runnymede: Magna Carta and American Constitutionalism* (Charlottesville: University Press of Virginia, 1968).

6. James Madison, "On Charters," *National Gazette*, January 19, 1792, in William M. Hutchinson, William M. E. Rachal, Robert A. Rutland, and J. C. A. Stagg, eds., *The Papers of James Madison*, 17 vols. to date (vols. 1–10, Chicago: University of Chicago Press, 1962–1977; vols. 11–, Charlottesville: University Press of Virginia, 1977–), 14: 191–192 (quote at 191). [Hereafter cited as *Madison Papers*.]

7. Thomas Jefferson to James Madison, December 20, 1787, in *Madison Papers*, 10: 335–339.

8. Thomas Jefferson to James Madison, March 15, 1789, in *Madison Papers*, 13: 13–16.

9. Paradoxically, Jefferson in his later years resisted the activist uses of judicial review pioneered by the United States Supreme Court under his adversary—and distant

cousin—Chief Justice John Marshall. See generally Richard E. Ellis, *The Jeffersonian Crisis: Courts and Politics in the Young Republic* (New York: Oxford University Press, 1971).

10. [Alexander Hamilton], *The Federalist No. 78*.

11. James Morton Smith, *Freedom's Fetters: The Alien and Sedition Acts and Civil Liberties* (Ithaca: Cornell University Press, 1955; rev. ed., 1963); for a contrasting perspective less convinced that libertarian views of freedom of speech and press existed before 1798–1800, see Leonard W. Levy, *Emergence of a Free Press* (New York: Oxford University Press, 1985).

12. Robert C. Palmer, "Liberties as Constitutional Provisions, 1776–1791," in William E. Nelson and Robert C. Palmer, *Liberty and Community: Constitution and Rights in the Early American Republic* (New York University School of Law Linden Studies in Legal History) (New York: Oceana Publications, 1987), 55–148; and Donald S. Lutz, "The U.S. Bill of Rights in Historical Perspective," in Schechter and Bernstein, eds., *Contexts of the Bill of Rights*, 3–17.

13. 32 U.S. (7 Peters) 248 (1833).

14. Recent scholarship on the history of the federal Bill of Rights between 1791 and the twentieth-century explosion of constitutional law protecting rights—what some scholars have called "the forgotten years"—suggests that previous scholars deemed a period of history barren regarding the Bill of Rights if their research turned up no judicial decisions *upholding* claims of individual rights.

15. Anthony Lewis, "If Madison Were Here," *The New York Times*, December 13, 1991, p. A39, col. 1. See also Michael J. Lacey and Knud Haakkonsen, eds., *A Culture of Rights: The Bill of Rights in Philosophy, Politics, and Law—1791 and 1991* (Cambridge: Woodrow Wilson International Center for Scholars and Cambridge University Press, 1991); and Lawrence M. Friedman, *The Republic of Choice* (Cambridge, Mass.: Harvard University Press, 1990).

16. Henry Adams, *History of the United States during the Administrations of Thomas Jefferson, 1801–1809* (1889–1891; New York: Library of America, 1986), 5. See generally Donald W. Rogers with Christine Scriabine, eds., *Voting and the Spirit of American Democracy: Essays on the History of Voting and Voting Rights in America* (Urbana: University of Illinois Press, 1992).

17. On African-Americans, see, e.g., Taylor Branch, *Parting the Waters: America in the King Years, 1954–1963* (New York: Simon & Schuster, 1988); Richard Kluger, *Simple Justice* (New York: Alfred A. Knopf, 1975); and David Garrow, *Bearing the Cross: Martin Luther King and the Southern Christian Leadership Conference* (New York: William Morrow, 1986). On women, see, e.g., Cynthia Harrison, *On Account of Sex* (Berkeley: University of California Press, 1988). For two contrasting views of the role of the American Civil Liberties Union in American life, see Samuel Walker, *In Defense of American Liberties* (New York: Oxford University Press, 1990) (a favorable history of the ACLU and its predecessor, the Emergency Committee on Civil Liberties); and Richard E. Morgan, *Disabling America* (New York: Basic Books, 1986) (a critical account of the "rights industry" in modern America). On the Free Speech League, see John Wertheimer, "Free Speech Fights" (Ph.D. diss., Princeton University, 1991), which investigates ideas of free speech and free press in the years predating the World War I Sedition Act

cases, generally regarded as the beginning of modern First Amendment law. On the NAACP Legal Defense Fund, the literature, again, is vast; see, e.g., Kluger, *Simple Justice*, and Genna Rae McNeill, *Groundwork* (Philadelphia: University of Pennsylvania Press, 1983) (a biography of Charles Hamilton Houston, a founder and principal organizer of the Fund).

18. The literature is enormous. See, e.g., Laurence H. Tribe, *American Constitutional Law*, rev. ed. (Mineola, N.Y.: Foundation Press, 1988); Michael J. Perry, *The Constitution, the Courts, and Human Rights* (New Haven: Yale University Press, 1982); Archibald Cox, *Freedom of Expression* (Cambridge, Mass.: Harvard University Press, 1981); Archibald Cox, *The Role of the Supreme Court in American Government* (New York: Oxford University Press, 1976); Archibald Cox, *The Court and the Constitution* (Boston: Houghton Mifflin, 1987); and Michael Kent Curtis, *No State Shall Abridge: The Fourteenth Amendment and the Bill of Rights* (Durham: Duke University Press, 1986). For attacks on these approaches to constitutional law, see, e.g., Charles Fairman, "Does the Fourteenth Amendment Incorporate the Bill of Rights? The Original Understanding," *Stanford Law Review* 2 (1949): 5–139; Robert H. Bork, *The Tempting of America: The Political Seduction of the Law* (New York: Free Press/Macmillan, 1990); Christopher Wolfe, *The Rise of Modern Judicial Review* (New York: Basic Books, 1986); and, among many books and articles by Raoul Berger, *Government by Judiciary: The Transformation of the Fourteenth Amendment* (Cambridge, Mass.: Harvard University Press, 1977).

19. Daniel J. Boorstin, *The Americans*, 3 vols. (New York: Random House, 1958–1973); Thomas R. Hughes, *American Genesis* (New York: Viking Press, 1989); and David Halberstam, *The Powers That Be* (New York: Alfred A. Knopf, 1980).

20. See Merrill D. Peterson, *The Jefferson Image in the American Mind* (New York: Oxford University Press, 1960); and Trevor Colbourn, ed., *Fame and the Founding Fathers: Essays of Douglass Adair* (New York: W. W. Norton for the Institute of Early American History and Culture, 1974).

21. See the essays collected in David Thelen, ed., *The Constitution and American Life* (Ithaca: Cornell University Press, 1988), 135–374. This valuable and illuminating collection originally appeared as vol. 74, no. 3, of the *Journal of American History* (December 1987), commemorating the bicentennial of the Constitution.

22. For a useful road map to the literature of the Bill of Rights focusing on its origins and their jurisprudential significance, see Gaspare J. Saladino's "The Bill of Rights: A Historiographical Essay," in Schechter and Bernstein, eds., *Contexts of the Bill of Rights*, 65–109 and his sequel, in Patrick T. Conley and John P. Kaminski, eds., *The Bill of Rights and the States* (Madison: Madison House, 1992), 461–514.

23. Friedman, *Republic of Choice*.

24. See, e.g., James Davison Hunter, *Culture Wars* (New York: Basic Books, 1991); and R. Laurence Moore, *Religious Outsiders and the Making of America* (New York: Oxford University Press, 1986).

25. On *Miranda*, see Liva Baker, *Miranda: Crime, Law, Politics* (New York: Atheneum, 1983).

26. Harold M. Hyman, *American Singularity* (Athens: University of Georgia Press, 1984).

27. *Civil Rights Cases,* 109 U.S. 3, 20 (1883); Tribe, *American Constitutional Law,* 1688 n. 1.

28. On the first decade of civil rights enforcement, see generally Robert J. Kaczorowski, *The Politics of Judicial Interpretation: The Federal Courts, Department of Justice and Civil Rights, 1866–1876* (New York: Oceana Publications, 1985).

29. 103 U.S. at 22.

30. Id., at 20.

31. Id., 24–25.

32. *Jones v. Alfred H. Mayer & Co.,* 392 U.S. 409 (1968), discussed in Tribe, *American Constitutional Law,* 331–334.

33. See, e.g., Berger, *Government by Judiciary.*

34. See the argument of Donald S. Lutz, presented in his two books *Popular Consent and Popular Control: Whig Political Theory in the Early State Constitutions* (Baton Rouge: Louisiana State University Press, 1980) and *The Origins of American Constitutionalism* (Baton Rouge: Louisiana State University Press, 1988), paralleled by Robert C. Palmer, "Liberties as Constitutional Provisions, 1776–1791," in William E. Nelson and Robert C. Palmer, *Liberty and Community: Constitution and Rights in the Early American Republic* (New York University School of Law Linden Studies in Legal History) (New York: Oceana Publications, 1987), 55–148.

35. 32 U.S. (7 Peters) 243 (1833).

36. Eric S. Foner, *Reconstruction: America's Unfinished Revolution, 1863–1877* (New York: Harper & Row, 1988), 586–587.

37. The leading case is *Munn v. Illinois,* 94 U.S. 113 (1877). See William J. Novak, *Intellectual Origins of the State Police Power: The Common Law Vision of a Well-regulated Society,* University of Wisconsin, Madison, Legal History Program, Working Papers, ser. 3, 3:2 (Madison: Institute for Legal Studies, University of Wisconsin, Madison, Law School, 1989).

38. 198 U.S. 45 (1906).

39. 268 U.S. 652 (1925).

40. 283 U.S. 697 (1931). See generally Fred W. Friendly, *Minnesota Rag* (New York: Random House, 1981).

41. 299 U.S. 353 (1937).

42. 310 U.S. 296 (1940).

43. 330 U.S. 1 (1947).

44. *Adamson v. California,* 221 U.S. 67 (1947). (Admiral Dewey Adamson had no connection with the Navy; his parents had named him for Admiral George Dewey, the victor in the battle of Manila Bay of 1898, and, after Theodore Roosevelt, the most popular hero of the Spanish-American War.) On *Adamson* and the struggle between Justices Black and

Frankfurter for which it is remembered, see James F. Simon, *The Antagonists: Hugo Black, Felix Frankfurter, and Civil Liberties in Modern America* (New York: Simon & Schuster, 1989), 176–179.

45. 211 U.S. 78 (1908).

46. 367 U.S. 643 (1961).

47. 372 U.S. 335 (1963). See Anthony M. Lewis, *Gideon's Trumpet* (New York: Random House, 1964).

48. 378 U.S. 1 (1964).

49. 378 U.S. 478 (1964).

50. 384 U.S. 436 (1966). See Baker, *Miranda.*

51. 387 U.S. 1 (1967).

52. Laura Kalman, *Abe Fortas: A Biography* (New Haven: Yale University Press, 1990), 251–253.

53. 408 U.S. 238 (1972).

54. 428 U.S. 153 (1976).

55. See the works cited in note 18.

56. 163 U.S. 537 (1896). The definitive monograph is Charles A. Lofgren, *The Plessy Case: A Legal-Historical Interpretation* (New York: Oxford University Press, 1987).

57. 332 U.S. 631 (1948).

58. 339 U.S. 637 (1950).

59. 339 U.S. 626 (1950).

60. The best study of Warren's career and jurisprudence is G. Edward White, *Earl Warren: A Public Life* (New York: Oxford University Press, 1982).

61. 347 U.S. 483 (1954) (*Brown I*); a follow-up case, known as *Brown II*, 349 U.S. 294 (1955), ordered the implementation of *Brown I*. Kluger, *Simple Justice,* is the definitive study; see also J. Harvie Wilkinson III, *From Brown to Bakke* (New York: Oxford University Press, 1978).

62. 369 U.S. 186 (1962). *Baker* was the first of a growing line of Supreme Court decisions applying the "one person, one vote" principle to institutions of government ranging from the United States House of Representatives, *Wesberry v. Sanders,* 376 U.S. 1 (1964), to the New York City Council and Board of Estimate, *Board of Estimate of City of New York v. Morris,* 109 S.Ct. 1433 (1989).

63. 429 U.S. 190 (1976). The intermediate standard defined by Justice Brennan in *Craig v. Boren* was endorsed by all but one member of the Court; then-Associate Justice William H. Rehnquist dissented. The *Craig* standard tried to strike a balance between the competing methods of judicial review of legislative objectives and legislative means: under *rational basis* review, the legislative objective need only be legitimate and the means only rationally related to its achievement to permit the upholding of the challenged statute or

program. By contrast, *strict scrutiny* review requires the state to demonstrate a compelling state interest plus the necessity of the challenged means to achieving that objective.

64. A leading defense of affirmative action is Melvin Urofsky, *A Conflict of Principle* (New York: Charles Scribner's Sons, 1991); an influential attack is Nathan Glazer, *Affirmative Discrimination* (New York: Basic Books, 1978). See the discussion in Wilkinson, *From Brown to Bakke.*

65. In 1973, however, Marco De Funis had argued that he had been wrongly denied admission to the University of Washington Law School, claiming that the school, under its affirmative action program, had admitted black and other minority students with academic records inferior to his. De Funis's suit charged that the university's affirmative action program violated the equal protection clause. Because the school admitted De Funis while his case was pending, and because he was about to graduate when the case reached the Supreme Court, the Justices dismissed the case as moot. *De Funis v. Odegaard,* 416 U.S. 312 (1974).

66. 438 U.S. 265 (1978).

67. *Firefighters Local 1784 v. Stotts,* 104 S.Ct. 2576 (1984).

68. See, e.g., Jonathan Kozol, *Savage Inequalities* (New York: Crown, 1991); Studs Terkel, *Race* (New York: New Press, 1992); Alex Kotlowitz, *There Are No Children Here* (New York: Doubleday, 1991); Andrew Hacker, *Two Nations* (New York: Charles Scribner's Sons, 1992); Gerald David Jaynes and Robin M. Williams, eds., *A Common Destiny: Blacks and American Society* (Washington, D.C.: National Academy Press, 1989); Derrick Bell, *And We Are Not Saved* (New York: Basic Books, 1987); and Derrick Bell, *Faces at the Bottom of the Well* (New York: Basic Books, 1992).

69. On these statutes and the cases interpreting them, see William Gillette, *The Right to Vote: Politics and the Passage of the Fifteenth Amendment* (1965; rev. ed. with new epilogue, Baltimore: Johns Hopkins University Press, 1969), 166–190; and Tribe, *American Constitutional Law,* 335–340.

70. Ward E. Y. Elliott, "Fifteenth Amendment (Judicial Interpretation)," in Leonard W. Levy, Kenneth Karst, and Dennis Mahoney, eds., *Encyclopedia of the American Constitution,* 4 vols. (New York: Free Press/Macmillan, 1986), 2: 727–728. See generally, e.g., Ward E. Y. Elliott, *The Rise of Guardian Democracy: The Supreme Court's Role in Voting Rights Disputes, 1845–1969* (Cambridge, Mass.: Harvard University Press, 1969); and Steven F. Lawson, *Black Ballots: Voting Rights in the South, 1944–1969* (New York: Columbia University Press, 1976).

71. See, e.g., Eric S. Foner, "From Slavery to Citizenship: Blacks and the Right to Vote," at 55–65, and Linda Faye Williams, "The Constitution and the Civil Rights Movement: The Quest for a More Perfect Union," in Rogers with Scriabine, eds., *Voting and American Democracy,* 97–107.

72. *Presley v. Etowah City,* U.S. Supreme Court, docket No. 90-711 (decided January 27, 1992).

73. Deborah L. Rhode, "Nineteenth Amendment," in Levy, Karst, and Mahoney, eds.,

Encyclopedia of the American Constitution, 3: 1315–16. But see Mary Fainsod Katzenstein, "Constitutional Politics and the Feminist Movement," in Rogers with Scriabine, eds., *Voting and American Democracy,* 83–95.

74. E.g., Joan Hoff, *Law, Gender, and Injustice: A Legal History of U.S. Women* (New York: New York University Press, 1991); Catherine MacKinnon, *Toward a Feminist Theory of Jurisprudence* (Cambridge, Mass.: Harvard University Press, 1990); and Susan Faludi, *Backlash* (New York: Crown, 1991). Hoff's notes and bibliography provide a valuable guide to the extensive literature on this theme.

75. Michael Tomasky, "Think Locally, Act Locally: Chicago Politics and the Nuisance of Presidential Primaries," *Village Voice,* March 31, 1992, at 29–31. Katzenstein's essay (written in 1989), cited in note 73, presaged the developments in 1991–1992.

76. Philip G. Schrag, *Behind the Scenes: The Politics of a Constitutional Convention* (Washington, D.C.: Georgetown University Press, 1985).

77. Between November 1972, the first Presidential election affected by the Twenty-sixth Amendment, and November 1988, participation by those eighteen to twenty-four has ranged from a high of 49.6 percent in 1972 to a low of 36.2 percent in 1988. By comparison, in 1972 the rate of participation by all age-groups was 63.0 percent; in 1988 it had fallen to 57.4 percent. In midterm congressional elections, the participation of those eighteen to twenty-four dropped significantly, with a high of 24.8 percent in 1982 and a low of 21.9 percent in 1988; comparable participation figures for all ages are 48.5 percent in 1982 and 46.0 percent in 1988. U.S. Department of Commerce, Bureau of the Census, *Voting and Registration in the Election of November 1988* (Washington, D.C.: Government Printing Office, 1989), 2. See also Thomas H. Neale (analyst in American national government, Government Division, CRS), *The Eighteen Year Old Vote: The Twenty-sixth Amendment and Subsequent Voting Rates of Newly Enfranchised Age Groups,* Report No. 83-103 GOV (Washington, D.C.: Congressional Research Service of the Library of Congress, May 20, 1983). We gratefully acknowledge the aid of then-Rep. S. William Green (Republican–New York) and his staff in obtaining this information.

78. See the listing in Richard A. Davis, *Proposed Amendments to the Constitution of the United States of America Introduced in Congress from the 91st Congress, 1st Session, Through the 98th Congress, 2nd Session, January 1969–December 1984,* Report No. 85-36 GOV (Washington, D.C.: Congressional Research Service of the Library of Congress, February 1, 1985), 314. [Hereafter Davis, *Proposed Amendments.*]

79. See Jeffrey H. Birnbaum and Alan S. Murray, *Showdown at Gucci Gulch: Lawmakers, Lobbyists, and the Unlikely Triumph of Tax Reform* (New York: Random House, 1987).

80. E.g., George Bush's 1988 promise, "Read my lips—no new taxes!"—which came back to haunt him during the 1992 Presidential campaign. Sidney Blumenthal, *Pledging Allegiance: The Last Presidential Campaign of the Cold War* (New York: HarperCollins, 1990).

81. Edmund Wilson, *The Cold War and the Income Tax* (New York: Farrar & Rinehart, 1962).

82. See the muckraking study by David Burnham, *A Law unto Itself* (New York: Random House, 1990).

83. The most accessible and lucid exposition of the theory is Stanley S. Surrey and Paul R. McDaniel, *Tax Expenditures* (Cambridge, Mass.: Harvard University Press, 1985).

84. On judicial appointments, see Henry J. Abraham, *Justices and Presidents: A Political History of Appointments to the Supreme Court,* 3d ed. (New York: Oxford University Press, 1991).

85. For this estimate, and for a scathing analysis of Senatorial campaign contributions, see Philip M. Stern, *The Best Congress Money Can Buy* (New York: Pantheon, 1988). For the House version of the problem, see Brooks Jackson, *Honest Graft: Big Money and the American Political Process* (1988; rev. ed., Washington, D.C.: Farragut, 1990). To be sure, not all Senators have to raise and spend such large sums of money. When Senator William Proxmire (Democrat–Wisconsin) retired in 1987, he was fond of pointing out that he had won reelection in 1980 with a campaign budget of under five hundred dollars.

86. Herbert L. Abrams, *"The President Has Been Shot"* (New York: W. W. Norton, 1992).

87. Tribe, *American Constitutional Law,* 173–195, is an admirably concise and clear synthesis. Clyde E. Jacobs, *The Eleventh Amendment and Sovereign Immunity* (Westport: Greenwood Press, 1972); and John V. Orth, *The Judicial Power of the United States: The Eleventh Amendment in American History* (New York: Oxford University Press, 1987), are two leading discussions. See also Calvin R. Massey, "State Sovereignty and the Tenth and Eleventh Amendments," *University of Chicago Law Review* 56 (1989): 61–153, and the studies cited at 61 n.2. The high points of the Eleventh Amendment's remarkably inconsistent doctrines are these: the amendment does not bar federal courts from considering litigants' appeals—on federal constitutional grounds—from state court convictions under laws arguably unconstitutional. Nor does it prevent federal courts from hearing suits against a state official acting under state authority but arguably violating the Constitution. Under certain circumstances (though exactly what they are remains a focus of bitter disagreement), a state may be deemed to have consented to suit. But these generalizations mask a host of exceptions, qualifications, and conditions—all attesting to "the theoretical incoherence of eleventh amendment jurisprudence." Orth, *Judicial Power,* 152.

88. Jane J. Mansbridge, *Why We Lost the ERA* (Chicago: University of Chicago Press, 1986).

CHAPTER 12
"WITH ALL THE COOLNESS OF PHILOSOPHERS": PROPOSALS TO REWRITE THE CONSTITUTION

1. Thomas Jefferson, Letter to C. W. F. Dumas, September 1787, in John P. Foley, ed., *The Jeffersonian Cyclopedia . . .* (New York: Funk & Wagnalls, 1900), 198.

2. Thomas Jefferson to Samuel Kercheval, July 12, 1816, reprinted in Merrill D. Peterson, ed., *Jefferson* (New York: Library of America, 1984), 1395–1403 (quote at 1401). Jefferson wrote Kercheval to encourage replacement of the inadequate Virginia constitution of 1776, which he had criticized for forty years.

3. Ibid., 1401.

4. Adrienne Koch, *Jefferson and Madison: The Great Collaboration* (New York: Alfred A. Knopf, 1950), 62–96, is a lively and useful account of this debate.

5. The states' constitutions provided ample support for these views. By the time of the Federal Convention, New Hampshire (1776 and 1784), South Carolina (1776 and 1778), and Massachusetts (1779 [rejected] and 1780) had each framed a new constitution twice. The "independent republic of Vermont" (which did not become a state until 1791) had also adopted two constitutions (1777 and 1786). Under the septennial review process written into its 1776 constitution, Pennsylvania had endured a bitter but unsuccessful campaign for revision in 1783 and was about to face another in 1790. Finally, in the years following the adoption of the United States Constitution, Georgia, Delaware, Pennsylvania, New Hampshire, and South Carolina replaced their constitutions. Willi Paul Adams, *The First American Constitutions*, trans. Rita and Robert Kimber (Chapel Hill: University of North Carolina Press for the Institute of Early American History and Culture, 1980); Donald S. Lutz, *Popular Consent and Popular Control: Whig Political Theory in the Early State Constitutions* (Baton Rouge: Louisiana State University Press, 1980); Donald S. Lutz, *The Origins of American Constitutionalism* (Baton Rouge: Louisiana State University Press, 1988); and Richard B. Bernstein with Kym S. Rice, *Are We to Be a Nation? The Making of the Constitution* (Cambridge, Mass.: Harvard University Press, 1987), ch. 2. For the record after 1789, see, e.g., Robert F. Williams, ed., *State Constitutional Law: Cases and Materials* (Washington, D.C.: American Commission on Intergovernmental Relations, 1988), 5–34, 423–464.

6. See Sanford Levinson, "Accounting for Constitutional Change (Or, How Many Times Has the United States Constitution Been Amended? (a) < 26; (b) 26; (c) > 26; (d) all of the above)," *Constitutional Commentary* 8 (1991): 409–431.

7. The only full-length study is John R. Vile, *Rewriting the United States Constitution: Proposals from Reconstruction to the Present* (New York: Praeger, 1991). Vile's book is a useful compendium of suggestions and has aided the preparation of the present discussion. It suffers, however, from an elastic definition of "proposals for rewriting the Constitution," a term that sometimes stretches to include focused recommendations for changing particular institutions, such as Congress or the Presidency, and sometimes contracts to cover suggestions for a full reframing of the nation's fundamental law. Vile also misses opportunities to make intellectual, political, cultural, and historical connections between the disparate proposals he addresses. Vile's 1992 study, *The Constitutional Amending Process in American Political Thought* (New York: Praeger, 1992), came to hand too late to be used in the preparation of this book.

8. Jacob Shallus was assistant clerk of the Pennsylvania General Assembly. John C. Fitzpatrick, "The Man Who Engrossed the Constitution," in U.S. Constitution Sesquicentennial Commission, *History of the Formation of the Union Under the Constitution* (Washington, D.C.: U.S. Government Printing Office, 1941), 761–769, was the first to identify Shallus as the calligrapher of the "original" Constitution. See Arthur Plotnik, *The Man Behind the Quill: Jacob Shallus, Calligrapher of the United States Constitution* (Washington, D.C.: National Archives and Records Administration, 1987).

9. See Trevor Colbourn, ed., *Fame and the Founding Fathers: Essays of Douglass Adair* (New York: W. W. Norton for the Institute of Early American History and Culture, 1974).

10. Max Farrand, ed., *The Records of the Federal Convention of 1787,* rev. ed. in 4 vols. (New Haven: Yale University Press, 1937, 1966), 1: 281–311 (June 18, 1787; all accounts).

11. On Yates's and Lansing's refusal, see Abraham G. Lansing to Abraham Yates, Jr., August 26, 1787, Abraham Yates, Jr., Papers, The New York Public Library, Rare Books and Manuscripts Division, quoted in Bernstein with Rice, *Are We to Be a Nation?,* 196–197.

12. Alexander Hamilton, "Plan of a constitution for America," ca. September 1787, Alexander Hamilton Papers, The New York Public Library, Rare Books and Manuscripts Division. The text of the Madison transcription is reprinted in Farrand, *Records,* 3: 619–630.

13. Farrand, *Records,* 2: 646 (September 17, 1787).

14. The principal study of Hamilton's administrative thought and achievements is Lynton K. Caldwell, *The Administrative Theories of Hamilton and Jefferson* (1944; rev. ed., New York: Holmes & Meier, 1990). See also Leonard D. White, *The Federalists* (New York: Macmillan, 1948); Forrest McDonald, *Alexander Hamilton: A Biography* (New York: W. W. Norton, 1979); Gerald Stourzh, *Alexander Hamilton and the Idea of Republican Government* (Stanford: Stanford University Press, 1970); Joanne B. Freeman, " 'Very Busy and Not a Little Anxious': Alexander Hamilton, First Secretary of the Treasury," in Stephen L. Schechter and Richard B. Bernstein, eds., *Well Begun: Chronicles of the Early National Period* (Albany: New York State Commission on the Bicentennial of the Constitution, 1989), 71–79; Joanne B. Freeman, " 'Mine is an Odd Destiny': Alexander Hamilton (1755–1804)," in Stephen L. Schechter and Richard B. Bernstein, eds., *New York and the Union: Contributions to the American Constitutional Experience* (Albany: New York State Commission on the Bicentennial of the United States Constitution, 1990), 439–457; and Harvey Flaumenhaft, *The Effective Republic: Administration and Constitution in the Thought of Alexander Hamilton* (Durham: Duke University Press, 1992).

15. Hamilton's 1787 plan languished in his and Madison's papers—although it resurfaced in the early 1800s as the question of what he had proposed became a sensitive political and historical issue. Volume 3 of Farrand, *Records,* contains numerous letters to and from Hamilton and Madison concerning Hamilton's June 18 speech and the plan he offered in it.

16. The principal suggestions, adopted in 1788 by state ratifying conventions as recommendations to the First Congress, were collected and reprinted as a pamphlet by the Richmond, Virginia, printer Augustine Davis; the pamphlet is reprinted in Stephen L. Schechter and Richard B. Bernstein, eds., *Contexts of the Bill of Rights* (Albany: New York State Commission on the Bicentennial of the United States Constitution, 1990), 112–146; in Linda Grant DePauw, Charlene Bangs Bickford, Kenneth R. Bowling, and Helen E. Veit, eds., *The Documentary History of the First Federal Congress, March 4, 1789, to March 3, 1791,* 9 vols. of 20 projected (Baltimore: Johns Hopkins University Press, 1972–), 4: 1–48; and in Helen E. Veit, Kenneth R. Bowling, and Charlene Bangs Bickford, eds., *Creating the Bill of Rights: The Documentary Record from the First Federal Congress* (Baltimore: Johns Hopkins University Press, 1991), 1–53.

17. For a comprehensive listing of all calls for a second convention in this period, see

Russell L. Caplan, *Constitutional Brinkmanship: Amending the Constitution by National Convention* (New York: Oxford University Press, 1988), 32–61.

18. Samuel Eliot Morison, Frederick Merk, and Frank Freidel, *Dissent in Three American Wars* (Cambridge, Mass.: Harvard University Press, 1970), ch. 1; and James M. Banner, Jr., *To the Hartford Convention* (New York: Alfred A. Knopf, 1970).

19. Drew R. McCoy, *The Last of the Fathers: James Madison and the Republican Legacy* (Cambridge: Cambridge University Press, 1989); and Caplan, *Constitutional Brinkmanship*, 46–52.

20. See Richard E. Ellis, *The Union at Risk* (New York: Oxford University Press, 1987); and Caplan, *Constitutional Brinkmanship*, 50–51.

21. Charles Robert Lee, *The Confederate Constitutions* (Chapel Hill: University of North Carolina Press, 1963); Emory M. Thomas, *The Confederate Nation, 1861–1865* (New York: Harper & Row, 1979); and the splendid brief study by Don E. Fehrenbacher, *Constitutions and Constitutionalism in the Slaveholding South* (Athens: University of Georgia Press, 1989). Marshall De Rosa, *The Confederate Constitution of 1861* (Columbia, Mo.: University of Missouri Press, 1991), accepts the argument of the Confederate constitution's framers that they were seeking to restore the "original intent" of the framers of 1787. See the review by Thomas C. Mackey, forthcoming in the *American Journal of Legal History*.

22. The full text of the Confederate Constitution of 1861 is most easily consulted in Henry Steele Commager, ed., *Documents of American History*, 9th ed. (New York: Appleton-Century-Crofts, 1973), doc. 201, at 376–384. It is also reprinted as an appendix to De Rosa, *Confederate Constitution*, and in the body of Lee, *Confederate Constitutions*. Thomas, *Confederate Nation*, 309–322, reprints an excerpted text.

23. The drafting committee grafted the first eight amendments of the Bill of Rights into Article I, sections 9 and 10; they added the Ninth and Tenth Amendments to Article VI as sections 5 and 6; they inserted the operative language of the Eleventh Amendment into Article III, section 2; and they incorporated the Twelfth Amendment into Article II, section 2.

24. See the brief but useful discussion in Caplan, *Constitutional Brinkmanship*, 57–58.

25. Fehrenbacher, *Constitutions and Constitutionalism*, 62–65.

26. Donald Nieman, "Republicanism, the Confederate Constitution, and the American Constitutional Tradition," in Kermit L. Hall and James W. Ely, Jr., eds., *An Uncertain Tradition: Constitutionalism and the History of the South* (Athens: University of Georgia Press, 1989), 201–224.

27. Nieman, "Republicanism."

28. Thomas, *Confederate Nation*.

29. Morton Keller, *Affairs of State: Public Life in Late Nineteenth-century America* (Cambridge, Mass.: Belknap Press of Harvard University Press, 1977).

30. On post-Reconstruction and twentieth-century calls for a second convention, see Caplan, *Constitutional Brinkmanship*, 58–78.

31. See Henry W. Bragdon, *Woodrow Wilson: The Academic Years* (Cambridge, Mass.:

Harvard University Press, 1967), and the relevant chapters in Arthur S. Link, *Wilson: The Road to the White House* (Princeton: Princeton University Press, 1947).

32. Woodrow Wilson, *Congressional Government: A Study in American Politics* (Boston: Houghton Mifflin, 1885); Johns Hopkins University Press reprinted the book in 1981, with an introduction by Walter Lippmann (written for a reprint in the 1950s).

33. Walter Bagehot, *The English Constitution* (1867; Oxford and New York: Oxford University Press, 1924).

34. Ironically, in his *Constitutional Government in the United States* (New York: Columbia University Press, 1908), Wilson turned away from his 1885 strictures on the Constitution, accepting and even praising the workings of the constitutional system. And, throughout his meteoric political career (which spanned only ten years—from 1911, when he became Governor of New Jersey, to 1921, when he left the Presidency), Wilson never revived his 1885 proposals for constitutional change.

35. Vile, *Rewriting the United States Constitution,* is a useful compilation and provides a careful, though not integrated, analysis of the various proposals he identifies.

36. On Cram, see Vile, *Rewriting the United States Constitution,* 75–78. See also Ralph A. Cram, *The End of Democracy* (Boston: Marshall Jones, 1937).

37. Henry Hazlitt, *A New Constitution Now* (New York: Whittlesey House, 1942; rept., with new introduction focusing on Watergate, New York: Arlington House, 1974); Alexander Hehmeyer, *Time for Change: A Proposal for a Second Constitutional Convention* (New York: Farrar & Rinehart, 1943); and Thomas K. Finletter, *Can Representative Government Do the Job?* (New York: Reynal & Hitchcock, 1945). See Vile, *Rewriting the United States Constitution,* 85–87, 90–93.

38. Rexford G. Tugwell, "Constitution for a United Republics of America," *Center Magazine* 3 (September–October 1970): 11–45 (a profile of Tugwell by Harry S. Ashmore appears at 2–8, Tugwell's introduction at 11–23, the text of the proposed "Constitution for a United Republics of America" at 24–45, and an interview at 50–62). See also Rexford G. Tugwell, *A Model Constitution for a United Republics of America* (Santa Barbara: Center for the Study of Democratic Institutions, 1970).

39. The most famous of Tugwell's books is Rexford G. Tugwell, *The Democratic Roosevelt* (New York: Doubleday, 1958). His posthumously published memoir is Rexford G. Tugwell, *To the Lesser Heights of Morningside* (Philadelphia: University of Pennsylvania Press, 1981).

40. Rexford G. Tugwell, *The Emerging Constitution* (New York: Harper's Magazine Press, 1974), xxxi.

41. Tugwell, *Emerging Constitution,* 595 (Article I, Rights and Responsibilities, Part A, Rights, § 1), 596 (Part B, Responsibilities, § 1).

42. Vile, *Rewriting the United States Constitution,* 109. See generally, 106–110.

43. Frank K. Kelly, *Court of Reason: Robert Hutchins and the Fund for the Republic* (New York: Free Press, 1981), 650, quoted in Vile, *Rewriting the United States Constitution,* 110.

44. Letter from Henry Steele Commager to Richard B. Bernstein, November 1, 1971, photocopy in Henry Steele Commager Papers, Amherst College Library, Amherst, Mass.

45. Ibid.

46. Stanley I. Kutler, *The Wars of Watergate: The Last Crisis of Richard Nixon* (New York: Alfred A. Knopf, 1990), 9.

47. See Vile, *Rewriting the United States Constitution*, 115–124.

48. *A Bicentennial Analysis of the American Political Structure: Report and Recommendations of the Committee on the Constitutional System* (Washington, D.C.: Committee on the Constitutional System, 1987), inside front cover.

49. Charles M. Hardin, *Presidential Power and Accountability: Toward a New Constitution* (Chicago: University of Chicago Press, 1974).

50. Ibid., 3.

51. Ibid., 5.

52. Charles M. Hardin, *Constitutional Reform in America: Essays on the Separation of Powers* (Ames: Iowa State University Press, 1989), ix–x.

53. Ibid., ix.

54. In addition to *Bicentennial Analysis,* see Donald L. Robinson, ed., *Reforming American Government: The Bicentennial Papers of the Committee on the Constitutional System* (Boulder: Westview, 1985); James L. Sundquist, *Constitutional Reform and Effective Government* (Washington, D.C.: Brookings Institution, 1986; rev. ed., 1992); and Donald L. Robinson, *Government for the Third American Century* (Boulder: Westview, 1989).

55. *Bicentennial Analysis,* 2.

56. Ibid., 3.

57. Ibid., 5–7.

58. Ibid., 8–9.

59. Ibid., 10–14. See *Buckley v. Valeo,* 424 U.S. 1 (1976).

60. Ibid., 14–16.

61. Mark P. Petracca, Lonce Bailey, and Pamela Smith, "Proposals for Constitutional Reform: An Evaluation of the Committee on the Constitutional System," *Presidential Studies Quarterly* 20 (1990): 503–532.

62. Ibid., 526. See also Vile, *Rewriting the United States Constitution,* 134–135, which discusses Petracca's 1988 paper that served as the basis for his 1990 article. For the response of a leading member of the CCS, see James L. Sundquist, "Response to the Petracca-Bailey-Smith Evaluation of the Committee on the Constitutional System," *Presidential Studies Quarterly* 20 (1990): 533–543.

Petracca was not alone in criticizing the CCS. James W. Ceaser, a political scientist at the University of Virginia, offered a vigorous defense of separation of powers and checks and balances, and rejected the CCS methodology as "radical in the worst sense [and] lacking in any scientific foundation," based on abstract reason rather than on experience and constitutional tradition. James W. Ceaser, "In Defense of Separation of Powers," in Robert A. Goldwin and Art Kaufman, eds., *Separation of Powers—Does It Still Work?* (Washington, D.C.: American Enterprise Institute, 1986), 168–193 (quote at 171, 179). See Vile, *Rewriting the United States Constitution,* 135–137. From the opposite end of the political spectrum, Jeanne Hahn denounced the prescription of the CCS as tending to concentrate political power in the hands of political, economic, and intellectual elites, which would only exacerbate the antidemocratic character of the Constitution. Jeanne Hahn, "Neo-Hamiltonianism: A Democratic Critique," in John F. Manley and Kenneth M. Dolbeare, eds., *The Case Against the Constitution: From Anti-Federalists to the Present* (New York: M. E. Sharpe, 1987), 145ff. See Vile, *Rewriting the United States Constitution,* 135.

63. E.g., Sundquist, *Constitutional Reform* (1986 ed.), 251.

64. Vile, *Rewriting the United States Constitution,* 133.

65. Barry Krusch, *The 21st Century Constitution: A New America for a New Millenium* (New York: Stanhope Press, 1992).

66. Telephone interview with Barry Krusch, September 21, 1992.

67. For a critical analysis of H. Ross Perot's "electronic town hall," see Richard B. Bernstein, "Hot-wiring the Constitution, 1787," *The New York Times,* July 17, 1992, p. A 27.

68. Wilson, *Congressional Government,* 332–333.

69. Herbert D. Croly, *The Promise of American Life* (1909; Indianapolis: Bobbs-Merrill, 1965), 316.

70. See generally Vincent Ostrom, *The Intellectual Crisis in American Public Administration,* rev. ed. (Tuscaloosa: University of Alabama Press, 1989); and John A. Rohr, *To Run a Constitution: The Legitimacy of the Administrative State* (Lawrence: University Press of Kansas, 1985).

71. Croly, *Promise of American Life,* 316.

Chapter 13
Riddles Without Answers: Issues of the Amending Process

1. In several telephone interviews, and particularly on June 24, 1992, Gregory D. Watson graciously reviewed our discussion of the history of the Twenty-seventh Amendment and contributed his detailed reminiscences of his part in that history. We are deeply grateful to him. For a detailed discussion, see Richard B. Bernstein, "The Sleeper Wakes: The History and Legacy of the Twenty-seventh Amendment," forthcoming in the *Fordham Law Review,* vol. 61, no. 3 (December 1992).

2. A valuable source which predates the ratification of the amendment is David C. Huckabee, "The Constitutional Amendment to Regulate Congressional Salary Increases: A Slumbering Proposal's New Popularity," *CRS Report for Congress* (Washington, D.C.:

Congressional Research Service of the Library of Congress, September 16, 1986). [Hereafter Huckabee, "Slumbering Proposal."] We thank Timothy L. Hanford, Esq., assistant minority tax counsel of the House Committee on Ways and Means, for drawing our attention to this study.

3. 70 Ohio Laws 409–410, May 6, 1873, reprinted in 138 *Congressional Record* S6836 (102d Cong., 2d sess., Senate, May 19, 1992) (documents supplementing remarks of Senator Robert C. Byrd). Watson notes that this reprint was the first time that Ohio's ratification was ever published in the *Congressional Record* or in any other formal journal kept by Congress.

4. Wyoming Legislature, J. Res. 3 (1978), reprinted in ibid.

5. In 1987, Paul Gann, coauthor (with Howard Jarvis) of California's Proposition 13 (an influential limit on state property taxes), founded a short-lived movement to submit the Compensation Amendment anew to more states' legislatures, and consumer activist Ralph Nader also briefly urged its adoption. And, in the early months of 1992, freshman Republican members of the House led by John Boehner (Republican–Ohio) took up the Amendment as one of their chief projects.

6. Journal of the Senate, State of Colorado, 54th General Assembly, 2d regular sess., 1984, at 966; quoted in Huckabee, "Slumbering Proposal," at 17.

7. Quoted in Don Phillips, "Proposed Amendment, Age 200, Showing Life," *Washington Post,* March 29, 1989, p. A23. See the useful compilation by the Library Services Division of the Congressional Research Service: *The Twenty-seventh Amendment: Congressional Pay and the Constitution—Background Material and Selected News Articles, 1987–1992,* Congressional Research Service of the Library of Congress, LRS92-3691, June 1992.

8. Telephone interview with Gregory D. Watson, June 24, 1992.

9. According to Watson, the following states have ratified the Amendment: Maryland (December 19, 1789); North Carolina (December 22, 1789); South Carolina (January 19, 1790); Delaware (January 28, 1790); Vermont (November 3, 1791); Virginia (December 15, 1791); Ohio (May 6, 1873); Wyoming (March 3, 1978); Maine (April 27, 1983); Colorado (April 18, 1984); South Dakota (February 21, 1985); New Hampshire (March 7, 1985); Arizona (April 3, 1985); Tennessee (May 23, 1985); Oklahoma (July 10, 1985); New Mexico (February 13, 1986); Indiana (February 19, 1986); Utah (February 25, 1986); Arkansas (March 5, 1987); Montana (March 11, 1987); Connecticut (May 13, 1987); Wisconsin (June 30, 1987); Georgia (February 2, 1988); West Virginia (March 10, 1988); Louisiana (July 6, 1988); Iowa (February 7, 1989); Idaho (March 23, 1989); Nevada (April 26, 1989); Alaska (May 5, 1989); Oregon (May 19, 1989); Minnesota (May 22, 1989); Texas (May 25, 1989); Kansas (April 5, 1990); Florida (May 31, 1990); North Dakota (March 25, 1991); Missouri (May 5, 1992); Alabama (May 5, 1992); Michigan (May 7, 1992); New Jersey (May 7, 1992); Illinois (May 12, 1992); California (June 26, 1992). Telephone interviews with Gregory D. Watson, June 24 and September 24, 1992. Watson notes several inaccuracies in the list prepared by the Archivist, *compare* Letter from Don W. Wilson, Archivist of the United States, to the Senate and the House of Representatives, May 17, 1992, reprinted in 138 *Congressional Record* at S6828 (102d Cong., 2d sess., Senate, May 19, 1992).

10. 1 U.S. Code, § 106 (b) (1984).

11. *Federal Register*, vol. 57, p. 21187–21188, May 19, 1992.

12. Quoted in Bill McAllister, "Across Two Centuries, a Founder Updates the Constitution," *Washington Post*, May 14, 1992, pp. A1, A5.

13. 138 *Congressional Record* at S6940 (102d Cong., 2d sess., Senate, May 20, 1992).

14. Ibid.

15. Ibid., S6950 (remarks of Senator Roth).

16. 138 *Congressional Record* E1456 (102d Cong., 2d sess., H.R., May 20, 1992), extended remarks of Representative Clay.

17. Tribe comment: quoted in Bill McAllister, "Madison's Remedy May Ignite Hill Pay Dispute," *Washington Post*, May 19, 1992, p. A17. Watson comment: telephone interview with Gregory D. Watson, June 24, 1992. See also Bernstein, "The Sleeper Wakes," n. 225 (on the first lawsuit to invoke the Amendment).

18. J. Jennings Moss, "House, Senate OK Amendment," *Washington Times*, May 21, 1992, p. A3.

19. Telephone interview with Gregory D. Watson, June 24, 1992.

20. Max Farrand, ed., *The Records of the Federal Convention of 1787*, rev. ed. in 4 vols. (New Haven: Yale University Press, 1937, 1966), 2: 629–630 (September 15, 1787).

21. Wilbur Edel, *A Constitutional Convention: Threat or Challenge?* (New York: Praeger, 1981), faces this point squarely.

22. For a thoughtful and elegant statement of this view, see Ruth Bader Ginsburg, "On Amending the Constitution: A Plea for Patience," *University of Arkansas at Little Rock Law Journal* 12 (1989–1990): 677–694. Judge Ginsburg is a member of the U.S. Court of Appeals for the District of Columbia Circuit.

23. Richard A. Davis, *Proposed Amendments to the Constitution of the United States of America Introduced in Congress from the 91st Congress, 1st Session, Through the 98th Congress, 2nd Session, January 1969–December 1984*, Report No. 85-36 GOV (Washington, D.C.: Congressional Research Service of the Library of Congress, February 1, 1985), 16, 23, 40 (Bush proposals); 115, 135, 136, 141, 142 (Quayle proposals).

24. See the excellent discussion in Stephen L. Schechter, "Amending the United States Constitution: A New Generation on Trial," in Keith G. Banting and Richard Simeon, eds., *Redesigning the State: The Politics of Constitutional Change in Industrial Nations* (Toronto: University of Toronto Press, 1985), 160–202.

25. On the defeat of the Equal Rights Amendment, see Mary Frances Berry, *Why ERA Failed: Politics, Women's Rights, and the Amending Process of the Constitution* (Bloomington: Indiana University Press, 1986); Jane J. Mansbridge, *Why We Lost the ERA* (Chicago: University of Chicago Press, 1986); and Gilbert Yale Steiner, *Constitutional Inequality: The Political Fortunes of the Equal Rights Amendment* (Washington, D.C.: Brookings Institution, 1985). On the successes of the 1960s and their consequences for later amendment politics, see Schechter, "Amending the United States Constitution."

26. Russell L. Caplan, *Constitutional Brinkmanship: Amending the Constitution by National Convention* (New York: Oxford University Press, 1988), vii. See also David C. Huckabee, "Constitutional Conventions: Political and Legal Questions," *CRS Issue Brief* (Washington, D.C.: Congressional Research Service of the Library of Congress, October 18, 1989). We are indebted to Timothy L. Hanford, Esq., assistant minority tax counsel of the House Committee on Ways and Means, for drawing this study to our attention.

27. See the chronology presented in Huckabee, "Constitutional Conventions."

28. 256 U.S. 368 (1921).

29. 307 U.S. 433 (1939).

30. Walter Dellinger, "The Legitimacy of Constitutional Change: Rethinking the Amendment Process," *Harvard Law Review* 97 (1983): 386–432, esp. 389–390.

31. 256 U.S. at 374.

32. Id., at 374–375.

33. Id., at 375.

34. *Idaho v. Freeman*, 527 F.Supp. 1105 (D.Idaho 1981), *vacated as moot sub nom. National Organization for Women, Inc. v. Idaho*, 103 S. Ct. 22 (1982).

35. Dellinger, "Legitimacy of Constitutional Change," 390–391.

36. Justice Frankfurter, speaking for himself and Justices Roberts, Black, and Douglas, filed a separate opinion rejecting the legislators' claim to have standing to bring the suit. 307 U.S. at 460–470.

37. Id., at 447.

38. Id., at 450.

39. Id., at 452.

40. *Coleman*, 307 U.S. at 459 (opinion of Black, Roberts, Frankfurter, and Douglas, JJ.).

41. 307 U.S. at 470–474 (Butler and McReynolds, JJ., dissenting).

42. Telephone interview with Gregory D. Watson, June 24, 1992.

43. Herman V. Ames, *The Proposed Amendments to the Constitution of the United States during the First Century of Its History*, in *Report of the American Historical Association for the Year 1896)*, vol. 2 (Washington, D.C.: Government Printing Office, 291–292 and 292 n. 1. [Hereafter Ames, *Proposed Amendments.*]

44. Samuel S. Freedman and Pamela J. Naughton, *ERA: May a State Change Its Vote?* (Detroit: Wayne State University Press, 1978), is the most detailed and thoughtful analysis. Dellinger, "Legitimacy of Constitutional Change," 421–427, argues that, even though history and the constitutional text provide no dispositive answer, substantive questions of public policy and constitutional legitimacy give great weight to the position that a ratification may *not* be rescinded.

45. See Dellinger, "Legitimacy of Constitutional Change," 420–421, calling for the Court to rule on the merits in an appropriate case to recognize a state's right to reconsider a vote to reject.

46. Compare Laurence H. Tribe, "A *Constitution* We Are Amending: In Defense of a

Restrained Judicial Role," *Harvard Law Review* 97 (1983): 433–445, esp. 440–445 (discussing and rejecting the concept of judicial review of amendments' substance), with Dellinger's rejoinder, id., at 446–450, and with Walter F. Murphy, "An Ordering of Constitutional Values," *Southern California Law Review* 53 (1980): 703–760, esp. 755–756 (urging judicial invalidation of an amendment contrary to the preeminent constitutional value of human dignity). See also Lester Bernhardt Orfield, *The Amending of the Federal Constitution* (Ann Arbor: University of Michigan Press, 1942), ch. 2, "Judicial Review of Validity of Amendments," 7–32.

47. Laurence H. Tribe, "Rule of Law: The 27th Amendment Joins the Constitution," *Wall Street Journal*, May 13, 1992, p. A15.

48. See, e.g., Thomas J. Curry, *The First Freedom: Church and State in America to the Passage of the First Amendment* (New York: Oxford University Press, 1986). *Contra*, Robert L. Cord, *Separation of Church and State: Historical Fact and Current Fiction* (New York: Lambeth Press, 1982).

49. John Pace, *Amendment to the Constitution: Averting the Decline and Fall of America* (Glendale: Johnson, Pace, Simmons & Fennell/Affiliation of League of Pace Amendment Advocates, 1985).

50. Telephone interview with Gregory D. Watson, June 24, 1992.

51. Telephone interview with Gregory D. Watson, June 24, 1992. For a brief discussion of proposals to amend Article V, see Peter Suber, *The Paradox of Self-amendment: A Study of Logic, Law, Omnipotence, and Change* (New York: Peter Lang, 1990), app. 1, at 321–331.

52. See also the useful summary in Paul J. Weber and Barbara A. Perry, *Unfounded Fears: Myths and Realities of a Constitutional Convention* (New York: Greenwood Press, 1991), 55–79. A detailed analysis covering all applications for a convention received between 1789 and 1949 is William Russell Pullen, "The Application Clause of the Amending Provision of the Constitution" (Ph.D. diss., University of North Carolina, Chapel Hill, 1951). We are indebted to Gregory D. Watson for alerting us to this reference.

53. Huckabee, "Constitutional Conventions."

54. In favor: "Symposium on the Article V Convention Process," *Michigan Law Review* 66 (1968): 837–1016. Literature opposed includes, e.g., Charles L. Black, Jr., "Amending the Constitution: A Letter to a Congressman," *Yale Law Journal* 82 (1972): 189–215; Gerald Gunther, "The Convention Method of Amending the United States Constitution," *Georgia Law Review* 14 (1979): 1–25; and Laurence H. Tribe, "Issues Raised by Requesting Congress to Call a Constitutional Convention to Propose a Balanced Budget Amendment," *Pacific Law Journal* 10 (1979): 627–640.

55. See J. R. Pole, *The Gift of Government* (Athens: University of Georgia Press, 1983); and John T. Alexander, *The Selling of the Constitutional Convention: A History of News Coverage* (Madison: Madison House, 1990).

56. Such is the hypothetical situation explored by Akhil Reed Amar, "Philadelphia Revisited: Amending the Constitution Outside Article V," *University of Chicago Law Review* 55 (1988): 1043–1104.

57. On the question of the District's character as a statelike entity, see the discussion of the D.C. Statehood Amendment in Chapter 8.

58. U.S. Department of Justice, Office of Legal Policy, *Report to the Attorney General: Limited Constitutional Conventions Under Article V of the United States Constitution* (September 10, 1987).

59. See also, American Bar Association, Special Constitutional Convention Study Committee, *Amendment of the Constitution by the Convention Method Under Article V* (Washington, D.C.: American Bar Association, 1974), paralleling Caplan's reasoning; Edel, *Constitutional Convention;* and Weber and Perry, *Unfounded Fears.*

60. Caplan, *Constitutional Brinkmanship,* 159–163.

61. Weber and Perry, *Unfounded Fears,* 105–125.

62. Ibid., 81–103. Gregory Watson agrees: "I don't see the whole country falling apart, because whatever a second convention did would have to go through the long, difficult ratification process, which would weed out any crazy ideas." Telephone interview with Gregory D. Watson, June 24, 1992.

CHAPTER 14
AMENDING AMERICA

1. Michael Lienesch, *New Order of the Ages: Time, the Constitution, and the Making of Modern American Political Thought* (Princeton: Princeton University Press, 1988).

2. See, e.g., Catherine Drinker Bowen, *Miracle at Philadelphia* (Boston: Atlantic/Little, Brown, 1966); and the introduction of former Chief Justice Warren E. Burger to the U.S. government's bicentennial pocket edition of the Constitution of the United States, reprinted in Richard B. Bernstein, "Charting the Bicentennial," *Columbia Law Review* 87 (1987): 1565–1624, at 1565–66; see also the critical discussion in ibid., 1566–68.

3. The leading studies are Michael Kammen, *A Machine That Would Go of Itself: The Constitution in American Culture* (New York: Alfred A. Knopf, 1986); and Michael Kammen, *Sovereignty and Liberty: Constitutional Discourse in American Culture* (Madison: University of Wisconsin Press, 1988).

4. Benjamin Franklin, speech to Federal Convention, September 17, 1787, in Max Farrand, ed., *The Records of the Federal Convention of 1787,* rev. ed. in 4 vols. (New Haven: Yale University Press, 1937, 1966), 2: 641–643.

5. This progression can be traced through J. Hector St. John de Crèvecoeur, *Letters from an American Farmer and Sketches of Eighteenth-century America* (New York: Penguin, 1984); Alexis de Tocqueville, *Democracy in America,* trans. by F. D. Reeve and ed. by Phillips Bradley, 2 vols. (New York: Alfred A. Knopf, 1945); James Bryce, *The American Commonwealth* (New York: Macmillan, 1888, and later eds.); John Gunther, *Inside U.S.A.* (New York: Harper, 1947); and Michael Barone, *Our Country: The Shaping of America from Roosevelt to Reagan* (New York: Free Press/Macmillan, 1991).

6. See Sanford Levinson, "Accounting for Constitutional Change (Or, How Many Times Has the United States Constitution Been Amended? (a) < 26; (b) 26; (c) > 26; (d) all of the above)," *Constitutional Commentary* 8 (1991): 409–431.

7. Bruce Ackerman first presented his arguments in "The Storrs Lectures: Discovering the Constitution," *Yale Law Journal* 93 (1984): 1013–62; and "Constitutional Politics/ Constitutional Law," *Yale Law Journal* 99 (1989): 483–547. His most elaborate and considered statement is *We the People, I: Foundations* (Cambridge, Mass.: Belknap Press of Harvard University Press, 1991). (Ackerman projects two further volumes, now in progress, *Transformations* and *Interpretations*.)

8. In 1803, when President Thomas Jefferson pondered whether to recommend the Louisiana Purchase to Congress, his principal concern was that the acquisition of new territory by treaty purchase might exceed the powers conferred on the federal government by the Constitution. He was ready to propose that Congress consider a constitutional amendment to authorize the treaty but changed his mind. Dumas Malone, *Jefferson the President: First Term, 1801–1805* (Boston: Little, Brown, 1970), 311–332.

9. The only book-length discussion of the subject is Henry Horwill, *The Usages of the American Constitution* (Oxford: Oxford University Press, 1924). Each of the examples given in the text, however, has received intensive study.

10. Maeva Marcus, *Truman and the Steel Seizure Case: The Limits of Presidential Power* (New York: Columbia University Press, 1977); and Alan F. Westin, *The Anatomy of a Constitutional Law Case:* Youngstown Sheet & Tube Co. v. Sawyer, *the Steel Seizure Case* (1958; New York: Columbia University Press, 1990).

11. For the most scholarly and responsible presentation of this view, see Stephen Halbrook, *That Every Citizen Be Armed* (Albuquerque: University of New Mexico Press, 1986).

12. Alexander M. Bickel, *The Least Dangerous Branch: The Supreme Court at the Bar of Politics* (Indianapolis: Bobbs-Merrill, 1962), 244.

13. Michael Kammen's massive cultural history of American constitutionalism, *A Machine That Would Go of Itself,* helped to inaugurate an approach to the study of American constitutional history that moves beyond the formal work of courts and other institutions of government. Kammen and other scholars have made this point more explicitly since the publication of that work. See, for example, Kammen, *Sovereignty and Liberty;* Garry Wills, "Talking Ourselves Out of a Fight," *William and Mary Quarterly,* 3d Ser., 44 (1987): 623–627; Louis Fisher, *Constitutional Dialogues: Interpretation as Political Process* (Princeton: Princeton University Press, 1988); Bernstein, "Charting the Bicentennial"; and Richard B. Bernstein, "*The Federalist* on Energetic Government: *The Federalist Nos. 15, 70, and 78,*" in Stephen L. Schechter, ed., and Richard B. Bernstein and Donald S. Lutz, contributing eds., *Roots of the Republic: American Founding Documents Interpreted* (Madison: Madison House, 1990), 335–380.

14. For scholarly works that analyze constitutional discourse from a range of perspectives, see, e.g., Bernard Bailyn, *The Ideological Origins of the American Revolution* (Cambridge, Mass.: Belknap Press of Harvard University Press, 1967, expanded ed., 1992); Bernard Bailyn, *The Origins of American Politics* (New York: Alfred A. Knopf, 1968); Bernard Bailyn, *Faces of Revolution: Personalities and Themes in the Struggle for American Independence* (New York: Alfred A. Knopf, 1990); Gordon S. Wood, *The Creation of the American Republic, 1776–1787* (Chapel Hill: University of North Carolina Press for the Institute of Early American

History and Culture, 1969); Herbert J. Storing, ed. with the assistance of Murray Dry, *The Complete Anti-Federalist*, 7 vols. (Chicago: University of Chicago Press, 1981); John Phillip Reid, *The Constitutional History of the American Revolution*, 3 vols. of 4 projected (Madison: University of Wisconsin Press, 1986–1991); John Phillip Reid, *The Concept of Liberty in the Age of the American Revolution* (Chicago: University of Chicago Press, 1988); John Phillip Reid, *The Concept of Representation in the Age of the American Revolution* (Chicago: University of Chicago Press, 1989); Ralph Lerner, *The Thinking Revolutionary* (Ithaca: Cornell University Press, 1987); Isaac Kramnick, *Republicanism and Bourgeois Radicalism* (Ithaca: Cornell University Press, 1990); and Joyce O. Appleby, *Liberalism and Republicanism in the Historical Imagination* (Cambridge, Mass.: Harvard University Press, 1992).

15. Even during the sectional crisis of 1848–1877, the one period of American history when constitutional discourse apparently failed, constitutional issues shaped both the secessionists' desperate fight to leave the Union and the Union's strategy to quell the rebellion. See Chapters 5 and 6. See also, e.g., J. G. Randall, *Constitutional Problems Under Lincoln* (Urbana: University of Illinois Press, 1926; rev. ed., 1953); Harold M. Hyman, *A More Perfect Union: The Impact of the Civil War and Reconstruction on the Constitution* (New York: Alfred A. Knopf, 1971); Emory M. Thomas, *The Confederate Nation, 1861–1865* (New York: Harper & Row, 1979); Harold M. Hyman and William E. Wiecek, *Equal Justice Under Law: Constitutional Development, 1835–1875* (New York: Harper & Row, 1982); Phillip S. Paludan, *"A People's Contest": The Union in the Civil War, 1861–1865* (New York: Harper & Row, 1989); and James M. McPherson, *Abraham Lincoln and the Second American Revolution* (New York: Oxford University Press, 1990).

16. The term is derived from Henry Adams, *History of the United States during the Administrations of Thomas Jefferson, 1801–1809* (1889–1891; New York: Library of America, 1986), 5.

17. These amendments are discussed in Chapters 3, 6, and 11.

18. Ackerman, "Discovering the Constitution," 1022. See also the works cited in note 7.

19. Ackerman, "Discovering the Constitution," 1022.

20. The Thirteenth, Fourteenth, Fifteenth, Eighteenth, Nineteenth, Twenty-third, Twenty-fourth, and Twenty-sixth Amendments.

21. Allan F. Sindler, *Unelected Presidents* (Berkeley: University of California Press, 1978); and Jules Witcover, *Crapshoot* (New York: Crown, 1992).

22. See, e.g., George H. Haynes, *The Election of Senators* (New York: Henry Holt, 1906), chs. 5–8.

23. Levinson, "Accounting for Constitutional Change," 413–431, discusses the growing jurisprudential argument over when and how Americans should invoke the amending process to add truly new materials to the constitutional framework as opposed to adapting the constitutional system via interpretation, custom, or usage.

24. See generally "New York University Supreme Court Project," *New York University Law Review* 59 (1984): 677–1929. The history of the project is recounted at 677–679. The lead article of the project, Samuel Estreicher and John E. Sexton, "A Managerial Theory of the Supreme Court's Responsibilities: An Empirical Study," ibid., 681–1003, was

published in revised and expanded form as Samuel Estreicher and John Sexton, *Redefining the Supreme Court's Role* (New Haven: Yale University Press, 1986).

25. Judith Best, *National Representation for the District of Columbia* (Frederick: University Publications of America, 1984), xiv.

26. Edmund Randolph, "Draught of a Constitution" [July 26, 1787], in James H. Hutson, ed., *Supplement to Max Farrand's Records of the Federal Convention of 1787* (New Haven: Yale University Press, 1987), 183–193 (quote at 183).

27. Robert F. Williams, ed., *State Constitutional Law: Cases and Materials* (Washington, D.C.: Advisory Commission on Intergovernmental Relations, 1988), esp. 21–35 and sources cited.

28. Professor Barry Cushman of St. Louis University Law School is completing a constitutional history of the New Deal; he rejects as overblown the traditional characterization of the Court as unflinchingly *"laissez-faire"* until the 1937 "switch in time" that defused the Court-packing plan. Although Cushman's analysis of the actual doctrinal history of the Supreme Court is persuasive, it is nonetheless important that the "conventional" story of the battle between creative uses of government power and *laissez-faire* constitutionalism has shaped constitutional law and the American people's understanding of how that law has developed over time.

29. For a brief but valuable discussion of the range of ways in which technological change can reshape politics and constitutional government, see Albert Gore, Jr., *Earth in the Balance: Ecology and the Human Spirit* (Boston: Houghton Mifflin, 1992), 208–209. The classic study of changes in American life is Daniel J. Boorstin, *The Americans,* 3 vols. (New York: Random House, 1958–1973). See also Thomas R. Hughes, *American Genesis* (New York: Viking, 1989); David E. Nye, *Electrifying America: Social Meanings of a New Technology* (Cambridge, Mass.: MIT Press, 1990).

30. See, e.g., Jonathan Schell, *The Time of Illusion* (New York: Alfred A. Knopf, 1976), (arguing that the awesome nuclear power of the Presidency was at the core of the abuses of power that culminated in the Watergate crisis); Francis D. Wormuth and Edwin B. Firmage, *To Chain the Dog of War: The War Power of Congress in History and in Law,* 2d ed. (Urbana: University of Illinois Press, 1989); and especially Harold Hongju Koh, *The National Security Constitution: Sharing Power After the Iran-Contra Affair* (New Haven: Yale University Press, 1990).

31. Kathleen Hall Jamieson and Karlyn Kohrs Campbell, *The Interplay of Influence: Mass Media and the Public in News, Advertising, Politics,* 2d ed. (Belmont, Calif.: Wadsworth, 1988); Edwin Diamond, *The Media Show: The Changing Face of the News, 1985–1990* (Cambridge, Mass.: MIT Press, 1991); Shanto Iyengar, *News That Matters: Television and American Opinion* (Chicago: University of Chicago Press, 1987); Robert M. Entman, *Democracy Without Citizens: Media and the Decay of American Politics* (New York: Oxford University Press, 1989); Edward Bliss, *Now the News: The Story of Broadcast Journalism* (New York: Columbia University Press, 1991); and Ellis Cose, *The Press* (New York: William Morrow, 1989).

32. Karlyn Kohrs Campbell and Kathleen Hall Jamieson, *Deeds Done in Words: Presidential Rhetoric and the Genres of Governance* (Chicago: University of Chicago Press, 1990); Kathleen Hall Jamieson, *Packaging the Presidency,* 2d rev. ed. (New York: Oxford University Press,

1992); Jeffrey Tulis, *The Rhetorical Presidency* (Princeton: Princeton University Press, 1988); Roderick D. Hart, *The Sound of Leadership* (Chicago: University of Chicago Press, 1984); and Mark Hertsgaard, *On Bended Knee: The Press and the Reagan Presidency* (New York: Farrar, Straus & Giroux, 1989). See also the most influential books voicing and celebrating this phenomenon: Theodore H. White, *The Making of the President 1960* (New York: Atheneum, 1961), and Theodore H. White, *Breach of Faith: The Fall of Richard Nixon* (New York: Atheneum/Reader's Digest Press, 1975).

33. See generally Jeffrey B. Abramson, F. Christopher Atherton, and Gary R. Orren, *The Electronic Commonwealth: The Impact of New Media Technologies on Democratic Politics,* rev. ed. (New York: Basic Books, 1990); Kathleen Hall Jamieson, *Dirty Politics: Deception, Distraction, and Democracy* (New York: Oxford University Press, 1992); Kathleen Hall Jamieson, *Eloquence in an Electronic Age: The Transformation of Political Speechmaking* (New York: Oxford University Press, 1988); Jamieson, *Packaging the Presidency;* Entman, *Democracy Without Citizens;* Ithiel De Sola Pool, *Technologies of Freedom* (Cambridge, Mass.: Harvard University Press, 1983); and Larry Sabato, *Feeding Frenzy: How Attack Journalism Has Transformed American Politics* (New York: Free Press/Macmillan, 1991). For an early and influential discussion, see Joe McGinniss, *The Selling of the President 1968* (New York: Trident Press, 1969).

34. Nathan C. Goldman, *American Space Law: International and Domestic* (Ames: Iowa State University Press, 1988); J. E. S. Fawcett, *Outer Space: New Challenges to Law and Policy* (Oxford: Clarendon Press of Oxford University Press, 1984); and Myres S. McDougal, Harold D. Lasswell, and Ivan A. Vlasic, *Law and Public Order in Space* (New Haven: Yale University Press, 1963).

35. The leading case is *Cruzan v. Missouri Department of Health,* 110 S.Ct. 2841 (U.S., 1990). See, e.g., David Rothman, *Strangers at the Bedside* (New York: Basic Books, 1991); Paul Ramsey, *Ethics at the Edges of Life: Medical and Legal Intersections* (New Haven: Yale University Press, 1978); Norman L. Cantor, *Legal Frontiers of Death and Dying* (Bloomington: Indiana University Press, 1987); and President's Commission for the Study of Ethical Problems in Medicine and Biomedical and Behavioral Research, *Deciding to Forego Life-Sustaining Treatment: A Report on the Ethical, Medical, and Legal Issues in Treatment Decisions* (Washington, D.C.: Government Printing Office, March 1983).

36. E.g., *Diamond v. Chakrabaty,* 447 U.S. 303 (1980) (life-forms can be patented under Constitution and federal patent laws). See David T. Suzuki and Peter Knudtson, *Genethics: The Clash Between the New Genetics and Human Values* (Cambridge, Mass.: Harvard University Press, 1989); and President's Commission for the Study of Ethical Problems in Medicine and Biomedical and Behavioral Research, *Splicing Life: A Report on the Social and Ethical Issues of Genetic Engineering and Human Beings* (Washington, D.C.: Government Printing Office, November 1982).

37. This phrase comes from James Russell Lowell's 1888 essay "The Place of the Independent in Politics"; see Kammen, *A Machine That Would Go of Itself.*

38. See the discussion in Chapters 12 and 13.

Index

About the Authors

RICHARD B. BERNSTEIN, adjunct associate professor at New York Law School, has written or edited twelve books on American constitutional history, including *Are We to Be a Nation? The Making of the Constitution* (with Kym S. Rice) and *Into the Third Century: The Congress, The Presidency, The Supreme Court* (with Jerome Agel). A graduate of Amherst College and the Harvard Law School, he is completing work for a doctorate in American history from New York University and has served on the faculty of Rutgers University, Newark. He has been co-curator of the New York Public Library's Constitution Bicentennial Project, historian of the New York City Commission on the Bicentennial of the Constitution, co-curator of the Congress Bicentennial Project of the Library of Congress, and research director of the New York State Commission on the Bicentennial of the U.S. Constitution. He currently serves as assistant editor of *The Papers of John Jay* and is completing a history of the First Congress. He lives in Brooklyn, New York.

JEROME AGEL has written and/or produced fifty books, including collaborations with Carl Sagan, Marshall McLuhan, Stanley Kubrick, and Isaac Asimov. His works include *The U.S. Constitution for Everyone, Why in the World: Adventures in Geography* (with George J. Demko), and the nonfiction novels *22 Fires* and *Deliverance in Shanghai*.